Descriptive

ENGLISH GRAMMAR

HOMER C. HOUSE · *and* ·
SUSAN EMOLYN HARMAN

Revised by

Susan Emolyn Harman

PROFESSOR OF ENGLISH LANGUAGE AND
LITERATURE, UNIVERSITY OF MARYLAND

Second Edition

PRENTICE-HALL, INC.
Englewood Cliffs, N. J.

Current printing (last digit):

40 39 38 37 36 35 34 33 32

Preface

The revised edition of DESCRIPTIVE ENGLISH GRAMMAR follows in the main the general plan of the first edition, though the greater portion of the text has been rewritten, and new exercise material and many new illustrations have been added.

The emphasis in the revision is definitely on the living language. Historical forms are cited only when they throw light on present-day usage. All sentences used for the illustrations and for the exercises in sentence analysis are taken from standard English, many of them from the classics. The material in the exercises in correcting substandard English comes chiefly from the oral and written speech of students registered in college English classes. By studying and comparing the two levels of English, the average student will be able to discover for himself that the best English is grammatical English.

The chief aim throughout the book has been to furnish the teacher and the student with material for a complete course in English grammar: the text covers the basic principles of Modern English usage. In both Part One and Part Two an effort has been made to place the responsibility of learning grammar upon the student. The approach is inductive: the student is encouraged to discover for himself the laws governing the behavior of his own language. The rules and definitions are presented somewhat formally in order to guide the student as he progresses from the simpler to the more difficult phases of syntax. They are not intended to be used for exercise in memory work. Once the student has learned the forms and the uses of the parts of speech as they appear in the various types of sentences in Modern English, he will be able to make his own rules and definitions.

The use that teachers and students make of this text will vary according to the previous training and needs of a given

group. It may be used for reference or for drill. It is not
presumed that the student using this book has had previous
knowledge of the subject. Part One will provide what he
needs to know of the particular parts of speech. Part Two
will explain the intricacies of syntax and afford quantities of
material for practice in sentence analysis and in the correction
of the more common violations of good usage.

While the method of using this book is left greatly to the
discretion of the teacher, it is important to note that the lessons in Part Two are so arranged that the simpler phases of
grammar come first. After Lesson I, each succeeding lesson
presents a new phase and reviews what has preceded. For
example, the lesson on infinitives not only treats the forms
and the uses of the infinitive but also reviews modifiers, complements, and the other verbals.

Most of the teachers using this book will find the diagraming a visual aid in objectifying the sentence units. The diagrams will show which are major and which are minor
(modifying) elements of each sentence. It is important, however, to remember that the diagram can only approximate the
complete analysis, and often needs to be supplemented by
parsing (oral or written) and by some explanatory annotations.

Acknowledgment is hereby made to the authors of important works on various phases of English study, particularly
Henry Sweet, Otto Jespersen, C. T. Onions, O. F. Emerson,
Albert Baugh, George O. Curme, and others whose works are
cited in the footnotes and listed in the Bibliography.

The diagraming is largely a replica or an expansion of that
used by the grammarians Reed and Kellogg (Charles E.
Merrill and Co.). Their system of diagraming appears the
simplest, as it is certainly the most generally known, of plans
hitherto employed.

I am indebted to a number of my students for supplying
many of the sentences used in the exercises in Part Two, and
to several of my colleagues and other teachers for valuable
suggestions for the revision. For detailed suggestions. illus-

trations, and valuable criticism special thanks are due to Dr. Katheryn P. Ward and Miss Marie Bryan of the University of Maryland; to Dr. Paul M. Wheeler of Winthrop College; and to Dr. Thomas D. Ordeman of Oregon State College.

I wish also to tender special thanks to a linguist of international fame, Professor John S. Kenyon, whose scholarly criticism of the first edition and detailed suggestions and emendations proved to be an invaluable guide in making the revision.

Finally, I must add a personal word concerning my deep obligation to the late Professor Homer C. House, the co-author of the first edition of DESCRIPTIVE ENGLISH GRAMMAR. He shared with me the planning of the revision, though he did not live to share the writing. Many of the changes that I have made, particularly the deletions and additions, were ones he had suggested or approved. I have transferred to the second edition the introduction on the English language and a number of other sections written by Professor House, for the first edition, making only a few minor alterations. The changes that I have made are ones which I believe he would have made had he lived to assist in the rewriting of the text. If the revision contains mistakes, they are mine, not his. With him and with all those who have aided me, I wish to share only what is good in this book.

SUSAN EMOLYN HARMAN

University of Maryland

Contents

Introduction

The English Language

The pattern of a language is seen in its grammar (word order, forms, and structure), rather than in its vocabulary. Modern English *words* have been derived from many sources; but English grammar is essentially of one type, and classifies our mother tongue clearly as of Germanic origin. The formation of its verb system, with its vowel changes in *ride, rode, ridden,* and in its dental suffix (*-d, -t,* or *-ed*) in *hear, heard; burn, burnt, deem, deemed,* is like that of all languages of the Germanic group, dissimilar in the main to that of Latin or Greek.

The pluralizing of English nouns by vowel change (*man, men; foot, feet; mouse, mice*) is essentially Germanic (or Teutonic).[1] So is the comparison of adjectives by *-er* and *-est;* so is the declension of pronouns; so is the compounding of words (*outcome, overlook, goldsmith, watchmaker, afterthought*). Also, in the main, in the order of words in sentences, English is much nearer the Germanic idiom than it is to the French or Latin.

The affiliation of English grammar with that of the Germanic languages is what we should expect from a knowledge of English history. The Old English language (also called Anglo-Saxon by some scholars, but designated in this text as Old English or O.E.)[2] was the speech of immigrants from what is now northern Germany, who settled in England dur-

---

[1] The formation of plurals by the addition of -*s* (*lord, lords*) is Germanic, and this scheme of plural formation has in most cases been extended to nouns of foreign origin. Germanic should not be confused with German. See sketch of Indo-European languages, p. 7.

[2] Most of our standard dictionaries use AS. (A.S., A.-S.) when listing Old English derivations.

ing the fifth and later centuries. Written first in the seventh century, the language was but little influenced by contact with other forms of speech (except those of the Danes, Swedes, and Norwegians, whose Germanic dialects were very similar to English) until the great Norman Invasion, which marked the closing years of the eleventh century. The language of England from the seventh to the eleventh century is now spoken of as Old English (Anglo-Saxon).

The Norman dialect of the French language, brought by the conquerors, did not supplant English. It fused with the latter in the course of centuries, adding richly to the English vocabulary but changing English grammar relatively little. English as spoken and written from the twelfth to the sixteenth century (called by scholars Middle English) does indeed show grammatical changes, but these are in the main not the result of foreign influence. They consist largely in the breakdown of inflectional systems of nouns and pronouns, in the "leveling" (or making identical) of the past indicative and past participle of verbs, and in similar phenomena making for grammatical simplicity. It is possible that contrast afforded by the French, a less highly inflected language than the English, and the necessity of finding an easy way to take care of a great influx of new words, hastened a tendency towards simplicity already existing, but it cannot be said that the Norman French has in any real sense remodeled English grammar.

The period of Modern English, dating from the beginning of the sixteenth century, about the time of the great Revival of Learning throughout Europe, shows a vocabulary vastly expanded by the incorporation of words from foreign sources (chiefly Latin and Greek) through a process of literary borrowing. Thousands of foreign words have been taken over, bodily or with slight changes, and made to do duty in English speech. *Interim, integer, genus, focus* are unmodified Latin. *Important, regent, correct* are Latin words shorn of suffix. *Telegraph, lexicon, politics* are slightly disguised Greek. The point to be emphasized here is that English has not become a Latin or a Greek language by borrowing hosts of words from classical literature. The idiom, the inwrought habit, the born-in-the-house spirit of our tongue, as seen in our modern grammar, is as soundly Germanic (i.e., as clearly *English*) as it ever was.

In his search for the explanation of a vast number of grammatical phenomena in Modern English, the scholar will go back and upward through the years and centuries, lighting upon many interesting things in the language of every period of the history of the English people. The forms of the Old English tongue will long hold his attention. But in Old English alone he will not find the answer to every question. Back of every system of written human speech there is a still older unwritten one, which is *like* yet *different*. In his attempt to find out what the pre-English was like, our scholar may have recourse to the methods of what is known as comparative grammar. This is a study of related languages for the light which the knowledge of each one of them throws on the phenomena of all the others. There are four other Germanic literatures of about the same antiquity as Old English; namely, Gothic, Old High German, Old Norse, and Old Saxon. The first of these, Gothic, was committed to manuscript about four hundred years earlier than any of its four sisters, and is therefore a veritable gold mine to Germanic scholars.

Gothic is not a parent of English; i.e., the latter is not descended from Gothic. But in the Gothic language, phenomena parallel to those of English (such as ablaut variation, reduplicating verbs, strong and weak declensions of nouns) are seen at a considerably earlier stage. Some knowledge of Gothic is essential to advanced English scholarship.

Old English and Gothic and Old Norse and Old Saxon and Old High German are sister languages, all derived from one older parent tongue, which scholars call pre-Germanic, or simply Germanic. This language was never written, but it must not be assumed from this fact that nothing is known about it. Pre-Germanic is a hypothetical language, to be sure, but scholarship has determined many of its forms to a practical certainty by comparing the later known phenomena and reasoning back to *what must have been*. It should be noted, however, that when a modern dictionary or other text cites a hypothetical form (one not actually found in any written language), the writer distinguishes it by an asterisk (*) placed before the word or root.

Even when, in our study of the grammatical secrets of English, we have come to pre-Germanic, we are not at the end of our resources. There are clear evidences of grammatical and phonetic relationship between the earliest Germanic tongues and Latin, Greek, Sanskrit (the language of the ancient Hindus), and other old languages of western Asia and Europe. All these have inflectional systems not totally unlike, similar uses for the cases of substantives, similar devices for distinguishing voice and mode, besides a remarkable correspondence in the very consonants and vowels which go to make up the primary forms of words. It is no waste of time for the English student to learn the forms and idioms of the classic tongues.

Pre-Germanic, then, is one of a group that includes Latin, Greek, Sanskrit, and a number of other languages, whose similarity points back to an identical origin in a very ancient mother speech called the Indo-European.

In concluding this brief analysis of the relationship of English to other tongues, the authors beg to explain that they are not here urging the readers of this text to engage in an extensive study of languages other than our own. Those who care to make such study are likely to pursue it without special urging, and others will find occupations which to them will doubtless seem more profitable. The purpose of the analysis is rather to explain why, in the following pages, somewhat frequent reference is made to Old and Middle English, and even to non-English tongues. Our essential business here is the examination of English grammar as it exists today and we must not, for a moment, lose sight of this fact. But when this very business can be facilitated by a brief glimpse at other forms, we may cheerfully avail ourselves of the results of the labor in many linguistic fields of a long line of devoted grammarians.

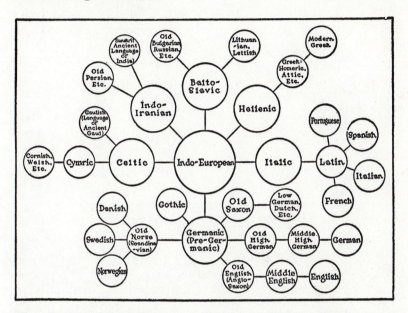

SKETCH OF THE INDO-EUROPEAN FAMILY OF LANGUAGES, SHOWING THE RELATION OF ENGLISH TO OTHER TONGUES.

Part One

GRAMMATICAL FORM

One

Terminology[1]

Grammar is the study of words and their function. In its wider sense it may include **phonology** (pronunciation), **morphology** (inflectional forms), **syntax** (the relation of words to other words in phrases, clauses, and sentences), and **semantics** (meanings of words). In its narrower sense it may deal only with the forms and with the uses of words. Since grammar is a science, it must describe and analyze the basic facts of speech, and explain and interpret the laws governing the behavior of language.

Historical grammar is a systematic study of the changes occurring in a language or a group of languages as they vary from generation to generation, from century to century. **Historical English grammar** is a study of the nature, the origin, and the growth of the English language from its earliest written form to the present time. It describes the characteristics of Old English (Anglo-Saxon), Middle English, and New (or Modern) English, and analyzes the variations and changes that occur in these three periods.

Descriptive grammar is a study of established facts and usages as they exist at a given time. A modern descriptive English grammar, as this text purports to be, deals with words and their functions in current English. It treats the

---

The terminology and the definitions given in this chapter and in the later chapters are the traditional ones, and no attempt has been made to expand the definitions of terms used in this text beyond their grammatical or linguistic significance.

most important facts of morphology and syntax of cultivated English of the present time. When historical facts are cited, it is for the purpose of throwing light on the standard level of English usage as it is spoken today in England and America.

A **sentence** (French, from Latin *sententia,* an opinion) is a group of related words containing a subject and a predicate and expressing a complete and independent unit of thought: (1) *Ducks swim.* (2) *A flock of wild ducks flew across the river.* (3) *I bought the book that you wrote.* The sentence may consist of the bare subject and predicate, as in the first of these illustrations; or of the subject and predicate with their modifiers, as in the second and third.

The **subject** of a sentence is a word or a group of words denoting that of which something is said. The subject may be a noun or any word or group of words substituting for a noun. The **predicate** is the word or group of words denoting that which is said of the subject. The predicate may be only a finite verb, or it may be a finite verb with its complements and modifiers. In *John is in the Navy, John* is the complete subject, and *is in the Navy* is the complete predicate. In *For a man to speak of himself is a difficult and delicate matter,* the subject is the phrase *For a man to speak of himself;* the complete predicate, *is a difficult and delicate matter,* consists of the verb *is* plus the noun *matter* with its adjective modifiers. In *That the earth is round has been proved,* the noun clause, *That the earth is round,* is the subject; and the predicate is the finite verb phrase *has been proved.*

A **phrase** is a group of related words without a subject or a predicate, acting as a single part of speech. Phrases may be classified as to their function (adverb, adjective, noun, verb) or as to their structure (prepositional, participial, gerundial, infinitive). The most common phrases are the verb phrases (*have come, will be seeing, might have been*) and the prepositional phrases (*at the seashore, in Europe, across the lake, in a bad humor, without reservation*).

A **clause** is a subdivision of a sentence containing a subject and a predicate. Clauses are traditionally classified as **independent** (or **principal**) and **dependent** (or **subordinate**), though these terms are somewhat loosely used when applied to noun clauses. In the sentence *Sin has many tools, but a lie is the handle which fits them all*, there are three clauses. The first two may be called independent (or principal) clauses; the third one is an adjective clause modifying the noun *handle*, and it may be called a dependent (or subordinate) clause, because it is dependent upon (or subordinate to) another clause. In *Straight is the gate, and narrow is the way*, there are two independent clauses, each of which might be a sentence if it stood alone without the *and*.[2] In the sentence *I said that I would go*, a noun clause is used as the object of the verb *said*, and the clause is in the predicate of the full sentence. *I said* cannot be regarded as a full clause, because the predicate is not complete with just the verb *said*. The clause *that I would go* is not in reality a dependent (or subordinate) member of the sentence, except perhaps for its meaning and function. Because the noun clause cannot stand alone and because of its dependence upon the full sentence for its meaning and construction, it is also generally classified as a dependent (or subordinate) clause.

In accordance with the general purpose of a sentence, it may be classified as **declarative, interrogative, imperative, or exclamatory.**[3]

A **declarative sentence** states a fact or makes an assertion and closes with a period: *Roger Ascham taught Queen Elizabeth Latin and Greek. I do not approve of wars.*

An **interrogative sentence** asks for information. It always closes with an interrogation mark. The question may be introduced by the verb or by an interrogative pronoun, an interrogative adjective, or an interrogative adverb; or it may

---

[2] The term *clause* is not usually applied to a simple sentence, but to any division of a complete sentence containing a subject and a predicate.

[3] Sentences are also classified by form as simple, **complex,** and **compound.** These will be defined and analyzed in Part Two of this text.

have the form of the declarative sentence, especially if an affirmative answer is expected or inferred: *Is your brother a soldier? Which book did you choose? Who is to be invited to your party? When did your sister leave? You saw* [did you not?] *the thief go through the window?*

An **imperative sentence** issues a command, a request, or imprecation. It, like the declarative sentence, closes with a period. The sentence is addressed to some person or some group of persons. The subject is usually implied: *Shut the door at once. Let us all pray for peace. O Lord, give us this day our daily bread.*

The **exclamatory sentence** expresses strong emotion: surprise, relief, grief, fear, hate, delight, etc. It closes with an exclamation mark, which often distinguishes it in the written form from the declarative, interrogative, and imperative sentences. It is often expressed in the form of an indirect (and sometimes a direct) question: *Frailty, thy name is woman! Long live the King! How could a father be so cruel!* [4]

Form (**Morphology**) and **Syntax** are the two principal phases of grammar to be treated in this text. Form has to do with the shape of words and the meanings and relationships that may result from inflection. *Child, boy, man* have singular forms; their plural forms are *children, boys, men.* In early English, form was much more important than it is today in differentiating the meanings of words. The gender, case, and number of a noun or a pronoun could be revealed in the form used. The noun, the adjective, and the adverb could usually be differentiated from one another and from the other parts of speech by their forms. But in Modern English these inflectional markings have been leveled (reduced, simplified) so that the form that a part of speech has in a sentence does not reveal as much as it once did, the inflectional meanings

---

[4] The interrogation mark may be used to close this type of sentence when the question requests a reply. The interrogative sentence asks for information; the exclamatory sentence exclaims the question. A question exclaimed is a rhetorical question, and no answer is expected from the one addressed; as, *And what is so rare as a day in June? Is this the man who scourged or feasted kings?*

in present-day English often being determined by the positions words occupy in sentences.

Function (or **Form**) **words** are sometimes called **morphemes** or **empty words.** They are words and phrases that have lost their original or individual meaning and serve only to show the relationship or the structure of **full words** (i.e., words having independent meaning of their own). *More* and *most* are function words when used to form the comparative and superlative degrees of adjectives and adverbs. *That* in *That the earth is round has been proved*, *is* in *The horse is a domestic animal*, *there* in *There are two of us*, *it* in *It is raining*, and *of* in *The Sea of Galilee is 14 miles long*, are all mere function words.

Inflection is the change, or modification, in the form of a word to indicate a change in its meaning. Verbs change their form (inflect) to show a change in tense (*see, saw*), person (*do, does; am, is*), number (*was, were*), voice (*give, is given*), and mode (*is, be*). Nouns and pronouns may change their form to show gender (*actor, actress*), or number (*boy, boys; man, men*), or case (*boy, boy's; he, his, him*). The inflection of a part of speech may be terminal (*boy, boys; red, redder; learn, learned*), or internal (*ride, rode; goose, geese*), or both terminal and internal (*sell, sold; bring, brought*). The inflection of a verb is usually called **conjugation;** that of the adjective and adverb, **comparison;** and that of nouns and pronouns, **declension.**[5] Prepositions, conjunctions, and interjections do not change their forms to show changes in meaning, and hence are called uninflected parts of speech.

Syntax (Greek *syn*, together, and *taxis*, arranging) means sentence structure: the orderly arrangement, relation, agreement of parts of the sentence in accordance with usage, or

---

[5] "The nominative was anciently held to be the primary and original form, and was likened to a perpendicular line from which the variations, or *oblique* cases, were regarded as fallings away (hence called *casus*, cases, or fallings); and an enumerating of the various forms, being a sort of progressive descent from the noun's upright form, was called a *declension*. By a later extension of meaning *case* was applied also to the nominative."

—*Webster's New International Dictionary.*

custom. It has to do with the use (or construction) of words, phrases, and clauses in a given sentence.

Parts of speech are the divisions into which words are classified according to their functions in a sentence. Most grammarians recognize eight parts of speech[6] in classifying all the words in the language which are used in connected discourse. Each part of speech has a special use (or part) in the make-up of the sentence of which it is a unit. The **noun** (the name of a person, place, or thing), the **pronoun** (a word substituting for a noun), and the **adjective** (a word qualifying a noun or pronoun) are generally associated with or thought to belong to the subject of the sentence or to substantives belonging to or relating to the subject. The **verb** (a word asserting action, being, or state of being) and the **adverb** (when a modifier of the verb) are felt to belong to the predicate of the sentence. The **preposition** ('a word placed before' to show relation between words) and the **conjunction** ('a yoking,' or connecting, word) show relationship or connect units within the sentence. The **interjection** (an ejaculation, an exclamation) is used to show emotion.

The same word may belong to more than one part of speech, the classification depending upon the use of the word, not upon its form. *Love* may be a noun (*Love rules the court*), or a verb (*Love your enemies*). *In* may be a preposition (*Duncan is in his grave*), or an adverb (*Come in*). *For* may be a preposition (*He came for the money*), or a conjunction (*Let another be judge, for I wish to enter the contest*).

A group of words (phrase or clause) may serve as a single part of speech. The infinitive phrase, for example, may be a noun (*To lie is wrong*), or an adverb (*He came to see me*), or an adjective (*I have an ax to grind*). The gerund is al-

---

[6] Some grammarians exclude the interjection from the list of the parts of speech; others separate the articles (*the, a, an*) from the adjective division; and others classify the expletive as a full part of speech. The number of parts of speech may, therefore, vary according to these or other similar exclusions and inclusions. School grammars generally recognize the traditional eight parts of speech, which will be discussed in Part One of this text.

ways a verbal noun and the entire phrase of which it is a part is frequently used for a noun: (*I enjoy playing baseball; I cannot approve of your going away*). Clauses may be used as nouns (*I know that you are my best friend*), as adverbs (*I go when I am invited*), or as adjectives (*I like the suit that you gave me*).

One part of speech may sometimes be converted into another by changing its form. An adjective by the addition of *-ness* or *-ty* may become a noun (*sweetness, purity*). Some nouns may become adjectives by adding *-ful* (*hopeful, cheerful*), or *-y* (*milky, fishy*), or *-ed* or *-d* (*talented, diseased*); or by adding other similar suffixes. The adjective may serve as a noun by ellipsis (*The good die young; Take the bitter with the sweet*). Some adjectives may become verbs by the addition of *-en* (*whiten, blacken, sweeten, thicken*), or adverbs by the addition of *-ly* (*slowly, rapidly*). The noun or pronoun in the possessive case may have the function of an adjective (*The boy's hat; My coat*). Other conversions of a similar nature will be treated more fully in the chapters devoted to the different parts of speech.

Usage is a term employed by linguists to classify speech habits or language peculiarities, to show what is or has been practiced at a given time by a stated group of users of a language. The term is frequently qualified to give us such expressions as *historical usage, Modern English usage, standard usage, current usage, British and American usage*, and so forth. The laws and rules of grammar are not always based upon historical facts or upon logic (as in mathematics and chemistry), but on current standard usage established by cultured and educated people whose influence is considered important.

Idioms and **idiomatic phrases** are terms used by grammarians, philologists, and lexicographers to explain or classify the unusual, the illogical, or the peculiar expressions in a language. Idiomatic expressions frequently defy grammatical analysis, and are, therefore, not easily translated into other words and phrases in the same language, or into other languages word for word without losing some of their highly specialized meaning. *Had better* in *You had better go at once* is an idiomatic expression. *It* in *It is snowing*, *there* in *There is a loaf of bread on the table*, and *How do you do?* in a formal salutation are all idiomatic expressions that occur very often in American English. When the terms *idiom* and *idiomatic* are used in this text, it is to be understood that they describe expressions that have been accepted through custom and usage as good English, even though these expressions may not always be used in such a way as to conform to the general and traditional rules of English grammar.

Solecism is a term used to describe a blunder in grammar or a construction not sanctioned by good usage. Any word or combination of words deviating from the idiom of the language or from the rules of syntax may be called a **solecism**; as, *He don't* for *He doesn't*, and *between you and I* for *between you and me*.

A **barbarism** is a word or phrase that is not in good use. It may be a newly coined word, a slang expression, a vulgarism, a provincialism, or any illiterate or unauthorized expression. *Ain't*, *orate*, *aviate*, *complected*, *gym*, *woozy*, *nowheres*, *attackted*, *unbeknownst*, and *irregardless* are all barbarisms, because these expressions are not used by cultured writers and speakers.

Colloquialisms are expressions used in ordinary conversation. They belong to the informal (popular or common) level of speech. Colloquial English admits words, phrases, forms, and constructions that would be out of place in formal oral or written speech. Because colloquial expressions without the aid of gestures, facial expressions, or tone of voice are often inexact, their use should be restricted to our informal communications. Colloquial English may include contractions, such as *I'll*, *you've*, *won't*, *shouldn't*, *can't*, and *don't*; or it may include such improprieties as *It is me; It is them; You are different than me.* When a colloquial expression becomes universally used, it may be regarded as standard English.

An **obsolete** expression is one that is no longer in use. An **archaic** expression is one that has the characteristics of a much earlier period and is on the way out of use. Any word is archaic if it is too old to be generally used. Poets frequently employ archaisms and thus prevent their becoming obsolete. Here are a few examples of obsolete or archaic English: *whilom, sikerly* (used by Chaucer for *surely*), *thilke* (for *that*), *methinks* (it seems to me), *hideth, wert, wast, quoth, thou, thy, thine, thee, ye, wrought* (for *worked*), *gotten, thrice, erstwhile, eftsoon.* To determine whether a word is obsolete or archaic, one must depend upon its classification in the standard dictionaries.

Two

Nouns

A noun is a name of anything. It may be the name of a person (*Joseph, boy, teacher*), an object (*box, toy*), a quality or condition (*purity, goodness, poverty*), a weight or quantity of something (*pound, ounce, pint, bushel*), a measure (*yard, rod*), an action (*movement, performance*), a state (*death*), an occurrence (*accident*), a sense impression (*sound, noise*), and a great many other sorts of things. Note that each of these headings (*person, object, quality, action,* etc.) is also a noun.

The term **substantive** is used to denote a noun or any word or combination of words used as a substitute for a noun; as, a pronoun (*I am **He** that liveth; **That** is my book, and **this** is yours*); an adjective (*Blessed are the **merciful**; The **poor** and the **rich**, the **weak** and the **strong**, the **young** and the **old** have one common father*); an adverb (*But an eternal **now** does not always last*); a verbal phrase (***Never to have suffered** is a misfortune*); or a clause (*The question is, **"Who locked the door?"***).

CLASSES OF NOUNS

In Old English, as in Latin, Greek, and German, nouns are identified and classified according to form, and are declined according to fixed inflectional patterns in the various declensions. But in Modern English, form does not play an important part in the identifying or the classifying of nouns for inflectional purposes, since most nouns are now declined alike, form and gender having very little influence on the inflection of substantives.[1] In the transition from the grammatical gender pattern of Old English to the natural gender distinction of Modern English, nouns have lost their various declensional classification, and are now somewhat arbitrarily classified (1) as to **form** and (2) as to **meaning.**

Nouns Classified as to Form

When classified as to form, nouns are generally grouped into (1) **simple,** (2) **compound,** and (3) **phrasal (or group) nouns.**

1. The **simple nouns** include all primary nouns in the language; that is, those which have not been formed by combining two separate words (*boy, boat, house, man, wife, brother, ship*).[2]

2. **Compound nouns** are those which have been formed by combining two or more words having individual meaning of their own when standing alone. The compound nouns may be formed by combining two nouns (*bookcase, bathroom, sunflower, firecracker, moonlight, thunderstorm*), or an adjective and a noun (*blackbird, greenhouse, blindfold, blacksnake, bluefish*), or a verb and a noun (*washrag, scarecrow, earthquake, breakfast, leapyear*), or an adverb and a verb (*outcome, downfall, outcast, walkout, outlet*); or by other similar combinations.

3. **Phrasal nouns**[3] are *groups* of related words, written sep-

---

[1] There are a few nouns in Modern English which show irregularities in the formation of gender and number (*man, men; woman, women*); but these are mainly survivals of Old English inflections, or they are borrowed nouns which have retained their original forms for differentiating gender and number (*alumnus, alumni; alumna, alumnae*). These irregularities will be treated later in this chapter under the Inflection of Nouns.

[2] The simple nouns may include derivative nouns; that is, nouns formed by adding suffixes to other nouns, or to adverbs, adjectives, and verbs; or to the stems of any of these parts of speech. Such words as *goodness, worship, worshiper, width, kingdom, reading, actor, actress, childhood, judgment, commission, function, pity*, etc. are strictly speaking not compound nouns, since they are not individual words joined to make new names.

[3] Phrasal nouns are sometimes called compound nouns, and the differentiation of the two classes is not important grammatically, the chief difference being that the component parts are run together in the compound nouns; and these are

arately or with hyphens, serving for the names of persons, places, things, or ideas (*Alfred the Great, King George VI, Commander in Chief, White House, Holy Writ, Duke of Windsor, son-in-law, maid-of-honor, fountain pen, attorney-general, forget-me-not*).

The first two classes are in the main regular in their inflectional changes. The group nouns, however, show some irregularities when declined for number. These irregularities will be treated later in this chapter in the discussion of Number of Nouns.

Nouns Classified as to Meaning

According to the meaning they represent, nouns may be divided into several classes: **common** or **proper, concrete or abstract, collective, individual, mass, material,** etc.

A **common noun** is the name of a class of objects: *ship, insect, city, teacher, object.* The name *city* is common to thousands of places. It does not distinguish one from another. The common noun may name a mass of objects or a material: *iron, pewter, soil.* It may name a number of things collected to represent one object or group: *army, fleet, committee, jury, flock, herd.* It is more often an individual noun, and denotes only one object in the singular, and more than one in the plural.

A **proper noun** (Latin *proprius*, one's own) is an individual name: *Woodrow Wilson, Birmingham, John the Baptist.* The name *Woodrow Wilson* was legally the property of a particular man. It was 'proper' to him only. The proper noun may be a person's full name, his Christian name, or his surname; or it may be just his nickname: *Edgar Allan Poe, Arnold, Joe, Slim Jim, Red Grange, Donald Duck, Orphan Annie.*

In the written texts the proper noun is differentiated from the common noun by being capitalized. The following are

---

kept separated by hyphenation or by being written as individual words in the phrasal nouns; e.g., we write *sunflower*, but *Holy Writ; mankind,* but *human being.*

NOUNS   **23**

proper nouns and should be capitalized: *Adam Bede* (a book);
Hull House (a home); *Mars* (a planet); *The Missouri* (a bat-
tleship); *Lassie* (a dog); *Big Ben* (a timepiece); *Black Beauty*
(a horse); *England, Egypt,* and *Lake Superior* (geographic
names); *Bambi* (an animal); and many other names of similar nature.

Through popular usage proper nouns change into common
nouns. *Calico, china* (porcelain), *mackinaw, boycott* were
once proper names, but they have now lost their individuality. These nouns are no longer capitalized. A few proper
nouns retain the capitalization when they change into common nouns, especially if some of the proper noun quality is
retained: *The Milton of this age, the John Does, the Shake-
speares, a Milton, a Lucifer, a Hitler.*

Unless personified, names of the seasons (*spring, summer,
fall, winter*), names of diseases (*measles, mumps, smallpox*),
names of flowers (*tulips, roses, crocus, marigold*), names of
educational subjects[4] (*physics, mathematics, history, psychology*), and names of the points of the compass (*west, northwest,
east, south*) are common nouns, and hence are not capitalized.

All nouns in the English language are either **proper** or **common**; and by a different kind of classification all **proper** and
common nouns may be classified as either **concrete** or **abstract**.

A **concrete noun** (Latin *concretus*, grown together) names
a person, place, or thing which exists as a tangible and definite substance. *Boy, house, car, tree,* and *book* are concrete
nouns.

An **abstract noun** (Latin *abstrahere*, to draw from) names a
quality, a condition, or an activity thought of separately and
hence *abstracted* from the concrete substance to which it
belongs. Every concrete substance, animate or inanimate,
possesses qualities or attributes which can be named by abstract nouns; e.g., *blueness* may be 'abstracted' from eyes, a

---

[4] Names of languages are always capitalized (*Latin, Greek, French, English,
German*). Also the names of particular courses of study are proper nouns, and
should be capitalized (*English I, Educational Psychology, American History 7*).

violet, the sky, the sea, or a piece of linen cloth. Many adjectives may be converted into abstract nouns by the addition of certain noun suffixes, such as *-ness, -ty,* or *-th: sweetness, goodness, purity, quaintness, loyalty, truth, security.* Verb forms may also be converted into abstract nouns: *conversation, ignorance, writing, speech, action, activity.* It is well, however, to remember that not all abstract nouns are derived from other parts of speech. Many common and important abstract ideas have individual names of their own. *Energy, joy, love, fever, disease, thunder, summer, faith, beauty, age,* and *hope* are all abstract nouns which are not derived from other parts of speech, though some of them may now have adjective and verb uses.

Because nouns have a way of suggesting complex meanings, and because there are degrees of abstractness and concreteness, the same word may have a concrete meaning in addition to its abstract one. Abstract nouns are not usually pluralized, but whenever an abstract noun takes on concrete meaning, it may have both the singular and plural forms. Observe the abstract and concrete qualities in the following: *I have no acquaintance with the arts; All of my acquaintances live in the East; Writing is an art; We studied reading, writing, and arithmetic; This book contains all of the writings of Mark Twain.*

The minor classifications of nouns are usually subdivisions of the common and concrete nouns, though they may be also proper or abstract.

A collective noun is sometimes called a noun of multitude. It names a group of persons, places, or things gathered together into a unit: *swarm, majority, audience, number, crowd, committee, Congress, bunch, the Senate, nation, United States, crowd.* The collective noun in the singular number usually takes a singular verb, though it requires a plural verb if the individuals in the group are thought of as acting separately. In *The Jury has its report ready,* the collective noun *jury* is singular in meaning, because the group is thought of as a unit.

In *The jury were in their seats before we arrived*, the members of the *jury* are thought of as individuals, each in his own seat. We may say *All the crew were ill*, or *The crew is now assembled;* also *The number of men present was not large*, or *A great number of prisoners have been released.*

Sometimes the collective noun in the plural is thought of as a single unit: *United States.* In *The United States is a democratic nation*, the subject is plural in form, but usually regarded as having singular meaning. The plural form and plural meaning of *state* is seen in *The New England states are very small.*

The plural form of a collective noun usually denotes more than one group; as, *All the committees have been appointed, and each committee must prepare a report for our next meeting.* Occasionally the collective noun in the plural has a meaning entirely different from the singular: *letters, morals, spectacles,* etc.

The **individual noun** names a unit which represents or belongs to a class of objects: *bear, tree, dog, man.*

The **mass noun**, sometimes called a material noun, names a bulk or *mass* or quantity of matter or an aggregation of things united in one body: *iron, pewter, flour, water, bread.* Mass nouns in the singular are usually modified by *much* and *little*, rather than by *many* and *few.* The plural form of a mass noun may have a meaning entirely different from the singular, and yet represent a mass idea: *news, clothes, irons, weeds.* Sometimes the plural form takes a singular verb; as, *Your news is sad.*

INFLECTION OF NOUNS

The **inflection**, modification in form, of nouns is largely employed to denote difference in gender, case, and number. In strict logic, it cannot be said that these differences are always indicated by modifications. The feminine of *boy* is *girl*—not a modification of the word *boy*, but an entirely different word. The nominative and the objective cases **of** *boy* have the same form. The singular and plural forms of *sheep* are alike.

Gender of Nouns

Gender is the classification of nouns and pronouns according to the sex (or the absence of sex) denoted.

The word *gender* (from Latin *genus*) originally meant *race* or *kind;* and in the Indo-European languages it was not always an expression of sex distinctions. In the older languages there were usually three, though sometimes only two, genders, and all nouns had to belong to one of these genders so as to have a fixed declensional pattern. Since all the modifiers of nouns in the languages having these gender distinctions had to agree with the nouns they modified in gender, number, and case, it was important for the users of the languages to know all the inflectional markings for each gender. In Latin the word *lingua* (tongue, language) is feminine gender; the word *cnimus* (mind, mood, spirit) is masculine gender; and the word *bellum* (war) is neuter gender. An adjective modifying *lingua* must follow the feminine gender pattern. Adjectives modifying *animus* must follow the masculine declension; and those modifying *bellum* must follow the neuter declensional pattern. In Modern English, however, the words *tongue, language, mind, mood, spirit*, and *war* denote no sex, and hence are all classified as neuter nouns. They possess no peculiar inflectional markings which one must remember when using them. When nouns are classified, as they are in Latin, Modern German, and Old English, for inflectional purposes; that is, to show grammatical distinctions, they are said to have **grammatical gender**. When nouns are classified to express sex distinctions, as in Modern English, they are said to have **natural gender**.

The **masculine gender** denotes the male sex: *man, hero, bridegroom, rooster, uncle, duke, actor.*

The **feminine gender** denotes the female sex: *woman, heroine, bride, hen, aunt, duchess, actress.*

The **neuter gender** denotes a lack of sex: *book, language, war, mind, river, chair, love, virtue.*

Nouns and pronouns which refer to persons or animals of undetermined sex are said to be of **common,** or **indefinite, gender:** *child, calf, student, singer, chicken, swimmer, cousin, citizen, bear, writer.*

Ways of Showing Gender. The distinction between masculine and feminine is indicated in the following ways:

1. By different words: *bachelor, maid; brother, sister; father, mother; gander, goose; husband, wife; king, queen; son, daughter; uncle, aunt; wizard, witch;* etc.

2. By different endings, with or without change in the spelling of the stem of the word:

a. Many feminine nouns are differentiated from corresponding masculine forms by the suffix *-ess: author, authoress;*[5] *abbot, abbess; actor, actress; baron, baroness; count, countess; duke, duchess; emperor, empress; host, hostess; murderer, murderess,*[5] *Negro, Negress; poet, poetess;*[5] *prince, princess; waiter, waitress;* etc.

b. Certain nouns, mostly proper, borrowed directly from Greek, Latin, French, Spanish, Italian, etc. retain their original gender terminations, with or without Anglicized spelling: *Augustus, Augustine; Carl, Caroline; don, donna; equestrian, equestrienne; Joseph, Josephine; Harry, Harriet; testator, testatrix;* etc.

c. A few nouns of Old English origin append a masculine suffix to a feminine base: *bridegroom, bride; widower, widow.*

3. By compounding an element of known gender with another element: *billy goat, nanny goat; Englishman, English-*

---

[5] Present usage tends to discard such feminines as *authoress, poetess, murderess,* etc., in favor of the corresponding masculine forms, that is, to treat the masculine as common gender.

woman; gentleman, gentlewoman; milkman, milkmaid: merman, mermaid; manservant, maidservant; and so forth.

CASE

Case (French *cas*, from Latin *casus*, falling, happening)[6] is the distinction or mark of distinction which denotes the grammatical relation of a noun or a pronoun to other words in a communication. In Old English and in other highly inflected languages, the function of a noun or pronoun can usually be determined by its case form. In Modern English, however, case markings for both nouns and pronouns have been greatly reduced, nouns having only two and pronouns only three case forms. Most grammarians still recognize three cases for nouns: **nominative, possessive** (or **genitive**), and **objective** (or **accusative**). Two of these must be determined by word order or by context, not by inflectional markings.[7] The **nominative** and **objective cases** in Modern English nouns are always identical, the difference in forms between these cases appearing only in pronouns. The **possessive** (or **genitive**) **case** of nouns is marked by the addition of the apostrophe and *s* (*'s*) or by the *s* and the apostrophe (*s'*) to the nominative. The three cases, then, to be considered in the study of nouns and their functions are the **nominative,** the **possessive,** and the **objective.**

The **nominative case** is sometimes called the **subjective case,** because its primary function is to name the subject of a finite verb. With the loss of case inflections in the development of our language, the nominative case performs some of the functions which belonged to other cases in Old English.

The Uses of the Nominative Case

1. Subject of sentence or clause (subject of finite verb):

---

[6] For explanation of the connection in the idea of 'falling' with that of the grammatical case, see note 5, p. 15.

[7] Jespersen classifies nouns as possessing two cases: the common case (the nominative and objective forms being alike) and the genitive. See his *Essentials of English Grammar,* pp. 138–139, for a fuller treatment of this subject.

(1) The *sun* has set. (2) *John* (or *He*) has gone. (3) *Mary* came when the *teacher* called. (4) I know that my *Redeemer* liveth. (5) The *library* purchased the book which my *father* wrote.

2. Predicate nominative (subjective complement):

(1) I will be the *pattern* of all patience. (2) You may come as my *guest*. (3) We are *men*, my liege. (4) He was elected *chairman*.

3. Direct address:[8]

(1) *Mary*, may I borrow your book? (2) I thank you, *gentlemen*, for this cordial reception. (3) *Mr. chairman*, I rise to a point of order.

4. Explanatory modifier (an appositive of a noun or pronoun in the nominative case):

(1) This is Mount Vernon, the *home* of George and Martha Washington. (2) We, the *people* of the United States, believe in democracy. (3) There were only three applicants for the position; namely, *Mary*, *Henry*, and *Joe*.

5. Nominative by pleonasm:

(1) *Father*, *mother*, *brother*, *sister*—all are dead. (2) The *smith*, a mighty man is he.

6. Nominative absolute (*absolute* from Latin *absolvere*, to untie, to unloose) so named because it is *free* or *unloose* from the rest of the sentence:

(1) The *teacher* being ill, we had no school today. (2) The *day* being stormy, we stayed at home.

7. Nominative of exclamation:

(1) *Darkness and devils!* Saddle my horses. (2) *Heavens!*

---

[8] A noun or pronoun in this construction is sometimes said to be in the **vocative case.** The term *vocative* ('calling') is borrowed from Latin grammars. In *Woe unto you, ye lawmakers*, there is good proof that the nominative had this function in early Modern English. The *ye* must not be construed as an appositive of *you*, since *ye* is in the nominative case, and *you* is in the objective case after the preposition *unto*.

can this be true?   (3) O *liberty! liberty!* how many crimes
are committed in thy name.

The **possessive case** (in many grammars called the **genitive case**), as the name suggests, is now used chiefly to denote
ownership (possession), source, or a similar relation.

The possessive case relation between nouns and pronouns
was expressed in the oldest English only by the inflected
genitive form, distinguished in Modern English nouns by the
final *s* or *z* sound, written *'s* or *s'*, and in pronouns by the
forms *my, mine, our, ours, thy, thine, your, yours, his, her, hers,
its, their, theirs,* and *whose.*

In late Old English the *of-phrase* (the preposition *of* and
its object) began to be used along with the inflected genitive
and its equivalent, and now this so-called phrasal (or periphrastic) form can be used in most instances as a substitute
for the inflected one.   The inflected possessive now always
precedes its noun, and the phrasal one almost always follows
it.   We may say *The **President's** sons are all married,* or *The
sons **of the President** are all married.*

Uses of the Possessive Case

Nouns in the possessive case are used as adjective modifiers
to express the following relations:

1. Possessive: *Sarah's* hat, *Brown's* farm, the *farmer's* pig,
   the *bird's* nest, the *dog's* bone, etc.

In this classification the idea of possession is used in a
somewhat broader sense than mere ownership, which belongs
strictly to persons, and is extended to include various sorts of
attachments or connections (*the **earth's** surface*); authorship
(***Byron's** poems*); origin, parenthood, or other close relationship (*the **preacher's** oldest son; my **sister's** husband*); manu-
facture (***Smith Brothers'** Cough Drops*).   All of these meanings may well have been extended from the idea of possession
or ownership.

2. Subjective:[9] They awaited the *President's* arrival; The *officer's* actions were very strange.

The subjective meaning always depends upon a noun containing some verbal idea. *Arrival* and *actions* in the illustrations given above are two such nouns, and the possessive case forms represent the subjects of the action named in the nouns they modify. The subjective idea can be made obvious by an equivalent sentence in which the corresponding verb is substituted for the verbal noun, and a nominative is substituted for the possessive form: *They waited until the President arrived; The officer acted very strangely.*

3. Objective:[9] the *soldier's* discharge, *Caesar's* murderers, the *thief's* arrest, *Othello's* punishment.

The analysis of the objective use of the possessive case is parallel to that of the subjective. In the objective, which likewise always depends upon a verbal noun, the noun in the possessive case contains the object of the verbal idea, and the objective relation can likewise be shown by replacing the possessive with an objective case form. Observe that the possessive case forms given under **3** above become the objects of finite verbs in the following: *The Army discharged the soldier; The conspirators murdered Caesar; The officer arrested the thief; The state punished Othello.*

4. Descriptive: a *year's* leave, a *week's* vacation, an *hour's* delay, a few *minutes'* rest, *Job's* patience, the *men's* chorus, a *woman's* reason, a *girl's* college, a *stone's* throw, *Friday's* newspaper.

This use of the possessive case is closely related to that of possession or ownership, and some of the examples given above might be classed as possessive.

The **objective** (or **accusative**) **case** is sometimes called the **object-case,** because its primary functions in present-day

---

[9] These constructions correspond to the Old English **subjective genitive** (the doer of an act) and the **objective genitive** (the receiver of an act), the terminology being that used in Latin grammars.

English are to name the receiver (or object) of a transitive verb and the object of a preposition. It has, however, other important uses. In Old English, as in Latin, Greek, and German, the majority of transitive verbs took objects in the accusative, though there were verbs which took objects in the genitive, dative, and instrumental cases. With the leveling of case inflections in the Middle English period, the accusative extended its scope and supplanted the other cases in all object relations, including the *object* of the preposition.

In Modern English grammars, and particularly in our American English grammars, the term *accusative* is being supplanted by the term *objective*. But in historical language studies and in almost all the grammars of foreign languages, the term *accusative* survives as the name of the *object-case* in the declensions of nouns and pronouns. It is well for the student to know that, whenever in Modern English the terms *accusative* and *objective* are used to name any of the following relations, they have identical meaning.

Uses of the Objective Case

1. Object complement (direct object of a transitive verb):

1. He killed the *bear*. 2. He praised her *taste*, and she commended his *understanding*.

2. Objective complement (noun or pronoun in the predicate referring to the object complement):

1. I will make thee *ruler* over many things. 2. I consider this man an *expert*. 3. They named the baby *Mary*.

3. Object of preposition (the principal term of a prepositional phrase):

(1) Charity begins at *home*. (2) The months of *July* and *August* were named after *Julius Caesar* and *Augustus Caesar*.

4. Explanatory modifier (an appositive of a noun or pronoun in the objective case):

(1) We have a building of God, a *house* not made with

hands. (2) We gave our neighbors, the *Sheldons*, some fruit. (3) I sent the peaches to Arthur Brooks, our *gardener*. (4) Whom will you send, *Mary* or *Anne?*

5. Adverbial objective (the indirect object and other nouns used as adverbs):

(1) Give a *man* a horse he can ride. (2) Give *John* and the *guests* the two biggest pieces of cake. (3) *Home* they brought their warrior dead. (4) She carried the basket two *miles*.

6. The subject of an infinitive:

(1) God never made his work for *man* to mend. (2) I want *you* to sing at my wedding.

7. The subjective complement of an infinitive whose subject is in the objective case:

(1) I want the Captain to be my *escort*. (2) I invited John and his wife to be my *guests*.

8. Retained object complement (object of a verb in the passive voice):

(1) I was given a sabbatical *leave*. (2) He was taught *reading*, *writing*, and *arithmetic*.

9. Cognate object (sometimes a normally intransitive verb becomes transitive and takes a noun related to the verb as its object):

(1) I dreamed a bad *dream*. (2) He lived a full *life*. (3) She danced three *dances*. (4) I sang three *songs*.

10. The object of a verbal (participle, gerund, or infinitive):

(1) The lady playing the *piano* is my sister. (2) I enjoy having *guests*. (3) I want to meet *John* and his *wife*.

NUMBER OF NOUNS

Number is the property of a word which indicates whether one or more than one object is designated. A noun or other substantive indicating one person, object, or idea is in the

singular number; a substantive indicating more than one is in the **plural number.**[10]   Some exceptions to this last statement are found in collective nouns that have singular forms but indicate groups of more than one (*committee, family, herd*). But the group can often be pluralized (*committees, families, herds*).   *Cattle* formerly a collective noun is now no longer treated as collective, but as an ordinary plural, of common gender and plural construction.

The plural is differentiated from the singular by the addition of *-s* or *-es;* by the addition of *-en;* by mutation (change of vowel); and, in foreign words, by various changes based upon foreign inflections.   A few nouns show no difference in singular and plural, the number being determined by the context.   In Old English, plurals were formed by the addition of *-as, -an, -u, -ru,* etc. endings, as well as by mutation. The *-as* ending, modified in Modern English to *-es* and *-s,* is now the suffix most generally employed in plural formation, having been extended to most words from Old English that once had other plural endings, and to all fully naturalized loan-words.   The *-an* (now become *-en, -n*) is seen in *oxen, children, kine, brethren,* of which *children* and *brethren* show traces of the old *-ru* declension, and *kine* (plural of *cow*) and *brethren* exemplify mutation.   *Shoon* for *shoes, eyen* for *eyes, hosen* for *hose* are now archaic.

Mutation (Latin *mutatio* from *mutare,* to change) was a phenomenon vigorously alive in a period preceding the earlier records of the English language, and is still active in Modern German, being referred to in German grammars as **umlaut** (literally, "around sound").   It consists, in the larger number of instances, in the "raising" of a low (guttural) vowel, *a* (pronounced *ah*), *o, u,* to meet the higher level of a high (palatal) vowel, *i, e,* in the syllable following.   Thus one may suppose a singular *man* (pronounced *mahn*), plural

---

[10] In some of the ancient languages a dual number also is found.   It refers to two persons or two objects.   Certain pronouns in Old English show singular, dual, and plural forms.

*manī[11] (pronounced *mahnee*). In pronouncing the vowel *a* in the plural, the tongue would be unconsciously raised towards the position it must occupy (near the hard, or front, palate) in pronouncing the *ī* (pronounced as *ee* in *see* or as *i* in *machine*) vowel of the plural. The result would be *menī. But after the *ī* of the plural had raised the vowel as sounded, the changed vowel would itself be felt to indicate the plural sufficiently, and the ending would be dropped; hence singular *man*, plural *men*. Similarly *gōs*, *gēsī, *gēs* (English *goose, geese*) and many others.

The same phenomenon of mutation (umlaut) operated in the formation of verbs from nouns, adjectives, and other verbs; in the formation of abstract nouns from adjectives, etc.[12]

Rules for Pluralizing Nouns

I. *a*. Most nouns form their plurals by adding -*s* to the singular: *apple, apples; boy, boys; flower, flowers; girl, girls; tree, trees; toe, toes;* etc.

b. Nouns ending in silent -*e* preceded by a fricative (a hissing, or "rub," sound) add an extra syllable in taking on the -*s: bridge, bridges; cage, cages; corpse, corpses; prize, prizes;* etc.

II. *a*. Nouns ending in a fricative (hissing, or "rub," sound), -*s*, -*z*, -*x*, -*ch*, -*sh*, add -*es* to the singular to form their plurals, thereby adding a syllable: *bench, benches; box, boxes; church, churches; lens, lenses; match, matches; tax, taxes; witch, witches;* etc.

b. But nouns ending in -*th* are exceptional, usually adding -*s* only: *moth, moths; mouth, mouths; oath, oaths; path, paths; youth, youths;* etc.

---

[11] The asterisk before a word means that it is a supposed pre-Old English form.

[12] For a good table of umlaut changes in the pre-English, see Bright's *An Anglo-Saxon Reader*, pp. xvii ff. For a full explanation of mutation, see Moore and Knott's *Elements of Old English*, 8th ed. (Ann Arbor, 1940), pp. 63–66.

III. *a.* Many nouns ending in -*f* or -*fe* change *f* to *v* and add -*es* or -*s* to form their plurals: *beef, beeves; calf, calves; knife, knives; life, lives; shelf, shelves; wolf, wolves; wife, wives;* etc.

b. However, many nouns ending in -*f* or -*fe* merely add -*s* to form their plurals, without change in the consonant: *belief, beliefs; cliff, cliffs; gulf, gulfs; grief, griefs; kerchief, kerchiefs; roof, roofs; waif, waifs;* etc.

IV. Nouns ending in -*y* preceded by a consonant change *y* to *i* and add -*es* to form their plurals:[13] *army, armies; body, bodies; country, countries; lady, ladies; spy, spies; worry, worries;* etc.

V. Nouns ending in -*y* preceded by a vowel form their plurals regularly by adding -*s*: *abbey, abbeys; alley, alleys; boy, boys; chimney, chimneys; key, keys; journey, journeys; monkey, monkeys; turkey, turkeys;* etc.

VI. Nouns ending in -*o* may add -*s* or -*es* to form their plurals:

a. If the final -*o* is preceded by a vowel, the plural is regularly formed by adding -*s* to the singular: *cameo, cameos; embryo, embryos; folio, folios; radio, radios; studio, studios; trio, trios;* etc.

b. Some nouns ending in final -*o* preceded by a consonant add -*es* to form their plurals: *echo, echoes; embargo, embargoes; hero, heroes; Negro, Negroes; potato, potatoes; tomato, tomatoes; tornado, tornadoes;* etc.

c. But the following add only -*s*: *alto, altos; banjo, banjos; canto, cantos; contralto, contraltos; dynamo, dynamos; libretto, librettos; piano, pianos; solo, solos; soprano, sopranos; torso, torsos;* etc.

d. A few nouns offer alternative plurals, the -*es* being more

---

[13] Proper nouns retain the *y* and add -*s*; as, *Marys, Davys, Henrys, Mrs. Rays.* See Rule XVI, p. 41.

common; but the increasing tendency is to add only -*s*: *buffalo, buffaloes* (or *buffalos*); *calico, calicoes* (or *calicos*); *cargo, cargoes* (or *cargos*); *domino, dominoes* (or *dominos*); *halo, haloes* (or *halos*); *hobo, hoboes* (or *hobos*); *motto, mottoes* (or *mottos*); *volcano, volcanoes* (or *volcanos*); etc.

VII. A few nouns become plural by change of the stem vowel (of stem and suffix in *women* and *brethren*):[14] *brother, brethren; dormouse, dormice; foot, feet; goose, geese; louse, lice; mouse, mice; man, men; titmouse, titmice; tooth, teeth; woman, women.*

VIII. Nouns of foreign origin form their plurals in various ways:

a. Many words of Latin origin follow the Latin declensions; but many have acquired Anglicized plurals:

1. Nouns ending in -*a* change -*a* to -*ae*: *antenna, antennae* (or *antennas*); *alumna, alumnae; formula, formulae* (or *formulas*); *larva, larvae; nebula, nebulae* (or *nebulas*); *vertebra, vertebrae* (or *vertebras*); etc.

2. Nouns ending in -*us* change -*us* to -*i*: *alumnus, alumni; bacillus, bacilli; cactus, cacti* (or *cactuses*); *focus, foci* (or *focuses*); *fungus, fungi* (or *funguses*); *radius, radii* (or *radiuses*); *stimulus, stimuli* (or *stimuluses*); *syllabus, syllabi* (or *syllabuses*); *terminus, termini* (*terminuses*); etc.

3. Nouns ending in -*um* change -*um* to -*a*: *agendum, agenda; bacterium, bacteria; curriculum, currlicula* (or *curriculums*); *datum, data; dictum, dicta* (or *dictums*); *erratum, errata; medium, media* (or *mediums*); *memorandum, memoranda* (or *memorandums*); *stratum, strata* (or *stratums*).

4. Singulars in -*x* become plural by change of -*x* to *c* and the addition of -*es*: *appendix, appendices* (or *appendixes*); *index, indices* (or *indexes*); *matrix, matrices* (or *matrixes*); *radix, radices* (or *radixes*).

b. Words of Greek origin usually retain their declensional

[14] The vowel change in the plural in these nouns is called mutation or umlaut. It was caused by a final high vowel (ī) after the stem (O.E. *fēt* comes from a still older form *fotī*). See Mutation, p. 34.

ending; but Anglicized plurals for some of these are now favored:

1. Nouns ending in *-on* become plural by changing *-on* to *-a: automaton, automata* (or *automatons*); *criterion, criteria* (or *criterions*); *ganglion, ganglia* (or *ganglions*); *phenomenon, phenomena.*

2. Singulars ending in *-is* change *-is* to *-es* in becoming plural: *antithesis, antitheses; analysis, analyses; basis, bases; crisis, crises; ellipsis, ellipses; hypothesis, hypotheses; oasis, oases; parenthesis, parentheses; synopsis, synopses; thesis, theses.*

c. A few nouns of Italian origin retain their foreign plurals in English; but some have acquired Anglicized plurals: *bandit, banditti* (or *bandits*); *dilettante, dilettanti* (or *dilettantes*); *libretto, libretti* (or *librettos*); *virtuoso, virtuosi* (or *virtuosos*).

d. Certain nouns of Hebrew origin add *-im* to the singular to form their plural: *cherub, cherubim* (or *cherubs*); *seraph, seraphim* (or *seraphs*).[15]

e. French nouns ending in *-eau* add *-x* or *-s* to form their plurals (both plurals pronounced as *-z* in English): *beau, beaux* (or *beaus*); *tableau, tableaux* (or *tableaus*); *manteau, manteaux* (or *manteaus*); *plateau, plateaux* (or *plateaus*).

IX. *a.* Some nouns have two plural forms with a difference of meaning:

Singular	*Plural*
brother	brothers (of the same family, related by blood) brethren (of the same social or religious group)
cloth	cloths (fabrics) clothes (garments)
die	dies (coining stamps) dice (gambling cubes)
genius	geniuses (persons of phenomenal intellectual power) genii (guardian deities, spirits)

---

[15] *Cherubims* and *seraphims* are double plurals, once in common use, as in the Bible of 1611; but these plurals are now regarded as *obsolete or erroneous.*

index { indexes (tables of contents)
        { indices (mathematical or other abstract signs)

penny { pence (quantity in value; *sixpence*)
        { pennies (separate coins)

pea { peas (taken separately)
      { pease (collectively)[16]

X. A number of nouns have singular and plural forms alike:[17] *bellows, chamois, corps, deer, grouse, heathen* (or *heathens*), *Japanese, salmon, sheep, series, Sioux, species, swine, trout, vermin,* etc.

XI. *a.* Many nouns of abstract or very general meaning are singular in form and use, logically admitting of no plural:[18] *algebra, assimilation, bashfulness, chemistry, courage, geometry, grammar, gravitation, honesty, mirth, peace, pride, status,* etc.

b. Some names of raw or manufactured materials do not ordinarily admit of plurals: *bread, butter, coffee, cotton, flour, hay, milk, zinc,* etc.

c. A few nouns have formed plurals with modified meanings: *beef, beeves; compass, compasses; custom, customs; divider, dividers; ice, ices; iron, irons; manner, manners; moral, morals; pain, pains; stagger, staggers;* etc.

XII. *a.* Names of numbers, measurement, quantity, etc. frequently use their singular forms in a plural sense, though many of them have plurals formed in the regular way: *a ton, two ton* (or *two tons*); *a gross, five gross; a dozen, three dozen; a yoke of oxen, five yoke of oxen; a score, fourscore;* etc.

b. The unchanged plural is regular in compound adjectives

---

[16] Formerly *peas* was used to indicate a definite number, as contrasted with the collective plural *pease.* Modern usage favors *peas* as plural in all senses.

[17] Some words have singular and plurals alike in the written form, but in spoken English have regular plurals. Consult *Webster's New International Dictionary* for the pronunciation of the singular and plural forms of *chamois, corps,* and *Sioux.*

[18] The abstract noun *courtesy,* when it means an act of courtesy, may be pluralized. Similarly *mercies* equals acts of mercy; and *kindnesses,* acts of kindness. The nouns *algebra, chemistry, geometry, grammar,* and the like are pluralized only when they are used to designate textbooks.

denoting number, quantity, etc.: *a quart, two-quart jar; a mile, two-mile race; a foot, a three-foot pole; a gallon, a five-gallon keg; an inch, two-by-four-inch board;* etc.

XIII. A few nouns in English have plurals with singular meaning: *acoustics,*[19] *aeronautics, amends, analytics, civics, economics, esthetics, ethics, eugenics, linguistics, mathematics, measles, molasses, mumps, obsequies, optics, obstetrics, news, poetics, physics, phonetics, politics, rickets, statistics, stamina,*[20] *whereabouts,* etc.

XIV. *a.* A number of nouns are plural both in form and in use: *aborigines, alms,*[21] *alps, annals, Apocrypha, ashes, archives, banns, clothes, dregs, eaves,*[21] *embers, entrails, fireworks, head-quarters, Hebrides, hysterics, lees, means, morals, nippers, oats, pliers, pincers (pinchers), proceeds, remains, riches,*[21] *scissors, shears, smallpox (small pocks), shambles, shingles* (a disease), *snuffers, stocks, suds, thanks, tidings, tongs, trousers, tweezers, victuals, wages,* etc.

b. Some nouns made from adjectives have no corresponding nouns in the singular: *betters, goods, matins, nuptials, odds, shorts, valuables, vespers, vitals.*

XV. Compound nouns usually form their plural by pluralizing the fundamental word of the compound:

a. The final part is pluralized:

1. When what precedes it describes the final element: *attorney-generals, Englishmen, footsteps, goosequills, goldsmiths, ground hogs, pickaxes, trade-unions, wood mice, workmen,* etc.

2. When words have been in use so long that they are not now regarded as compounds: *handfuls, mouthfuls, spoonfuls, touchdowns,* etc.

---

[19] Words ending in *-ics* are from Greek adjectives, and hence have no singular forms. Compare *betters, sweets, sours, bitters,* etc. Some of the nouns ending in *-ics* are construed as either singular or plural in meaning. The student should consult his dictionary when in doubt as to the number of any noun.

[20] *Stamina* is an old Latin plural, now construed as singular.

[21] Historically *alms, eaves,* and *riches* are singulars, though they now have plural meaning.

3. When the compounds are made up of words none of which may be regarded as the principal element: *forget-me-nots, Jack-in-the-pulpits, Johnny-jump-ups, touch-me-nots,* etc.

b. When the first part of the compound is described by what follows, the first element is pluralized: *aides-de-camp, brothers-in-law, courts-martial, hangers-on, maids-of-honor, men-of-war, sons-in-law,* etc.

c. A few words made up of two noun forms pluralize both elements: *Knights Templars, Lords Justices, Lords Provosts, menservants, women cooks,* etc.

XVI. *a.* Most proper nouns form their plurals by adding -s to the singular: *Brown, Browns; German, Germans; one Indian, two Indians; a Russian, two Russians; one Mary, two Marys; Shelley, the Shelleys;* etc.

b. Certain proper nouns ending in a fricative add *-es: Burns, Burnses; Dickens, Dickenses; Williams, Williamses; Cox, Coxes; Bush, Bushes;* etc.

c. Proper names with titles form their plurals (1) by pluralizing only the title, or (2) by pluralizing only the name:

1. The plural for *Miss* is *Misses;* for *Mr.* is *Messrs.;* for *Madam* is *Mesdames;* for *Master* is *Masters:*

Singular	Plural
Miss Smith	Misses Smith (or the Misses Smith) / Miss Smiths
Miss King	Misses King (or the Misses King) / Miss Kings
Madam Le Baron	Mesdames Le Baron / Madam Le Barons
Mr. Johnson	Messrs. Johnson (or the Messrs. Johnson) / Mr. Johnsons
Master Jones	Masters Jones / Master Joneses

2. *Mrs.* has no plural; hence the name must show the pluralization:

Singular	Plural
Mrs. Allen	Mrs. Allens
Mrs. Wright	Mrs. Wrights

3. When a title precedes two or more names, the title only is pluralized:

Singular	Plural
Dr. Bright and Dr. Mayo	Drs. Bright and Mayo
Professor Cross and Professor Mann	Professors Cross and Mann
Dean Emerson and Dean Lowe	Deans Emerson and Lowe
General Lee and General Grant	Generals Lee and Grant

XVII. Letters of the alphabet, numerical characters, and other small symbols used as nouns form their plurals by adding 's:

Singular	Plural
Dot this *i*.	Dot your *i*'s.
Cross the *t*.	Cross your *t*'s.
Cancel the 4.	Cancel the 4's.
One *and* too many.	Two *and*'s[22] too many.

XVIII. *a.* Many abbreviations are pluralized in the regular way by adding -s to the singular:

Singular	Plural
Bro. (brother)	Bros. (brothers)
Dr. (doctor)	Drs. (doctors)
lb. (pound)	lbs. (pounds)
MS. (manuscript)	MSS. (manuscripts)
Mt. (mountain)	Mts. (mountains)
St. (street)	Sts. (streets)
yd. (yard)	yds. (yards)

[22] Plurals of complete words are sometimes written by adding *s* without the apostrophe: "too many *ands* and *thats*."

b. The initial is doubled to signify the plural of certain abbreviations:

Singular	Plural
l. (line)	ll. (lines)
p. (page)	pp. (pages)
f. (and following page, line, chapter, etc.	ff. (and following pages, lines, chapters, etc.)

c. A few abbreviations have the same form for both singular and plural:

ft. (foot, or feet)	fig. (figure, or figures)
deg. (degree, or degrees)	Heb.⎫ Hebr.⎭ (Hebrew, or Hebrews)

DECLENSION OF NOUNS

The nominative and objective (or accusative) cases of Modern English nouns are always identical, difference in form between these cases appearing only in pronouns. The distinction, so far as nouns are concerned, though once marked by inflection, is now based solely upon function.[23]

The possessive (or genitive) singular is usually formed by adding the apostrophe and *s* ('*s*) to the nominative; the possessive (or genitive) plural, by adding *s* and the apostrophe (*s*') to the nominative. Variations, however, appear in some of the following paradigms:

	Singular	Plural	Singular	Plural
Nom.	girl	girls	child	children
Poss.	girl's	girls'	child's	children's[24]
Obj.	girl	girls	child	children
Nom.	woman	women	lady	ladies
Poss.	woman's	women's[24]	lady's	ladies'
Obj.	woman	women	lady	ladies

[23] For full discussion and illustration of the function of substantives, see **Part Two.**

[24] Nouns with -*n* or -*en* plurals and those which form their plurals by vowel change form the plural possessive by adding the apostrophe and *s* ('*s*) to the plural nominative.

	Singular	*Plural*	*Singular*	*Plural*
Nom.	lass	lasses	sheep	sheep
Poss.	lass's	lasses'	sheep's	sheep's[21]
Obj.	lass	lasses	sheep	sheep

	Singular	*Plural*
Nom.	Mr. Brown	Mr. Browns, or Messrs. Brown
Poss.	Mr. Brown's	Mr. Browns' or Messrs. Brown's
Obj.	Mr. Brown	Mr. Browns, or Messrs. Brown
Nom.	Mrs. Williams	Mrs. Williamses, or Mesdames Williams
Poss.	Mrs. Williams's	Mrs. Williamses', or Mesdames Williams'
Obj.	Mrs. Williams	Mrs. Williamses, or Mesdames Williams
Nom.	son-in-law	sons-in-law
Poss.	son-in-law's	sons-in-law's[26]
Obj.	son-in-law	sons-in-law

The possessive *'s* is sometimes omitted in words that end in *s* or words that end in sounds that cannot easily be pronounced with an additional *s*-sound, especially when the word following begins with an *s* or *s*-sound; as, *for goodness' sake; for conscience' sake; Moses' secret; Jesus' suffering.* It is, however, seldom, if ever, incorrect to add the *'s*, and it should be used if there is any uncertainty about the identification of the stem of the word; as, *Dickens's family, King James's Version of the Bible, the Woods's farm.*

[25] Nouns with plural and singular forms alike have singular and plural posessive forms alike also. The *sheep's wool* may mean the wool from one sheep or from a flock of sheep. It is important to observe here that the fewer inflections a noun has, the fewer meanings it is capable of conveying.

[26] In compound nouns the sign of the possessive is usually added to the last word of the compound; as, *son-in-law's, sons-in-law's.* And when two or more nouns or phrases represent a unit of possession, the possessive sign is attached to the last of the group; as, *Woodward and Lothrop's* store; *Blount and Northup's* Grammar and Usage; *Brown and Son's* Hardware, or *Brown and Sons'* Hardware; *the King of France's* war; *the Prince of Wale's* visit to America; *Frederick the Great's* time; *Charles* III*'s* reign.

Three

Pronouns

A **pronoun** (from Latin *pro,* meaning *for,* and *nomen,* meaning *name*) is a word used instead of a noun or a noun-equivalent. The meaning of a pronoun is restricted to relation or reference. It may name a person by his relation to the act of speaking: *I, you, he;* a thing by its relation of nearness or remoteness from the speaker: *this, that.* It may refer to a person or an object as already named: *who, which, that.* It may represent the unnamed answer to a question: *Who? What?* It may, with adjective significance, suggest quantity: *much, little, enough;* or number: *many, few, all;* or order: *former, latter;* or distribution: *each, either, neither.*

The word, phrase, or clause for which the pronoun stands is called the **antecedent** of the pronoun. Most pronouns have antecedent either expressed or implied,[1] and they should agree with their antecedents in person, number, and gender. In *John gave me his books, and I gave them to his sister, John* is the antecedent of *his;* and *books* is the antecedent of *them.* The possessive *his* is here used instead of the possessive form *John's;* and *them* is used instead of the common noun *books.*

The antecedent of a pronoun may be another pronoun or a phrase or a clause. In *Everyone has his wishes sometimes denied,* the antecedent of *his* is the pronoun *everyone.* In *He that will use all winds must shift his sail,* the pronoun *he* is the

---

[1] Pronouns which require no antecedents are sometimes construed as nouns. *Anything, none, anybody, another, one,* etc. are of this type. See Indefinite Adjective Pronouns, pp. 68–71.

antecedent of *that* and therefore also of *his*. In *It was wrong for you to lie, and you know it*, the phrase *for you to lie* is the antecedent of *it*. A clause is the antecedent of *that* in *He is telling the truth—that I know*.

CLASSES OF PRONOUNS

Pronouns are sometimes classified according to their structure as (1) **simple** (*I, he, you, who*, etc.), (2) **compound** (*myself, yourself, yourselves, himself, themselves, whoever, whosoever, anything, somebody*), and (3) **phrasal** (*each other, one another*).[2]

When classified as to use, pronouns are (1) **personal** (*I, you, he*), (2) **relative** (*who, that, which*), (3) **interrogative** (*who, what, which*), (4) **adjective** (*any, all, neither, few*), (5) **indefinite** (*none, something, everybody*), and (6) **reciprocal** (*each other, one another*). Some of these have important subdivisions, which will be treated under these major classifications.

Personal Pronouns

A **personal pronoun** is one which distinguishes (1) the speaker, (2) the person or thing spoken to, and (3) the person or thing spoken of (that is, the person or thing not speaking or spoken to). These are called **first, second,** and **third persons** respectively.

(1) The speaker employs *I, my, mine, myself*, or *me* instead of his own name. If he includes others when he speaks, he uses *we, our, ours, ourselves*, or *us*.

(2) In direct address *you, your, yours, yourself, yourselves* are used instead of the names of the person or persons addressed. In Biblical and poetic language *thou, thy, thine, thee*, and *ye* are sometimes employed in direct address, but these forms are not now in common use in either the popular or the standard (literary) level of our speech.

(3) *He, his, him, himself, she, her, hers, herself, it, its, itself*

---

[2] The compound pronouns are always written as single words without hyphens.

are used to refer to singular nouns previously mentioned, the gender of the pronoun agreeing with the gender of the noun it stands for. *They, their, theirs, them,* and *themselves* are used instead of plural nouns which have been previously mentioned or clearly implied.

Inflection of Personal Pronouns

The **personal pronouns,** like nouns, inflect for number and case; and the third person singular forms indicate gender. The first and the second persons and the third person plural do not denote gender, their gender being determined by their noun antecedents. Unlike nouns, most of the personal pronouns have different forms for the objective and nominative cases: *I—me, we—us, he—him, she—her, they—them.*

The inflection of pronouns is called **declension,** and the changing of the forms (and in some instances of the words themselves; as, *she* and *he, I* and *me, he* and *they, I* and *we*) to show changes in gender, case, or number is called **declining.** The forms given in the following declension of the personal pronouns show all of the inflectional changes of the simple personal pronouns.

Declension of Personal Pronouns

FIRST PERSON

	Singular	Plural
Nom.	I	we
Poss.	my, mine	our, ours
Obj.	me	us

SECOND PERSON

	Singular	Plural
Nom.	you	you
Poss.	your, yours	your, yours
Obj.	you	you

Old forms of the second person, still found in poetry, the Bible, prayer books, hymns, etc.:

	SINGULAR	PLURAL
Nom.	thou	ye, or you
Poss.	thy, thine	your, yours
Obj.	thee	you

THIRD PERSON

	SINGULAR			PLURAL
	Masculine	*Feminine*	*Neuter*	*Mas., Fem.,* and *Neut.*
Nom.	he	she	it	they
Poss.	his	her, hers	its	their, theirs
Obj.	him	her	it	them

Uses of the Inflectional Forms

Logically speaking, English has no inflectional plural for *I*, *my*, *mine*, and *me*. *We*, *our*, *ours*, and *us* are not modifications of the singular forms. *We* and its oblique case forms may mean several things:

(1) One *I* and one *you: Mary, shall we* (you and I) *accept this invitation?* (2) One *I* and one *he, she,* or *it: John and I were late; we had car trouble.* (3) One *I* and *they* (any number): *We were all exhausted before we reached our destination.*

The second person *you* now has fewer inflectional forms than any other of the personal pronouns, the same form *you* being used for nominative and objective singular and also for the nominative and objective plural. The older forms, some of which are not now in common use, showed fuller inflections and could indicate more exact meanings. *Thou, thy, thine, thee* were always singular; and *ye, your, yours, you* usually had plural meaning.[3] *You*, even when it is singular in

---

[3] *Thou, thy, thine,* and *thee* are not now used in standard (General American) English. Some religious sects, Quakers, for example, in an attempt to preserve the language of the King James Version of the Bible, still employ these archaic forms in their conversational speech. Often an observance of the correct case and number is not adhered to, *thee* being used for both the nominative and objective, sometimes having plural and sometimes singular meaning. The archaic forms should not appear in the same sentence with the modern *you* and *your.* Say *With my hand in yours* (not *thine*), *dear Lord, I will go where you want me to go.* The correct inflectional forms of *thou* are given in the declension chart above.

meaning, still requires the plural form of the verb. One must now take pains to say: *Mary, you were* (not *was*) *invited to bring your sister.* Here the context indicates that *you* is singular, but sometimes it is difficult to determine whether a singular or plural meaning is intended.[4] Often the adjective *all* is added to indicate the plural meaning: *You all are to leave when the bell rings.* *All* must never be used with *you* when the meaning is singular. One must not say *I didn't give you all a cup of coffee, did I?* when only one person is being addressed, as is the case in this sentence, where a (one) cup of coffee is to be served to one person.

The third person forms of the personal pronouns are more numerous and their uses more complicated than those of the second and first persons. The speaker or writer must keep in mind the gender and the number of the antecedent of *he, his, him; she, her, hers; it, its.* The third person plural forms (*they, their, theirs, them*) do not denote gender, but they always denote plural number, and their antecedents must always be plural.

The third person singular *he, his, him* and the plural *they, their, theirs, them* may refer to masculine antecedents or to nouns having common or unknown gender: *Every man should do his work; Each person should do his part; The student was ill, and the teacher sent him home; The husband and wife were invited, but they did not come; Every man, woman, and child must do his share of the sacrificing.*

The third person singular feminine gender forms (*she, her, hers*) are used to refer to nouns whose gender is known to be feminine or the personified names of objects that are thought of as having feminine characteristics: *Mrs. Roosevelt has written the story of her life; Each girl must be in her uniform before the gong sounds; Mother Earth has her charms.* The third person feminine plural forms are the same as the masculine:

---

[4] The reflexive and intensive forms indicate number but not gender: *Do your work by yourself* (or *by yourselves*); *See yourself* (or *yourselves*) *in this mirror.*

All the girls brought **their** *lunches, because* **they** *wished to have more time for play; The boys* (or *the boys and the girls*) *left* **their** *books at home.*

The third person singular neuter pronoun (*it, its*) has both a personal and an impersonal use. Its antecedent, when *it* has personal meaning, may be an inanimate object (*I wound the clock, but it would not run*), a bird (*The wren is cleaning its nest*), or an animal (*If the kitten has not been fed, you must feed it*). *It* may also be used to refer to a small child (*Put the baby in its crib, and let it go to sleep*). The plural forms of *it* (*they, their, theirs, them*) are the same as the masculine and feminine forms: *The flowers were picked only an hour ago, but* **they** *have wilted already.*

In addition to its personal use, *it* has a number of impersonal uses. *It* may serve as an indefinite subject for an impersonal verb: *It is raining; It is time to go home; It is a long lane that has no turning.* Sometimes *it* is the object of a verb derived from a noun, as in *Foot it, girls* and *He lords it over us. It* is used frequently as an introductory, or expletive subject (See Infinitives, pp. 328–329), the logical subject coming after the predicate: *It is my job to entertain the guests; It is true that he objected to my coming alone.* In a similar way *it* may anticipate the object complement: *I find it hard to be frank with you; I thought it best to tell you what I heard.* Sometimes *it* refers to a general truth, statement, or idea: *Of all sad words of tongue or pen, the saddest are these: "It might have been!"* *It* often stands for an idea expressed in the verb: *Those parents are most honored whose character best deserve it.* Often *it* is used in a demonstrative sense: *You are it; If it is the maid at the door, let her come in.*

As a rule, the other personal pronouns (*you, he, she, we, they*) are not used in the indefinite and impersonal sense. Their antecedents should be clearly indicated. Careful speakers do not say **They** *make bricks in Florida* for *Bricks are made in Florida;* nor do they say **You** *should dress well if* **you** *want to be popular* for **One** *should dress well if* **he** (*one*) *wants to be popular,* or for *A young lady shculd dress well if she wants to be popular.*

The first person *we* should not be used loosely for the first person singular, though *we* may be used in the editorial or royal sense, when one is speaking for a group of persons including himself: *We want our customers to be satisfied.* The royal (or majestic) *we* once had a well defined use, and was employed by kings or other rulers when they spoke for their subjects or for a general group. Shakespeare's kings sometimes use the plural form *we* with a distinctly singular meaning. Observe the *we, us, our* in Claudius's speech to the Queen concerning Hamlet's killing of Polonius:

> O heavy deed!
> It had been so with *us,* had *we* been there:
> His liberty is full of threats to all;
> To you yourself, to *us,* to every one.
> Alas, how shall this bloody deed be answer'd
> It will be laid to *us,* whose providence
> Should have kept short, restrain'd and out of haunt,
> This mad young man: but so much was *our* love,
> *We* would not understand what was most fit.
>
> *Hamlet,* Act IV, i.

The alternative possessive case forms *mine, thine, yours, hers, ours,* and *theirs* are sometimes called **absolute possessives,** because they are normally used absolutely; that is, separately from the nouns they qualify. We may say *It is my book* and *Thy kingdom come;* but, if the possessive forms are used alone, we must say *This book is* **mine** and **Thine** *is the kingdom.* In religious texts and in poetry, however, we may find *mine* and *thine* employed for the sake of euphony before words beginning with vowels even when they immediately precede the nouns they modify; as, *Mine eyes have seen the glory. Thine eyes are stars of morning. Mine* and *thine* are the original possessives (genitives), the shorter forms *my* and *thy* being used before consonants, and in time becoming the standard forms. The same practice was observed in

my-mine, thy-thine, no-none, as with the article *a-an* in present-day speech.[5]

The possessives *my, thy, her, our, your, its,* and *their* are
never correctly used in the absolute function; and they are
sometimes classed as adjectives because they must always
modify expressed nouns, and they must immediately precede
the nouns they modify.[6] The absolute forms ending in *-rs*
are sometimes called **double possessives,** the *-s* being added
to the possessive plural ending in *-r: our-s, your-s, their-s.*
Hers and *its* are later forms, the final *-s* having been added to
the singular by analogy with the genitive plural of the older
forms.

COMPOUND PERSONAL PRONOUNS
(SELF-PRONOUNS)

Forms of the Self-Pronouns

The **compound personal pronouns** are formed by adding
-self to the singular and *-selves* to the plural forms of the simple personal pronouns. The first person (*myself, ourselves*)
and the second person (*yourself, thyself, yourselves*) are formed
by adding *-self* to the singular possessives (*my, thy, your*) and
-selves to the plural possessives (*our, your*). The third person
singular (*himself, herself, itself*) is formed by adding *-self* to
the objective singular forms (*him, her, it*), and the third person plural is formed by adding *-selves* to the objective plural
form (*them*). *Oneself* (earlier *one's self*) did not appear until
the Modern English period (16th c.).[7] The forms made
from the objective case are the earlier, being found in Old
English along with *me self, us self, thee self, you self.* In Middle English *me self* and *thee self* came to be pronounced like

---

[5] See Wright's *An Elementary Historical New English Grammar,* § 199, p. 106,
and § 328, p. 154.

[6] The masculine singular *his* is used without any inflectional modification in
the absolute construction, as in *These books are his.*

[7] For a fuller treatment of the history and development of the reflexive personal
pronouns, see Wright's *An Elementary Middle English Grammar,* § 377, p. 158,
and *An Elementary Historical New English Grammar,* § 323, p. 154.

myself and *thyself* respectively and the objective *her* and *herself* made no change because the genitive and objective forms were alike. Hence there arose in Middle English the new forms *myself* and *thyself*, and by analogy *ourself*, *yourself* (later *ourselves*, *yourselves*), *hisself*, *itsself*, *theirselves*. The last three of these new forms dropped out of standard English before the end of the fifteenth century.

Declension of Reflexive and Intensive Pronouns

Personal pronoun plus *self*, plural *selves*

FIRST PERSON

	SINGULAR	PLURAL
Nom.	myself	ourselves
Poss.	———	———
Obj.	myself	ourselves

SECOND PERSON

	SINGULAR	PLURAL
Nom.	yourself thyself	yourselves
Poss.	———	———
Obj.	yourself thyself	yourselves

THIRD PERSON

	SINGULAR			PLURAL
	Mas.	*Fem.*	*Neut.*	*Mas., Fem.,* and *Neut.*
Nom.	himself	herself	itself	themselves
Poss.	———	———	———	———
Obj.	himself	herself	itself	themselves

The Uses of the Self-Pronouns

The uses of the **compound personal pronouns** are numerous and complicated, and only the main features can be treated in a text of this type.[8] The two most common (the two

---

[8] For a full treatment of the uses of the self-pronouns, see H. Poutsma, *A Grammar of Late Modern English*, Part II, Section I, B, Chapter xxiv, pp. 830–874.

traditional classifications) are (1) **reflexive** and (2) **intensive** (or emphatic). Broadly interpreted these classifications may be extended to include all of the **self-pronouns**.

REFLEXIVE USES

The **reflexive pronoun** has a function of its own in the sentence; its antecedent (the word it refers to and stands for) is a noun or pronoun (usually the subject of the sentence, though not always) which precedes it in the sentence. Its function may be seen in the following illustrations:

1. Object of verb: (1) I can defend *myself*. (2) He praises *himself* too highly. (3) Know *thyself*. (4) Put *yourself* in my place.

2. Object of preposition: (1) Lay up for *yourselves* treasures in heaven. (2) He confessed that no one could black his boots to suit him except *himself*. (3) We found the boys playing by *themselves* in your garden. (4) My teacher told me to think for *myself*.

3. Indirect object (adverbial objective): (1) Riches make *themselves* wings. (2) I made *myself* a new dress. (3) John bought *himself* a new car.[9] (4) She gave *herself* a shampoo.

4. Predicate nominative (subjective complement): (1) He is not quite *himself* this morning. (2) No woman could be *herself* under those conditions.

INTENSIVE USES

The **intensive,** or **emphatic,** pronoun is an appositive, an explanatory modifier, and has in Modern English, as in Old English and Middle English, an intensive or identifying force. Its position in the sentence depends somewhat upon the noun or pronoun being intensified or identified. Because it func-

---

[9] In sentences like (2) and (3), the simple personal pronoun may sometimes be preferred. See Note 10, p. 56

tions as an appositive, it usually follows immediately the word it identifies or emphasizes, but it may, when it is an appositive of the subject of the sentence, be placed after the predicate; as, *I myself saw you;* or *I saw you myself.* When the word being intensified is the direct object, the object of a preposition, or the subjective complement, the intensive usually follows the noun or pronoun it is identifying or emphasizing: *I saw the employer himself about my promotion; I invited the president himself to send a representative; That statement was made by Mary herself; It was the students themselves who voted for this change.*

The **intensive,** like the **reflexive,** is formed by adding *-self* (*-selves*) to the possessive or the objective forms of the simple personal pronouns. In their compound forms, however, the reflexive and intensive pronouns are not inflected, and their uses are always nominative or objective, their case meaning being determined always by their function in the sentence. The possessive meaning may be denoted by inserting a word or a phrase between the parts of the compounds. *My own, your own, his own, her own, our own, their own,* when followed by *self* (or *selves*) may be construed as phrasal possessives. In strict analysis, *self* (or *selves*) in the expressions *my own self, your own self, our own selves,* etc. should be regarded as a noun limited by the possessive form of the simple personal pronoun and the adjective *own,* the possessive meaning being merely implied.

The function of the compound personal pronoun is limited to the intensive or reflexive uses. The *self*-pronouns should not be used loosely to replace personal pronouns. One should not say *John and myself are coming,* or *May I go with Mary and yourself to the party?* In these sentences the *self*-pronouns are neither reflexive nor intensive. *Myself* is sometimes used as a dodge when the speaker wants to avoid using *I,* or when he is not sure whether to use the nominative or objective case form of the personal pronoun. It is important to remember that the intensive and reflexive pronouns should not be used unless they reflect, identify, or intensify.[10]

RELATIVE PRONOUNS

A **relative pronoun** performs a dual function in the sentence of which it is a part: it takes the place of a noun in the clause it introduces, and at the same time joins and relates that clause to the rest of the sentence. In *This is the man who sells flowers, who* is the relative pronoun, used as the subject of the adjective (relative) clause, *who sells flowers.* Its conjunctive and substantive meaning may be seen by omitting the relative and substituting *and he* (a conjunction and a pronoun), as in *This is the man, and he sells flowers.* The relative pronoun makes the clause it introduces an adjunct to some noun-word in a preceding clause, and hence the clause it introduces is always adjectival.

The relative pronoun differs from other pronouns in that its antecedent is always in a preceding clause; and hence it cannot be a member of a simple sentence. The noun-word it stands for, its antecedent, may be in a principal clause or in a preceding subordinate clause. In *This is the cat that killed the rat that ate the malt that lay in the house that Jack built,* there are four relative pronouns, each introducing an adjective clause. The first clause, *that killed the rat,* modifies the noun *cat,* the predicate nominative in the principal clause

---

[10] In Old English the simple personal pronouns could be used with reflexive meaning, and there are some survivals of this use in Modern English; as, *Now I lay me down to sleep; He built him a new home in the country; I brought my cat with me; Look behind you; We gazed about us.*

In the indirect object function the reflexive or the simple personal pronoun may be used after certain verbs. In *I made myself a new dress,* and in *John bought himself a new car,* the *myself* could be replaced by *me,* and *himself* by *him.* The simple personal pronouns *me* and *him* may be said to have reflexive meaning in sentences of this type. In the other illustrations in group 3 above, however, the simple personal pronouns ought not to replace the *self*-pronouns. After the verbs *give, sell, lend,* and many others that usually imply another person as the subject, the simple personal pronouns do not convey reflexive meaning. One should say *Give me* (not *myself*) *that big book,* and *I could lend you* (not *yourself*) *the car.*

of the full sentence; but the other three relative clauses modify nouns used in adjective clauses.

Classification of Relative Pronouns

When classified as to form, relative pronouns are **simple** or **compound.** The **simple relatives** are *who, which, what, that,* and sometimes *as* and *but.*[11] The **compound relatives** are formed by adding *-ever* or *-soever* to the simple relatives *who, which,* and *what* (*whoever, whosoever, whichever, whichsoever, whatever,* and *whatsoever*).

When classified as to meaning, relative pronouns are either **definite** or **indefinite.**

The **definite relatives** (*who, which,* and *that*) stand for and relate to definite persons or objects named in foregoing clauses. Their antecedents are usually expressed: *This is the house **that** I bought; I prefer food **which** is highly seasoned; Mother found the book **which** you recommended; My dog, **which** is a Chow, barks at tramps; I wrote the sentence **which** you just quoted.*

The **indefinite relatives** (*what, whatever, whatsoever, whichever, whichsoever, whoever, whosoever*)[12] usually include or imply their own antecedents, *what* being equivalent to *that which* or *those which,* and *whoever* being equivalent to *he who,* or *they who,* etc. Observe the indefinite relative meaning in the following: *Whatever is, is right; Take **whichever** is the lightest; Do **what** is right; Do you see **what** I see? **Whoever** would find pearls must dive deep.*[13] Generally when the antecedent of an indefinite relative is expressed, it is an indefinite noun-

---

[11] *As* and *but* are used as relatives in the following sentences: *The teacher purchased such books as were needed; He has the same office as I had; I do not know anybody but would vote for you.* *As* and *but* are really conjunctions used in sentences of this type to do the work of relatives.

[12] *Whoso* for *whosoever* and *whatso* for *whatsoever* were common indefinite relatives in the 16th century: *Whoso keepeth the law is a wise son; Whoso mocketh the poor reproacheth his Maker; Whatso I do, I would that ye do.* These forms are now regarded as archaic.

[13] For fuller analysis of sentences containing indefinite relatives, see Part Two, Adjective Clauses.

word forced into the sentence for rhetorical effect; as, *Whatever you think should be done, do it; Whoever samples this cake, he is sure to want more.* In both of these sentences, the antecedents could be omitted, and the sentences would be more natural by their omission. Usually when the antecedent is supplied, the indefinite relative tends to become more definite; as, **He who** (= *Whoever*) *goes to war, must expect to fight.* Occasionally, however, the simple definite relatives *who* and *which* are used with indefinite meaning with antecedents unexpressed: **Who** *steals my purse steals trash* (Shakespeare); *You may take* **which** *you prefer.* In sentences of this sort, however, the compound indefinite pronouns are more usual.

Declension of Relative Pronouns

SINGULAR AND PLURAL

Masculine and Feminine

Nom.	who	whoever,	whosoever
Poss.	whose	whosever,	whosesoever
Obj.	whom	whomever,	whomsoever

Neuter

Nom.	which	whichever,	whichsoever[14]
Poss.	[whose][15]	———	———
Obj.	which	whichever,	whichsoever
Nom.	what	whatever,	whatsoever[14]
Poss.	———	———	———
Obj.	what	whatever,	whatsoever

Masculine, Feminine, and Neuter

Nom.	that
Poss.	[whose][15]
Obj.	that

---

[14] The indefinite relatives (*what, whatever, whatsoever, whichever, whichsoever*) have no possessive forms. The phrasal forms substitute for the inflectional possessives: *of what, of whatever, of whatsoever, of whichever, of whichsoever.*

[15] *Whose* is sometimes employed as the possessive of *which* and *that* to avoid an awkward construction with *of which.* When the phrasal form is used for the possessive case of *that*, the preposition always has postposition: *that . . . of.* Example: *This is the book that I spoke of.*

Person, Number, and Gender of Relative Pronouns

Relative pronouns, like the personal pronouns, agree with their antecedents in person, number, and gender; but, unlike the personal pronouns, the relatives never indicate person, number, or gender by a change of form, these modifications in meaning being determined wholly by their antecedents. In *It is I who am at fault,* the relative pronoun *who* agrees with its antecedent, *I,* in person and number. In *Every girl who brings her mother may enter free, who* agrees with *girl,* its antecedent, in person, number, and gender. In *Men who are strong should be brave,* the gender, person, and number of *who* can be determined only by its antecedent *men,* a plural, third person, masculine noun. In *Houses that are made of brick are durable, that* agrees with its antecedent *houses,* and may be said to possess third person, plural number, and neuter gender meaning.

When the relative pronoun is the subject of its own clause, it governs the number and person of its predicate verb, and hence it is important for the relative pronoun in this construction to have the same person and number meaning as its antecedent. The gender modification of the relative is also important if there is a personal or reflexive pronoun referring to it. In *It was Mary who came by herself,* the third person, feminine gender reflexive pronoun *herself* refers to *who,* the subject of the clause, the gender, number, and person being expressed in the antecedent noun, *Mary,* which is third person, singular number, feminine gender. In *I am one of the men who vote for the candidate and not for the party,* the antecedent of *who* is *men,* not *one;* and, therefore, the verb in the relative clause must be plural to agree with its subject *who.*

Case of Relative Pronouns

The **case** of the relative pronoun is determined by its use in its own clause, and not by its antecedent. *Who* and the compounds formed with *who* (*whoever, whosoever*) are the only relatives having nominative, possessive, and objective case forms, all the others having nominative and objective forms alike and having no inflectional possessive forms. *What, which,* and *that* are indeclinable. *Whose,* the regular possessive of *who,* is sometimes used for the possessive of *which* and *that.* *Of what* is sometimes used to express possessive meaning. The following sentences illustrate various case uses of simple and compound relative pronouns:

A. Nominative Case:

  a. Nominative case is used as the subject of the relative clause:

    (1) He laughs best *who laughs last.* (2) A charity *which is not broad* is no charity at all. (3) They are silent griefs *that cut the heart-strings.* (4) I shall do *what is right.* (5) *Whatever begins* also ends. (6) Take *whichever pleases your fancy.* (7) *Whoever lies on the ground* cannot fall.

  b. Nominative case is sometimes used as a subjective complement (predicate nominative) in the relative clause:

    (1) *Whoever you are,* your sins will find you out. (2) I am *what I seem.* (3) *Whatever the gift is,* I shall refuse it.

B. Possessive Case:

The possessive case frequently introduces the relative (adjective) clause:

    (1) This is the man *whose car was stolen.* (2) The dog *whose master was killed* died of grief. (3) The three books *whose bindings are poor* should not be in circulation. (4) *Whosesoever sins ye remit,* they are remitted unto them; and *whosesoever sins ye retain,* they are retained. (5) He *whose tongue is loudest* thinks least.

C. Objective Case:

  a. The objective case form of the relative pronoun may be the object of the verb in the adjective clause:

    (1) He chose twelve *whom he named apostles.* (2) God rules the world, *which he created.* (3) *Whatever he asks,* grant it. (4) You may refuse *whichever you dislike.* (5) This is the house *that I bought.*

b. When a relative pronoun is used as the object of a preposition, it is always in the objective case:

(1) This is the book *that I referred to.* (2) I know the place *of which you speak.* (3) Comfort is the soil *on which human beings thrive.* (4) *Unto whomsoever much is given,* of him shall much be required.

Omission of the Relative Pronoun

In restrictive clauses the relative pronoun is frequently omitted when it is the direct object, or the object of a preposition:

(1) I examined the books *you purchased.* (2) The man *you saw* is my brother. (3) These are the students *I referred to in my lecture.* (4) This is the group *I shall go with to your party.*

And it is sometimes omitted in rapid conversation and in poetry when, if expressed, it would be the subject of a clause, as in the following:

(1) 'Tis distance *lends enchantment.* (2) I bought all the sugar *there was in the store.* (3) It is the medicine *makes me ill.*

Sentences of this type are not very common in standard literary prose. Observe that some of these sentences may be improved by the insertion of a *that* or a *who* before the verbs in the relative clauses, and the subjects must be supplied before the sentences can be fully analyzed.

Uses of Relative Pronouns

Who, whose, whom. The relative pronoun *who,* as a rule, is used only when the antecedent is one or more persons: *Where are the masters who could have taught Shakespeare? There never was but one man whom I would trust with my latchkey; No person ever lived whose virtues satisfied all men's desires.*

Who, however, is sometimes used to refer to inanimate objects personified and to animals when they are given human characteristics: *O Time, who waiteth not, teach us to be up and doing; My dog Fido, who can dance to music, is not a thoroughbred; Lois owns a horse who loves children.* In restrictive clauses, like the one in the last illustration, *that* would be more usual, and *which* could be used here.

Which, whose, of which. The relative *which* is applied to animals or things: *Virtues are the spices and salt which season a man; This is the city in which Grant lived; Death is the black camel which kneels at every man's gate.* In earlier English, *which* referred to persons also: *Our Father, which art in heaven, Hallowed be thy name.* Modern versions of the Bible often have substituted *who*, which was not used commonly as a relative pronoun until after the sixteenth century. In early English *the which* is often used for *which: He spied the oll, the which he hastily caught up.*

The possessive *whose* is often used of animals and things, as well as of persons: *I own a parrot whose tongue has never been split; We saw rocks whose surface glistened with mica; Mountains on whose barren breast the labouring clouds do often rest.* *Of which* is sometimes used instead of *whose* to relate to neuter antecedents; and, though grammatically possible, it is likely to be cumbersome: *These trees, the tops of which are dead, should be pruned.*

That. *That* is the oldest of the relative pronouns, having come from the Old English demonstrative *sē, sēo, ðæt*, which alone or along with the indeclinable *ðe*, was used as a relative. The relative *that* now refers to persons, animals, or things: *A man that is young in years may be old in hours; A dog that barks at everybody is a nuisance; A government that is hated seldom lasts.*

Often there is little choice between *who* and *that* or *which* and *that.* The relative *that*, being older, is likely to have a more familiar and traditional ring, and *who* or *which* replacing *that* often sounds more formal. *Who* and *which* are usual in nonrestrictive clauses. *That* is generally preferred in restrictive clauses, and is rarely used to introduce the nonrestrictive clause. *That* seems to retain some of its Old English demonstrative meaning even in the relative use, and tends to point out: *This is the man that I voted for.* Hence, in restrictive clauses after superlatives and exclusive adjectives, *that* is preferred: *The sweetest flower that blows; Ho, everyone that thirsteth, come ye to the waters. The only thing that we fear is this; They are silent griefs that cut the heart-strings.* If the antecedent of the relative pronoun is the demonstrative pronoun *that*, or is a word qualified by the demonstrative adjective *that*, the relative pronoun must not be *that*. Say *That dress which I gave you* (not *That dress that I gave you*) *is silk.* Also prefer *The that which you used* (not *That that that you used*) *is an adjective.*

As and *but* are primarily conjunctions, but they are sometimes used as relative pronouns. *As* has the function of a relative after *such* and *same*, and may refer to persons, animals, or things: *Name such persons as you know to be capable; Such as I have, I give unto you; He has the same qualifications as I have; My examination was the same one as you had.* *As* is common in contracted clauses, especially when its predicate verb is omitted; as, *You have the same opportunities as I* (*have*). *But* is sometimes used with the force of a negative relative when it is the equivalent of *that not: There is not a man here but knows the story; There is no fireside but has a vacant chair.*

The relative pronoun *what* is sometimes classified with the compound relative pronouns, because it generally conveys a compound or double meaning, being equivalent to *that which, those which,* or *the thing* (or *things*) *which: Do what I do; What are vices in one age seem fashions in the next; Riches and affluence are what are desired by men of the world.* *What* is always neuter, and is more commonly used in the singular than the plural. It is not declinable, but it has nominative and objective uses. The relative *what* should be carefully dis-

tinguished from the interrogative *what*, which may introduce
a direct or an indirect question, but not an adjective (relative) clause.

The compound indefinite relatives ending in *-ever* and
-soever are intensive or emphatic forms of the simple relative
pronouns, the *-soever* compounds being more intensive and
more formal than those ending in *-ever*. The *-ever* relatives
are, however, more commonly used in current English to
express the indefinite meanings: *All men admire **whatever** is
good and true; **Whoever** will excel in arts must excel in industry; My sister will like **whichever** you select; **Whosesoever** sins
ye forgive, shall be forgiven; **Whosoever** shall smite you on the
right cheek, turn to him the other also.*

Indefinite Relatives as Adjective Modifiers. By analogy
with the interrogative adjectives *who, which,* and *what,* some
of the indefinite relative pronouns modify nouns which repeat
the antecedents belonging in the principal clause. Since
these words have adjective and relative uses, they are sometimes called **relative adjectives**: *Take **what** aid you can get;
You must order **whatever** equipment you need; **What** men he
had were then off duty; You may choose **whichever** room
suits you; **Which** way I am traveling is a secret.*

Indefinite Relative in Concessive Clauses. The indefinite
relative pronoun sometimes introduces a concessive clause,
and has no antecedent expressed or understood, though
doubtless the idiom is an outgrowth of an older form in which
the antecedent was present: ***Whoever** said it, it is not the
truth* means *Though any person soever said it, it is not the
truth.* Similarly, ***Whichever** you take, you will be disappointed*
means *Though you take either, you will be disappointed.* These
pronouns may be called **conjunctive pronouns**: they are pronouns which join and subordinate adverb clauses having
concessive meaning. Unlike the other relative pronouns,
they do not introduce adjective clauses. For the analysis
of the concessive clause introduced by the indefinite relative,
see Part Two, Lesson XIV.

INTERROGATIVE PRONOUNS

The **interrogative pronoun** is one that introduces a question, either direct or indirect. In *Who is going to your party?* the speaker is asking a direct question of the one (or ones) addressed; but in *Tell us who is going to your party*, the speaker is asking for information in an indirect way. The direct question may be a full sentence (*What day of the week is this?*); or it may be only a part of a sentence (*He said, "What have I done to offend you?"*). The indirect question always has a noun function within a sentence: *I know what you did last night; Tell me whom you saw at the circus; Whom she will choose is no concern of mine.*

The interrogative pronouns are *who, which,* and *what.*[16] The interrogative *who* is declined like its corresponding relative for case only (nominative: *who*, possessive: *whose*, objective: *whom*), its person, number, and gender being determined by the context of the sentence in which it occurs. *Which* and *what* are indeclinable, but they may have adjectival use corresponding to *whose*, the possessive case form of *who: Which house is yours? What information have you received today?* The nominative and objective uses of *which* and *what* must be determined by their use, not by form: *Which* (nominative) *is yours? Which* (objective) *did you choose? What* (nominative) *are your plans for tonight? What* (objective) *do you have in your basket?*

Who is used to ask for information concerning persons: *Who is he? Who discovered America?* In standard literary speech *who* is restricted to nominative uses, and *whom* to the objective constructions; but in informal speech, *who* is often used where the rule calls for *whom*. But careful speakers do not, as a rule, use *who* to introduce an interrogative sentence unless it has a nominative function. *Whom* is the form

---

[16] *Whether* meaning *which of two* was in common use as an interrogative pronoun in Middle English and early Modern English. From the Scripture we get *Whether is the greater, the gift or the altar?* This interrogative use of *whether* is now obsolete.

approved by our cultivated writers when it is the object of a verb (*Whom did you see in town?*), or is the object of a preposition (*Whom are you going with to the party?*).

Which is used in a selective sense. It asks the identity of one or more persons or things in a definite group; as, *which person?* or *which thing?* The answer to a *which* question will point out, locate, or identify. In *Which of the ties may I have?* the answer might be *This one, That one, The red one,* or *The checked one.* Similarly, in *Which house do you live in?* one might answer *This one, That one, The white one,* etc.

What is used to ask for more general information than *which.* It inquires concerning the identity of an object or the matter in question, or concerning the calling or social status of persons. *What is the name of your novel? What is this green stuff which you have in this bottle? What is your profession? What is John, a doctor or a lawyer?*

The interrogative pronoun is generally used to ask for information, but it is sometimes used to introduce a rhetorical question; i.e., a question which does not require an answer. It may be used to state a negative generalization, or to express an indefiniteness or uncertainty on the part of the speaker: *What do I want anyway? Who are you to be giving me orders? Who does not crave sympathy? Who can refute a sneer?*

The interrogative pronoun differs from the personal and relative pronouns in having no expressed or implied antecedent. The antecedent of the interrogative pronoun is the answer to the direct or indirect question which it introduces. If the answer to *Who are you?* is *Joe Brown,* then *Joe Brown* may be considered the antecedent of *who.* The one who asks the question is requesting some one else to supply the antecedent for the interrogative pronoun.

ADJECTIVE PRONOUNS

A group of words having definitive meaning, and hence adjective force, are often employed substantively, in which construction they are called **adjective pronouns**. Of this group are the following: *this* (pl. *these*), *that* (pl. *those*), *some, one, many, much, enough, few, little, same, such, other, another, any, either, neither, both, each, several, former, all,* etc.

Adjective pronouns, when classified as to meaning, are **definite** or **indefinite**.

Definite Adjective Pronouns

The **definite adjective** pronouns include the **demonstratives** and the **absolute possessives** of the personal pronouns.

This and *that* and their plurals, *these* and *those*, are demonstrative adjectives[17] when they modify nouns (*This book is mine; These books are mine*); but they are demonstrative pronouns when they stand for nouns (*This is my book; These are your books*). The **demonstratives** are used to designate or point out some definite person, place, or thing referred to or intended. *This* and *these* point to objects near at hand; *that* and *those* point to what is more distant or remote.

In earlier English, *yon, yond, yonder* were common demonstratives, and were used either as adjectives or as pronouns. They are now restricted in the main to poetic diction and to the adjective function: *yon celestial skies, yond man, yonder ivy-mantled tower*, etc.

When preceded by the definite article (*the*) used in its generic sense,[18] the words *former, latter, first, second, last, one,* and *other* have demonstrative force: *The former is better; The first shall be last, and the last shall be first; No man can serve two masters: for either he will hate the one, and love the other; or else he will hold to the one, and despise the other.*

The **absolute possessive** forms of the personal pronouns usually indicate definite meaning because they replace nouns naming definite objects:[19] *mine, thine, yours, hers, ours, theirs,* and *his. Your dog is larger than mine, but mine is two months*

---

[17] See Demonstrative Adjectives, Chapter Four, p. 74.
[18] The generic the is discussed under **Articles**, p. 76.
[19] The absolute possessives are discussed under *Case of Personal Pronouns,* pp. 56–57.

older than yours. Frequently the absolute possessives are used in sentences with the demonstratives: *This is* **mine,** *and that is* **his.** *Give me that book; it is* **mine.**

Indefinite Adjective Pronouns

Pronouns which point out objects less clearly than the demonstratives and do not substitute for nouns previously mentioned but rather for some noun-word, phrase, or statement understood or implied are called **indefinite pronouns.** These pronouns have no fixed meaning except one of relation or limitation. The **indefinites** may include adjective pronouns denoting indefinite meaning (*few, some, any, much, enough,* etc.) and a number of words which have no adjective function in present-day speech (*none, everybody, somebody, anything, something, aught, naught, nought, nothing,* etc.).

The indefiniteness of the indefinite pronouns may be noted when they are compared with the personal, the relative, or the demonstrative pronouns, which usually convey very definite meanings. The pronouns *he, she, you, I, we, these, those, that,* etc. stand for definite persons or objects, but *some, few, everybody, something, enough, much, anything, none, nothing* substitute for nouns having very general or indefinite meanings.

In use also, the indefinites differ from personal and relative pronouns in that they do not require definite antecedents. They stand for nouns that name persons, places, or things which are not definitely and often not even clearly identified. Because the indefinites do not have definite antecedents, some grammarians prefer to classify them as **indefinite nouns.**

Most adjectives which name the quality or the quantity of substance or designate the number of objects can substitute for nouns, and are classified variously in our school grammars; as, **indefinite pronouns, indefinite nouns, adjective pronouns, nouns,** etc.[20] In *The race is not to the swift, nor the battle to*

---

[20] A few adjectives when pluralized like nouns by adding an *-s* acquire highly specialized meanings; as *sweets* for candy, *goods* for wares or merchandise, *bitters*

the strong, swift and *strong* are descriptive, not definitive, adjectives used substantively; and they may be classified as adjectives substituting for nouns or as adjective pronouns.

Inflectional Forms and Uses of Adjective and Indefinite Pronouns

Some of the adjective pronouns and some of the indefinites inflect for number (*one-ones, other-others, this-these, that-those*); and a few denote possession by inflectional change (*one's, other's, others', everybody's,* etc.). Some are always singular (*each, another, nothing*); and some are always plural (*several, many, few, both*). Many of the adjective and indefinite pronouns are, however, indeclinable (*all, some, none, either, neither, little,* etc.); their case, gender, and number must be determined by the context.

Somebody else, anybody else, no one else, someone else, etc. may now be regarded as compound (or phrasal) indefinites, though *else* has generally been construed as an adjective qualifying the pronoun it follows. In current English, the phrasal compounds are all singular in form and meaning, and their possessives are formed like the possessive singular of nouns by adding the apostrophe and *s* to the nominative singular forms (*somebody else's, anybody else's, no one else's,* etc.). In earlier English, the apostrophe and *s* were added to the substantive part of the compound and not to the adjective *else;* but *somebody's else, no one's else,* etc. are rarely found in written English, and seldom heard in oral speech. Usage has fully established *somebody else's, no one else's,* etc.

A number of the indefinites resemble collective nouns in being singular in form and suggesting a number of individuals; and, as with the collective nouns, the verbs they govern and the personal pronouns referring to them are sometimes singular and sometimes plural. In *None but the brave deserves the fair, none* is singular; but, in *None of the men have brought*

---

for liquors, etc. Since these pluralized forms are the names of concrete objects, they are not true pronouns, but are nouns derived from adjectives. They are, therefore, better classified as nouns. See Chapter Two, p. 20.

their wives, none is clearly plural. Similarly *some* and *all* are singular or plural, and their number must be indicated by the verbs and pronouns following them. They are plural in *All of the boys have eaten their lunches,* and in *Some of these students are lazy and deserve to fail;* but they are singular in *Hope lost, all is lost,* and *Some of this food is spoiled, and should be thrown out.*

The compound and phrasal indefinites which have been formed by combining modifying adjectives and substantives require special attention. *Everyone, everybody, someone, somebody, anyone, anybody, no one, nobody,* often suggest a plural meaning in the distributive sense, though they govern singular verbs, and logically pronouns referring to them should be singular also; but in substandard speech, the reference pronouns used with these indefinites are more often plural than singular. Our most exact writers, however, take pains to use singular pronouns in referring to any of the indefinites governing singular verbs. The confusion of number in the use of these indefinites is probably due to the fact that the English language has no common gender form for the personal pronoun in the third person singular; and the third person plural pronoun (*they, their, them*) is sometimes substituted, especially in informal speech, even when its antecedent is clearly singular. The masculine third person singular pronoun (*he, his, him*) is the approved common gender pronoun for the third person singular, though in popular speech it is avoided, because it often seems more formal and more restricted in meaning than the plural forms. The singular pronoun in this construction denotes, as a rule, a more exact meaning. Thus *Everybody must leave his notebook* conveys a more logical and more exact meaning than *Everybody must leave their notebook.* One cannot, strictly speaking, say *their notebook* unless the entire class is preparing one notebook. The substitution of the plural noun after *their* does not, therefore, always make for clearness.

Sometimes the gender of the indefinites is indicated by the

modifiers of the pronouns: *Everyone of the girls made her formal debut* before she was twenty-one. *Every one of the boys has sold his ticket.* In formal speech, it is correct to use *his* or *her* to indicate that the singular antecedent is to include both sexes: *Everyone in this church should be willing and anxious to do his or her share of the sacrificing.* In less formal English, however, the *or her* is usually omitted, and *his* is construed as indicating common gender. It is well to remember that *he, his, him* may be used to indicate masculine or common gender. *She* and *her* must be used only when the antecedent is known to be feminine: *Everybody in the sorority should be invited to bring her escort.* It is incorrect to say *Everyone of the teachers had her salary increased,* unless the teachers are all women, since *her* excludes all the male members of the group. *His,* having common gender function, may be substituted for *her* and include both men and women teachers.

The indefinite pronoun *one (one's)* in current English is used interchangeably with *he (his, him)* as a reference pronoun or as an antecedent for *he (his, him)*. Some rhetoricians strongly recommend the repetition of *one (one's)* when there is no noun antecedent. It seems somewhat pedantic and a bit forced to have to say *One must be in one's room before one can feel that one is safe* instead of the more natural *One must be in his room before he can feel that he is safe.* Similarly, *One ought to have one's dentist examine one's teeth regularly* seems less natural than *One* (or *Everyone*) *ought to have his dentist examine his teeth regularly.*

Each other and *one another* are called **reciprocal pronouns,** because they express mutual action or relation on the part of the persons indicated by the subject. They are always treated as phrasal (or compound) pronouns; and they cannot be separated and used as adjectives to express the reciprocal relation. Like the reflexive pronouns, they seldom, if ever, have nominative case function. They always reflect to the subject or to a preceding noun or pronoun. *Each other* and *one another* are now used interchangeably to refer to two or more persons. However, in earlier English, *each other* was restricted to two persons, and *one another* was used only when more than two persons were involved: *Mary and I like each other; Little children, be good to one another.* While this distinction is logical enough, it is not now strictly observed in either oral or written speech.

Four

Adjectives

An **adjective** is a word used with a noun or other substantive as a modifier[1] to describe or define it.

TYPES OF ADJECTIVES

Adjectives may be classified as to form, meaning, and derivation, each classification having a number of subdivisions.

Form

When classified as to form, adjectives may be said to be **simple** or **compound**. The **simple adjectives** are those whose primary function is adjectival: *good, tough, young, old, sweet, hale,* etc. The **compound adjectives** are words or phrases combined to describe or define noun-words: *alive, asleep, cocksure, aware, homesick, sunfast,* etc. Sometimes the component parts of the compound adjectives are joined by hyphens: *head-strong, far-fetched, blue-green, twice-told, has-been, would-be, two-pound, ten-story, six-foot, cut-and-dried, happy-go-lucky, matter-of-fact, long-drawn-out, never-to-be-forgotten, out-of-the-way, up-to-date, down-at-the-heels,* etc.

Meaning

When classified as to meaning, adjectives are **descriptive** or **definitive,** some of each class having definite and some indefinite application.

---

[1] To modify is to change. *Red apples* are not the same thing as *apples.* **Red** apples have a quality which apples as a whole do not possess, and there are fewer of them in the world. The prefixing of *red* adds to the qualities, and limits the quantity of *apples. Three men* is more definite than *men,* and less extensive.

A **descriptive adjective** names a quality, feature, or characteristic of the thing modified: *red apples,* **honest** *men,* **brave** *leaders,* **ugly** *ducklings,* **sour** *cherries,* **sweet** *apples,* **smug** *people,* **tall** *buildings.*

A **definitive adjective** limits the application or scope of a substantive by specifying quantity or number: *that boy,* **much** *grain,* **three men,** *some day, time* **enough,** etc. Definitive adjectives may be subdivided as follows:

1. The **demonstrative adjective** limits the substantive it modifies by pointing out: *this, that, these, those, yonder, yon, latter, former, both, same,* etc. When the demonstrative has the function of a noun, it is called a **demonstrative pronoun;** as, *This is my house.* But it is a demonstrative adjective when it limits a noun which immediately **follows it:** *Those books are mine; That house is for sale.*

2. **Numeral adjectives** limit the meaning of **nouns by show-**ing how many or in what **order** things **are to be** considered. Numerals may be (1) **definite** and denote the **exact** number (*one, two, first, second,* etc.); or (2) they may be **indefinite** and denote number in a general sense (*few, many, all*).

(1) The **definite numerals** are **cardinals, ordinals,** and **multiplicatives.** The **cardinals** are the primary, or counting, numbers, answering the question *How many? One, two, three, twenty-five, fifty,* etc. are cardinals. The **ordinals** indicate the serial order, position in rank, of individual persons, objects, or ideas, answering the question *Which one of the list, or group? First, second, third, twenty-fifth, fiftieth,* etc. are ordinals. The **multiplicatives** indicate how often the object is repeated; e.g., *triple, double, treble, quadruple,* etc.

(2) The **indefinite numerals** suggest number without indicating precisely what the number is: *All men must die;* **Few** *students came; He has been here* **many** *times; I have lived here* **several** *years; Countless, any, numerous, innumerable,* etc. are other indefinite numerals.

Large numbers (*twenty* upwards; e.g., *hundred, thousand,* etc.) were in Old English employed as substantives, the nouns which in Modern English they would modify being genitives dependent upon them; as, *twenty of sheep, a hundred of men, ninety of ships, a thousand of miles.* Of course, any modern cardinal or ordinal numeral may be used in the substantive position, the noun which it would normally modify being suppressed: *Three came where only **two** were expected; I choose the **third** from the end.*

It is notable that all ordinals except *first* and *second* are derived from corresponding cardinals: *third* from *three, fourth* from *four, thousandth* from *thousand.* *First* is derived from the stem of *fore.* *Second* is a borrowed word, coming through the French from Latin *secundus.* It means literally *following* (e.g., *every **second** day* equals *every **following** day*). *Once, twice,* and the archaic *thrice* are adverbs based on *one, two,* and *three.* *Twain* is a variant of *two,* coming from the masculine of the Old English numeral, as *two* is from the feminine neuter.

3. **Indefinite adjectives** may suggest indefiniteness of quantity or number: *Some people, some trouble, some time, some place, any place, every place, no place, any man, much effort, all ages,* etc. Many of these have pronominal function, and when so used are called **indefinite adjective pronouns:**[2] *Some of my people, some of our trouble, some of his time, much of our effort,* etc. Some indefinite adjectives do not have pronominal use (e.g., *alone, else, every, no, only, sundry,* etc.), and are, therefore, never used except when they qualify nouns.

4. **Pronominal adjectives** are words which are normally pronouns used as modifiers of nouns.[3] These may be personal, relative, and interrogative adjectives: *My house is for sale;*

---

[2] For fuller treatment of these Indefinites, see Pronouns, pp. 68–71.
[3] For a discussion of adjectives having pronominal function, see Adjective Pronouns, pp. 66–72.

Whatever money I give must be used for food; Which answer should I give?

THE ARTICLES

The **articles** *the* and *a* (*an*) belong to the general class of adjectives called definitive. One of them, *the,* is more definite than the other, *a* (*an*). Hence *the* is called the definite article, and *a* (*an*), the indefinite: *Give me a book from the shelf; Give me the book on that shelf.*

Origin and Function of *The*

1. *The* is in late Old English *ðe,* the masculine form of the demonstrative pronoun *ðæt* (pronounced much like its modern English form, *that*).[4] *The* is still in meaning a weakened form of the demonstrative *that. The man on the corner* nearly equals *That man on the corner. The* has demonstrative force when emphasized or stressed: *Is he the Churchill? Are you the singer?*

2. *The* has a generic meaning when it is used with singular nouns to indicate the class or kind of objects, as in the well known aphorism: *The child is father of the man,* and in kindred expressions. Here *the child* means *any child* (almost *childhood*). Other examples of the generic *the* are: *The poet* (*any poet, every poet*) *hath the child's sight in his breast; The oak shall send his roots abroad.*

The generic *the* is used before an adjective to give it substantive function: *The valiant never taste of death but once. The weakest go to the wall. The meek, the poor, the rich, the wicked are in our midst.* In this function, *the* gives the adjective a plural substantive meaning. Some adjectives do not make good nouns (*canine, juvenile, human*), and hence are not, as a rule, used with the generic *the.*

---

[4] For an account of the origin of *the* and its relation to *that, he, she,* and other forms, see Skeat's *An Etymological Dictionary of the English Language,* and also the *Oxford English Dictionary,* at *the* and *that.*

3. *The* is sometimes used as part of a proper name or title: *The United States of America, The Honorable James Sterling, The Hudson Bay Company, The Soviet Union.*

The *ye* in archaic expressions such as *ye olde men* and *Ye Barstowe Inn* is the result of a misconception. An Old English character þ, written for the sound *th*, looked somewhat like the letter *y*, for which it has been mistaken. *Ye* in these phrases should be pronounced *the*. It has nothing to do with the personal pronoun. See *Webster's New Collegiate Dictionary.*

The Indefinite Article *A* (*An*)

A and *an* are in effect two forms of the same word, of which *an* is the earlier, or original. The *n* is retained before a word beginning with a vowel sound: *an apple, an old song.* *A* is used before a word beginning with a consonant sound: *a man, a better chance.*

The rule for the choice of *a* or *an* is regular and without exception if we regard only the initial sound of the following word regardless of the spelling. Thus we say and write *a man, a unit, a useful tool, a ewe, a yew tree, a European, such a one;* and *an hour, an honest man, an honor, an heir.* If we pronounce *h* in *humble, herb, homage, hostler, Humphrey,* we may say and write *a humble, a herb, a homage, a hostler, a Humphrey;* if we do not pronounce *h*, we say *an hostler, an humble and contrite heart,* etc.

A few expressions have become stereotyped from earlier pronunciation; and we sometimes find, especially in British speech, *an historical novel,* dating from a time when the unaccented *h* was silent; *such a one, one* (now pronounced *wŭn*) having been formerly sounded like *own*, as it still is in *only* and *alone;* and *an union, an eulogy,* formed when these words began with the vowel sound (diphthong) *ĭu*, since then changed to *yū*. But present good usage demands none of these older forms, and the best usage follows the rule strictly.[5]

---

[5] See *Webster's New International Dictionary,* Second Edition, at *an,* and H. W. Fowler, *Dictionary of Modern English Usage,* p. 1.

In etymology, *an* (*a*) is the unstressed form of *one*. Old English *ān* (*one*), when unstressed, became *an;* when stressed, it became *one.*[6]

In meaning, the **indefinite article** indicates that the noun with which it is used is one of a general class: *a book, an ornament, a struggle, an effort.* It is used with collective nouns: *a corps, an army, a squadron.*

In such expressions as *a few weeks, a good many* (or *a great many*) *people*, the *a* seems to modify a plural noun. However, in the earlier construction from which such forms are derived, the *a* modified *few* and *many*, these being treated as substantives, and *weeks* and *people* as nouns in the genitive case (*a few of weeks, a great many of people*). One still sees the same relation in *a dozen of those eggs, a good many of my friends.*

Omission of the Article. Both the definite and the indefinite articles limit the scope or application of the nouns they modify, and they must not be omitted when the sense of the noun requires limitation. The definite article, *the*, restricts the meaning of the noun it modifies to a particular individual or object: *The man was here.* The indefinite article, *a* (*an*) restricts the application of the noun it modifies to one of a class: *A man was here.* When a noun is used in its broadest sense, neither article should be used: *Man was created by God.*

1. The article should be repeated before each of two or more nouns when they refer to different things and are joined by a coördinating conjunction: *I have a knife, a pencil, and a notebook; I got the money and the tickets.*

2. When two or more coördinate nouns mean the same person, the article is not repeated: *He is a stationer and bookseller; I am the secretary and treasurer; Mr. Cabbot is the preacher and teacher.*

3. When two or more adjectives modify different nouns,

---

[6] The present pronunciation of *one*, with initial *w*, arose from a 15th century local dialect. The regular form would sound like *own*, as now heard in *only* and *alone*.

expressed or understood, the article should be repeated: *I have a red, a white, and a blue umbrella;* or *I have three umbrellas—a red one, a white one, and a blue one; I bought a silk, a rayon, and a cotton dress; They have sold the black and the white pups.*

4. When two or more coördinate adjectives modify the same noun, the article should not be repeated: *I found a red, white, and blue handkerchief;* or *I found a handkerchief, a red, white, and blue one.* Similarly, *We sold the black and white pups;* or *We sold the pups, the black and white ones.*

5. The article should not be used before nouns following *kind of, sort of,* and *type of: This kind of man* (not *kind of a man*) *is rare; I like this kind of or sort of* (not *kind of a or sort of a*) *person; She is not that type of* (not *type of a*) *woman.*

PHRASES AND CLAUSES AS ADJECTIVES

1. The prepositional phrase frequently has adjectival function: *the man **on the box,** a feeling **of loneliness,** a love **of money,** a ring **of gold,** a coat **without seam,** a man **without honor,*** etc.

2. The participle is used as an adjective: *a **cutting** remark, a **moving** van, **stolen** fruit, **lost** hope, **burnt** bread, that child **being punished,*** etc.

3. The infinitive phrase may be used to limit a noun: *an ax **to grind,** an attempt **to escape,** a house **to sell,** a trap **to catch** mice, nothing **to do,*** etc.

4. Any clause describing or limiting a noun is an adjective clause: *This is the man **who paints portraits;** The house **in which I was born** is now for sale; The dress **which I bought** is too large; Denver, **where I live in the summer,** is the capital of Colorado; I must not tell you the reason **why I left the meeting.***

NOUNS AND ADVERBS AS ADJECTIVES

Most adjectives cannot be identified as such by their form. The fact that the same word may be used without modification as an adjective and as some other part of speech drives one to the test of function. In general, *any word which modifies a noun or its equivalent is an adjective.*

Nouns Which Modify Nouns. But here we meet difficulties in classification. What shall we say of such expressions as *fire department, desk pad, twelve-inch gun, August sale?* A glance at these will convince one that almost any noun can be made to modify another noun, the juxtaposition of the two assuming some relation of design, size, time, etc. Most grammarians would hesitate to call such words as these adjectives, since they name not a quality but substantive concepts. It will be observed that the relation set forth in these noun groups is transitory, variable, or accidental. Where the association of the two nouns is a permanent one, the tendency is for them to become joined into a compound noun; as *bookworm, flagstaff, armchair.*[7]

Proper Adjectives. Proper adjectives are proper nouns or words derived from proper nouns used to describe or define substantives: *New York styles, Hollywood beds, Shakespearean costumes, Augustan age, British citizen, American language, Chinese food, French wine, Italian cheese, Jewish refugees.* Where there is no change in the noun form, as in *Ohio coal,* the *Lincoln motor,* a *United States soldier,* etc., the term may be called in question; but there can be no question in respect to proper noun forms having adjective suffixes: *Germanic, Elizabethan, Icelandic, Swedish.*

All adjectives which are not **proper** may be classified as **common** adjectives. Proper adjectives, like the proper nouns from which they come, are always capitalized. When their origin is forgotten or disregarded, proper adjectives become common adjectives, and are then written with small letters: *tartarean situation, jovial laughter, roman type, mosaic figure, titantic undertaking, venetian blinds, manila paper, satanic manner, india ink,* etc.

---

[7] American printers are not, however, at all consistent in printing these forms as compounds. The function and meaning must be the determining factor here, not the form.

Adverbs as Adjectives. Some primary adverbs and a number of preposition-adverbs (adverbs derived from prepositions) have adjectival function: *This very day, the day after, my day off, the off side, the out fielder, off base, down payment, the man in,* etc. In the predicative position, the adverb is more common: *The man is in today and out tomorrow; My troubles are over; I have this day off.*

Adverbs which point out and have demonstrative meaning should not be used with the demonstrative adjectives: *This book* (not *this here book*) *is mine; That boy* (not *that there boy*) *borrowed my car; These apples* (not *these here apples*) *are sour.*

ADJECTIVE SUFFIXES

By the addition of suffixes (*-ful, -less, -y, -ly, -like,* etc.), many adjectives are formed from words which are other parts of speech. Among words so converted, it will be found that the nouns predominate, though many of the nouns employed as bases for adjectives are of active character, akin to verbs: *hopeful, useful, shiftless, lively, tireless, flighty.*

French, Latin, and Greek suffixes, including *-ous (-ious), -ant, -ent, -ate, -ac (-ic), -able (-ible), -esque, -ine, -ile (-il), -ive, -ory, -ose,* and others, appear in many English adjectives: *valorous, rampant,[8] fluent,[8] ornate,[8] cardiac, poetic, tolerable, edible, grotesque, canine, civil, juvenile, elective, introductory, verbose.*

Position of Adjective Modifiers

Adjectives are sometimes classified according to their position in the sentence; as, **attributive, appositive,** and **predicative.**

1. An adjective is said to be **attributive,** or **adherent,** when it modifies its noun directly and names an attribute of the noun. The **attributive adjectives** regularly precede the noun which it describes or limits: *Brave men are needed; Fine*

---

[8] These adjectives are participial forms, *-ant* and *-ent* in their origin being present participle endings, and *-ate* coming from a perfect participle.

words butter no parsnips. As a rule, the one-word adjective precedes its noun, but in certain standardized phrases it follows the noun which it limits or describes; as, *life everlasting, no interest whatever, food enough,* *something else,* etc. A descriptive phrase or clause preceding the noun it modifies is usually hyphenated, and considered as a one-word (compound) adjective: *a never-to-be-forgotten experience,* *a pay-as-you-go plan.*

2. An **appositive adjective** usually follows its noun, and, like the noun in apposition, adds to its noun and explains it. The **appositive adjective** may be restrictive (*A teacher untrained in phonetics is as useless as a doctor untrained in anatomy*); or it may be nonrestrictive (*A blacksmith, swarthy and muscular, was leisurely working the long handle of his bellows*).

3. An adjective may be **predicative** when it is used as a subjective or as an objective complement. The **predicative adjective** as subjective complement follows linking verbs: *Our hoard is little, but our hearts are great; I became weary; The fruit tastes sour; The stick was made smooth; The man was found dead.*

The **predicative adjective** may be used to complete the meaning of the transitive verb and limit or describe the direct object: *The teacher made us uneasy; We found the child asleep; The news drove the man insane.*

Adjectives having distributive or quantitative meaning are not ordinarily used predicatively: *Each man* (not *man is each*); *some people* (not *people are some*); *every citizen* (not *citizen is every*).

Order of Adjectives

1. When two or more adjectives precede or immediately follow a noun, the definitive adjectives usually precede the descriptive ones. The articles (*the, a*), the demonstratives (*this, that*), the possessives (*my, your, his, our, their,* etc.), and the numerals are placed before other adjectives in a

series, the articles usually preceding all other definitives: *the first hard rain, the first big word, a great big apple, my good old friend, three little pigs, the first intelligent remark.* In a few stock phrases, however, the article follows another adjective: *half a day, such a problem, not a man, many a time.*

2. When adjectives are of the same rank, the longest ones usually come closest to the noun: *a fine progressive citizen, a big blond actress, an old dilapidated building.*

3. When a cardinal and an ordinal come together, the ordinal is usually placed first: *the first ten, the last three,* etc. There is, however, some authority for placing the cardinal first; e.g., *the ten first, the three last.*

4. Adjectives derived from nouns or nouns functioning as adjectives usually come next to the nouns they limit; *a cold November rain, an intelligent Civil War veteran, a southern Texas farmer, fat beef cows, an old race horse.*

5. Compound nouns in the adjective function, especially the long hyphenated ones, come next to the words they limit: *a hot blackberry pie, a never-to-be-forgotten scene, a small matter-of-fact individual.*

6. When the adjectives are of the same rank and length, the one closest to the noun in meaning is placed next to the noun: *a big fat man, a large black bear, a tall, lean, lank soldier.*

In a few stereotyped phrases, the order of the adjective is fixed by rhythm and usage: *each and every one of you, black and white prints, the great and small ones, a day or so, more or less interest, bruised black and blue,* etc.

Misplaced Adjectives

Above all, adjectives must be so placed that the meaning is clear and accurate. One should not say *I had a hot bowl of soup,* when he wishes to convey the idea that the soup, and not bowl, was hot. The adjective modifiers, whether words, phrases, or clauses, should, as a rule, come as close as possible to the nouns they limit: *We bought the fruit which we had for breakfast from a street vender* (not *We bought the fruit from a street vender which we had for breakfast*). *Only the men smoked* (not *The men only smoked*, unless *only* is to be construed as an adverb limiting *smoked*).

Inflection of Adjectives

In Old English, as in Modern German, adjectives had inflectional modification to indicate number, gender, case, and degree of comparison. In addition, there was a distinction of weak and strong declensions, based upon the use of the adjective with another defining word or without it. In Middle English, most of these declensional distinctions were lost, the general tendency of the language being to drop all suffixes. Except for *this* and *these* and *that* and *those*, which still show number distinction, and which are really pronominal in their quality, adjectives in Modern English do not change their forms to show changes in number, case, or gender; and only a few adjectives of the pronominal class possess meanings which indicate number. *One, every, each*, and a few others modify singular nouns; while *several, few, many, innumerable*, etc. modify only plural substantives. No English adjective is now capable of indicating gender or case. The only inflection of adjectives common to both Old and Modern English is **comparison**.

Comparison of Adjectives

Most descriptive adjectives and a few definitive adjectives (*few, much, little, many*) have degrees of comparison. In comparing objects with each other, the forms of adjectives are changed or modified to show degree of quality, quantity, or relation. There are three degrees of comparison: 1. The **positive**, 2. the **comparative**, and 3. the **superlative**.

1. The **positive degree** is the simplest form of the adjective and denotes a simple quality, quantity, or relation. It has no special ending: *strong, old, mighty, liberal*. It describes

without expressing or suggesting any comparison: *I am strong; He is old; The sword is mighty; American institutions are liberal.*

2. The **comparative degree** denotes an increase or diminution of the quality, the quantity, or the relation expressed in the positive form: *I am stronger than you; He is older than I; The pen is mightier than the sword; American institutions are more liberal than Chinese.* The comparative degree is used when two things are compared, or when one object is compared with one group or one class of objects. A true comparative is always followed by *than,* expressed or understood: *I am older than you; Your book is better than mine; Some remedies are worse than the disease.*

3. The **superlative degree** is applied to persons, objects, or groups possessing a quality or quantity in the highest or the lowest degree: *I am the strongest person in my class; He is the oldest of the children; The mightiest men sometimes fall; He is the most liberal citizen in this community; I am least of the Apostles.* The superlative degree is used when one thing is compared with all other things of the same class: *This is the best book (of all the books) I have read this winter.* It is usually employed when three or more objects are compared.

A number of adjectives having superlative forms are now used to convey emphatic or intensive meaning: *Dearest Mother; our kindest regards; a most lovely lady.*

Methods of Comparison

To denote degrees of superiority adjectives are regularly compared by adding *-er* and *-est,* or by the use of the adverbs *more* or *most* as modifiers of the positives of adjectives capable of showing differences of degree. To denote inferiority, the method of comparison is limited to the periphrastic, or phrasal, pattern, *less* and *least* being used as modifiers of the positive forms. If an adjective is not compared by one of these methods, it is said to be **irregularly compared.**

I. Regular Comparisons. The pattern of comparison to indicate degrees of superiority is determined in the following ways:

1. Adjectives of one syllable are regularly compared by adding to the positive form -*er* for the comparative, and -*est* for the superlative: *great, greater, greatest.* The only exceptions to this rule are a few monosyllables which are difficult to pronounce with the -*er* and -*est* suffixes: *just, like, off, real, wrong, wan.* One must say *I am more like* (not *liker*) *my father than he is.*

2. Adjectives of more than two syllables are regularly compared by the employment of the function words *more* and *most: comfortable, more comfortable, most comfortable; precious, more precious, most precious.* One must say *I am more comfortable than I was* (not *comfortabler than I was*).

3. Some adjectives of one and two syllables have both patterns of comparison, usually the *more* and *most* pattern being employed to show special emphasis: *calm, calmer, calmest;* or *calm, more calm, most calm; kind, kinder, kindest* (or *kind, more kind, most kind*); *narrow, narrower, narrowest* (or *narrow, more narrow, most narrow*). Adjectives used in the appositive position are generally compared with *more* and *most: I never knew a man more calm or more kind than you.*

4. For phonetic reasons many adjectives ending in -*al*, -*ar*, -*ard*, -*ed*, -*en*, -*erse*, -*ful*, -*ic*, -*il*, -*is*, -*ive*, -*ose*, -*ous*, -*om*, -*que*, -*st*, -*ure*, etc. are compared by the employment of *more* or *most* rather than by the addition of the suffixes -*er* and -*est*. We seldom attempt to put -*er* or -*est* on any of the following: *equal, frugal, vulgar, awkward, constant, diseased, talented, sudden, brazen, terse, useful, comic, stoic, dramatic, poetic, fertile, hostile, bovine, canine, roguish, English, boyish, active, verbose, porous, buxom, just, honest, antique, secure.*

5. Compound adjectives are sometimes compared by inflecting the first element of the compound: *well-known, better-known, best-known; worldly-minded, worldlier-minded* (or *more worldly-minded*), *most worldly-minded*. Sometimes the second element of a compound word receives the *-er* and the *-est: lonesome, blood-thirsty, worldly-wise*, which may have the *-er* and *-est* pattern also, or perhaps a mixture of the two, as with *worldly-minded*, where the comparative may have the *-er*, and the superlative *most*. Adjectives which are limited to the predicative and appositive positions are always compared with the function words *more* and *most;* e.g., *afraid, alone, aware, alive*, and others like these: *I am more afraid than I was; The strongest man on earth is he who stands most alone* (Ibsen).

6. Some adjectives have mixed patterns, the comparative being formed on one pattern, and the superlative on the other: Many adjectives which are not regularly compared with *-er* or *-est* have superlative forms in *-est* and the comparative with *more*. Often the *-est* superlative is preferred when the adjective has pronominal function, or when it is preceded by the definite article (*the*): *He is the handsomest of the boys; You are the cruelest woman alive; She is the cheerfullest person I know; That is the cleverest of all your tricks.*

II. **Comparison to Denote Inferiority.** The suffixes *-er* and *-est* and the function words *more* and *most* are limited to denoting degrees of superiority. When adjectives are compared to show diminution of quality or quantity, the adverbs *less* and *least* must be used: *famous, less famous, least famous; slow, less slow, least slow; useful, less useful, least useful; kind, less kind, least kind;* etc.

The comparative degree with *less* is not very common. The adverb clause of degree following a negative is the more usual method of expressing this type of degree of comparison. Usage seems to prefer *I am not so tall as you* to *I am less tall than you*. *You are not so old as I thought you were* is more usual than *You are less old than I thought*.

III. Irregular and Defective Comparisons. Adjectives having irregular comparison have lost some of their forms, which have been replaced by others of similar meaning, such as *good, better, best; bad (evil), worse, worst.* The old Teutonic positive for *better* and *best* was *bat-*, 'good,' and for *worse* and *worst* was *wers-*, 'evil'; and when these positive forms dropped out of the language, words of similar meaning were substituted.

Some adjectives having defective comparison have lost one and in some instances two of the degree forms. *Under, over,* and *other* are comparatives which have no superlative forms. *After, aftermost* and *nether, nethermost* have no positives. The comparatives *under, over, after,* and *nether* now denote relational rather than comparative meaning. Observe that *than,* expressed or understood, always follows the true comparative. *Former, elder, latter, utter,* and *outer* are comparative forms now used to express relational meaning and not degrees of comparison, and therefore are not followed by *than.*

The most irregular feature of the **irregular** and **defective comparison** of adjectives is the addition of the suffixes *-er* and *-est* or the employment of the function words *more* and *most* to forms that are already comparative. *Lesser* and *nearer* are sometimes called **double comparatives;** they are formed by adding *-er* to the older comparatives *less* and *near. Less* is now more common than *lesser* in denoting comparison; *lesser* is used in only a few expressions, such as the *lesser of two evils,* the *lesser third,* etc. *Lesser* is never followed by *than.* The suffix *-est* is now added to the earlier comparative form *near,* to make the superlative *nearest.* In earlier English *worse* also had a double comparative form, *worser.* Shakespeare made frequent use of *worser* as an emphatic comparative: *Let not my **worser** spirit tempt me.* It is also employed by some nineteenth-century poets. In Richard Hovey's *The Marriage of Guenevere,* we find the following:

There are *worser* ills to face
Than foemen in the fray.—Act IV, Sc. 3.

More and *most* shift to the suffix position in a number of words: *hindmost, inmost, outmost, utmost.* *Most* is sometimes added to comparative forms to make new superlatives: *furthermost, hindermost, innermost,*[9] *nethermost, outermost, uppermost,* etc.

A few superlatives of the irregular group are irregular because of the loss of internal letters or syllables or because of modified spelling. The dropping out of *-te-* in *latest* gives *last.* *Next* is a superlative derived from the Old English *nēhst* (*niehst, nyhst*), superlative forms of *nēah* or *nēh,* 'nigh.' *Next* is only the modern spelling for *nēhst,* which had the comparative form *near* (a contraction of O.E. *nēahra,* nigher, near).

Topmost has defective and irregular comparison. It has no comparative, and its formation is irregular. *Topmost* is a superlative based on an adjective denoting the highest degree in its simplest form. It is sometimes called a **double superlative;** and, strictly speaking, its form suggests a **triple superlative,** for *most* has two superlative markings, the *-m* and the *-ost.*[10]

Absolute Superlatives. A few adjectives, because of the character of their meaning, cannot logically admit of comparison. These are called **absolute superlatives.** Such words as *perfect, honest, everlasting, vertical, daily, endless, chief, round, right, erect, dead, eternal, correct, perpetual, principal, mortal, universal, matchless, infinite, holy, divine, unique, sincere, single, square,* and *empty* represent absolute quality in their simplest forms; and, when compared, the comparative

---

[9] For illustrations of other words having **double comparison,** see **Irregular Comparison of Adverbs,** pp. 171–173.

[10] The *-m* is an old superlative suffix found in certain ancestral forms; for example, Lat. *optimus, primus, summus.* The *-ost* (for an older *-est*) is the Old English superlative suffix. This double superlative is found in Old English *-emesta, -mesta,* which became Modern English *-most* and later *most.*

and superlative forms are based on modified meanings of these words, sometimes on meanings well established by usage. When we say that a person or a thing is more correct or more perfect than some other person or thing, we imply that the positive form is lacking in this absolute quality which the words *correct* and *perfect* are capable of conveying. One cannot be *more correct* (or *less correct*) or *more perfect* (or *less perfect*) than another person unless he can be compared with one who is not quite correct or less than perfect. Most of the adjectives classed as **absolute superlatives** are not confined to the single absolute meaning, but often mean 'approaching the quality' named; for example, *perfect* can mean 'approaching perfection'; *unique* can mean 'unusual.' *Most perfect, less* (or *least*) *perfect, most exact, most unique, most holy,* etc. are employed by good writers and cultivated speakers to emphasize the quality indicated. Observe the effective use of the absolute superlatives in the following:

1. Pearl-glint, shell-tint, ancientest, *perfectest* hues.—Sidney Lanier
2. That *divinest* hope which none can know of
   Who have not laid their dearest in the grave.—Marian Dix Sullivan
3. Imitation is the *sincerest* of flattery.—C. C. Colton

In Renaissance English, the **double comparatives** and **double superlatives** are not uncommon. The function words *more* and *most* were employed with words that were comparative or superlative to intensify the degree of quality indicated. Such expressions as *more richer, more fuller, more unkinder, most unkindest,* etc. may be found in Shakespeare, in the Bible, and in other Elizabethan texts:

1. This was the *most unkindest* cut of all.—Shakespeare.
2. After the *most straitest* sect of our religion I lived a Pharisee.—Bible.
3. I am *more better* than Prospero.—Shakespeare.

These expressions are not now found in approved standard English. The examples are cited here chiefly to show that they were once in good standing.

Adjectives Having Irregular or Defective Comparison

(Forms in brackets are archaic or obsolete.)

Positive	Comparative	Superlative
1. [aft]	after	aftermost
2. bad, ill, evil	worse[11]	worst
3. fore	former	foremost, first
4. fore [forth]	further	furthest, furthermost [forthmost]
5. good	better	best
6. hind	hinder	hindermost, hindmost
7. in	inner	innermost, inmost
8. late	later, latter	latest, last
9. little	less,[11] lesser[12]	least
10. much, many	more	most
11. [neath]	nether	nethermost
12. near, nigh	nearer, nigher	nearest, next, nighest
13. north, northern	more northern	northmost, northernmost
14. out	outer, utter [uttermore]	utmost, uttermost, outmost, outermost
15. old	older, elder	oldest, eldest
16.	other	......
17.	over	......
18. top	......	topmost
19.	under	......
20. up	upper	uppermost [upmost]

IV. Adjectives not Compared. Adjectives which do not admit of comparison are those which cannot indicate degrees of quality or quantity. Except for a few words, such as

---

[11] Observe that *less* and *worse* are the only comparatives in the above list not ending in *-r* or an *r* sound.

[12] *Less* is now used to refer to quantity; and *lesser*, to size.

much, little, many, few, etc., definitive adjectives are not compared. The articles (*the, a, an*), the demonstratives (*this, that, these, those*), and most numerals and quantitative adjectives (*two, three, each, several, every, daily, such, any, some, none,* etc.) have no degrees of comparison.

A number of Latin comparatives have come into the language and are employed to show relational meaning rather than degrees of quality or quantity. Such words are *anterior, exterior, excelsior, inferior, interior, prior, posterior, superior, ulterior, major, minor, junior, senior,* etc. These forms are **never** followed by *than,* as are English comparatives; hence, in their English use, they are not true comparatives. We must say *This is superior to* (or *inferior to*) *that;* but not *This is superior than* (nor *inferior than*) that.

Also a number of Latin superlatives have come into English with only a little modification of their forms. These usually convey superlative meanings, and are therefore rarely compared. Such words as *supreme* (Lat. *supremus*), *extreme* (Lat. *extremus*), and *prime* (Lat. *primus*) are from Latin superlatives, though they are not regarded as superlative forms in English. Their positive forms, if we may call these positive forms, are capable of conveying the highest degree of quality: *extreme remedies, extreme diseases, prime minister, prime virtues, supreme hour, supreme love,* etc. Occasionally these words do admit of the degree modification; e.g., *extremest* (*most extreme*), *supremest* (*most supreme*); but these superlative forms add little, if any, degree meaning to their basic forms, *extreme* and *supreme;* and they should be used with caution. See Absolute Superlatives above, p. 89.

Five

Verbs

A **verb** is that part of speech which expresses action (*run, walk, steal, kill, jump*), being (*am, become*), or state of being (*suffer, rejoice*).

A popular definition of verbs states that the verb asserts, or predicates. This is true only in the case of the "finite" phases of the verb; there being a class of verb forms, the "nonfinites," which lack the power of asserting.

A **finite** (Lat. *finitus*, limited) **verb** is one which asserts, or predicates. It is "limited" by person and number. In *The dog runs*, the verb *runs* is in the third person, singular number. Some verbs have more inflectional modifications (limitations) than others, chiefly because they have retained more of the earlier inflectional markings. The verb *be* has fuller inflections than other verbs and can indicate both person and number in the present tense (*I am, we are; he is, they are*).

A **nonfinite**, or **infinite**, **verb** is one which lacks the power to assert (i.e., predicate). It is not limited by person or number. *The dog running* (or *The dogs running*) makes no assertion; nor is the expression a sentence, having no predicate. There are three nonfinite verbs: (1) the **participle**, a verbal adjective; i.e., a word derived from a verb and modifying a noun: *An angel writing in a book of gold* (or *A book written by an angel*); (2) the **infinitive**, a verbal noun, often preceded by *to: To err is human;* (3) the **gerund**, a verbal noun; i.e., a word derived from a verb and having substantive use (often called the infinitive in *-ing*): *He wins his honors by deserving them.*[1]

CLASSES OF VERBS

Verbs may be classified according to their meaning as **transitive** and **intransitive**; and according to their form as **regular** and **irregular**, or as **strong** and **weak**.

In a **transitive verb** (Lat. *transitivus* from *trans*, across; and *ire*, to go), the action is conceived as "going across" or "passing over" from a subject or doer to an object or receiver; as, *He lifted the hammer.* Therefore, every transitive verb requires a receiver for the action which it expresses. In the active voice the subject is the actor, and the direct object is the receiver of the action of the verb. In the passive voice, the subject receives the action, as in *The hammer* **was lifted** *by him.* (See Voice of Verbs, pp. 107–108.) Such verbs as *own, possess,* and *have,* which show little action, require objects and hence are transitive; as, *I have* (*own, possess*) *a farm.*

An **intransitive verb** either shows no action at all (*He is a good man; She* **appears** *amiable*); or represents action as limited to the subject or agent; as, *She* **walks** *briskly; The scheme* **works** *well.*

A verb which is usually or naturally transitive may be converted into an intransitive one by withholding the name of the object, as in *He* **paints** *prairie landscapes* and *He* **paints** *well.* The representation of a verbal idea essentially transitive as customary or habitual, the object being unmentioned (*He* **smokes;** *Does he* **smoke?**) is sometimes described as **absolute.** A verb having absolute meaning will be listed in the dictionary as transitive and intransitive, its transitive meaning usually being given first, since its primary, or basic, meaning is the transitive one.

A verb which presents an idea that is normally intransitive

---

[1] For the forms and uses of the nonfinites, see Tenses of Nonfinite Verbs in this chapter; and for an analysis of the uses and meanings of participles, gerunds, and infinitives, see Lessons VIII, IX, and X, Part Two.

may take what is called a **cognate object**. The **cognate object** is in a sense identical with or akin to the verb which it follows. It is usually "cognate" (Lat. *co-*, with, *gnatus*, *natus*, born) in etymology with the verb. Examples are *live a life; do a deed; sing a song; sleep his last sleep; fight a good fight; dream a dream; run a race;* etc.

Many verbs are always intransitive and cannot in standard English take even the cognate object; e.g., *appear, be (am, is, are, was, were), belong, come, exist, go (went), occur, remain, seem, swoon,* etc.

A transitive verb which expresses causation may be called a **causative verb**; as, *to fell the tree (make the tree fall).* Many causative verbs were derived from older intransitive verbs, often with a change of vowel, as in the case of *fell* from *fall.*

In this way, *set* (to cause to *sit*) was derived from the pre-English (Germanic) *sat* (pronounced *sät, säht*), the past tense of *sitan* (the *-an* is the ending of the infinitive), by the addition of the causative suffix *-jan,* or *-ian.* The vowel *a* in the new verb *satjan*[2] (pronounced *sät-yän*) became modified to short *ĕ* by the principle of mutation, or umlaut (see Mutation, pp. 34–35), and the *y* doubled the *t* and later was dropped. The verb then was *settan,* the Old English form of *set,* to place. By a similar process we have *raise* (cause to *rise*); *lay* (cause to *lie*); *drench* (cause to *drink*); *bend* (cause to *bind*).

Causative verbs were also formed on noun and adjective bases: *meet* (to cause a *moot,* a gathering); *deem* (to form a *doom,* a judgment); *trim* (to make *trum,* strong); *fill* (to make *full*); *(de)file* (to make *foul*); *feed* (to cause to have *food*).

The causative verbs here listed are of very early origin, most of them appearing in Old English. But Modern English has the same power of making an intransitive verb causative (and hence transitive), though without suffix or change of vowel; as, to *run the machine* (i.e., make it *run*). Simi-

---

[2] The forms *sat* and *satjan* are actually found in Gothic, the Germanic tongue of which we have the earliest record.

larly, in *water the horse* and *air the room,* causative verbs are made from nouns without change of form. Since the fifteenth century, English has had the power of making a causative verb out of an adjective or a noun by adding the suffix *-en* (without change of vowel): *shorten, soften, darken, heighten, strengthen, hearten,* etc. Also, the French prefix *-en* is employed in the formation of causative verbs: *endear, enfeeble, enlarge.*

An **auxiliary verb** is a verb form which assists in the formation of voice, tense, mood, etc. of other verbs. *Shall* and *will* are used with infinitive forms to make up the future tenses: *shall see, will see.* *Do* and *did* are used with infinitives without *to* to form the emphatic present and past tenses and the imperative of other verbs: *do go, does go, did go.* *Do* and *did* are also used with the infinitive when there is no special emphasis implied to introduce interrogations: *Did he leave? Do you enjoy playing chess? Have* and *had* are used with the past participle to form the perfect tenses: *I have seen; I had seen; I have been; I had been.* The verb *be* (*am, are, is, was, were*) has more auxiliary uses than most verbs, three of which are well established and in common use: (1) It is employed as an auxiliary with the past participle of a transitive verb to form the passive voice: *Be seen; I am seen; They were seen.* (2) The present and past tense forms of *be* are sometimes employed with a few verbs like *go, come,* and *rise* instead of *have* and *had* to form the perfect tenses; as, *The book is gone; The sun was risen before we left.* (3) When followed by the present participle, the various finite forms of *be* are used to indicate definite time (i.e., to form the progressive tenses): *I am running; She is calling for help; We are talking about you.*

The **modal auxiliaries** (*may, can, might, could, would, should, ought, must*) are used to form the verb phrases indicating different attitudes or aspects of mood, such as ability, possibility, obligation, necessity, etc.: *I may go; I must go.*

A **copulative verb,** often called a **linking verb,** is a verb which is incapable of predication without the help of a noun or an adjective or some word or group of words used as a noun or as an adjective. The chief function of a copula is to announce the subject of a sentence and introduce and join it to some adjective or noun or the equivalent of one or the other of these, which will describe, define, or identify that which the subject names. Any intransitive verb which is incapable of asserting without a complement must be construed as a **copulative** (or **linking**) **verb.** The verb *be* (including all of its person, number, and tense forms) is the oldest and the most commonly used of the copulative verbs: *be, am, is, are, was, were, have been,* etc. Other verbs in general use which may be employed as linking verbs are *appear, come, become, feel, grow, look, keep, rest, remain, seem,* and *taste.* Many verbs having copulative use may also be full verbs. *Be* (*am, is, are,* etc.) is a full verb when it means exist, as in *The baby is on the bed.* In *Whatever is, is right,* the first *is* is a full verb; the second one is a copulative verb. Compare also *He appears intelligent* with *He appeared too early.*

A verb is said to be **impersonal** when it is used either without a subject or with a very indefinite one. *Methinks* (it seems to me), now archaic or poetic, is a good example of a verb without an expressed subject. The **impersonal verbs** are not inflected for person or number. They are always third person and always singular. In Modern English, impersonal verbs have the indefinite pronoun *it* preceding them and serving as the grammatical subject, as in *It is freezing; It is snowing; It rained yesterday.* Observe that the *it*-subject in these sentences has no meaning; its sole function is to announce the impersonal verb which follows it. In an inflected language, such as Latin, the verb would have no expressed subject; e.g., Lat. *pluit* (it rains).

A **reflexive verb** is one whose object denotes the same person or thing as its subject. In the following sentences, *absent, wash,* and *dress* have reflexive meanings:

(1) If one *absent* himself without excuse, he will be fined.

(2) You must *wash* yourself before you come to the table.

(3) The child is now large enough to *dress* himself.

Sometimes the object of a reflexive verb is not expressed, but is implied in the verb itself. A man may say *I am shaving myself*, or *I am shaving*, without altering the basic meaning of the verb. When the object complement is expressed, the reflexive verb is transitive; when it is not expressed, the verb is construed as intransitive, as in *Behave yourself while I am away* (where *behave* is transitive) and in *Behave for my sake* (where *behave* is intransitive).

Verbs are said to be **reciprocal** when they denote mutual action or relation. If a reciprocal verb is transitive, it will have one of the reciprocal pronouns for its object; as, *They fought one another; We love each other.* Sometimes an intransitive verb is capable of indicating reciprocity, as in *We quarreled; When shall we three meet again?*

FORMS OF THE VERB

English verbs are classified according to the method used in forming the past tense and the past (or perfect) participle. In most of our modern grammar texts, particularly those used in our elementary and secondary schools which deal only with the verb forms found in Modern English, all verbs are classified as either *regular* or *irregular*. In advanced grammars dealing with the origin and development of English words, verbs are classified, as they were in Old English and in the parent language (Germanic), as *strong* and *weak*. The two classifications are not always based on the same patterns of inflection, the chief likeness being that the strong and irregular verbs are in the main older forms than the weak and regular ones. On examining the weak and strong verbs treated in the following pages, the student will discover that some weak verbs are not "regular," and that some strong verbs are not entirely "irregular," in the way in which they form their past tense and past participle.

A **regular verb**, as the term is now somewhat generally applied to the classification of Modern English verbs, is one which forms its past indicative and past participle by adding the suffix *-ed, -d,* or *-t* to the present infinitive (or the present indicative) form; as, *work, worked, worked; hate, hated, hated; burn, burnt, burnt.*

An **irregular verb** is one that does not form its past indicative and past participle by adding *-ed, -d,* or *-t* to the stem-word; as, *ride, rode, ridden; awake, awoke, awaked; bleed, bled, bled; tell, told, told; set, set, set.*

It will be seen that all Modern English verbs may be classified as either **regular** or **irregular.** The terms defined below (**strong, weak, defective,** and **anomalous**) are useful in indicating types of verbs found in the Germanic from which many of our modern verbs are derived. The historical classification is useful in our study of the growth of English and in our appreciation and understanding of the language used by the great masters of English.

A **strong verb** is one which historically formed its past tense and past participle by vowel gradation ("ablaut") or by reduplication. The strong verbs represent the oldest verbs in the language, most of them being older than the English language itself. Many of the verbs which we now classify as "irregular" are little more than fossilized survivals of old Germanic "regular" strong verbs.

The most "regular" and most commonly used of the strong patterns surviving in the language may be recognized by the following characteristics: (1) the change of root vowel for the past tense; and (2) the addition of *-en, -n,* or *-ne* for the past participle, with or without change or modification of stem vowel; as, *rise, rose, risen; choose, chose, chosen; draw, drew, drawn; bear, bore, borne.*

Formerly all strong verbs formed their past participle by adding *-en, -n,* or *-ne* (and thus differed from the weak verbs, which added the *-d, -t* suffix); but many of our strong verbs of Old English origin have lost this inflectional marking:

sing, sang, sung; begin, began, begun. Some of the verbs which dropped the suffix now have only two distinct forms for the principal parts, the past participle often being like the past tense or like the present infinitive; as, *sit, sat, sat; get, got, got; run, ran, run; come, came, come.*

A **weak verb** is one which historically formed its past indicative and past participle by adding to the stem a suffix containing *-d* or *-t.* In Modern English the *-d* or *-t* suffix must be relied upon to identify the weak verbs, especially if one has no knowledge of the earlier forms, though some old weak verbs whose stem ended in *d* or *t* have lost their dental suffix and now resemble some verbs of strong origin (e.g., *read, read, read; feed, fed, fed; meet, met, met.*

All verbs which take the *-t, -d,* or *-ed* suffix may be classified as weak even though they, like the strong verbs, change the vowel for the past tense, the reasons for the vowel changes being different. The verb *fight, fought, fought* is a strong verb; it has the *-t* in its stem-form, and shows a change in tense by a change in vowel; the *-t* is not added to show change in tense. But the verbs *buy, bought, bought; teach, taught, taught; sell, sold, sold; bring, brought, brought;* and others like these which add the *-t* or *-d* are weak verbs, even though they show vowel change also. The difference in the vowel in *buy, bought* is due to umlaut; in *fight, fought,* it is due to ablaut.[3] It is worth noting that most, if not all, the weak verbs which show vowel change are of Old English origin. There were once many more of these, but, because they were very "irregular" weak verbs even in Old English, only those that were in general use survived the Middle English leveling with their irregular features.

When the weak verbs first entered the Germanic language, they were considered the "irregular" forms (or new forms), because they differed in their inflectional pattern from the strong, or old pattern. Therefore, we have the names *strong*

---

[3] For other illustrations of umlaut, see pp. 34–35; and for a full and scholarly treatment of ablaut, see Wright's *Old English Grammar.* pp. 105–111.

and *weak;* the strong verbs were the important and established ones, and were strong enough to retain their old inflectional patterns; that is, they resisted falling into the weak and simplified pattern.

Defective verbs are those that are deficient in some of their principal parts. They cannot be conjugated as full verbs can. As a rule, they have no infinitive and no participle, and are incapable of inflectional change. These include the preterit-present verbs *shall, will, can, may, must,* and *ought,* and a number of other verbs having only one or two forms, such as *quoth, beware, prithee, wit (wot), y-clept (y-cleped), worth, methinks (methought),* and *hight,* most of which are now archaic, or else used only in poetry or solemn style.

The **anomalous verbs** are full verbs whose principal parts are so irregular that they do not easily lend themselves to classification. *Be* and *go* can be called anomalous verbs, because their past tense forms *was (were)* and *went* are not formed from the infinitives *be* and *go. Did,* the past of *do,* is not formed on any recognizable pattern of either the strong or the weak verbs, and hence *do, did, done* may also be placed in the anomalous group. Observe that *be, go,* and *do* have "regular" strong participle forms.

A few verbs have **mixed inflection,** some of the forms following the weak pattern of conjugation, and others, one of the strong (ablaut) patterns. *Awake, awoke, awaked* has its past form *(awoke)* in the strong conjugation, and the past participle *(awaked)* in the weak conjugation. Such a verb can, of course, be classified as **irregular,** if we dispense with the **strong** and **weak** classifications.

Those verbs which make no change in form or pronunciation to denote changes in tense, such as *put, put, put; set, set, set; cost, cost, cost; burst, burst, burst;* etc., have leveled (or simplified) inflection. There are many verbs of this type (count them in any representative list of irregular verbs), and the number is increasing from time to time.

A List of Irregular Verbs[4]

The following list includes, in the main, verbs of Old English origin. Most of them are from strong verbs, though the list includes verbs like *deal, dealt, dealt; hear, heard, heard; read, read, read*, which are derived from Old or Middle English weak verbs which had in early English or have since developed irregular forms.

The principal parts of the verbs given are (1) the **simple infinitive,** (2) the **past indicative,** (3) the **past participle.** All forms that are rare or obsolete or colloquial are enclosed in parenthetical marks. Variant regular (weak) forms are italicized.

Present	Past	Past Participle
abide	abode	abode
arise	arose	arisen
awake	awoke	*awaked*
be	was, were	been
bear	bore	born, borne
befall	befell	befallen
beget	begot (begat)	begotten, begot
begin	began	begun
behold	beheld	beheld (beholden)
bend	bent	bent
bid	bade, bid	bidden, bid
bind	bound	bound
bite	bit	bitten
bleed	bled	bled
blow	blew	blown
break	broke (brake)	broken
breed	bred	bred
bring	brought	brought
burst	burst	burst
buy	bought	bought
cast	cast	cast
catch	caught	caught

---

[4] This list of irregular verbs is by no means complete. The student should consult his dictionary for the principal parts of irregular verbs not given here.

Present	Past	Past Participle
choose	chose	chosen
cleave	cleft (clove)[5]	cloven, cleft
cling	clung	clung
come	came	come
cost	cost	cost
creep	crept	crept
crow	crew, *crowed*[5]	*crowed* (crown)
cut	cut	cut
dare	durst, *dared*	dared
deal	dealt	dealt
dig	dug, *digged*	dug, *digged*
do	did	done
draw	drew	drawn
drink	drank	drunk
drive	drove	driven
eat	ate	eaten
fall	fell	fallen
feed	fed	fed
feel	felt	felt
fight	fought	fought
find	found	found
flee	fled	fled
fling	flung	flung
fly	flew	flown
forbear	forbore	forborne
forbid	forbad, forbade	forbidden
forget	forgot	forgotten, forgot
forgive	forgave	forgiven
forsake	forsook	forsaken
freeze	froze	frozen
get	got	got (gotten)
give	gave	given
go	went	gone
grind	ground	ground
grow	grew	grown

[5] Consult your dictionary for the differences in meaning and use of the regular and irregular forms of *cleave* and *crow*.

Present	Past	Past Participle
hang	hung, *hanged*[6]	hung, hanged
have	had	had
hear	heard	heard
hew	*hewed*	hewn, *hewed*
hide	hid	hidden, hid
hit	hit	hit
hold	held	held
keep	kept	kept
kneel	knelt	knelt
know	knew	known
lead	led	led
leave	left	left
lend	lent	lent
lie	lay	lain
light	lit, *lighted*[6]	lit, *lighted*
lose	lost	lost
make	made	made
mean	meant	meant
mow	*mowed*	mown, *mowed*
put	put	put
read	read	read
ride	rode	ridden
ring	rang	rung
rise	rose	risen
say	said	said
see	saw	seen
seek	sought	sought
sell	sold	sold
send	sent	sent
set	set	set
shake	shook	shaken
shear	*sheared* (shore)	shorn, *sheared*
shine	shone, *shined*	shone, *shined*
shoot	shot	shot
shrink	shrank, shrunk	shrunk, shrunken

[6] Consult your dictionary for differences in meaning and use of the regular and irregular forms of this verb.

Present	Past	Past Participle
shrive	shrove, *shrived*	shriven, *shrived*
sing	sang	sung
sink	sank	sunk (sunken)
sit	sat	sat
slay	slew	slain
sleep	slept	slept
sling	slung (slang)	slung
slink	slunk	slunk
smite	smote	smitten
speak	spoke	spoken
spend	spent	spent
spin	spun (span)	spun
spit	spit, spat	spit, spat
spread	spread	spread
spring	sprang, sprung	sprung
stand	stood	stood
steal	stole	stolen
stick	stuck	stuck
sting	stung (stang)	stung
stink	stunk, stank	stunk
stride	strode (strid)	stridden
strike	struck	struck, stricken (strucken)
string	strung	strung
strive	strove, *strived*	striven, *strived*
swear	swore	sworn
sweep	swept	swept
swim	swam (swum)	swum
swing	swung (swang)	swung
take	took	taken
teach	taught	taught
tear	tore	torn
think	thought	thought
thrive	throve, *thrived*	thriven, *thrived*
thrust	thrust	thrust
wake	woke, *waked*	waked (woken)
wear	wore	worn
weave	wove, *weaved*	woven, *weaved*

Present	Past	Past Participle
weep	wept	wept
win	won	won
wind	wound	wound
wring	wrung	wrung
write	wrote	written

INFLECTION OF VERBS

In highly inflected languages, such as Latin, Greek, German, and Old English, verbs had much fuller inflectional markings than English verbs have today. Since the Old English period, verbs, like nouns, pronouns, adjectives, and adverbs, have lost most of their terminal suffixes and other markings, such as vowel changes, which were once essential to indicate changes in tense, person, number, voice, and mode. The verb *be* is now the only verb in English which is capable of indicating number in the past indicative (*was*, *were*); and it is the only verb that has full inflection to indicate the three persons of the present tense, indicative mode (I *am*, you *are*, he *is*).

With the dropping of the inflectional markings, English acquired a number of substitutions which users of the language could employ to indicate differences in person, number, tense, mode, and voice. The auxiliary verbs *be, have, do, shall, will, may, can,* and *should,* when used with infinitives and participles, can denote with surprising accuracy what in the older languages had to be expressed by inflection. Strictly speaking, these periphrastic (phrasal) forms cannot be regarded as inflectional changes; but they are excellent substitutes for the stem and terminal markings of the inflected languages. Since verbs cannot be fully conjugated without the assistance of these auxiliaries, they must be considered in our study of the inflectional modifications of verbs. Any full verb in Modern English may show by inflection (i.e., change of form) or by substitution (periphrasis) modifications of **voice, mode, tense, person,** and **number.**

Voice

Voice is that modification of a transitive verb which indicates whether the subject is acting or being acted upon. When the subject of the verb represents the actor (or agent), the voice is said to be **active:** *John killed the bird.* When the subject receives or denotes the object to which the action is directed, the verb is said to be in the **passive voice:** *The bird was killed by John.*

Greek and Latin show relatively complete systems of inflection for active and passive meanings. English, however, shows no passive forms by inflection, passive meaning always requiring to be expressed by verbal phrases: *He had been cheated; They were left; I shall have been forgotten.*

In the sentence *Apollo strikes the lyre,* the transitive verb *strikes* is in the active voice, since the subject, *Apollo,* is represented as acting. In *The lyre is struck by Apollo,* the predicate verb (*is struck*) is in the passive voice, since the subject, *lyre,* is represented as being acted upon. It should be observed that *is struck* is not an intransitive verb, but a transitive verb in the passive voice. That which in the former sentence was the direct object has now become the subject,[7] but the action still passes over from a doer or agent to a receiver.

Intransitive verbs have no voice.[8] In *My son lives in Chi-*

---

[7] Not always is it the former direct object which becomes the subject when the verb is changed from the active to the passive voice. The new subject may have been the indirect object: *I denied him the privilege; He was denied the privilege.* In the second sentence, *privilege* is called the "retained" object. Some grammarians have objected to this construction, considering it of questionable propriety; but it has been used by a great number of classic English writers, and is still freely employed by recognized masters of the tongue.

[8] A verb normally intransitive may, however, take on a transitive form and meaning when reënforced by a preposition: *They laughed; They laughed at* (=*ridiculed*) *him. Him,* while technically the principal term of the prepositional phrase *at him,* is in effect the object of the verbal group *laughed-at,* which may be made passive: *He was laughed at.* This form is authentic English, though the construction may become awkward, as in *I was run off from by my elder brother.*

cago, lives is neither active nor passive, but an intransitive verb. When an intransitive verb is made transitive by giving it a cognate object, it may then have voice: *Most of his life was lived in Chicago.*

Mode

Mode (Lat. *modus*, manner), or **mood,**[9] is the modification of the verb that shows the manner in which the verbal idea is conceived—whether as a fact, a supposition, a desire, a command, etc.

The three modes of finite verbs generally recognized by grammarians are the **imperative,** the **indicative,** and the **subjunctive.** These were originally distinguished by inflection, but in Modern English neither in form nor in meaning are the three distinct.

Imperative Mode

The **imperative** (Lat. *imperare*, to command) **mode** expresses a command or a request:

(1) *Give* me that dagger!   (2) *Help* thou mine unbelief.
(3) *Do come* to see us!   (4) *Don't come* near me!   (5) *Beware* my fangs!

USES OF THE IMPERATIVE

The imperative is used in addressing one person or a group of persons. It is always in the second person and always in the present tense. It has no inflectional markings to show number: *Fight, you coward! Fight on, my merry men all.* In the first sentence, the verb is singular; and in the second it is plural. The number is determined by the context, and not by the form.

Like the indicative, the imperative may have periphrastic forms instead of the simple forms. *Do* may be used with the

---

[9] The native word *mood* (O.E. *mōd*, mind, feeling) is also a generally accepted form for *mode*. It doubtless originated in the idea that mode expressed the *mood*, or *temper*, of a verb.

present infinitive to emphasize or vary the intensity of the emotion of a request or a command; as, *Do stop that noise! Please* (usually construed as an elliptical clause) is now felt to be an auxiliary verb to be used in polite commands or requests: *Please do as you are told.*

The passive voice of the imperative is the auxiliary *be* coupled with the past participle: *Be saved. Be warned.*

Sentences containing verbs in the imperative mode may be closed with the exclamation mark or with the period. If the sentence conveys strong emotion, the exclamation mark should be used: *Get away! Stop that noise!* Requests and polite commands are properly closed with the period, as in *Awake, arise, or be forever fallen. Please* (or *Do*) *accept our hospitality.*

In Renaissance English the subject of an imperative verb, when expressed, was sometimes placed after the verb: *Go ye therefore and teach all nations. Be ye therefore wise as serpents, and harmless as doves.*

Indicative Mode

The **indicative mode,** so far as it differs from the others, is used to state a fact or ask a question concerning a fact:

(1) They *have* their reward. (2) *Do* they *have* their reward? (3) How old *are* you? (4) The child *has been injured.*

USES OF THE INDICATIVE MODE

Since the majority of our communications are uttered as facts, not as suppositions, nor as commands, the indicative is generally considered the normal form of the finite verb. Every full verb has six tenses in the indicative mode; and if a verb is transitive, it will have a full passive voice conjugation of these six tenses. (For the tense forms of the indicative in the active and passive voices, see conjugation of *give*, pp. 152–153.)

In Latin and in early English, the indicative mode had

more restricted uses than it has today. With the leveling of the subjunctive and imperative mode forms, the indicative has usurped many of the functions formerly belonging to the other modes, particularly those belonging to the subjunctive. The indicative is now used for communicating all facts and all questions concerning facts. Any statement, whether true or false, which a speaker presents as a fact requires the indicative mode. Thus if one announces: *Good books are never read,* the verb must be in the indicative, because the announcer is presenting his idea as a fact.

The **indicative** is not restricted to independent clauses; for all subordinate clauses presenting ideas as facts have verbs in the indicative. In the following sentences, the verbs in the principal clauses and also the verbs in the subordinate clauses are in the indicative:

> (1) I *know* that John *is* a democrat. (2) When a woman once *dislikes* another, she *is* merciless. (3) My friend *is* so gray that he *looks* much older than he *is.* (4) Though her features *are* regular, her face *is* not beautiful. (5) If I *am* Sophocles, I *am* not mad; and if I *am* mad, I *am* not Sophocles. (6) I *know* a man who *believes* that the moon *is made* of green cheese.

Subjunctive Mode

The **subjunctive mode** expresses an idea as desirable, supposable, conditional, or the like:

> (1) Would she *were* mine. (2) If you *were* my father, would you reprove me for this? (3) *May* the Lord *bless* and *keep* you. (4) If she *be* not for me, What care I how fair she *be?*—George Withers. (5) If it *were* done when 'tis done, then '*twere* well It *were* done quickly.—Shakespeare.

SUBJUNCTIVE VERSUS INDICATIVE

The subjunctive mode, which was once a highly inflected mode, capable of indicating person, number, and tense, has now only a few forms which differentiate it from the forms of the other modes. It has no inflectional endings to indicate person, number, or tense. Except for the verb *be*, its main differentiating feature in form is the loss of *-s* in the third person singular, present tense, and the shift from *has* to *have* in the third person singular, present perfect tense:

Indicative: 1. He *goes* to work early every morning.
2. He *has gone* away and *has left* no address.
Subjunctive: 1. If a man *die*, shall he live again?
2. Is it essential that he *have* a witness?

The **modal subjunctive**, or **potential subjunctive**, is now more common than the inflected subjunctive (see uses of Modal Auxiliaries, pp. 129–131.):

1. *May* you *have* all that you deserve.
2. I had hoped that he *might win* one of the prizes.

The subjunctive has four tenses (**present, past, present perfect**, and **past perfect**),[10] but the times which these tenses denote are not identical with the corresponding indicative forms. The meaning of the past subjunctive forms is not, as a rule, past, but present or future, as in *If I were your father, I would punish you*, where *were* is past subjunctive indicating present time. In *Though he were dead, yet shall he live again*, the past subjunctive *were* denotes future time, equivalent to *though he should die*.

Both the present and the past subjunctives are used to indicate present or future time. The present tense is employed when there is some hope or likelihood of realization of ideas expressed, as in *God be with you till we meet again*, where the present tense form *be* is used. When the ideas expressed by the subjunctive suggest unlikelihood of realization, the past tense is more often used; as *I wish he were coming*, where *were*

---

[10] For the subjunctive forms of the verb *be*, see conjugation of the verb *be*, pp. 150–151. The subjunctive forms of other full verbs may be ascertained by examining the conjugation of *give* in the subjunctive mode. Chapter Six, pp. 154–155.

is the correct tense form to use (One infers here that he is not coming). The past perfect subjunctive is employed to indicate past time: *Had I but known what I now know.*

USES OF THE SUBJUNCTIVE

The word *subjunctive* (Lat. *subjunctivus,* subjoined), like many other grammatical terms, is likely to be misleading in that it cannot, with strict regard for its etymology, be applied to all uses of the mode. It is true that many or perhaps most of the clauses in which it is used are "subjoined" (i.e., subordinated) to other clause ideas expressed or understood. But the subjunctive mode is employed in a number of independent constructions.

Subjunctive in Principal Clauses

1. Expressing a wish in the third person (prayer and imprecations), as in *Thy kingdom come,* where the meaning is clearly optative.

2. Expressing a curse or blessing: *Family ties be damned; God bless you and keep you* (compare with imperative in *O God, save my son!*).

3. Expressing a command in the first or third person (hortative): *Raise we now our hearts and voices; Come one, come all.*

4. *Had,* the past subjunctive of *have,* is seen in the expressions *had rather, had better* (or *had best*), *had as lief* (more common *had as soon*). The verb *had* here has an old meaning 'would hold,' or 'would consider,' in which *would* is the past subjunctive of *will.* In spite of adverse criticism by those ignorant of the history of the construction *had rather, had better,* and *had as lief* are in the best of usage. *Would better,* used by a few to avoid *had better,* violates the prevailing use of *would* in the first person, and has never become general. But *would rather* is older than *had rather,* is logical, and in equally good use. The contractions *I'd, he'd, you'd, they'd,* *rather* are indistinguishable from the contracted form of *had rather*.[11] The following are typical idiomatic sentences:

(1) I *had rather go* with you than stay here alone. (2) You *had better watch* your step. (3) You *had best* go now. (4) I *had rather be* a dog and bay the moon, Than such a Roman. —Shakespeare.

Subjunctive in Subordinate Clauses

1. In noncommittal conditional clauses (without implied opinion as to probability of fact or fulfillment), the present tense of the subjunctive is used, sometimes with present meaning, and sometimes with future meaning. In the following, *be* refers to present time:

Be he alive or *be* he dead,
I'll grind his bones to make my bread.

The indicative is now more commonly employed in noncommittal clauses (see Conditional Clauses in Part Two, Lesson XIV).

2. The subjunctive is used in clauses following *as if* and *as though*, as in *He looked as if* (or *as though*) *he* **were** *ill; It looks as if* (or *as though*) *it* **were** *snowing*.

3. Conditions contrary to fact regularly require the subjunctive:

(1) If I *were* an American, as I am an Englishman, I would never lay down my arms (*were* is past subjunctive, present time). (2) If I *had been* an American, I would never have laid down my arms (*had been* is past perfect subjunctive, past time).

4. In concessive clauses expressing a supposition (not as a fact), the subjunctive is used:

(1) *Be* it ever so humble, there's no place like home! (present subjunctive *be* denotes present, or rather universal,

---

[11] For an excellent treatment of these forms, see George Curme, *A Grammar of the English Language*, Vol. III, Syntax, pp. 399 ff.

time). (2) Though he *slay* me, yet will I trust in him (present subjunctive *slay* denotes future time).

5. The purpose clause (often with the negative) frequently requires the subjunctive:

> (1) Judge not that ye *be* not *judged.* (2) Let him that thinketh he standeth take heed lest he *fall.*

6. After the conjunctions *till, until, before, ere,* and others of similar meaning, the subjunctive is employed to express a supposed future occurrence:

> (1) One jot or one tittle shall in no wise pass from the law, till all *be fulfilled.* (2) Come ere my heart *break.* (3) Tarry at Jericho until your beards *be grown.* (4) If I were you, I would wait till he *came.*

In all these sentences but the last, the indicative is more usual. In the last example the form of the subjunctive *came* is now like that of the indicative, but the verb is shown to be subjunctive by expressing a supposition, not a fact, and by past tense expressing future time.

7. In the conditional clause of "future less vivid," the subjunctive is sometimes used:

> (1) He could plan battles if war *became* necessary. (2) He would come to your party if you *invited* him.

8. In clauses after verbs of wishing, advising, demanding, warning, and the like, corresponding to the optative subjunctive in principal clauses (see **1** under Subjunctive in Principal Clauses), the subjunctive is usually preferred:

> (1) I desire that he *be* appointed (present subjunctive, future time). (2) O that it *were* possible! (The wish is implied in *O;* the past subjunctive *were* denotes present time.) (3) I wish he *were* here (past subjunctive, present time). (4) I wish you *would sing* for us (past subjunctive, present or future time). (5) I demand that this subject *be dropped* (present tense, present time). (6) I wish you *had been* there (past perfect subjunctive, past time).

9. Legal judgments and similar hortative expressions (corresponding to the subjunctive of command in principal clauses) require the subjunctive:

(1) The decision of the court is that the property *be sold* to the highest bidder. (2) I move that the question *be put* to a vote. (3) Be it resolved that the secretary *send* a copy of this letter to the President.

10. In noun clauses stating obligation or propriety, the subjunctive is employed:

(1) It is proper that he *obey* his father. (2) Is it necessary that this food *be rationed?*

Potential Subjunctive *vs.* Potential Indicative

Verb phrases of the so-called modal auxiliaries *may-might, can-could, should-would, must,* etc. and the infinitives of other verbs have encroached upon the provinces of both the indicative and the subjunctive. The verbs in *I can do it; You must go;* and *He could help,* present ideas on the whole indicative. Whereas, in *May there be no moaning of the bar,* and *Oh, that mine enemy would write a book!* the meaning is clearly subjunctive.

These phrases are by some grammarians regarded as constituting a fourth mode, called the **potential.** The word *potential* suggests power or ability (*I can sing*). But the potential phrases are used also to express ideas of permission (*You may leave me now*), compulsion (*They must fight*), obligation (*He should apologize*), possibility (*It may rain*), and perhaps some modifications or refinements of these. Predicate verbs made up with the modal auxiliaries do not tell us what the subject does, but what it can, may, might, or could do.

When the potential verb phrases are used to express realities (i.e., fact-ideas), the modal classification should be **potential indicative,** as in *I can sing that song without the music.* But if the modal auxiliaries are used to express non-realities (i.e., thought-ideas, suppositions), the modal classification should be **potential subjunctive,** as in *May you live to be a hundred.*

Tense

Tense (from O.F. *tens* from Lat. *tempus,* time) is the form a verb takes to indicate the time of the action or the state of being; as, **present** (*he speaks*), **past** (*he spoke*), **future** (*he will speak*).

Grammatical tense (a verb form) must be carefully differentiated from actual time, for the two are not always identical. For example, the past tense does not always indicate past time, nor does the present tense always indicate present time. Observe that *sings* (present tense form) in *He sings every Sunday in our church,* denotes a duration of time starting in the past and extending through the present into the future. In *I am leaving town tomorrow,* the present tense *am leaving* denotes future time, and is equal to *shall leave.* In *I wish John were here, were* is the past subjunctive form used to denote present time. In *If I had my music, I could sing this song for you now* (or *tomorrow*), *had* is past subjunctive used to denote present (or future) time.

Because the idiom of our language is somewhat complicated in respect to the uses of tense, some study of the various tense forms, together with the meanings, both usual and exceptional, is necessary to an understanding of the subject.

Modern English has six tenses, three of which are **simple** (or **basic**) **tenses,** and three of which are **compound** (or **perfect**) **tenses.** The simple tenses are the **present,** the **past** (or **preterit**), and the **future.** The compound (or perfect) tenses are the **present perfect,** the **past perfect,** and the **future perfect.** The **perfect tenses** represent the action of the verb as completed at a present, a past, or a future time. The word *perfect* means completed; hence the **present perfect tense** denotes action completed at the time the speaker is making his statement, as *I have finished the job.* In *I had finished eating* *before you arrived,* the finite verb *had finished* indicates that the action was completed at some time in the past. Similarly, *will have left* in *She will have left before you arrive,* denotes an action to be completed in the future.

Forms of the Tenses

Of the six tenses in common use in the living language, only two are inflected: the **present** (*sing, walk*) and the **past** (*sang, walked*). The other four must indicate the time of the action periphrastically; i.e., by employing certain phrasal combinations. The **simple future** tense is formed by a combination of *shall* or *will* with the present infinitive without *to: I shall go; He will go.* The **future perfect tense** is a combination of *shall* or *will* and the present perfect infinitive without *to: I shall* (or *you, he, they will*) **have lived** here a year in June. The present and past perfect tenses are formed by combining the present and past finite forms of *have* (*have, has, had*) with the past participle of a verb, as in *I have left; I had left; He has gone; He had gone; They have left; They had gone.*

In addition to these simple and perfect (compound) tenses in Modern English, there are a number of so-called expanded tenses of later origin, such as the **definite** (**progressive, or continuous**) **tenses,** the **emphatic tenses,** and the **potential** (or **modal**) **tenses.** The **progressive tenses** are formed by combining the present and past finite forms of the verb *be* with the present participle of a principal verb: *I am running; I was running; He is walking; He was walking; We are studying; We were studying.* The **emphatic tenses** are formed by using the present and past finite forms of *do* (*do, does, did*) with the simple infinitive: *I do study; I did study; She does work here; She did work here.* The **potential** (or **modal**) **tenses** (simple and compound) are formed by combining the present and past forms of the modal auxiliaries (*may-might, can-could,* etc.) with the present or the present perfect infinitive forms of principal verbs: *I may sing; I might sing; I can go; I could go; I can have finished; I could have finished.*

In Old English full verbs had only two tenses (the present
and the past) to indicate the time of the action or of the state
of being. The four tenses which have been added to the
regular conjugation of verbs correspond to tenses found in
Latin grammars; but Latin had distinctive inflectional markings to indicate differences in tense. In Modern English, all
tenses except the indefinite (or simple) present and the indefinite (or simple) past must be formed by combining the
various forms of the auxiliary verbs *shall, will, do, be, have,*
etc. with the simple or perfect infinitive forms or with the
present or past participle of principal verbs. Of the phrasal
tense forms, the future is the oldest and the most basic; and
it is, therefore, always listed in our English grammars as one
of the three simple (or basic) tenses.

Uses of the Tenses

As we have learned earlier in our study of verb inflections,
the names which we assign to the grammatical tenses do not
always describe the time of the action or the time of being or
state of being represented by the verbs. There is consider-
able overlapping of the functions of the tenses, which can
best be explained by an examination of the uses of the various tenses.

PRESENT TENSE

Of the six tenses examined under Forms of the Tenses (see
pp. 117–118), the present is the one which requires most consideration because it is the most loaded with meanings and
functions. The **present tense** represents an action, being,
or state of being; as:

1. Habitual action or being, extending from some point in
the past through the present into the future:

(1) I *live* in the country.   (2) I *sing* for a living.   (3) A
blind man *makes* these rugs.   (4) He *paints* landscapes.

The habitual action may be emphatic or potential:

(1) I *do try* to be on time. (2) I *can sing* well enough.

2. Definite time (= continuous, or progressive, time) especially stressing an act going on or in progress when the thought is expressed:

(1) The maid *is eating* her lunch. (2) Your baby *is sleeping*.

3. Gnomic time, general truths, etc.:

(1) Barking dogs seldom *bite*. (2) A triangle *is* a figure bounded by three lines. (3) Five times five *is* twenty-five. (4) Great haste *makes* great waste.

4. Future time, as in Old English, sometimes with an accompanying adverb to point to a future time:

(1) I hope it *does* not *rain* tonight. (2) My train *leaves* in a half an hour. (3) If a man *die*, shall he live again.

Some linking verbs (*be, am, are, is, go, is going*, etc.) followed with a completing infinitive phrase are employed commonly to denote future action:

(1) It *is going to rain*. (2) She *is to arrive* at noon tomorrow. (3) This show *is going to please* the young people.

5. Historical present is employed in narration, book reviews, reports, etc., to represent past events:

(1) Hamlet *dies* in the last scene of the play. (2) Then Jack *begins* to climb the bean stalk. (3) After Othello *learns* that Desdemona is innocent, he *takes* his own life.

PRESENT PERFECT TENSE

The **present perfect tense** lays stress upon the completion of an action at the time when the speaker expresses the thought. Like the present tense, the present perfect has extended its meanings and functions somewhat beyond the perfection of an act in the present. It may indicate any of the following time meanings:

1. An act just completed, often with the help of an accompanying modifier:

(1) The doctor *has* just *arrived*. (2) I *have* this very minute *finished* reading your note. (3) At last, you two *have found* each other. (4) He *has* finally *learned* our secret.

2. An action beginning in the past and continuing into the future:

(1) I *have been hearing* too many political speeches. (2) I *have been sitting* here in this chair since noon. (3) He *has lived* in my apartment for over a year. (4) I *have known* him for many years.

3. An action completed at any time before the present:

(1) I am sure I *have seen* him before. (2) I *have bought* two dresses since you got yours. (3) The director *has appointed* the committees, and they are studying these problems. (4) *Have* I not *seen* you elsewhere?

Past Tense

The **past tense** is generally employed to represent an action or state of being as having occurred or existed before the present; but in some of its special uses, the past tense is not restricted to denoting past action. The following are the chief time meanings of the past tense forms:

1. Past indefinite time:

(1) He *threw* the ball. (2) He *lived* in Athens.

2. Past definite time may be expressed with the assistance of a modifier specifying the time, or with the progressive (or definite) tense forms of the past tense:

(1) He *threw* the ball the instant he received it. (2) The bell *rang* two minutes before noon. (3) He *was throwing* the ball as I came by. (4) I *was eating* when our guests arrived.

3. The past tense is employed to express an action or state of being as a habit or a custom:

(1) She *wrote* novels. (2) He *directed* an orchestra.
(3) He *lived* well. (4) He *was* a real artist.

4. The past tense is also used to convey general truths, historical facts, and the like:

(1) Shakespeare *was born* in 1564 and died in 1616. (2) The Druid priests *required* human sacrifice. (3) The Greeks *were* the schoolmasters of the ancient world. (4) Job *was persecuted*. (5) Our Anglo-Saxon ancestors *came* from Germany.

5. The past tense of the subjunctive mode is used to represent an action as occurring at the present time or at some future time:

(1) If I *told* this, who would believe me? (2) If I *were to* (or *should*) *resign* tomorrow, would you leave? (3) He could plan battles if war *became* necessary.

PAST PERFECT TENSE

The **past perfect tense** represents an action as completed at a past time. It may denote that an action occurred at an indefinite or definite past time, as the following examples illustrate:

1. Indefinite past time:

(1) I *had seen* the show once before. (2) That child *had* never *been* to a circus. (3) He *had signed* the contract before he left for Europe.

2. Definite (continuous) time, action continuing from a point of time in the past to another past time:

(1) I *had been hearing* strange noises for some time before I called the police. (2) It *had been snowing* all day.

In hypothetical clauses, the past perfect of the subjunctive may also be employed to denote past definite time:

If I *had had* this money yesterday, I could have bought that dress for you.

FUTURE TENSE

The **future tense** is used to represent an action or a state of being as yet to take place or come into existence:

> (1) I *shall leave* within an hour.   (2) He *will be* here tomorrow.

As we have already observed, our earliest English had no future tense pattern, future time being indicated by the present tense forms.   Some Old English verbs were more capable than others of conveying future meaning, particularly those that had subjunctive uses.   *Shall* and *will* were two such verbs, and they took on rather naturally the future meaning which they now possess.   In all levels of English, the present tense is still employed to denote future time, especially when the future idea is closely associated in the mind of the speaker with the present time, as in the following:

> (1) I *am going to sing* at his wedding.   (2) I *teach* in the new building tomorrow.   (3) The guests *are about to depart*. (4) John *sails* next week.

In sentences such as these, the verbs *am going*, *teach*, *are*, and *sails*, are all present tense forms representing a more immediate future action or state of being than the indefinite future tense.   The future meaning is not, however, indicated by the forms of the verbs, but by or with the assistance of words or phrases used with them.   Once more we must remind ourselves that the name of a tense (i.e., grammatical tense) is not identical with the time of the action or the state of being indicated by the verb forms.

Since the Old English period, the language has established a future (grammatical) tense which requires no assistance from accompanying modifiers to denote future time.   The auxiliaries *shall* and *will* are now generally recognized as the signs of the future tense; and when these auxiliaries are used with the simple infinitive (the infinitive without *to*), they are generally employed to denote an action or a state of being yet to come.

The **future tense,** as we have observed before, is formed, not by inflectional change of the verb form, but by a combination of verb forms (the auxiliaries *shall* and *will* followed by the infinitive of the verb to be conjugated). This type of inflection is called **periphrastic (or phrasal) inflection.**

Originally *shall* and *will* were separate verbs with independent meanings, not mere auxiliaries, as in present-day English. In Old English they had nothing in common except the idea of implied futurity, which idea they had in common with a number of verbs. *Shall* (and its past *should*) had the meanings of commanding, owing, obligation, necessity; and *will* (and its past *would*) was used to convey a wish, a desire, a promise, a threat; therefore, a volition—voluntary action or exercise of the will. Almost all, perhaps all, the modern uses of *shall* and *will* have developed from these basic meanings; and in some of their present-day uses they retain some of their original meanings. Observe that in *I shall fall,* the auxiliary *shall* denotes pure futurity; but in *Shall I feed the cat now or later?* *shall* denotes mild obligation, and is about the equivalent of *should.* Likewise, in *I shall be obliged to buy a new dress for your party,* *shall* retains its older meaning of obligation, and the verb phrase *shall be obliged to buy* is almost the equivalent of *must buy.*

Similarly, *will* has developed different meanings and uses. In *You will be late,* *will* has lost its sense of volition; but in *Will you buy the meat for supper, if I buy the dessert?* *will* retains some of its volition meaning; and *Will you buy?* is nearly the equivalent of *Are you willing* (or *Will you be willing*) *to buy?*

The **progressive (or definite)** forms of the future tense represent an action as going on or continuing at a specified or implied future time:

(1) He *will be seeing* me at noon tomorrow. (2) I *shall be studying* this problem all evening.

Uses of *Shall* and *Will*. When *shall* and *will* are used to denote future time and nothing else, they are the distinctive signs of the future tense, and they belong in the inflection of every full verb. But these auxiliaries are not restricted to this form-word function; they may in a different use be **modal auxiliaries** and denote obligation, necessity, volition, promise, determination, etc. The rules governing the uses of the two types of auxiliaries are not the same in respect to the personal subjects governing verbs containing *shall* and *will*. The meaning to be conveyed must be the determining factor. A few suggestions concerning the proper uses of the future and modal auxiliaries may guide the student in choosing the right auxiliaries to express his thoughts in the forms established by the best usage.

1. When mere futurity is intended, *shall* is correctly used for the first person, *will* for the second and third:

> (1) I (We) *shall arrive* on Monday. (2) You (He, They) *will reach* Chicago by noon. (3) You *will* all *be going* to her wedding. (4) He (She, It, They, You) *will arrive* next week. (5) They *will come* early if you invite them. (6) I *shall drown* if no one *will help* me.

In these sentences *shall* and *will* perform no function except to indicate futurity.

2. When the future idea is reënforced by one of determination, promise, intention, desire, prophecy, threat, command, and other similar meanings on the part of the speaker, the auxiliaries are reversed, *will* being used with the first person, and *shall* with the second and third:

> (1) I *will tell* the truth and nothing but the truth. (2) I *will give* you this car when I get my new one. (3) We *will punish* every one of the culprits. (4) You *shall do* as I say from now on. (5) Thou *shalt* not steal. (6) You *shall have* a new dress as soon as I get my check.

Observe that *shall* and *will* have modal meaning in these sentences; and in some of the sentences a modal auxiliary

like *must* or *ought* could be used for *shall* and *will*. (See Uses
of Modal Auxiliaries, pp. 129–132.)

Some exceptions to rules 1 and 2 should be mentioned here:

  a. In military commands, official correspondence, and
  formal orders, *will* is used with the second and third
  persons instead of *shall* as a form of courtesy, as in
  the following:

  (1) Each teacher *will send* his list of absences to the head
  of his department. (2) John Doe *will report* to the Colonel
  immediately. (3) The regiment *will* now *advance*.

  b. Shall is used instead of *will* with the first person when
  willingness or intention is expressed in the predicate
  verb (*wish, please, desire,* or the like), or by an adjective in the predicate expressing willingness, intention,
  or desire (e.g., *glad, happy*), as in the following:

  (1) I *shall be glad* to serve on your committee. (2) We
  shall be pleased to see you. (3) We *shall be willing* to accept
  those terms.

  But when willingness is indicated in a modifying adverb, *will* is used:

  I *will gladly share* the expenses of the trip.

3. In questions, *shall* may be used with the second person
to denote pure futurity. Here the form of the question an-
ticipates the form of the answer:

  Question: *Shall* you *go?* Answer: I *shall.*

But *will* is used when volition is indicated:

  Question: *Will* you *be* so kind as to hand me that book?
  Answer: Surely, I *will.*

Should and Would as Past-Future Auxiliaries. The past-
future tense, sometimes called the **secondary future tense**, is
employed to represent an action as having occurred in the
past as opposed to the present. In other words, the **past-**

future denotes future time to some past time expressed or implied. *Should* and *would* as the past tense forms of *shall* and *will* are the auxiliaries employed in the past-future tense. They follow the same rules as *shall* and *will* when they are used to denote pure futurity; that is, *should* is used with the first person, and *would* with the second and third. Like *shall* and *will*, their uses as pure future auxiliaries are not identical with their uses as modal auxiliaries. (See Uses of Modal Auxiliaries, pp. 129–132.)

1. The past-future tense is most frequently used in indirect discourse and in reporting speech, as in the following:

> (1) I did say that I *should return* by August 1. (2) He said that he *would retire* next month. (3) She was afraid that he *would fail* to pass the oral examination. (4) I said that I *should enjoy living* in Paris.

Observe that *should* and *would* are pure past-future auxiliaries in these sentences. They have lost their original meanings of obligation, compulsion, volition, desire, etc. In the direct discourse form or in reported speech as in the present, the future auxiliaries *shall* and *will* are employed, as in the following:

> (1) He said: "I *shall return* by August 1." (2) He says that he *will retire* next month. (3) She is afraid he *will fail* to pass the oral. (4) I say that I *shall enjoy living* in Paris (or, I said: "I *shall enjoy living* in Paris").

2. When the first person with *shall* or *should* in direct discourse becomes the second or third in indirect, *shall* or *should* may be retained, as in the following:

> (1) He says, "I *shall drown* unless you help me." (2) He says he *shall drown* unless I help him.

When the direct speech is reported in the **past-future,** *should* instead of *would* may be used with the third person:

> (1) He said: "I *shall drown* unless you help me." (2) He said that he *should* (or *would*) *have drowned* if I had not helped him.

The explanation for the retention of *shall* and *should* in the indirect discourse in sentences such as these is that the second and third persons represent the first in the direct discourse.

3. But when *will* is used with the first person in direct address to denote desire or volition, *will* and *would* are retained in the indirect:

(1) He says, "You *will drown*." (2) He says that you (he, they) *will drown*. (3) He says that he will not go (Direct address: "I *will* not *go*").

When these sentences are reported indirectly in the past tense, *would* replaces *will:*

(1) He said that he *would drown*, but he did not drown. (2) He said that he *would* not *go*, but he did go.

4. In indefinite relative clauses and in other clauses expressing expectation, purpose, manner, concession, and condition, *shall* and *should* may be used with all three persons to denote pure futurity:

(1) Whoever *shall exalt* himself, shall be abashed; and he that *shall humble* himself, shall be exalted. (2) He was anxious that I *should meet* you before we begin this work. (3) If you *should see* John in town, tell him to come home. (4) Though thou *shouldst bray* a fool in mortar, yet will not his foolishness depart from him.

Will and *would* are generally used in subordinate clauses expressing a wish or voluntary approval:

(1) If Joe *would go* with our children, no one would worry. (2) If I *will sing* my song, will you sing yours? (3) They hoped that we *would celebrate* their anniversary. (4) We judge as we *would be* judged. (5) If you *would be* wealthy, think of saving as well as getting.

In the main, these sentences represent somewhat formal speech, and illustrate in some instances correct but not common uses of *shall* and *should* and *will* and *would*. In present-day speech, mere futurity in dependent clauses is more often expressed by the present tense. In purpose clauses *may* and *might* are commonly used to denote action yet to come.

The Past-Future Perfect Tense. *Should* and *would* as past tense forms of *shall* and *will* in the **past-future perfect** denote that an action is future to some past time specified or implied for the termination of the action. In this use, *should* and *would* are pure future auxiliaries (i.e., form-words), not notional verbs, as they are when they denote obligation, compulsion, volition, or desire. Observe the past-future meaning in the following:

> (1) They *would have asked* me if they had wanted my advice. (2) He said that he *would* not *have been surprised* at anything you said. (3) I *should have gone* to that party if the invitation had arrived earlier. (4) I believe you *would have enjoyed* the program.

TENSES OF THE MODAL AUXILIARIES

In Old English, *may*, *can*, and *shall* are preterit forms of still earlier pre-Germanic strong verbs. They all had present meanings very similar to those they have today. Historically these forms are old perfect tenses which shifted their meanings and tense to the present. Other verbs of this same group of the so-called preterit-presents are *owe* (*own*, *owe*), archaic *mote* (may), and *wot* (I know, he knows). The shift in meaning and tense can be seen in *wot*, which formerly had the meaning of *I have seen* but came to mean *I know*, since what I have seen I now know.

After the old preterits became presents, new past tenses were formed on the pattern of weak (or regular) verbs; and hence *may-might*, *can-could*, *shall-should*, *owe-ought*, *mote-must*[12] (*So mote it be*,—Masonic formula), *wot-wist* (*What I shall choose I wot not; I wist not that he was the high priest*).

---

[12] Observe that all the new past forms have the weak verb suffix -*t* or -*d*. *Mote-must* does not appear to show the addition of a -*t* suffix in its present form; but the *s* in *must* is the effect of a phonetic law in Germanic which turns a *t* before another *t* into *s*; hence the O.E. *most* equals *mot* + *t*. The new past of O.E. *witan*, *wat* followed the same law, the *s* in *wist* representing a shift from an earlier *t* (*wit* + *t*). Also *wast* (knowest) is the equivalent of *wat* + *t*.

Uses of the Modal Verbs

May-Might. *May* and its past *might* are now restricted to expressing possibility or permission, or a wish (in the subjunctive). *May* and *might* are indicative when they are used in statements of facts, and subjunctive when they are employed to denote suppositions.

The time which *may* and *might* are capable of expressing is not restricted to the time denoted by the tenses they belong to. With the assistance of adverbial modifiers, either verb may denote present, past, or future time; but the simple present tense and the simple past tense forms (i.e., *may go* and *might go*) are generally used to denote future time, the difference of meaning measuring a difference in the degree of possibility, the present tense being more definite and more positive than the past, chiefly because the present tense forms are likely to be used to convey facts, and therefore be indicative, whereas the past forms are often subjunctive and convey mere suppositions. Observe the distinction in the following:

(1) He *may succeed* (fair or strong possibility). (2) He *might* possibly *succeed* (weak probability, usually with a contingent *if*-clause). (3) He *may be* a college graduate (He probably is). (4) You *may leave* now (indicative mode, permission). (5) You *may go* tomorrow, if you have finished your work (a promise). (6) You *might go* tomorrow if someone would come for you (weak probability).

Observe the time distinction in the present perfect form *may have succeeded* and the past perfect *might have succeeded* in the following sentences:

Present Perfect: He *may have succeeded* (doubt).
Past Perfect: He *might have succeeded*, had he tried harder (He did not succeed).

In noun clauses in which sequence of tenses must be preserved (a present depending upon a present, a past depending upon a past), the distinctions between *may* and *might* are preserved by careful speakers and writers:

(1) He *says* he *may go* (Both verbs are in the present). (2) He *said* that he *might go* (Both verbs are past tense forms). (3) If we *sell* this house, we *may move* into an apartment (Both verbs are present tense forms denoting future time). (4) I *might have gone*, if I *had been invited* (Both verbs are past perfect tense forms denoting past time).

Can-Could. *Can* was once an independent verb meaning *know*. It is now used to denote or assert ability or power. Its preterit *cou(l)-d* has dropped the *n* of *can*, and through false analogy with the past tenses of *shall* and *will* has acquired the *l* before the *-d*. Observe that *should* and *would* came from words having stems ending in *-l* (*shall* is from O.E. *scal*, *sceal*, from the infinitive *sculan;* and *will* is from O.E. *willan*).

Can is used only in the indicative, and in tenses where the indicative of *may* is used. *Could* may be used in the indicative or the subjunctive. It is indicative when it asserts something as a fact; it is subjunctive when it asserts a thought idea (i.e., a supposition). Observe the tense and time meanings in each of the following, and note which statements have verbs in the indicative and which in the subjunctive:

(1) I *can sing* this song for you. (2) He *cannot have arrived* yet. (3) He *could not have been elected*, had he tried. (4) Father said that I *could go* home with you. (5) If I *could sing* that song, I would sing it for you. (6) I had hoped that I *could see* my way clear to finance this project for you. (7) We *could have won* that game if we had had proper coaching.

Must-[Had to]. *Must* is now used to express necessity or obligation. It is always indicative, and except in rare cases it is always employed to denote present or future time. Unlike *can* and *may*, it possesses no past (or rather there is no present form, *must* being historically past). The past meaning of *must* in present-day speech, particularly in the spoken language, is generally rendered periphrastically by the phrase *had to*, the past of *have to* (must). Observe the tense and time meaning in the following:

> (1) He *must go* now (present time). (2) You *must* (or *have to*) *go* home tomorrow (future time). (3) He *had to go* away before I arrived (*had to* here denotes obligation in the past; *was obliged to* could also be used here as a past of *must*.)
> (4) *Must* we (or Do we *have to*) *leave* now?

Ought is a preterit-present verb of a later origin than the others generally listed in the group of modal auxiliaries derived from earlier past forms. *Ought* differs in its use from the other modal auxiliaries in one respect: it is always followed by the infinitive with *to*. *Ought* denotes obligation, and is a stronger expression of obligation than *should*, but not so strong as *must*. It has no past tense form, but it may express past meaning when it is combined with the perfect infinitive.

> Present or Future Time: He *ought to go* now (or tomorrow).
> Past Time: He *ought to have gone* with his children to get the ice-cream.

Ought has no past participial form, and hence it should never be used after *had* in such expressions as *had ought* and *had ought to have*. Say *You ought to leave here at once* (not *You had ought to leave here at once*); and *You ought not to have been seen* (not *You hadn't ought to have been seen*). To put *had* before *ought* is as illogical as to put *had* before *could, must,* or *would;* yet no one ever says *had could, had must,* or *had would.*

Shall-Should.[13] When *shall* has the force of *must,* or is used in the expression of obligation, compulsion, or necessity, it may be regarded as a modal auxiliary. In this use it retains some of its original meaning and may be regarded as a no-

---

[13] For the uses of *shall* and *should* in denoting mere futurity, see Future Tense, pp. 124–129.

tional verb; i.e., a verb having a meaning of its own. *Should* is now used as a modal auxiliary chiefly to denote obligation or condition. In conveying obligation, *should* is similar to *must* and *ought*, but does not express the compulsion which *must* denotes, nor the moral obligation or duty of *ought*. All three auxiliaries generally convey present or future time. Observe the tense forms and the time meanings which *should* denotes in the following sentences:

(1) You *should be ashamed* of yourself. (2) You *should know* better than to trust an enemy. (3) *Should* I *fail* to get this money, what must I do? (4) I am anxious that he *should hear* your story.

The past subjunctive *should* is frequently used to express obligation modestly or politely, as in the following:

(1) I *should be studying* (compare *I must be studying*). (2) We *should not stay* longer (compare *We ought not to stay longer*). (3) Now you know that children *should not fight* (compare *should not fight* with *ought not to fight* and *must not fight*).

Will-Would. The uses of *will* and *would* to denote futurity have been treated in the forms and uses of the future tense (see pp. 122–128). They were once independent verbs; but are in the living language seldom used except as modal auxiliaries to denote volition, obligation, intention, or wish; or as mere function words to denote futurity.

1. *Will* and *would* are full verbs in the following:

(1) Whatever God *wills*, is holy, just, and good. (2) *Would* (= I *wish*) that mine enemy would write a book!

2. They are modal auxiliaries in the following:

(1) This basket *will hold* a bushel. (2) He *would not come* when we sent for him. (3) My father *would* certainly *disapprove* of your doing that. (4) If you *would put* more time on your work, you *would get* better marks. (5) If you *would sing* that song, you *would make* a hit.

TENSES OF THE NONFINITE VERBS

In addition to the finite (or principal) verbs, the tenses of which we have examined in the preceding pages, there are three nonfinite (infinite, not limited) verb forms, which have voice and tense inflection.

The nonfinites are the **participle,** the **gerund,** and the **infinitive.** When these are employed as grammatical units in sentences (i.e., as nouns or modifiers), they are called **verbals.** The gerund is always a verbal, but the participle and the infinitive are also employed in forming the periphrastic tenses of principal verbs.

The Participle

The **participle** has three tenses: the **present, the past,** and the **present perfect.** The present perfect has two forms for denoting action completed: the **definite** and the **indefinite present perfect.** The **definite** (or progressive) form belongs only to intransitive verbs or to transitive verbs in the active voice.

The participle of an intransitive verb has four tense forms, all of which may be used as adjectives or as parts of verb phrases. Every intransitive verb having full conjugation will have tense forms corresponding to the ones given for *fall* in the table below:

Present: *falling*
Present Perfect Indefinite: *having fallen*[14]
Present Perfect Definite (Progressive): *having been falling*
Past: *fallen*

---

[14] Some intransitive verbs, particularly those denoting motion (*go, fall, come, rise, arrive,* etc.) sometimes have the auxiliary *being* instead of *having* in the present perfect tense; as, *being gone, being fallen, being come, being risen,* etc. The *having*-forms are more regular, and in present-day speech are more common than those with *being;* as, *having gone, having fallen, having come,* etc. Observe that *being come* denotes action completed in the present; and this form should not be confused with the present tense form of transitive verbs in the passive voice; as, *being forgotten, being taught, being seen,* etc.

The participle of a transitive verb has six different forms to denote time, three of which are in the active voice, and three in the passive voice. Observe the tense and voice forms of the participle of the transitive verb *see* in the table below:

ACTIVE VOICE	PASSIVE VOICE
Present: *seeing*	*being seen*
Present Perfect Indefinite: *having seen*	*having been seen*
Present Perfect Definite (Progressive):	
having been seeing	———————
Past: ———————	*seen*

The Formation of the Tenses of the Participle. The **present participle** of an intransitive verb and that of a transitive verb in the active voice may be formed by adding *-ing* to the simple infinitive: *see + ing*. The **present tense of the passive voice** is formed by combining *being* (the present participle of the verb *be*) with the past participle of a principal verb: *being + seen*.

The **indefinite present perfect tense** is a combination of *having*, the present participle of *have*, and the past participle of a principal verb: *having + seen*. The **definite** (or **progressive**) **perfect** is a combination of *having been* (the present perfect participle of *be*) and the present participle of a principal verb: *having been + seeing*. The **present perfect passive** is a combination of *having been* (the present perfect participle of *be*) and the past participle of a principal verb: *having been + seen*.

The **past participle** is the form listed in the dictionary and in school grammars as the third principal part of a full verb. It has no fixed form, unless it is a regular verb, in which case it will end in *-t*, *-d*, or *-ed*, and one of these endings will be added to the simple infinitive, which is considered the stem-form of a principal verb. Many verbs of Old English origin have past participles ending in *-n*, or *-en;* as, *seen, fallen,* etc.

The Gerund

The **tenses of the gerund** are the same as those of the participle, except that the gerund has no past tense form. The present tense form, which ends in *-ing*, is the most commonly used of the gerund forms, being the oldest and the most thoroughly established in the noun function. The ending *-ing* of the gerund is **not** borrowed from the *-ing* of the participle. The gerund has had the ending *-ing* (O.E. *-ung*) from the earliest record of English; the present participle did not acquire the ending *-ing* until after the twelfth century, but previously ended in *-inde, -ende,* or *-ande.* Originally the gerund was treated as a noun (and not as a verb form, as it is in Modern English). As a noun it could take the plural inflection *-s,* and it could have adjective modifiers (nouns and pronouns in the genitive case). It was not construed as a verb, nor as a part of a verb; it could not denote tense meanings, nor take an object.

After the participle took the form of the gerund, the gerund tended to assume some of the functions of the participle and to have forms other than its original *-ing* (O.E. *-ung*) suffix form. The *-ing* form of the gerund in present-day English is always treated as a verb form, and all of its expanded forms may be found in the full inflection of a principal verb. Like the participle, it has tense modification, and may have voice (if it is a transitive verb) and adverb modifiers. In addition, it may have adjective modifiers (See Part Two, Lesson IX).

The gerund forms of any full verb correspond to those of *see* in the table below:

Active Voice	Passive Voice
Present: *seeing*	*being seen*
Present Perfect Indefinite: *having seen*	*having been seen*
Present Perfect Definite (Progressive): *having been seeing*	

It should be noted that the gerund has no past tense form, as does the participle.[15]

---

[15] When the past participle has the function of a noun, it should be construed as an adjective (verbal adjective) used as a noun. *The wounded* (i.e., *wounded people*) *lay dying in the street.* For other illustrations of the participle used as a noun, see Part Two, Lesson VIII, pp. 294–296.

The Infinitive

The infinitive has two tenses, the present and the present perfect. Intransitive verbs and transitive verbs in the active voice have two forms which may be employed to denote the time of action which each of these tenses represents: the simple (or indefinite) form and the definite (or progressive) form. The passive voice has only one form for each tense: the indefinite present and the indefinite present perfect.

Intransitive verbs have infinitive forms corresponding to the ones given below for the verb *fall:*

Present Indefinite (Simple Infinitive): *(to) fall*
Present Definite (Progressive): *(to) be falling*
Present Perfect Indefinite: *(to) have fallen*
Present Perfect Definite (Progressive): *(to) have been falling*

Transitive verbs have four forms in the active voice and two in the passive voice. These correspond to the tense forms listed for *see* in the table below:

Active Voice

Present Indefinite (Simple Infinitive): *(to) see*
Present Definite (Progressive): *(to) be seeing*
Present Perfect Indefinite: *(to) have seen*
Present Perfect Definite (Progressive): *(to) have been seeing*

Passive Voice

Present Indefinite: *(to) be seen*
Present Perfect Indefinite: *(to) have been seen*

The **indefinite** (or **simple**) **infinitive** is the oldest of all the forms of the infinitive now in common use; and except for the verb *be*, which has a very irregular present and past tense conjugation, the simple infinitive is identical with the first person, present tense form of the verb it represents. In our dictionaries and school grammars, the simple infinitive is listed as the primary (or basic) form of the verb, all the other forms being derived from or based upon it. To conjugate any full verb, one must know the simple infinitive of the verb in question and its inflectional pattern.

Origin and Forms of the Infinitive. In Old English the infinitive had only two distinctive forms: the simple (or **noun**) **infinitive** and the **gerundial infinitive**. The **noun-infinitive** was recognized by its ending *-an* (O.E. *drincan*, drink), and the **gerundial infinitive** by its dative ending *-ne* (e.g., O.E. *to drincanne*) and by the preposition *to*, which always preceded it. The **noun-infinitive** was a neuter noun, and could have nominative or accusative function, but it was not used as a modifier. The **gerundial infinitive** had restricted use. It was employed mainly to express purpose; it was not used as the subject or object of a verb.

In Middle English, when the noun-infinitive lost its suffix (O.E. *-an;* M.E. *-en*) the only distinctive infinitive form was the infinitive with *to*. In time the *to* was felt to be the sign of the infinitive, and was attached to it in its other verbal uses. In Modern English the *to* is treated as a mere function word except when it is used to show relationship between the infinitive it governs and some other sentence element, as in *He came to get the money* (= *He came for the money*), where *to* shows relationship between two grammatical units, *came* and *get the money*.

The infinitive without *to* is now used with the future and modal auxiliaries (*shall, will, should, would, may, can, must,* etc.) and with *do* and *did* in forming certain periphrastic tenses of finite verbs. In earlier English these auxiliary verbs were full verbs, and the noun-infinitive which followed any one of these was the direct object.

When the infinitive in its verbal function is used as an objective complement after such verbs as *see, make, hear, feel,* and the like, the *to* is usually omitted, as in *I saw him leave; I heard her sing; She made me laugh.*

The infinitive as a verbal is also used without *to* after certain prepositions, such as *but* and *except;* as, *He does nothing but stare at us; I will do anything you ask except sing that song.*

The **expanded tenses** of the infinitive represent somewhat recent formations. These are formed by combining the present or perfect infinitives of the verb *be* or *have* with the present or past participle of principal verbs. The **present definite (progressive) infinitive** consists of the present infinitive of *be* plus the present participle of the principal verb: (*to*) *be + seeing*, (*to*) *be + falling*. The **present perfect indefinite infinitive** consists of the present infinitive of *have* plus the past participle of a principal verb: (*to*) *have + seen*, (*to*) *have + fallen*. The **present perfect definite (progressive) infinitive** consists of the present perfect infinitive of the verb *be* plus the present participle of a principal verb: (*to*) *have been + seeing*, (*to*) *have been + falling*.

The **present tense of the passive voice** is formed by combining the present infinitive of *be* and the past participle of a principal verb; (*to*) *be + seen*. The present perfect passive infinitive consists of the present perfect infinitive of *be* plus the past participle of a principal verb: (*to*) *have been + seen*.

SEQUENCE OF TENSES

Sequence of tenses has to do with the tenses of verbs in certain subordinate constructions in relation to that of verbs in principal ones. As a rule, the tenses of verbs in dependent elements (clauses or verbal phrases) are influenced by and adjusted to the tenses of predicate verbs in principal clauses.

The tenses that measure time from the standpoint of the present to some past or future time; that is, from the time the speaker is stating his thoughts to some other time past or yet to come, are sometimes called the **primary tenses**. These are the present, the past, the present perfect, and the future Those tenses that measure time in relation to some past or future time are called **secondary tenses**. These are the past perfect and the future perfect. If one of the secondary tenses depends upon one of the primary tenses for its meaning (or measure of time), as it usually does, it must conform (or be adjusted) to the tense of the principal verb. If we say *When* *he had come* (or *If he had come*); or *When he had driven through the city* (or *When he had been driving through the city*), our verbs *had come, had driven,* and *had been driving* are denoting time as relative to some other past time; and if we follow these verbs with principal clauses, we must use past tense forms so that the action which they denote as completed in the past can be measured by (or based upon) some other past action.

The future action expressed in a future perfect tense is based upon some other future action, which may be expressed by the simple future tense or by the present tense denoting future time. If we say *I shall have finished eating my lunch;* or *I shall have been eating for an hour;* or *He will have been in Europe a year,* it is necessary for us to furnish primary verbs (in this case, present or future) in dependent clauses so that these verbs may measure time from some action yet to come to the time of the action which they denote.

For the sake of brevity, the primary tenses are sometimes suppressed; but the primary tense meaning must be implied or suggested by the context; as, *I shall have finished this job by noon.* Here the primary future tense meaning is indicated by the phrase *by noon,* which suggests a point of time in the future, which serves as a basis for measuring the extent of the action, which begins a moment after the present time and extends to noontime. Rephrased, this sentence means *I shall work until noon, at which time I shall have finished this job.*

Verbs are said to have **natural sequence** when they indicate the natural or logical time relations existing between the actions which they denote. The present perfect naturally precedes the present, and the future naturally follows the present, as in the following:

(1) When he *has finished,* he *may go.* (2) He *has* not *asked* me what we *are having* for lunch. (3) When I *finish* this exercise, I *shall leave.* (4) When he *has finished,* he *will depart.*

When it is desired to make clear the relation of time between the main and the subordinate verb, the tense of the subordinate verb is independent of that of the main verb—and in such a case there is no sequence of tenses. Observe the two tenses in each of the following:

(1) I *sing* because I *love* to sing. (2) I *sang* because I *love* to sing. (3) I *sang* because I *had been invited* to sing. (4) I *shall sing* in Chicago because I *had promised* to sing there before I *was invited* to sing in your town.

In indirect quotations[16] a present main verb is followed by a verb in any tense in the noun clause:

He says he
{
writes, is writing
wrote, was writing
has written, has been writing
had written, had been writing
will write, will be writing
will have written
}
his reply.

But a past principal verb is followed by the past or the past perfect:

He said he
{
wrote
was writing
had written
had been writing
}
his reply.

There is one exception to this rule: after a past tense a general truth or a permanent fact is usually expressed by a subordinate verb in the present tense, as in *He said that honesty is the best policy;* and *He knew that the earth is round.* Sometimes the past tense is preferred as a means of shifting the responsibility for the truth of a statement. Observe, however, that there is sometimes a difference in meaning between the past and present tenses in clauses of this type; e.g., *He said that he was a member of the Communist party;* and *He*

---

[16] We may have in effect the indirect quotation not only after *say* and *said,* but after such expressions as *He believes, thinks, is certain,* e.g., *He is certain he will* (or *did*) *succeed; He was certain he had succeeded* (or *would succeed*); etc.

*said that he **is** a member of the Communist party.* Compare also *He said you **were** sick* with *He said you **are** sick.* In subordinate clauses like these, the proper sequence must depend upon logic, not upon grammatical tense.

The modal auxiliaries follow the same rules in denoting proper sequence of tenses as other verbs; i.e., the grammatical present tense forms normally follow present tenses, and the grammatical past tense forms follow past tenses, as in the following:

> (1) I *may go* if I *have* (not *if I had*) the money. (2) I *might go* if I *had* (not if *I have*) the money. (3) He *could write* legibly if he *tried* (not *tries*). (4) I *say* this in order that I *may* (not *might*) *convince* you. (5) I *said* that in order that I *might* (not *may*) *convince* you.

The danger of error in the use of the modal verb forms lies in the tendency to make careless substitution of the past forms (*might, could, would, should*) for present or future tense forms (*may, can, will, shall*). We have observed earlier in our treatment of tenses of verbs that both the present and past forms of the modal verbs are capable of denoting future time, but when sequence of tenses is to be considered, the present and the past forms should be differentiated.

PERSON AND NUMBER

The person and number of verbs depend upon the person and number of their subjects, the law being that the verb must agree with its subject in these particulars. English has preserved few terminal markings that denote person and number, and often both must be determined by the context, not by the forms of the verb.

In verbs other than *be*, there is only one form in which modern English inflection shows a differentiation in form to indicate person and number; namely, the third person singular of the present tense, indicative mode, which adds -*s* to the simple form used for the other persons of the singular and for all persons of the plural. The modal auxiliaries (*may, might, can, could, should, would, must, ought*) do not even have the -*s* ending for the third person singular form. Agreement in English is, therefore, less significant than in more fully inflected languages, such as Latin, Greek, and Old English. Excluding the past tense forms of *be* (*was* and *were*), English has no past tense inflection to denote person or number; e.g., I *rode*, you *rode*, he *rode*, we *rode*, you *rode*, they *rode*.

In the subjunctive mode, the verb *be*, the most highly inflected verb in English, has no markings to denote person or number, the form *be* serving for all persons and both numbers in the present tense, and the form *were* for all persons and both numbers in the past tense. Other verbs have no inflection to show person and number in the subjunctive.

In the conjugation of *be*, English has preserved three distinctive forms (*am, are, is*) for the singular indicative, but one of these, the second person *are* is like the form used for all three persons of the plural. Highly inflected languages, like Latin and Greek, have separate forms for each person in the singular and a form for each person in the plural. Old English could differentiate between the second person plural and the second person singular, a distinction that modern English is now incapable of making. When the singular pronoun *thou* became archaic, the verb form which it governed became archaic also. The blunder in substandard speech in *You was* (or *Was you?*) for *You were* (or *Were you?*) may be regarded as an error either in person or number. It is logically correct for the singular meaning, but violates usage, and hence must be avoided. When *you* became a substitute for *thou* in the singular, it kept its plural verb form (compare with German *Sie sind* and *du bist*). Sometimes the adjective *all* is placed immediately after *you* to specify plurality, as in *You all are invited to come*. *You are invited* is ambiguous when no qualifying word is expressed or implied to indicate the number of the subject, and therefore the number of the verb *are invited* could be either plural or singular. Such ambiguity results from the inflectional leveling of both the pronoun-subject and the verb.

As we have seen earlier, *shall* (*should*) and *will* (*would*) when used correctly to denote pure futurity differentiate the first person from the second and the third, but these uses are not always observed; and they show no differentiation between the singular and the plural number.

Principles Determining the Person and Number of Verbs

1. Personal pronouns are the only words in English capable of indicating by inflection both person and number. Most nouns have singular and plural forms to indicate differences in number; but all nouns must be construed as being third person, unless they are appositives of personal pronouns, such as *We, the people; you, the president; I, the oldest citizen.* Here the pronouns, not the nouns, denote the person.

2. A relative pronoun must agree with its antecedent in person and number; and when the relative pronoun is the subject of a clause, its predicate verb must agree with it in person and number. Observe the number of the verb in the relative clause in each of the following:

(1) He who *fights* and *runs* away may live to fight another day. (2) It is I who *am* at fault this time. (3) It is you who *are* criticizing the program. (4) It is these men who *have* sacrificed for us.

Failure to recognize the correct antecedent of a relative pronoun may result in error: *I am one of those who favor* (not *favors*) *equal wages for equal service.* In this sentence the verb in the adjective clause must be plural, because the antecedent of *who* is *those*, not *one.* The point is, that there are some persons, perhaps several, who favor equal wages, and I am one of them. In *I am the only one of those who favors the measure*, the antecedent of *who* is *one*, not *those;* and hence *favors* is the correct form.

3. Determining the number of a noun which may have

either singular or plural meaning without change of form requires special attention. Collective nouns take singular verbs when the idea is of the group as a whole, as in *The party is leaving at daybreak;* but a plural verb is required, if the idea is of the individuals composing the group, as in *The party were of all ages and both sexes.* Because the collective nouns more often than not convey numbers as a unit, they are usually followed by singular verbs, as in the following:

> (1) The class *has been* examined.   (2) A large army *is* a protection.   (3) Congress *has adjourned.*   (4) The herd of cattle *was sold* with the farm.

4. Singular nouns with plural modifiers require singular verbs, as in *The father, with his sons, has been honored.* It is well to remember that *with, together with, beside, including, in addition to, along with, accompanied by, as well as,* and phrases like these, following singular nouns do not make those nouns plural; e.g., *The captain, in addition to the members of the crew, was rescued.* If we substitute *and* for *in addition to,* the adjunct modifier becomes coördinate with the singular noun, and the subject becomes plural and requires a plural verb.

5. In question sentences, the verb may precede its subject, but it must agree with it in person and number, as in *Were you* (not *Was you*) *speaking to me? Are* (not *Is*) *John and Alice invited?* Also in declarative sentences when the subject follows the verb, special care must be exercised to see that the subject and verb agree in number; as, *In our club are* (not *is*) *a captain and a general; There are* (not *is*) *a grapefruit and an orange in the refrigerator.*

6. The number of the verb following compound subjects depends upon the idea suggested by the conjunction:

And (suggesting addition) is commonly followed by a plural verb: *The fool and his money are soon parted.* But where the parts of the subject are thought of as a unit or as representing one idea in two or more words, the singular may be used, especially when two nouns connected by *and* present an idea usually expressed by what is referred to in rhetoric books as hendiadys ("one through two"), two coördinate nouns being the equivalent of a noun with a modifying adjective; as, *Bread and butter* (= bread with butter) **is all I** *want for my lunch.* But *bread and butter* **are sold** *here* contains a plural subject, and the verb must be plural. Kipling's *The tumult and shouting* **dies** (note the singular verb) is not to be construed as faulty grammar. The compound subject is equivalent to *the tumultuous shouting.*

Also when two nouns referring to the same person are joined by *and,* the verb should be singular, as in *The owner and manager of the business* **is** *John Smith.*

7. Singular nouns joined by *or, nor, neither . . . nor,* and *either . . . or* take singular verbs:

(1) Neither the party nor the nation *knows* where it stands. (2) Either this boy or that girl *is* to blame. (3) Neither Mary nor her sister *is* attending class.

If one of these conjunctions joins pronouns representing different persons or joins a singular and a plural substantive, the one nearer the verb determines the person and number of the verb:

(1) Either you or I *am* to blame. (2) Either the chief or his subordinates *are* responsible. (3) Either he or you *are* to blame.

8. The form of the noun is not always indicative of its number meaning, for some plural forms take singular verbs, and some singular forms require plural verbs. The following suggestions may help the student in determining the number meaning of the more troublesome forms:

a. Some nouns plural in form are always singular in meaning, and hence require singular verbs: *news, whereabouts, measles, ethics, economics, summons;* e.g., *The news* **is** *good today.*

b. Some nouns are plural in form and singular in meaning (they represent one object or one collection or mass) and require the plural verb: *scissors, coffers, tidings, riches, trousers;* e.g., *My scissors **are not** sharp. Your trousers **are being pressed.***

c. Plural nouns indicating sums of money, distance, measurement, and the like require singular verbs: *Two thousand dollars **is** too much to pay for that car; Two miles **is** too far for me to walk before breakfast.*

9. The indefinite pronouns *anybody, everybody, anyone, nobody, someone, many a one,* etc. regularly take singular verbs: *Everyone **is** present; Many a one **has** attempted that feat and failed.*

The adjectives *each* and *every* modifying a singular or a compound subject are followed by singular verbs:

(1) Every student *has* voted. (2) Every bud, stalk, flower, and seed *displays* a figure, a proportion, a harmony, beyond the reach of art. (3) Every man, woman, and child in this town *is* contributing to the support of this enterprise.

10. *None* is one pronoun which needs special attention. It has both singular and plural meaning, though many speakers and writers take pains to make the verb following *none* singular (see Indefinite Pronouns, pp. 68–71). The following sentences show correct uses of *none:*

(1) None of the women *have invited* their husbands.
(2) None (= not one) of the women *has invited* her husband.
(3) None of the vegetables *are* (or *is*) fresh.

11. The expression *more than one,* though plural in meaning, regularly takes a singular verb; and if a noun follows, as in *more than one man,* which is singular too, the number of both the verb and the noun being influenced by the singular *one,* which is closer to the verb than *more,* as in *More than one person **has failed** to solve this problem.* If *more* is followed by a plural noun, the verb is naturally plural: *More teachers than one have failed to solve this problem.*

12. If the subject of the sentence is singular and the predicate nominative is plural, the verb must agree with the subject, not the predicate nominative: *It was they; It is we; It was the children who annoyed you.*

13. When an affirmative subject is followed by a negative one, the verb agrees with the affirmative: *The boy, not the parents, is being punished.*

14. Titles and names of books, ships, countries, etc., though plural in form take singular verbs:

1. The *Last of the Mohicans,* which starred your friend, *has had* a long run. 2. The *Chicago News,* which reviewed that story, *is* a good newspaper. 3. Why *has* the United States failed? 4. *Is* Ibsen's *Ghosts* in our library?

15. Clauses, verbals, or other groups of words serving as subjects require singular verbs: *When to quit business and enjoy their wealth is the problem never solved by some.*

Conjugation

The **conjugation** (or **inflection**) of a verb is the systematic arrangements of its forms. All English verbs that are complete in voice, mode, tense, person, and number, as most transitive verbs are, may be conjugated according to the same scheme, provided that one knows the stem-forms which appear in the present infinitive (or indicative), the past indicative, and the past participle. These forms constitute what are called **principal parts.**

The **principal parts,** or stem-words, may show three distinct forms, as in *rise, rose, risen* (an original ablaut verb); or two, as in *bind, bound, bound* (an ablaut verb in which leveling has occurred between the past indicative and the past participle); or only one basic form, a suffix (*-d, -t,* or *-ed*) being added for the past indicative and the past participle, as in *fill, filled, filled.* It is also possible to find a set of verb forms identical in all three principal parts, as in *set, set, set* (an original weak verb in which phonetic influences have operated to obliterate the suffix in the past indicative and the past participle).

For convenience, however, it is customary in listing or describing verbs to give as principal parts three forms, unless (as in the cases of *can, must, beware,* and *quoth*) one or more forms should be actually lacking. Some grammars list the present participle as a fourth principal part, but since the present participle shows no variation in its formation, *-ing* always being added to the present infinitive, it is not necessary for one to include it when listing the principal parts of verbs.

With the following synopsis of the verb *give* as a basis, the student can make for himself a conjugation to fit nearly any verb in the language, provided he knows the principal parts of the verb he wishes to conjugate.

A full conjugation of the irregular verb *be* is given first below, because its finite and infinite forms appear oftener than the forms of other auxiliary verbs used in the conjugation of principal verbs, and because its forms are more varying than those of the other assisting verbs.

The infinite forms (participles and infinitives) of the verb *be* are placed before the finite ones so that the student may become familiar with these and be able to recognize them when they appear in the various periphrastic tenses of the different modes.

It is important to note that the verb *give* is a transitive verb, and therefore has both active and passive voice inflection. An intransitive verb, such as *fall, seem, come, go,* has no voice modification, and will have only those forms listed for the active voice of *give*. The expanded tense forms (the progressive and emphatic) are included in the conjugation given for *be* and *give*, because they are now recognized as standard and important tense forms of the inflection of any full verb. The potential pattern is given to show the proper uses of the present and past tense forms of the modal auxiliaries (*may-might, can-could*, etc.).

CONJUGATION OF THE VERB *BE*

Principal Parts: be (am, are, is), was (were), been

Infinitives
{ **Present:** (to) be
Present Perfect: (to) have been }

Participles
{ **Present:** being
Past: been
Present Perfect: having been }

INDICATIVE MODE

PRESENT TENSE

I am	we are
{ you are / thou art[17]	you (ye) are
he (she, it) is	they are

PAST TENSE

I was	we were
{ you were / thou wast	you (ye) were
he (she, it) was	they were

FUTURE TENSE

I shall be	we shall be
{ you will be / thou wilt be	you (ye) will be
he (she, it) will be	they will be

PRESENT PERFECT TENSE

I have been	we have been
{ you have been / thou hast been	you (ye) have been
he (she, it) has been	they have been

---

[17] The forms with *thou* are now archaic or restricted to poetry and solemn style. We hear them used in prayer and see them in the prose and poetry of the greatest literary masters of the 16th, 17th, and 18th centuries.

PAST PERFECT TENSE

I had been   we had been
{you had been   you (ye) had been
{thou hadst been
he (she, it) had been   they had been

FUTURE PERFECT TENSE

I shall have been   we shall have been
{you will have been   you (ye) will have been
{thou wilt have been
he (she, it) will have been   they will have been

SUBJUNCTIVE MODE

(Forms in italics differ from corresponding indicative forms.)

PRESENT TENSE

If[18] I *be*   If we *be*
{If you *be*   If you (ye) *be*
{If thou *be*
If he (she, it) *be*   If they *be*

PAST TENSE

If I *were*   If we were
{If you were   If you (ye) were
{If thou *wert*
If he (she, it) *were*   If they were

PRESENT PERFECT TENSE

If I have been   If we have been
{If you have been   If you (ye) have been
{If thou *have been*
If he (she, it) *have been*   If they have been

---

[18] *If* is used in the paradigm because subjunctive clauses are frequently introduced by it; but the student should know that it is not a part of the subjunctive inflection; *though, lest, as if, as though,* etc. may introduce subordinate clauses containing verbs in the subjunctive mode. The subjunctive forms are also used in principal clauses (see Uses of Subjunctive Mode, pp. 112–116).

PAST PERFECT TENSE

If I had been	If we had been
⎰If you had been	If you (ye) had been
⎱If thou hadst been	
If he (she, it) had been	If they had been

IMPERATIVE MODE

PRESENT TENSE

Be (you, thou)   Be (you, ye)

POTENTIAL INDICATIVE[19]

PRESENT TENSE

I may[20] be	we may be
⎰you may be	you (ye) may be
⎱thou mayst (mayest) be	
he (she, it) may be	they may be

PAST TENSE

I might be	we might be
⎰you might be	you (ye) might be
⎱thou mightst (mightest) be	
he (she, it) might be	they might be

PRESENT PERFECT TENSE

I may have been	we may have been
⎰you may have been	you (ye) may have been
⎱thou mayst (mayest) have been	
he (she, it) may have been	they may have been

---

[19] In the living language, the forms of potential subjunctive are identical with those of the potential indicative; the *thou*-forms are archaic in both modes.

[20] Most of the other modal auxiliaries (*can-could, will-would, shall-should*) follow the same pattern as *may-might. Ought* has similar inflection, but it is always followed by the infinitive with *to;* as, **Present:** *ought to be;* **Past:** *ought to have been. Must,* like *ought,* has no inflectional modifications: the form with *thou* is *must* (not *mustest*).

PAST PERFECT TENSE

I might have been	we might have been
{ you might have been { thou mightst (mightest) have 　been	you (ye) might have been
he (she, it) might have been	they might have been

CONJUGATION OF THE VERB *GIVE*

Principal Parts: give, gave, given

INFINITIVES

ACTIVE VOICE	PASSIVE VOICE
Present Indefinite: (to) give	(to) be given
Present Definite, or *Progressive:* (to) 　be giving	_____
Present Perfect Indefinite: (to) have 　given	(to) have been given
Present Perfect Definite, or *Progressive:* (to) have been giving	_____

PARTICIPLES

Present Indefinite: giving	being given
Present Perfect Indefinite: having 　given	having been given
Present Perfect Definite, or *Progressive:* having been giving	_____
Past: _____	given

A Synopsis of the Indicative Mode

ACTIVE VOICE	PASSIVE VOICE

PRESENT TENSE

Indefinite: I give	I am given
Definite, or *Progressive:* I am giving	I am being given
Emphatic: I do give	_____

PAST TENSE

Indefinite: I gave	I was given
Definite, or *Progressive:* I was giving	I was being given
Emphatic: I did give	_____

FUTURE TENSE

Indefinite: I shall give   I shall be given
Definite, or *Progressive:* I shall be
giving

_____

PRESENT PERFECT TENSE

Indefinite: I have given   I have been given
Definite, or *Progressive:* I have been
giving

_____

PAST PERFECT TENSE

Indefinite: I had given   I had been given
Definite, or *Progressive:* I had been
giving

_____

FUTURE PERFECT TENSE

Indefinite: I shall have given   I shall have been given
Definite, or *Progressive:* I shall have
been giving

_____

The first person singular form in the synopsis of *give* suggests the pattern for the full conjugations of each tense in the indicative and subjunctive modes. In a few instances the form changes to denote person or number. The following variations should be noted:

1. The indefinite and emphatic present have distinctive forms for the third person singular. The suffix *-s* (or *-es*) is added to the first person form; e.g., *He (she, it) gives; He (she, it) does give.*

2. The progressive and all the tenses in the passive voice follow the inflection of the verb *be;* e.g., *I am giving* (or *am given*); *He (she, it) is giving* (or *are given*); *We (you, they) are giving* (or *are given*).

3. In the present perfect tense, *have* becomes *has* in the third person singular; e.g., *He (she, it) has given* (or *has been giving*).

4. In the future and future perfect tenses, the second and third persons follow the pattern given for the future tense of *be,* and have *will* instead of *shall;* e.g., *You*

will *give; He* *will* *have given; They* *will* *be giving.* For the modal uses of *shall* and *will,* see Uses of the Modal Auxiliaries, pp. 129–132.

POTENTIAL INDICATIVE MODE[21]

ACTIVE VOICE	PASSIVE VOICE

PRESENT TENSE

Indefinite: I may[22] give

Definite, or *Progressive:* I may be giving

I may be given

_____.

PAST TENSE

Indefinite: I might give

Definite, or *Progressive:* I might be giving

I might be given

_____.

PRESENT PERFECT TENSE

Indefinite: I may have given

Definite, or *Progressive:* I may have been giving

I may have been given

_____.

PAST PERFECT TENSE

Indefinite: I might have given

Definite, or *Progressive:* I might have been giving

I might have been given

_____.

A Synopsis of the Subjunctive Mode

ACTIVE VOICE	PASSIVE VOICE

PRESENT TENSE

Indefinite: If [23] I give

Progressive: If I be giving

If I be given

_____

---

[21] The potential indicative and the potential subjunctive forms are alike. In the living language, none of the modal auxiliaries inflect to denote person or number.

[22] Any of the modal auxiliaries having present and past forms may be substituted for *may* and *might.* See note 20, p. 151.

For the use of the archaic forms with *thou,* see conjugation of *be,* p. 149; and for the uses and meanings of the modal auxiliaries, see Tenses of the Modal Auxiliaries, pp. 128–131.

[23] For an explanation of the use of *if* with the subjunctive forms, see note explaining the *if* in the conjugation of the verb *be* in the subjunctive, p. 150.

PAST TENSE

Indefinite: **If I gave**   If I were given
Definite, or *Progressive:* **If I were giv-**
ing   If I were being given

PRESENT PERFECT TENSE

Indefinite: **If I have given**   If I have been given
Definite, or *Progressive:* **If I have**
been giving   _____

PAST PERFECT TENSE

Indefinite: **If I had given**   If I had been given
Definite, or *Progressive:* **If I had been**
giving   _____

IMPERATIVE MODE
PRESENT TENSE

Indefinite: **give**   Be given
Definite, or *Progressive:* **Be giving** _____
Emphatic: **Do give**   _____

Six

Adverbs

The **adverb** is perhaps the most difficult of all the parts of speech to put within the limits of a definition which will cover all its numerous and varied uses and meanings. The name *adverb* (Latin *ad verbum*, to the verb) suggests only one of its many uses, though doubtless its earliest and primary function was to qualify the verb. But since the earliest English period, the adverb has been used to qualify a verb, an adjective, or another adverb (or any adverb-equivalent); and in addition the adverb has been gradually extending its functions to those usually performed by other parts of speech.

Forms and Derivation of Adverbs

When classified as to form and origin, adverbs are of two general types: **1. primary** and **2. derivative**.

1. The **primary adverbs** are the oldest in the language and the most general in meaning. They were adverbs in Old English or became adverbs before the end of the Middle English period. Their original, or primary, function was to qualify verbs, though they now are used to modify other parts of speech. Primary adverbs have no suffixes or other markings to distinguish them from the other parts of speech; and most of them are not inflected for comparison, and many of them are monosyllabic. The following are **primary adverbs:** *hence, here, how, never, not, since, soon, then, there, thus, twice, too, where, whence.*

2. The **derivative adverbs** may be identified by their suffixes (*-ly, -wards, -ways, -wise*), or by their compound or phrasal nature, being formed by combining or joining words in various ways. Some adverb compounds are very old, dating back to earliest English, and some are very new. The older compounds, those formed in the Old English and in the Middle English periods, can sometimes be recognized because the elements of the compounds are usually written as single words; the more recently formed ones usually have their component parts joined by hyphens, or written as phrases.

In Old English the oblique cases (and therefore all cases except the nominative) could have adverbial function, and nouns and their modifying adjectives (*mid way, mean time, some times, straight way*) developed into compound adverbs: *midway, meantime,* etc. Prepositions which always went with certain nouns joined with those nouns to make new adverbs. In the following adverbs, the prefixes *a-, for-, in-, per-,* and *to-* were once prepositions: *aboard, ahead, apart, apiece, forsooth, indeed, perchance, today.* Adverbs and adjectives often attached themselves to prepositions to convey new or special adverbial meanings: *hereafter, forever, thereby, thereat, whereby, wherein, anew, amid, awry, anon.* Also adverbs joined with adverbs to make new adverbs: *however, whenever, wherever, wheresoever, whensoever.* Occasionally an adverb joined with a noun to make a new adverb: *naught, nought* (O.E. *nāwiht* from *n- a- wiht,* not a whit). More recent adverb formations have various combinations: *heretofore, inasmuch, insomuch, nevertheless, notwithstanding, pell-mell, perhaps, willy-nilly.* Sometimes an entire phrase functions as a single adverbial modifier: *to and fro, hand in hand, by and by, in general, in short, to boot, to wit, in vain, of late, off and on, now and then,* etc.

No rule can be given to aid one in determining which of the derivative adverbs are to be written solid, which with hyphens, and which as phrases. The older the compound, the more likely it is that the individual elements are written as single words without hyphens. The hyphenated adverbs usually belong to the middle stage in the development of compounds. The dictionary is really the only final authority on such matters. Our standard dictionaries list *back and forth, backwards and forwards, by and by, here and there, hither and thither, in vain, in truth, in and out, now and then, off and on,* and *up and down* as phrases; but *inasmuch, insomuch, nevertheless,* and *notwithstanding* as single words without hyphens.

Old and New Forms of Adverbs. Most adverbs, whether new or old, like adjectives, are derived from other parts of speech. Many are formed by the addition of the suffix *-ly:* (1) to adjectives: *bold—boldly, calm—calmly, quiet—quietly;* (2) less frequently to nouns: *week—weekly, part—partly, name —namely, order—orderly.* This is now the usual way of forming adverbs from adjectives or from nouns having adjectival meaning. Any recently coined adjectives, such as *peppy* and *snappy,* would thus be made into adverbs by adding *-ly;* e.g., *peppily, snappily.* Hence, the *-ly* is now the living (or productive) adverb suffix.

It must not be assumed, however, that all adverbs must end in *-ly,* for the language has numerous adverbs formed in past times in other ways. Nor should one assume that all words ending in *-ly* are adverbs. The words *beastly, costly, deadly, fatherly, friendly, godly, homely, kingly, likely, manly, slovenly, seemly, timely, womanly, ugly,* and several others are adjectives in common use; and some words in *-ly* serve equally well as adjectives and as adverbs; e.g., *daily, early, monthly, only, weekly, yearly.*

There is an important group of adverbs in good use without the ending *-ly,* sometimes called **flat adverbs,** such as *bright, deep, fair, fast, first, hard, high, ill, late, long, loud, low, quick, right, sharp, strong, thick, wide.* A common misunderstanding is that these are "adjectives used as adverbs," because, through language leveling, they have become identical in sound and in spelling with corresponding adjectives.

But they are true adverbs, and have always been so. In Old English and Early Middle English, these adverbs were distinguished from corresponding adjectives by the ending -*e*, pronounced as an extra syllable that was lacking in the adjective. Thus in Old English the adjective *bright* had one syllable and the adverb *brightė* had two; and so with the others. The difference lasted until Chaucer's time, who wrote *Bright was the sun*, and *Her face shone so brightė.* After his day the sound of final -*e* was lost, and the adverb became like the adjective. But the adverb *bright* is still an adverb in its own right, not an adjective used as an adverb.

Many of the flat adverbs have taken on the -*ly* ending, so that there are now double forms in common use: *bright—brightly, deep—deeply, fair—fairly, hard—hardly, high—highly, just—justly, late—lately, low—lowly, quick—quickly, right—rightly, slow—slowly, strong—strongly, thick—thickly, wide—widely, wrong—wrongly.* Observe that all the flat forms have identical adjective forms in common use; and *lowly* (an -*ly* form) serves equally well as an adjective or as an adverb, but with somewhat modified meaning.[1]

The choice between the two forms is not a matter of correct and incorrect, but often of meaning or style. Compare *He worked hard* with *He hardly worked; He threw the ball high* with *He was highly esteemed; He has come late* with *He has come lately; He turned right* with *He turned rightly* ('properly'); *Drive slow* with *Proceed slowly.* Several of the flat adverbs do not immediately precede the verbs they qualify. We can say *He walked out slow* or *He slowly walked out*, but not *He slow walked out.* Often the flat adverbs belong to a more familiar style than the ones ending in -*ly*. Sometimes the shorter form seems to convey a more forceful meaning than

---

[1] A few flat adverbs have identical adjective forms, but do not have the -*ly* adverb forms; e.g., *fast, ill,* and *long.* Observe their use in the following: *One behaves ill* (not *illy*, though sometimes heard in substandard English). *It rained all night long* (not *longly*). *We must move fast* (not *fastly*). Except in their transitional use, *first* and *last* are preferred to *firstly* and *lastly,* as in *You go first* (not *firstly*), *and I shall come last* (not *lastly*).

the -*ly* adverb. Our local road signs may request us to *drive slow* or to *drive slowly*. Both according to the history of the forms may be regarded as correct. The shorter form is often felt to be more commanding.

Certain adverbs existed in Old English without distinctive ending and mostly without corresponding adjectives; as, *far, forth, nigh, here, hither, in, out, there, thither, thus, too, up, well, where, whither*, and others. Since these are primary adverbs, the addition of the -*ly* is not permitted: *far* (not *farly*); *forth* (not *forthly*); *much* (not *muchly*); *nigh* (not *nighly*); *thus* (not *thusly*); *too* (not *tooly*).

A few adverbs like *maybe* and *willy-nilly* are survivals of entire clauses or sentences. The adverb *maybe* is elliptical for *it may be*. Hence *Maybe you are right* is equivalent to *It may be that you are right*. *Willy-nilly* is a corruption of *will he, or will he not* (or *will ye, or will ye not*). In earlier English, it was a subjunctive expression of doubt, and meant *whether he will or will not*. It is now archaic.

Adverbs Classified as to Meaning

When classified as to meaning, most adverbs can be put into the categories of **time, place, manner, degree,** and **cause.** In addition to these major classes, there are the so-called modal adverbs which express **negation, affirmation, assertion, probability, doubt,** etc. Adverbs which do not modify and which do not convey any of these meanings may be **independent, introductory,** or **functional (expletive).**

Adverbs of time may express present time (*now, immediately, instantly, today*); past time (*ago, already, before, lately, then, yesterday*); future time (*afterwards, by and by, hereafter, soon, tomorrow*); duration of time (*always, continuously, ever, incessantly, never, still, while*); or frequency of time (*again and again, daily, frequently, often, periodically, sometimes*). Adverbs of time may denote number and be multiplicatives (*once, twice, thrice*), or ordinals (*first, second*).

Adverbs of time usually modify verbs. They answer the question *When?* or *How long?* or *How many times?*

1. Present time: (a) Do it *now*. (b) Go *immediately*. (c) I am leaving town *today*.

2. Past time: (a) *Then* burst his mighty heart. (b) He came *yesterday*. (c) They have *already* left. (*d*) I have been in this house *before*.

3. Future time: (a) I shall come *soon*. (b) Father plans to arrive *tomorrow*. (c) *Hereafter* prepare your own meals. (d) He will arrive *sometime*.

4. Duration of time: (1) We shall be *continuously* annoyed. (2) Mother is *still* in the hospital. (3) She is *never* at home. (4) He is *always* in trouble.

5. Frequency of time: (1) Our papers are delivered *daily*. (2) She is absent *frequently*. (3) He goes to church *occasionally*. (4) We shall see this sort of thing happening *again and again*.

6. Multiplicative time: (1) I visited him in that house *once*. (2) He came to see me *twice*.

7. Ordinal time: (1) I want to speak to Mother *first*.   (2) John will sing *next*.

The types of time expressed by the adverbs in these illustrations are by no means complete, but they should serve to show the difficulty of pressing all grammatical phenomena into a few names and specific categories.

It is well to remember that the time expressed in the adverb should be in agreement with the time (or tense) of the verb which the adverb modifies. For example, *ago* has past time meaning, and should not be used with present time verbs (i.e., with the present or the present perfect tense). One should say *It was a year ago*, not *It has been a year ago*.

Adverbs of place and **direction** may denote place where (*above, below, near, here, there, where, upstairs*); motion to (*forward, onward, hither, thither, whither*); and motion from (*away, hence, thence, whence*).

Adverbs of place usually modify verbs. They answer the question *Where?* or *In what direction?* or *From what direction?* The following illustrate:

   1. Adverbs of place where: (1) I study *here*. (2) Our guests sleep *upstairs*. (3) I have been *there*. (4) Put it *there*. (5) Leave your books *below*.

   2. Adverbs of direction: (1) Come *hither*. (2) Go *thither*. (3) Go *hence*. (4) Turn *left*. (5) Move *forward*. (6) Move *onward*. (7) Go *away*.

Adverbs of place sometimes have demonstrative meaning:[2] *there, here, hither, thither.*

Adverbs of manner usually go with verbs of action, and they denote the way or manner of the action expressed in the verb. Manner adverbs are the most numerous of adverbs, largely because they can be made from simple and compound adjectives and from the present and past participles by adding the suffix *-ly* (*gladly, happily, carefully, gracefully, nicely, charmingly, learnedly, pointedly, whole-heartedly,* etc.). In addition to the derived adverbs, there are a number of primary and simple adverbs which denote manner: *better, fast, faster, hard, how, ill, loud, so, straight, right, well,* etc.).

Adverbs of manner usually modify verbs. They answer the question *How?* or *In what way?* Note the meaning and the position of the adverbs in the following sentences:

   (1) Do it *thus*. (2) *So* shalt thou live. (3) Listen *carefully*. (4) He guessed *right*. (5) He supported us *whole-heartedly*. (6) She works *fast*. (7) She entertains *charmingly*.

Adverbs of degree denote measure or extent, and answer the question *How much?* or *How little?* or *To what extent?* Many of the degree adverbs are primary or flat adverbs (*far,*

---

[2] Adverbs having demonstrative meaning are derived from Old English pronouns, and express adverbially the meaning conveyed by *this* and *that*. Some of the demonstrative adverbs express place: *there, here, hither, thither;* and some express time: *then, hence, thence;* or manner: *thus.*

just, little, more, very, too, altogether, all, quite, enough, rather, almost), and many of them are made from adjectives denoting measure or extent by the addition of the suffix -*ly* (*completely, barely, scarcely, excessively, partly, nearly*.

Adverbs of degree usually modify adjectives or adverbs:

(1) John is *very* tall. (2) He walks *too* slowly. (3) I was *almost* asleep. (4) This food is good *enough* for kings.

They may also modify prepositions, prepositional phrases, or conjunctions:

(1) He came *just* before noon. (2) I am *partly* at fault. (3) I shall call the role *exactly* at twelve o'clock. (4) The speaker left the stage *just* as we arrived.

Adverbs of degree sometimes modify verbs, especially compound verb forms which contain a present or a past participle:

(1) He succeeded *completely*. (2) Rejoice *greatly*. (3) He was *highly* elated. (4) They are *somewhat* subdued. (5) The place was *completely* deserted. (6) I was *rather* disappointed in the program.

A few simple adverbs may be employed to express **cause or reason**: *consequently, hence, therefore, then, wherefore, why*. They usually modify verbs, but they may qualify clauses or entire sentences. They may or may not be interrogative adverbs:

(1) *Consequently* I am leaving. (2) *Why* did he go? (3) *Wherefore* didst thou doubt? (4) *Therefore* I am referring this case to you.

Modal adverbs may express affirmation or assertion (*yes, indeed, certainly, surely, truly, undoubtedly*), negation (*nay, no, not, never, nowise*), or doubt and probability (*perhaps, perchance, maybe, possibly*). These adverbs may modify verbs, clauses, or sentences:

1. Affirmation and assertion: (1) *Indeed*, I shall go. (2) I am *certainly* interested in the case. (3) *Yes*, I shall go.

2. Negation: (1) Are you coming with me? *No.* (2) I shall *never* go. (3) He is *not* at fault.

3. Probability and doubt: (1) *Perhaps* you are wrong. (2) *Maybe* I shall see you tomorrow.

Complex Adverbs

When classified as to their function, adverbs are said to be **simple** or **complex.** The simple adverbs include all primary and derivative adverbs whose sole function is to limit, describe, or qualify verbs, adjectives, adverbs, or adverb-equivalents. The **complex adverbs** are dual in their nature: they modify and also perform some other function in the sentence. If they modify and join clauses or sentences, they are called **conjunctive adverbs.** If they modify and introduce an exclamation, they are sometimes called **exclamatory adverbs.** If they modify and interrogate, they are called **interrogative adverbs.** Adverbs which have lost their power to qualify are called **independent, introductory, or functional adverbs.** In this class are the expletives and a number of words which once had full adverb meaning and function, but now serve only as introductory particles.

Uses of the Complex Adverbs

The **conjunctive adverb** is an adverb which performs a double function: it serves both as an adverb and as a conjunction. Those adverbs that coördinate sentence units are called **transitional** (or **illative**); and those that subordinate clauses are called **relative adverbs.**

The transitional (or illative) adverbs are mainly used to join clauses, sometimes full sentences.[3] They introduce an inference (sequence, consequence, or result) based on the thought presented in a preceding clause of equal rank. The following are the most common of the transitional adverbs: *accordingly, also, consequently, furthermore, hence, however,*

---

[3] The transitional adverbs may introduce and join closely related sentence thoughts, as in **Yet,** *I am not at fault;* **Next,** *let us examine the material we have.*

likewise, moreover, nevertheless, next, notwithstanding, now, only, so, then, therefore, thereupon, still, whereas, wherefore, whereupon, yet. Also, adverb phrases are in common use as transitional elements; e.g., *on the contrary, in conclusion, in brief, inasmuch as, on the other hand.*

Observe the transitional (illative, conjunctive) nature of the italicized words in the following:

(1) Rash counsel is unprofitable to him that gives it; *therefore*, be ready to hear, careful to contrive, but slow to speak.
(2) Charity and pride have different aims; *yet* both feed the poor. (3) I do not approve your plan; *however*, I shall not oppose it.

Relative adverbs are more complex in their function than the other types of adverbs: they modify verbs, adjectives, and adverbs; and in addition they relate, subordinate, and join clauses. They may be adverbs of time, place, manner, degree, cause, means, etc.; and they may be used to introduce and join adjective or adverb clauses to other clauses.

In form the relative adverb may be **simple** (*as, after, before, ere, than, that, the, since, until, when, where, whither*) or **compound** (*whenever, whereby, wherever, whithersoever*). The compound forms are usually more indefinite in meaning than the simple ones. Observe their use in the following:

(1) I shall go *when* the bell rings. (2) I shall go *whenever* you are ready. (3) I will go *where* you go. (4) I will go *whithersoever* you lead.

The relative adverb may introduce an adverb clause expressing time, place, manner, or degree; or it may introduce an adjective clause that modifies a noun denoting time, place, manner, cause, reason, means, etc.

A relative adverb that introduces an adjective clause may be converted into a prepositional phrase containing a relative pronoun. The antecedent of the relative pronoun will be the substantive in the main clause that the entire adjective clause modifies. In *The castle where I was born lies in ruins*, *where* is the relative adverb introducing an adjective clause modifying *castle*. In this sentence *where* can be converted into *in which* without altering the sense of the sentence, and the converted form may aid in the analysis of the sentence, the adjective function being sometimes more easily recognized with the *which* or *that* clause than with the *where* clause.

If used to introduce an adverb clause, the relative adverb may be converted into two prepositional phrases, one containing a relative pronoun, the other the antecedent of the relative pronoun. In *I shall go when the bell rings*, *when* is the relative adverb in the adverb clause *when the bell rings*. In this sentence *when* may be converted into two prepositional phrases, and the sentence will then read *I shall go **at that time at which** the bell rings*. The expansion of *when* does not change the meaning of the sentence, though the shorter communication is simpler, more natural, and often more forceful. If the relative adverb correlates with an adverb in another clause, each adverb may be converted into a prepositional phrase, but the relative adverb always converts into the phrase containing the relative pronoun.

The following sentences contain relative adverbs, some of which introduce adjective clauses; others introduce adverb clauses:[4]

1. Time: (1) Oats are ripe *when* the straws turn yellow. (2) *Whenever* a sultan visits his friends, he is carried on four men's shoulders. (3) Christmas is the time *when* we exchange gifts.

2. Place: (1) *Where* law ends, tyranny begins. (2) There is home *where* my thoughts are sent. (3) I shall go *wherever* you go.

3. Manner: (1) I speak *as* I am taught. (2) He works *as if* (or *as though*) he enjoyed working. (3) Live with men *as* you live with God.

---

[4] For other illustrations and a fuller analysis of clauses containing relative adverbs, see Part Two, Adjective Clauses, pp. 349–396, and Adverb Clauses, pp. 390–420.

4. Degree: (1) It is as old *as* the hills. (2) So faintly you came tapping *that* I scarce was sure I heard you. (3) *The* longer she stands, the shorter she grows. (4) He is older *than* his cousin.

5. Cause: You know the reason *why* I am leaving.

6. Means: You take my life in taking the means *whereby* I live.

Correlative adverbs are pairs of adverbs that are regularly used together to correlate and join clauses: *as . . . as, so . . . as, the . . . the, then . . . when, there . . . where, so . . . that.* Of such correlatives one in each pair is a **relative adverb** in the subordinate clause, and the other is a simple adverb with demonstrative meaning in the principal clause. Each pair of the correlatives can be expanded into prepositional phrases, one of which will contain a relative pronoun, and the other its antecedent. *Then . . . when* may be converted into *at the time (moment, day, hour) at which;* and *there . . . where* is the equivalent of *at (or in) that place (town, spot, house) in (or at) which.* The correlatives *as . . . as* and *so . . . as* may express a manner or degree correlation; and hence they may expand to mean *in the manner in which* or *to the degree at which.*[5]

The order of clauses expressing time, place, and manner relations joined by correlative adverbs may vary. Observe that many sonnets, particularly Shakespeare's, are of the *when . . . then* type:

> **When** I consider everything that grows
> Holds in perfection but a little moment,
> . . . .
> **Then** the conceit of this inconstant stay
> Sets you most rich in youth before my sight.

The order of the degree clauses is more fixed by usage; and in sentences containing the *the . . . the* clauses, the subordi-

---

[5] For further discussion and analysis of sentences containing correlative adverbs, see Conjunctions, pp. 187–193. Also see Part Two, Adverb Clauses, pp. 390–420.

nate clause always comes first. In the *as . . . as* clauses, the main clause normally comes first. *So . . . as* and *so . . . that* are not limited in their use to correlating degree clauses, being sometimes used to express manner relations; and hence the order of the clauses they join is not so standardized; but *so* in each of these pairs always introduces or belongs in the principal clause, and *as* and *that* belong in the subordinate clauses. In ordinary speech the degree (subordinate) clause generally comes second.

Interrogative adverbs are simple adverbs performing a dual function: They modify verbs, adjectives, and adverbs, and introduce direct and indirect questions. *When, where, why, how, whence,* and *whither* are the most common interrogative adverbs used to inquire concerning time, place, manner, cause, and degree.

	Direct Questions	*Indirect Questions*
Time:	*When* does he go?	I wonder *when* he is going.
Place:	*Where* are you?	He asked *where* I was.
Manner:	*How* will they accomplish this?	I should like to know *how* they will accomplish this.
Reason:	*Why* is he so downcast?	He will not tell me *why* he is so downcast.
Degree:	*How* old are you?	I must not tell *how* old I am.
	How fast does the train go?	We do not know *how* fast the train goes.

Exclamatory adverbs, like the interrogatives, have a dual nature: They are indefinite adverbs of degree used in exclamatory expressions:

(1) *How* beautifully that bird sings! (2) *How* rich, *how* poor, *how* abject, *how* august, *how* wonderful is man!

Independent and functional adverbs are adverbs which through long use have lost their qualifying force, and have become independent or mere functional words. These are broadly classified as **independent** (or **introductory**) **adverbs or as functional** (or **expletive**) expressions.

1. Adverbs may be independent, and stand grammatically alone, not modifying any particular word, phrase, or clause. Sometimes they suggest vague modal or illative relation or have the force of weakened interjections: *Well, I wonder what he means.* *Well, my boy, what's the news?* *Now, that is strange!* *I am to do, then, as I please with the funds?* *Well, now,* and *then* have here lost not only their primary meaning indicating time or manner, but they have also lost their force as qualifiers. This use is common in informal speech, especially in direct discourse of the substandard level. Usually such an adverb can be dropped from the sentence without affecting it in any way whatever; and, because it has no real function in emphasizing, clarifying, or modifying the thought expressed, it should be employed with caution.

2. An adverb or an adverb phrase or a symbol representing an adverb may be used to introduce an appositive or a list of items or a series of illustrations: *namely, as, expressly, especially, specifically, notably, to wit, in other words, for example (e.g.), videlicet (viz.), that is (i.e.),* etc. In *Two things show the wisdom of a nation; namely, good laws and a prudent management of them, namely* is an expletive (a mere functional) adverb.

3. The expletive *there* is an adverb employed as a mere warning that the normal order of the subject and predicate is to be reversed: *There were twenty persons there (in the room).* Observe that the first *there* is the expletive; the second *there* is a pure adverb denoting place.

4. The independent adverb may convey an entire communication, especially one of affirmation or negation (*yes, no, certainly, never,* etc.): (1) *Are you moving to California?* *No* (or *Yes*). (2) *Will you tell me exactly what happened?* *Certainly.* In these illustrations, *no, yes,* and *certainly,* convey full sentence thoughts. They are sometimes called pro-sentence adverbs.

Nouns, phrases, and clauses function as adverbs. Almost all of the meanings and the relationships that the simple adverbs can express can also be expressed by nouns used adverbially (adverbial objectives), by phrases (prepositional and verbal), and by clauses.[6]

Some phrases and clauses by compounding or by ellipsis have become simple adverbs; e.g., *today* (*to day*),[7] *upstairs* (*up the stairs*), *howbeit* (*however that may be*), *maybe* (*it may be*), *albeit* (M.E. *al be it*, although it be).

Comparison of Adverbs

Comparison is the only inflectional modification that adverbs have, and many do not have that Most of the primary adverbs indicating time, place, cause, assertion, affirmation, negation, and illation are not compared; e.g., *also, as, first, never, now, only, than, that, then, there, thence, thither, thus, too, twice, so, still, very, where, whence, while, why, yes,* and many others. The exceptions to this rule are a few adverbs expressing time and position, which may inflect to show degrees of nearness or of remoteness of time or place: *early, far, frequently, late, nearly, often, rarely, seldom, soon.*

Adverbs, like adjectives, have three degrees of comparison: the **positive,** the **comparative,** and the **superlative.** The formation and uses of these degrees are similar to those of adjectives. Most flat adverbs indicating quality, particularly those of manner, are compared regularly by adding to the positive form the suffixes *-er* (or *-r*) for the comparative and *-est* (or *-st*) for the superlative, or by employing the function words *more* and *most* or *less* and *least.* A few adverbs corresponding to adjectives having irregular comparison are defective in their comparison, or have acquired comparative and superlative forms based on other positive forms.

---

[6] For fuller treatment and an analysis of nouns, phrases, and clauses used adverbially, see Part Two, Adverbial Objectives, pp. 27–281; Prepositional Phrase, pp. 222–228; Clauses, pp. 390–420.

[7] *Today, tomorrow,* and *yesterday* have acceptable noun functions, and may inflect, like nouns for case and number: *I have today's report. Tomorrow's sun may never rise. O for yesterdays to come!*

1. Most adverbs of one syllable and a few two syllable adverbs, especially those having forms of corresponding adjectives, are compared by adding *-er* (or *-r*) and *-est* (or *-st*) to the positive: *cheap, cheaper, cheapest; early, earlier, earliest; fast, faster, fastest; hard, harder, hardest; late, later, latest.*

2. Most adverbs ending in *-ly* and other adverbs of two syllables or more are compared with the function words *more* and *most: beautifully, more beautifully, most beautifully; clearly, more clearly, most clearly; seldom, more seldom, most seldom.*

3. Some adverbs have two positive forms, one with and one without the *-ly* suffix. The two forms may or may not have identical meaning. The positives without the *-ly* usually form comparatives and superlatives with the suffixes *-er* and *-est;* and the ones with the *-ly* ending, with the adverb modifiers *more* and *most.* Observe the two patterns in the following:

Positive	*Comparative*	*Superlative*
cheap	cheaper	cheapest
cheaply	more cheaply	most cheaply
high	higher	highest
highly	more highly	most highly
loud	louder	loudest
loudly	more loudly	most loudly

Other adverbs like these are *deep-deeply, fair-fairly, low-lowly, near-nearly, quick-quickly, right-rightly, wide-widely, wrong-wrongly.*

4. Irregular comparison of adverbs corresponds quite closely to the phases of irregular comparison of adjectives. The student would do well to reëxamine irregular adjective comparison (p. 91), and observe wherein forms are identical and wherein they are different. The following are the most common of the adverbs having irregular comparison:

Positive	Comparative	Superlative
badly, ill	worse	worst
far	farther	farthest
forth	further	furthest
	(furthermore)	
late	later	latest, last
little	less	least
much	more	most
nigh, near	nigher, nearer	nighest, nearest, next
(rathe)	rather	(rathest, ratherest)
well	better	best

Of these, some are more irregular than others. Neither *badly* nor *ill* is related in origin to *worse* and *worst*. *Ill* is now seldom used as an adverb except in literary language, being generally replaced by *badly*.

In Middle English *far* had regular comparison: *fer, ferrer, ferrest*. The *th* is intrusive; its origin is probably based on the *th* in *further, furthest*, which has the *th* in the positive *forth*.

Furthermore, though a double comparative in form, does not now denote comparative meaning. Observe that it is never followed by *than*.

Last, a contraction of *la(te)st*, usually denotes position, while *latest* denotes time. *Last* may function either as an adjective or as an adverb; but *latest* is largely restricted to the adjective use.

Near is an old comparative, a short form of the Old English *nēahra*, nigher. The old superlative form *nehst* is now spelled *next*. The word *near* is therefore a comparative form which now functions as a positive. It has acquired the new comparative *nearer* and the new superlative *nearest*.

Rather is in common use as a comparative, though *rathe*, its positive, and *rathest* (*ratherest*), its superlative, are now obsolete. *Rather* when used for *somewhat* denotes relational meaning. Observe the two uses of *rather* in the following:

Comparative Meaning: (1) I would *rather* go than stay. (2) I had *rather* be a dog and bay the moon than such a Roman.

Relational Meaning: (1) I was *rather* tired last night. (2) I know her *rather* well. (3) I am *rather* glad that your father did not come.

The very common use of *rather* to mean *somewhat* or *in some degree* suggests that it may be on its way out as a true comparative. *Rather* following *or* is used in still a different sense. *Or rather* is a mere expletive (introductory conjunction) in *This is my house, or rather my place of abode.*

Well now replaces the lost positive of the adverb *better*, *best*. It should not be confused with the adjective positive *good*, which cannot function as an adverb.

Seven

Prepositions

A **preposition** is a particle (word or a word-equivalent) used with a noun or pronoun (and usually placed before it) to form a phrase, which phrase usually performs the function of an adjective or an adverb: *a letter **from** home, riding **on** a horse, anxious **about** her son, go farther **into** the stream.*

While prepositions are particles (subordinate, uninflected elements), they have distinct character, suggesting position (*at, above, on, in*), direction (*to, toward*), time (*at, during*), limit of motion (*to, into*), source (*from, of*), etc. In general, a preposition shows relation between one element of a sentence and another called its **object.**

The **object** of the preposition is the principal term in the prepositional phrase. The phrase may contain only the preposition and its object, or it may contain modifiers of either or both. In *I came **from** town,* the prepositional phrase contains only the preposition *from* and its object, the noun *town.* In *His chair was always **in** the warmest nook,* there are two modifiers of the object of the preposition, the article *the* and the descriptive adjective *warmest.* In *He arrived **just before** Christmas,* the adverb *just* restricts the preposition *before.* In *He works **only at** night, only* modifies the entire prepositional phrase.

The **object** of the preposition is normally in the objective case: *With **whom** are you living? I came with **him**; This is* *the woman of **whom** you spoke.* Occasionally the possessive form of the noun or pronoun is used as the object of a preposition. This occurs when the **double genitive (possessive)** meaning is conveyed: *These pictures **of his** are to be sold at auction.* The meaning here is that the pictures possessed (owned) by some person are to be sold at auction, not pictures (likenesses) of the person referred to here, as would be indicated if *of him* were substituted for *of his.*

The **object** of a preposition may be any grammatical unit substituting for a noun. In *I shall stay till **after Christmas,*** the prepositional phrase *after Christmas* may be treated as the object of the preposition *till.* The infinitive phrase is often used as the object of a preposition, as in *I am about **to leave you,*** where *to leave you* is the object of *about.* The gerund or the gerund phrase may also be the object of a preposition: *He is interested in my **being invited**; He wanted his wife to be submissive without **seeming so.***

Participles and adjectives sometimes substitute for nouns, and become the objects of prepositions: *Only friends of the **deceased** were there; Be kind to the **poor** and **helpless.***

An adverb substituting for a noun and a modifying demonstrative adjective may be the object of a preposition: *It is a mile from **here** (i.e., this place) to your house; You must be on duty from **now** (i.e., this time) till noon.*

A noun clause may be the object of a preposition: *The dispute about **who should be invited** was very unpleasant; My going there will depend upon **whether or not I can be released from duty.***

DERIVATION AND FORM

Simple Prepositions

The oldest and the most frequently used prepositions in English are those which are the simplest in form, many of them being monosyllabic: *after, at, but, by, down, ere, for, in of, off, on, over, since, through, to, till, under, with.*[1] All of these were once adverbs which could be prefixed to verbs, and therefore were called **prepositions** (= before position). *At, by, down, for, in, of, on, over, through, under, up,* and *with* are prepositions when they govern nouns or pronouns, but they are adverbs when they merely modify verbs and do not show relationship between words.

a. In the following sentences the italicized words are prepositions:

> (1) I live *by* the mill. (2) He came *down* the hill. (3) The thief was *in* my room. (4) We walked *through* the woods.

But the same words are adverbs in the following sentences:

> (1) I shall come *by* early tomorrow. (2) He came *down* after supper. (3) The thief came *in* after I left the house. (4) We must carry this project *through.*

b. *After, but, for, since,* and *till* are prepositions when they govern nouns or noun-equivalents:

> (1) They came *after* sunset. (2) There was no one *but* the janitor to assist us. (3) My brother has not been here *since* Christmas. (4) You must work *till* noon.

They are pure conjunctions or relative (conjunctive) adverbs when they introduce and join clauses:

> (1) They came *after* (= relative adverb) the sun had set. (2) There were no volunteers to help, *but* (= pure coördinating conjunction) the janitor assisted us. (3) I insist upon doing this, *for* (= pure subordinating conjunction) you need my help. (4) My brother has not been here *since* (= relative adverb) he left Christmas Eve. (5) You must work *till* (= relative adverb) I return.

c. If the preposition introducing an adjective phrase loses its object, or its object is omitted to avoid verbal repetition,

---

[1] For some statistics on the nine most used prepositions in standard English, see Charles C. Fries, *American English Grammar*, pp. 110–114.

the preposition may function as an adjective in the appositive position:

(1) Prepare for the life *beyond* [this life]. (2) I have a stateroom on the deck *below* [this deck]. (3) The apartment *above* [this one] is for rent. (4) The sentences *above* [these] contain adjectives. (5) The day *after* [the day mentioned] was my birthday.

Compound Prepositions

Prepositions have been formed from time to time by combining words into compounds to show relations which the simple (or primary) prepositions could not express. The **compound prepositions** represent the middle stage in the development of prepositions, many of them being of Old and Middle English origin. They have been formed and are still being formed by various combinations.

a. Sometimes a preposition attaches itself to another preposition or to an adverb to show a relation not adequately conveyed by either when used alone or separately. *Into* is a compound of *in* and *to; upon* is from *up* and *on; within* is from *with* and *in;* but these words in their compound forms are not synonymous with *in to, up on,* and *with in.* Compare the two forms in the following sentences:

1. a. He came *in to* see us.
   b. He came *into* the station.
2. a. Mother came *up on* the fast train.
   b. We came *upon* them suddenly.
3. a. I have no tools to work *with in* this house.
   b. I shall be there *within* an hour.

This compounding began in Old English with the joining of some of our oldest prepositions: *But* (O.E. *be-ūtan*) represents a contraction of *be* (by) and *ūtan* (out); and *about* (from O.E. *a-be-ūt-*) is formed by joining two English prepositions with an adverb: *a* (on) *be* (by) -*ūt* (out).

b. Primary prepositions are sometimes compounded with nouns, adjectives, and adverbs to convey relations between words that were once expressed by inflectional forms of nouns or pronouns. Many of these compounds are very old and are so familiar that the component parts of the words are not easily recognized, most of them being of Old or Middle English origin. A number of these have the prefix *a-* (on, in) and *be-*(by): *aboard, across, along, amid, amidst, among, amongst, around, below, before, behind, beside, besides, between, betwixt, beyond.* The adverb *out* (O.E. *ūt*) is sometimes attached to a noun or to a preposition as a prefix or as a suffix to form compound prepositions: *outside, without, throughout.*

In expressions like *o'clock* (*of the clock*) and *a-hunting* ("*A-hunting we will go*"), the prepositions *of* and *on* (O.E. *an*) contracted to *o'* and *a-*, and in the course of time attached themselves to the substantives they once governed, though they still retain some of their prepositional meaning.

c. A number of our more recently acquired prepositions are derived from verbs, usually from the present or past participial forms of verbs. Many of these retain much of their original verbal meaning. Examples are *barring, concerning, considering, during, excepting, including, notwithstanding, pending, regarding, respecting, saving, touching, except, past,* and *save.*[2]

Some of these may also function as conjunctions having subordinating or transitional force. *Notwithstanding* (a compound of the adverb *not* and the verbal *withstanding*) is a true preposition when it means *in spite of;* it is a subordinating conjunction when it means *although;* and it is a transitional (conjunctive) adverb when it means *nevertheless, yet,* or *however.*

Verbals and other parts of speech functioning as prepositions are sometimes called **secondary prepositions.** Their chief function in the language is not that of showing relation between grammatical units.

---

[2] *Save* (Lat. *salvus*, whole, uninjured; hence *safe.* M.E. and O. Fr. *sauf*, except) is now used chiefly in poetry. The English form *save* is probably from the imperative form of the verb.

Phrasal Prepositions

A **phrasal preposition** consists of two or more words written separately but used as a single unit to show relation between a noun or a noun-equivalent and some other sentence element. Phrasal prepositions may be formed by combining prepositions with other parts of speech (adjectives, adverbs, conjunctions, verbs, etc.): *according to, along with, as for, as to, because of, instead of, out of, regardless of,* etc. The most common of the phrasal prepositions are the fossilized prepositional phrases of abstract meaning followed by prepositions, such as *by virtue of, by means of, in accordance with, in addition to, in front of, in regard to, in spite of, out of regard for,* and *with reference to.* Sometimes by ellipsis (the omission of a word of obvious meaning), two prepositions are brought together and have the value of one; as, *from over the hill* (from a place over the hill), *from under the porch* (from a place under the porch).[3]

Sometimes it is difficult to determine whether an expression is one prepositional phrase made up of a phrasal preposition and its object, or is two prepositional phrases, the second phrase modifying the object of the first preposition; and often the differentiation is not an important one. Usually the prepositional meaning can be tested by substituting a simple or compound preposition for the phrasal one. In such expressions as *beyond the reach of art, in the course of human events, in the middle of the stream, at the point of death,* and *at the top of the hill,* the words *reach, course, middle, point,* and *top* have the function and meaning of nouns. The phrases that follow them may be regarded as adjective phrases.

Meanings and Uses of Prepositions

In an analytic language, such as Modern English, the inflectional markings are usually reduced to a minimum, and

---

[3] It sometimes seems more logical to regard the first preposition in phrases like these as governing (having for its object) a prepositional phrase. See Object of Preposition, p. 175.

the meanings and relations of words to each other depend largely upon relational words (prepositions, relative adverbs, conjunctions) to indicate not only most of the meanings once conveyed by case forms but also all the various new relations that have developed as English has grown out of a dialect into the very rich and flexible language that it now is. Our prepositions have contributed more to this richness and flexibility than any other single part of speech. All of our complex thoughts and most of our simplest communications are conveyed with the aid of prepositions. One needs only to attempt to write a short letter or a theme or even a telegram without using prepositions to discover the importance of the preposition in the communication of ideas. The exactness of the expression of thought may depend entirely upon the choice of prepositions and upon the positions they are given in sentences. No one speaks or writes accurately or effectively who is indifferent to the meanings of prepositions and the various relationships they express. Prepositions must not be tossed about carelessly.

Only a few of the various and multitudinous meanings and relations that prepositions are capable of conveying can be classified and tabled in a text of this sort, and a long and extended listing of the usual and unusual meanings of prepositions would be of little value. The dictionary is the best authority on the meanings and uses of words. The relations mentioned below and the examples given may suggest a pattern for classifying meanings not listed here. The student should study the italicized phrases in the examples, and note the use and meaning of each preposition. Observe that the same preposition may convey several different meanings:

Accompaniment: May I go *with you?*

Agency: The books were sold *by John.*

Association: Self-denial is a kind of holy association *with God.* —Pope.

Addition: Put the lettuce *with the tomatoes,* and make a salad.

Affirmation: *By all means,* seize this opportunity.

Apposition: The state *of New York* is called the Empire State.

Cause or **reason:** *Because of the accident,* we were late.

Comparison: Truth, *like gold,* shines brighter by collision.

Concession: *Even with money and friends,* he is not popular.

Condition: *Only on my terms* will I accept your offer.

Degree: I am older than you *by ten years.*

Description: The girl *with blue eyes* won the prize.

Direction: Go *toward the gate.*

Design: Youth is the proper time *for love.*

Instrument: Spread your butter *with this knife.*

Manner: He walks *with a limp.*

Material: My house is made *of brick.*

Means: He travels *by plane.*

Measure: We must sell the material *by the yard.*

Objective Genitive: The loss *of honor* is the loss *of life.*

Partition: Half *of the world* may be wrong.

Place: I am staying *at the Statler Hotel.*

Possession: Swords *of Caesars,* they are less than rust.

Purpose: I am giving this lecture *for your benefit.*

Quality: Hamlet called Claudius a king *of shreds and patches.*

Respect: These apples are good *for pies.*

Separation: God hath deprived her *of her wisdom.*

Source: The poet gathers fruit *from every tree,* Yea, grapes *from thorns,* and figs *from thistles,* he.—Sir William Watson.

Subjective Genitive: For this is the cry *of a thousand souls* that down to the pit have trod.—Leonard H. Robbins.

Time: Shakespeare was born *in 1564* and died *in 1616.*

Value: I do not set my life *at a pin's fee.*—Shakespeare.

Position of the Preposition

The prescribed and the most common position for the preposition (Lat. *prae,* before, and *positus,* position) is before its object; and since its function is to show relation between two grammatical units, it normally follows one of these units and precedes the other. In actual speech, however, the prepositional phrase does not always follow the word it modifies, nor does the preposition always precede the word it governs. Both should be so placed that the correct meaning is conveyed effectively.

When the preposition governs an interrogative pronoun introducing a direct or an indirect question, the preposition is frequently placed at the end of the clause or sentence:

> (1) What did you do that *for?* (2) Your mother will know what you are up *to.* (3) I wonder what you are thinking *about.*

If we transpose the prepositions in sentences like these to the prescribed positions; i.e., before their objects, we may fail to convey the intended meaning, or we may secure awkwardness, vagueness, and even absurdity. Usage will hardly justify one's choosing any of the following sentence patterns even though the preposition is placed according to the prescribed rule before its object:

> (1) *For* what did you do that? (2) Your mother will know *to* what you are up. (3) I wonder *about* what you are thinking.

If the relative pronoun in a prepositional phrase is understood, the preposition must be placed in a post-position to its implied object:

> (1) This is the man I used to work *for.* (2) These are the persons I have been visiting *with.* (3) This is the sort of machine I am used *to.* (4) I shall be glad to have anything you can do *without.*

When the relative pronoun is *that* or *as*, the preposition must also come in the post-position: and it frequently closes the sentence:

> (1) This is the book that I referred *to.* (2) Is this the man you were speaking *of?* (3) We are such stuff as dreams are made *on.*

When the unexpressed antecedent of a relative pronoun is the object of a preposition and the relative pronoun itself is governed by another preposition, the preposition governing the relative pronoun must be placed in postposition: *I am certainly interested in what you are talking about.* This sentence expanded would read *I am interested in that which (in the subject which) you are talking about.*

Detached Prepositions. The preposition loses its prepositional nature when it has no object (expressed or understood) to govern, and becomes an adverb. In *We shall depend upon you, upon* is a preposition; but, if the object of the preposition becomes the subject of this verb in the passive voice, then *upon* becomes an adverb: *Can you be depended upon?* Similarly, when a relative clause is condensed into an infinitive or participial phrase, the preposition that ended a clause may revert to its earlier function as an adverb and modify the verbal. Such an adverb is usually placed at the end of the verbal phrase, which phrase is often placed at the end of the sentence. The following are examples of such condensation:

(1) This is a good house to live *in*. (2) He is a very hard person to talk *to*. (3) Give me a good pencil to write *with*. (4) Suggest something interesting for me to be thinking *about*. (5) I know the man referred *to*. (6) I certainly have nothing to be ashamed *of*. (7) The children showed some interest in every subject spoken *of*.

It is important to observe here that sentences such as these end in adverbs, not true prepositions. Since most of the primary prepositions were adverbs before they were prepositions, the shift back to the adverb function is an easy one to make. These are sometimes called **preposition-adverbs.**

With a certain type of verbs, especially intransitive verbs, which can take on transitive meaning with the aid of a preposition-adverb, the preposition is sometimes placed immediately after its object instead of immediately before it, as in *Think this matter over before you write me,* and in *You must read the book* **through** *before condemning it.*   In these sentences *over* and *through* have the stress (accent) and force of adverbs; but they may be said also to show relation between the nouns they follow and the verbs they modify.

Even though one may cite numerous examples of good idiomatic English sentences that end in prepositions, it is important for one learning English to be constantly aware of the fact that this is the exception rather than the rule for the position of the preposition.   The normal place for the preposition is before the word it governs; and it should be placed in this position, unless a writer or speaker has good reason for transposing it.   In reality, only a very small percentage of the prepositions we use in our standard level of English are placed in postposition; and there are fewer in written than in spoken English.   To realize this, one need only count the number of prepositions in *pre-position* and those in *post-position* of any article, story, or poem by a reputable writer.

Functions of Prepositional Phrases

Since the primary function of the preposition is to show relation between grammatical units, the phrase that it introduces is normally a modifier substituting for either an adjective or an adverb; and it is, therefore, capable of performing most, if not all, of the functions belonging to the adverb and the adjective.   When a prepositional phrase has any other function than that of the adverb or adjective, its use may be regarded as exceptional or special.   (For a fuller treatment of the functions of the prepositional phrase, see Lesson II in Part Two.)

Eight

Conjunctions

A **conjunction** (from Lat. *con*, together, and *jungere*, to join) is a word or a word-equivalent used to join words, phrases, or clauses; and in continuous discourse, the conjunction may be employed to join sentences or even paragraphs.

Conjunctions do not "govern," as prepositions do. Contrast *John and I sang* (where *and* is a conjunction) with *John sang with me* (where *with* is a preposition). *And* merely connects *John* and *I;* whereas *with* may be said to govern *me*, throwing the pronoun into the objective case. Again, contrast *He does this for me* (where *for* is a preposition) with *He does this, for he believes it to be right* (where *for* is a conjunction). In the former sentence *for* governs *me*, making it objective; whereas in the latter sentence *for* introduces (while it does not govern) an entire statement, and leaves the pronoun *he*, which follows it, in the nominative case.

Pure conjunctions do not "modify," as adverbs do. Contrast *I came, for I was called* (where *for* is a conjunction) with *Why did you come?* (where *why* is an interrogative adverb). Here again, *for* has no modifying force (though the clause as a whole does modify *came*), whereas *why* (meaning *for what reason*) modifies the verb *did come*.

A word which modifies and connects (or relates) grammatical units or thoughts cannot be called a **full** (or **pure**) **conjunction**, but may be called a **secondary** (or a **half**) **conjunction**. The **conjunctive adverbs** (e.g., relative, illative, and transitional adverbs) are **secondary conjunctions.** They join and modify or relate ideas. In *I came when I was called,* the two clauses *I came* and *I was called* are joined by *when,* a relative adverb, which can be expanded into two prepositional phrases (*at the time* and *at which*), one modifying the verb *came* and the other modifying *was called.*

Sometimes the same word may be used as a preposition, as an adverb, as a full conjunction, or as a secondary (or half) conjunction, the differentiation in function depending upon the particular use the word has in a given sentence. Observe the use of *since* in each of the following:

Preposition: We have had no news *since* Sunday.

Adverb: John was in town during the holidays, but no one has seen him *since.*

Full (or *Pure*) *Conjunction: Since* you will not listen, I will say no more.

Secondary (or *Half*) *Conjunction:* I have not seen your brother *since* he moved into town.

Origin and Form of Conjunctions. Originally all conjunctions were other parts of speech, the conjunction being the most recent addition to the parts of speech now studied in our language classes. Most of our conjunctions came from prepositions, which they most resemble in function and meaning. *And, but, for, before,* and *after* were prepositions before they were conjunctions, and all of these with the exception of *and* are prepositions in good standing in present-day speech.

A few conjunctions, however, are derived from other parts of speech, such as verbs (*provided, supposing*), adverbs (*so, than, then, though, yet*), nouns (*while* from the O.E. noun *hwīl,* time), pronouns (*whether* from the O.E. interrogative pronoun *hwæðer,* which of two), adjectives (*both, either,* and the demonstratives *the* and *that*). A few conjunctions are made up from other parts of speech by contractions (*as* is a contraction of *also,* and *or* of *other*), or by compounding the words in a phrase or a sentence, such as *because* (from *by* + *cause*) and *albeit* from an entire clause (*al* + *be* + *it,* although it be).

Classes of Conjunctions

Conjunctions may be classified according to their form as simple, compound, and phrasal; or according to their function as coördinating and subordinating; or in various ways according to the meanings that they are capable of denoting, such as accumulation, affirmation, alternation, cause, concession, condition, degree, manner, purpose, place, result, time, etc.

The simple conjunctions are single words used to join grammatical units. Our oldest conjunctions are in the main the shortest and simplest ones (*and, if, but, or, though, lest*), because most of these are derived from simple (or primary) prepositions.

The compound conjunctions have been formed by combining two or more words into compounds. A few of the compound conjunctions are of Old English origin, though most of them are modern formations. *Because, although, notwithstanding, unless,* and *nevertheless* are compound conjunctions because they have been formed by combining two or more words. Consult the dictionary for the origin and primary meaning of these words.

The phrasal conjunctions are those connectives that are made up of two or more separate words, each group of words serving as a single grammatical unit to join words or groups of words. *As if, as though, in case that, inasmuch as, in order that, provided that, supposing that,* and *so that* are phrasal conjunctions in common use in standard and literary English.

A coördinating conjunction connects words, phrases, clauses, or sentences of equal rank and usually of the same order. In *Mary and Jane enjoyed the game,* the coördinating conjunction *and* joins two substantives. In *Let us go to the mountains or to the seashore,* the connective *or* joins two prepositional phrases. In *I go, but I shall return,* the conjunction *but* joins two like (coördinate) clauses.

The elements joined by the coördinating conjunction need

not, however, be of the same order. In *He came swiftly and with buoyant steps*, the conjunction *and* joins a simple adverb and an adverbial prepositional phrase.

Coördinate grammatical units may be joined by **full (or pure) conjunctions**, such as *and, or, nor, but;* or they may be joined by conjunctive (transitional, illative) adverbs, such as *however, nevertheless, notwithstanding*, or by adverbial phrases having illative meaning, such as *as well as, in other words, on the other hand*.

A **subordinating conjunction** always joins clauses of unequal rank; that is, a principal clause with a subordinate clause. In *He will win if he keeps his courage, He will win* is the principal clause (sometimes called the **independent, or main clause**); and *if he keeps his courage* is a subordinate (sometimes called **dependent**) **clause** of condition, performing the function of an adverb, and modifying *win*. The conjunction *if* does not modify any word, but it does subordinate the clause it introduces to the clause it follows. In most school grammars, the subordinating conjunctions include the **pure (or full) conjunctions**: *if, unless, because, since, for,*[1] *as, that, in order that, though, although, but that;* and with somewhat extended meaning they are made to include relative adverbs, the **secondary (or half) conjunctions**, which modify, introduce, and subordinate clauses: *after, when, where, while, as, than, that*, etc.

Correlative conjunctions are like other conjunctions except that they are used in pairs, the first of the group introducing and emphasizing the relation of the elements to be joined by

---

[1] *For* is a coördinating conjunction when it joins clauses of equal rank, as in *For ye suffer fools gladly, seeing ye yourselves are wise.*—Bible. In earlier English *for* was in common use as a coördinating conjunction, and there are many examples of this use in the Bible and other texts belonging to the Renaissance period. Consider the following, both of which are taken from the Bible: (1) *For if I have boasted anything to him of you, I am not ashamed.* (2) *Speak, Lord, for thy servant heareth.* In present-day English *for* is chiefly employed to introduce a subordinate clause of reason or cause. See Analysis of Adverb Clauses, p. 410. **2.**

the second. *Both . . . and, either . . . or, neither . . . nor,* and *whether . . . or not* are frequently used to correlate coordinate words, phrases, or clauses, as in the following:

(1) *Both* hill *and* dale resounded. (2) *Either* Hamlet was mad, *or* he feigned madness admirably. (3) He was *neither* tall *nor* thin. (4) She *neither* spoke *nor* wept.

Sometimes an adverb is used with a conjunction to introduce and emphasize two or more coördinate ideas. *Not (only) . . . but (also), not . . . nor,* and *never . . . nor,* are the most common of the coördinating correlatives:

(1) *Not only* the men *but also* the women and the children had to walk. (2) He was *not* of an age, *but* for all times. (3) Nature *never* rhymes her children, *nor* makes two men alike. (4) We must *not* fear adversity, *nor* must we cease to expect it.

Both the coördinating and the subordinating conjunctions may be grouped or classified according to the meanings they convey. Sometimes the same conjunction may belong to more than one group, since it may be capable of denoting two or more meanings. For example, *as, because, for,* and *since* may each be used to express two or more meanings. *As,* for example, may introduce and subordinate a clause of time, manner, cause, or degree. Even conjunctions like *and* and *for* may have more than one meaning.

Coördinating Conjunctions

The **coördinating conjunction** may join grammatical units and introduce and express any of the following meanings: 1. **cumulative** (addition), 2. **alternative** and **disjunctive** (choice), 3. **adversative** (contrast), 4. **transitional** (illation). These meanings may be conveyed by pure coördinating conjunctions or by adverbs having transitional or illative function.

1. In common speech, the **cumulative** (or additive) ideas are most often joined by the pure conjunction *and*,[2] or by certain words or phrases used as conjunctions, of which the following are the most common: *as well as, also, besides, furthermore, in addition, likewise, moreover.* Observe the cumulative meaning suggested by the conjunctions in the following:

> (1) Two *and* two make four. (2) The wind blew, *and* the rains fell. (3) All the world's a stage, *and* all the men and women merely players.—Shakespeare. (4) Men *as well as* boys need this type of exercise.

2. Alternative and **disjunctive** thoughts are usually expressed by employing the coördinating conjunctions *or, nor, whether . . . or, either . . . or,* and *neither . . . nor;* or by employing the conjunctive adverbs *otherwise* and *else.* Observe the adversative or disjunctive meaning in each of the following:

> (1) We must not fear adversity, *nor* must we cease to expect it. (2) You must interview this candidate *whether* you want to *or not.* (3) We must hurry; *otherwise* we shall be late. (4) *Neither* a borrower *nor* a lender be.

3. The chief function of *but* is to convey **adversative** (contrasting) ideas:

> (1) Not daggers *but* ballots are the proper weapons. (2) Applause is the spur of noble minds, *but* the end of weak ones. (3) Individuals sometimes forgive, *but* society never does.

A number of the conjunctive adverbs (words or phrases) are used to join and convey contrasting ideas, the most com-

---

[2] Sometimes *and* indicates sequence: *He spoke, and lo, it was done. Human love soon wears threadbare, and then we die of cold.* In popular speech *and* is frequently used to express purpose: *Try and find an error. Go and see what that child wants. Send and get me a good substitute.* This use of *and* is an example of a widespread tendency called **parataxis**—one sentence element parallel to another in form, but subordinate to it in meaning. This extended use has been condemned by some grammarians without reason, for it is well established by usage. One example from Milton may serve to show that it is used even in highly literary speech: *At least to try and teach the erring soul.*

mon of these being *however, nevertheless, notwithstanding, on the contrary, on the other hand, still, whereas,* and *yet.* Observe that the conjunctive adverbs in the following examples convey about the same meaning as is conveyed when *but* is used

(1) These people are poor, *yet* they are honest. (2) I am old and feeble, *whereas* you are young and strong. (3) *However,* with the good has come the evil, too. (4) *On the other hand,* there are some advantages in being poor.

4. Though the essential grammatical business of the conjunction is exercised inside the sentence, and consists of connecting its parts, it may perform a more general (and rather rhetorical) service in linking the thoughts of entire sentences, or even of paragraphs, with what precedes it. Such connectives may be called **transitional** (crossing-over) or **illative** (reference) conjunctions because they stand as literary guide-boards, occurring at or near the beginning of sentences or paragraphs, and directing the mind towards the proper route.[3] They may be classified in various ways according to their meaning and use in the sentences in which they occur. They often replace or bring about an ellipsis of the pure coordinating conjunctions, which can usually be supplied when the sentences are analyzed. The general effect of these may be discovered by examining the words and phrases classified as to their meaning in the following table:

Continuous—straight on: *and, also, besides, furthermore, likewise, moreover, too.*

Alternation—choice of roads: *or, else, otherwise.*

Reverse—correction—pause for checking up: *but, however, nevertheless, notwithstanding.*

Conclusion—end of road: *consequently, hence, finally, so, then, therefore, wherefore, whence.*

---

[3] Frequently the transitional connectives are stereotyped prepositional phrases, such as *at any rate, at the same time, in addition, in conclusion, in short, in other words, on the contrary, on the other hand,* etc.

Subordinating Conjunctions

The connectives that introduce and subordinate clauses may be full (or pure) subordinating conjunctions and have no function in the sentence except to subordinate and join; or they may be words that have some other function in the sentence than that of joining, such as the relative adverbs, which modify and join; or they may be expletives (introductory words) that have almost no modifying and little connective force.

The **full** (or **pure**) **subordinating conjunctions** always introduce adverbial clauses, and the clauses they introduce may, therefore, modify whatever adverbs modify. The full subordinating conjunctions most frequently used are those that introduce clauses of **cause, reason, condition, concession, purpose,** and **result** or **effect.**[4]

Adverb clauses denoting **time, place, manner,** and **degree** are introduced by relative adverbs, sometimes called **secondary** (or **half**) **conjunctions,** because their primary function is not that of joining sentence units. They are more like relative pronouns than the pure subordinating conjunctions, and they can usually be converted into two adverbial phrases, one of which will contain a relative pronoun. In *I live where the snow falls*, the relative adverb *where* joins and subordinates the clause *the snow falls*. *Where* is here equivalent to two prepositional phrases, one modifying *live*, and the other *falls*. The meaning of the relative adverb may be seen in the following converted sentence: *I live in a country in which the snow falls*. Relative adverbs are like full (or pure) subordinating conjunctions in that they may introduce adverbial clauses, but they are unlike the pure subordinating conjunctions in that they may also introduce adjective clauses. In either type of clause, however, the relative adverb has the function of a connective, and hence in both of these functions it shows some kinship with the pure subordinating conjunc-

---

[4] Sentences containing clauses introduced by full (pure) conjunctions are classified and analyzed in Part Two, Lesson XIV.

tion, which always subordinates and joins a clause to another clause.[5]

The **expletive** (or **introductory**) **conjunctions** *that* and *but that* (negative of *that*), *if*, and *whether* are usually classed as subordinating conjunctions, but in reality they are mere form (function) words. Often the expletive *that* is not essential to the meaning of the clause it introduces, and can be omitted and frequently is omitted, especially when the noun clause that it introduces is the direct object. The expletive conjunction is restricted to introducing noun clauses. *That* in its expletive function resembles the relative pronoun (from which it probably had its origin) in sentences such as *We know that he speaks the truth*. Doubtless *that* was originally a stressed demonstrative, and the clause *he speaks the truth* was in apposition with *that*, as in *I know that* (*He speaks the truth*). The two clauses joined into a sentence without a pause, and the stressed demonstrative *that* (referring to the fact just stated) was reduced to an unstressed conjunction merely joining the two clauses. We still have the older demonstrative construction with different word order: *He speaks the truth; I know that.*

But that is used to introduce noun clauses after negative verbs. Originally *but* was a preposition governing the pronoun *that* followed by an explanatory clause: *I doubt anything* (or if negative, *naught*) *but that* (*you are invited*), out of which grew *I do not doubt but that you are invited.*

In formal and poetic diction *but* is sometimes used without the expletive *that*, as in *No doubt but ye are the people, and wisdom shall die with you.*—Old Testament.

Whether comes from the O.E. interrogative pronoun that meant *which of two*. It is now used chiefly to introduce indirect questions. *Whether* usually suggests alternation (choice), and may be followed by its correlative *or not* (or *or no*): *I*

---

[5] For a fuller treatment of relative adverbs, see Adverbs, Chapter Six, pp. 164–165. For an analysis of the various types of clauses containing relative adverbs, see Part Two, Lessons XI and XII, pp. 360–361 and 390–403.

must learn whether or not I am invited. The *or not* is frequently omitted in both the popular and the literary levels of speech.

If for *whether* dates back to the Old English period, but it is not so common in formal speech today as it once was. Its use, however, as an expletive can be justified by citing illustrations from literary texts:

> She doubts *if* two and two make four.—Prior.

> And he sent forth a dove from him, to see *if* the waters were abated from off the face of the ground.—Old Testament.

The **expletives** that introduce appositives are sometimes called **appositive conjunctions**. Their function is to introduce explanatory or illustrative material. The most common and the most useful of these are the following, some of which are borrowed from Latin: *as, by way of example, especially, for example* (or *e.g.,* abbreviation of *exemplum gratia*), *i.e.* (Lat. *id est,* that is), *in other words, namely, notably, or, particularly, scil.* (or *sc.,* Lat. *scilicet,* to wit), *such as, specifically, that is, that is to say, to wit, viz.* (Lat. *videlicet,* namely). Of these *as* and *or* can also function as full conjunctions. *As* is also used as a relative adverb (see Adverb Clauses, Part Two, pp. 394–395).

In its expletive function, *as* may introduce an appositive element:

> (1) *As* a singer, he had few equals.   (2) Washington's career *as* a soldier and statesman was lofty, fair, and patriotic.

It is also frequently used to introduce a subjective or an objective complement:

> (1) He was introduced *as* the hero of the day.   (2) The committee named John *as* the acting secretary.

Or, as we have already noted, is one of the three most used coördinating conjunctions, the other two being *and* and *but.*

In its expletive function, *or* shows some remote kinship to its use as a pure coördinating conjunction. Compare *The period, or dot, should be used here* (where *or* is an expletive, used merely to introduce the word *dot*, which explains the noun that precedes it) with *The period or the semicolon should be used here* (where *or* is a coördinating conjunction used to join two nouns, and suggests a choice (alternation—one or the other).

Observe that the expletive *or* always introduces a nonrestrictive appositive, which must be set off by punctuation marks, usually by commas or parentheses. If the punctuation marks are omitted, *or* must be construed as a coördinating conjunction, and hence suggests a choice of two objects or items. The expletive merely suggests a choice of names for the same objects.

Except for *as* and *or*, the expletives listed are more common in written than in spoken English. They are indispensable in formal dissertations, legal documents, and scientific treatises, where they introduce and tie illustrative material to what precedes.

Nine

Interjections

An **înterjection** (from Lat. *interjectus,* past participle of *interjictere,* to throw between) is a word or a group of words interjected (thrown) in a sentence to denote strong feeling or sudden emotion. The interjection, strictly speaking, is not a true part of speech. It does not enter into the construction of the sentence, nor is it grammatically related to other words in the sentence. It must always be construed as an independent element.

Often the interjection constitutes an entire sentence. In their more typical examples, interjections are involuntary and almost or quite physical records of reactions to emotional stimuli. Thus *Ah!* is in origin a mere gasp of pain or surprise; *Oh!* a resonated outburst of breath, almost a howl; *Pooh!* or *Pah!* a violent expulsion from the lips, as of an offensive substance or odor; *Hm!* a deliberate preparation for speech, much the same as clearing the throat; *Ha! Ha!* a nervous quaking of the diaphragm.

Akin to the above are sounds used conventionally as warnings: *Hush! (Sh!), Hist! (St!), Tut! Tut!* The last of these, often used as a mother's reproof to her child, is in origin one of the so-called "clicks" of some language. It is made by sucking the breath from the tip of the tongue placed against the upper teeth. The resulting familiar sound is imperfectly represented by the usual spelling of the interjection.

Hurrah! is an imitative word (possibly, with strongly

196

trilled *r*, of the sound of a drum) conventionalized into an expression of joy. *Alas!* goes back to a Latin compound of *Ah* and *lassus* (weary, fatigued, wretched). It means *wretched that I am. Alas! Oh!* and *Ah!* are often followed by nouns or pronouns with or without the preposition *for* or modifying adjectives: *Alas, poor Yorrick, Alas for me! Oh, wretched me! Ah me! Woe's me! Dear me!*

Oaths, curses, and bywords constitute one type of interjection. They represent a wide variety of feelings; and in the conversation of some are so habitual as to have slight emotional content.

Interjections are sometimes classified according to their form as **primary** and **secondary.**

The **primary interjections** are those expressions which have come into the language as reproductions of sounds made involuntarily when people are under the influence of emotional stimuli: *Ah! Alas! Hurrah! Ouch! Pah!* They have no use in the language except to convey emotional reactions.

In the written speech the degree of feeling that an interjection expresses can be indicated only by the punctuation which follows it. The exclamation mark is used to denote strong feeling; and the comma is employed when the emotional content is slight: *Oh! I cannot bear this torture. Oh, that is not very important.*

Words in common use as other parts of speech employed with the effect of interjections are sometimes called **secondary interjections,**[1] because their primary function is not that of denoting emotion. These can be recognized in the oral speech by the tone of voice with which they are uttered. In the written speech, the exclamation mark that follows them shows them to be ejaculations.

The imperative forms of verbs are frequently employed in ejaculating commands: *Behold! Begone! Bless us! Look*

---

[1] Many grammarians prefer to classify the so-called **secondary interjections** as verbs, adjectives, nouns, etc. used independently. Many of them, such as *Listen!* and *Stop that!* convey full thoughts. Strictly speaking, the interjection is not a sentence, nor a grammatical unit within a sentence.

out! Listen! Stop that! Adjectives and nouns are also employed to indicate sudden and strong feeling of approval or disapproval: *Fine! Horrible! Impossible! Good! Bravo! Horrors! Nonsense! Twaddle! Shame!* Similarly, adverbs are sometimes employed as interjections: *On! Forward! Away!*

In the substandard levels of speech slang expressions often have the force of interjections: *Beat it! Good night! Holy smoke! Skiddoo! Step on it! Yeah!*

PART TWO

SENTENCE ANALYSIS

The Elements of the Sentence

Analysis in grammar is the separation of the sentence into its component parts, or elements. To analyze a sentence is to identify and classify its constituent parts (words, phrases, clauses).

Parsing a sentence is (1) naming the parts of speech which constitute the various elements of the sentence, (2) accounting for the inflectional forms of all words that show inflection, and (3) explaining the relation each word has to any other word or words in the same sentence.

A **sentence** is an independent group of words which expresses a complete thought. Every sentence must contain a **subject** (expressed or implied) and a **predicate.** The **subject** is that of which something is said, asserted, predicated. The **predicate** is that which is said, asserted, predicated of the subject. The subject of a sentence must be a noun or a noun-equivalent; and the predicate must be or must contain a finite verb (one that is capable of asserting, having limits of person and number, which the nonfinite, or infinite, verbs lack). *Men walk* is a sentence; it contains a subject and a predicate: *men* is the subject, and *walk* is the predicate. *Be saved* is also a sentence, even though it contains only the passive verb form *be saved;* its subject (*you*) is implied.

The **elements** of a sentence consist of (1) the **simple subject** (a noun or a noun-equivalent), (2) the **simple predicate** (the finite, or predicate, verb), (3) the modifiers, which may be explanatory, adjectival, or adverbial, (4) the complements (subjective complement, objective complement, direct object), and (5) independent expressions, such as expletives, introductory words and phrases, and interjections.

The **simple sentence** contains one subject and one predicate, either or both of which may be compound. *Adams, Jefferson, and Monroe died on the Fourth of July* is a simple sentence: it contains one subject, which is compound, and one predicate. *This man went to Pilate, and begged the body of Jesus* is also a simple sentence: it contains one simple subject and one compound predicate.

The simplest sentences in the language contain only the noun-subject and the verb-predicate: *Dogs bark; Heat expands; Jesus wept.* The predicate verb may be any finite verb form found in the inflection of a full verb; as, *Napoleon was conquered; Jesus was betrayed; Men must die; Liars should be punished.* As a rule, however, the sentences which we actually use in our daily communication are not restricted to the simple noun-subject and the simple verb-predicate. We usually qualify or explain the simple subject and often complete our predicate verbs with complements and qualifying words, phrases, or clauses. It is important to remember that, if the simple subject or the simple predicate or any word belonging to either is explained or modified by a clause, the sentence is not a simple sentence.

Any sentence that contains one principal clause and one or more subordinate (or dependent) clauses is called a **complex** sentence: *I know that the earth is round* is a complex sentence because it contains the noun clause *that the earth is round*, which is in the predicate of the principal clause. *Death is the black camel which kneels at every man's gate* is a complex sentence: it contains a principal clause (*Death is the black camel*) and an adjective clause (*which kneels at every man's gate*); the latter modifies *camel*, a noun in the predicate of the principal clause.

A **compound sentence** is composed of two or more independent clauses, either or both of which may contain one or more adjective, adverb, or noun clauses. *Many meet the* *gods, but few salute them* is a compound sentence: it contains two simple independent clauses joined by the coördinating conjunction *but*. If a compound sentence contains a dependent clause, it is sometimes called a **complex-compound** (or **compound-complex**) sentence (see illustrations and references cited in Lesson XV, pp. 426–427).

Analysis by Diagraming

One may analyze, or dissect, sentences by pointing out the component parts and classifying them orally or in writing; or one may analyze sentences by diagraming them.

A **diagram** of a sentence is a graphic representation of the sentence, picturing the interrelations of its parts. It is used by the grammarian in much the same way as perpendicular and parallel lines, triangles, and circles are used by the mathematician. The diagram records and objectifies the constituent parts, or elements, of the sentence. It is exceptionally useful to both the student and the teacher in explaining the basic structure of a given sentence. It can, however, only approximate the complete analysis, and should be supplemented by parsing (oral or written) and explanatory annotations.

The sentences presented for analysis in Part Two of this text may be analyzed by written or oral parsing, or by diagrams accompanied with written or oral annotations. The authors strongly recommend the diagraming of sentences selected from those given for analysis in **Lessons I** through **XV**, chiefly because diagraming is a rapid method of recording and objectifying the major and minor elements of the sentence. Its use will save time for both the instructor and student. As a rule, a student must determine all of the constituent parts of a sentence before he can complete his diagram of it.

The system of diagraming employed and described in this text is one of the simplest and one of the most widely used of all the systems of diagraming now taught in the public and private schools of America.[1]   The lines used in diagrams are few, and their significance can be mastered in a very short time.   The mastery of sentence structure may prove more difficult.

The assignments which are given in the fifteen lessons presented in Part Two begin with the simplest types of sentences, and are so arranged as to introduce only a few new phases of sentence-structure in each lesson.   The simple sentence with all the elements that belong to it are presented in Lessons I–X inclusive.   The complex and compound sentences are analyzed and diagramed in Lessons XI–XV inclusive.   The exercises in parsing and in correcting violations of good usage and the review exercises are to be used whenever the instructor wishes to have additional oral or written assignments, or wishes to review work previously covered.

---

[1] The system of diagraming used in this text is the one now generally referred to as the Reed and Kellogg system.   It was presented in Reed and Kellogg's *Higher Lessons in English*, copyrighted first in 1877, by Alonzo Reed and Brainerd Kellogg.   The text is now published by Charles E. Merrill Co., New York.

LESSON I

Simple Sentences Containing Adjective and Adverb Modifiers

To diagram a simple sentence, one should draw a heavy horizontal line, and then divide it into two parts by a short vertical line. At the left of the bisecting line belongs the simple subject; at the right belongs the simple predicate:

1. Men walk.

$$\text{Men} \mid \text{walk}$$

This is a sentence. *Men* is the **subject**: that of which something is said, asserted, predicated. *Walk* is the **predicate**: that which is said, asserted, predicated of the subject.

When the subject or the predicate or both have modifiers, these are placed on lines drawn diagonally from the words they describe or limit:

2. These questions may be settled peaceably.

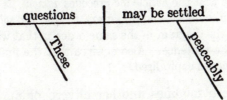

In this sentence, the demonstrative adjective *these* modifies *questions*, the noun-subject; and *peaceably* is an adverb expressing manner, modifying the verb-predicate, *may be settled.*

205

If a word has more than one modifier, these should, as a rule, be placed in the same order in the diagram as that which they have in the written or spoken sentence, as in the following sentence:

3. Young, active men walk rapidly.

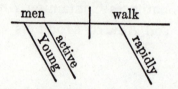

In this sentence the subject, *men*, is modified by the adjectives *young* and *active;* and the predicate, *walk*, is modified by the adverb *rapidly.* *Young, active men* is the complete subject; *walk rapidly* is the complete predicate.

Sometimes modifiers are transposed to secure variety, euphony, emphasis, or poetic effect, as in the following example:

4. Far away, faintly, solemnly tolls the ancient bell.

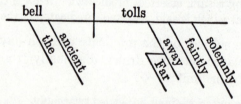

Observe that the article *the* precedes *ancient*, as it does in the spoken sentence, and that *away, faintly*, and *solemnly* are placed in the diagram in the same order as that which they have in the sentence. Also observe that the first word in the sentence is capitalized.

If an adverb modifies another adverb or an adjective, it should be placed (see *far* in the above sentence) on a line drawn first parallel with the base line and then down and parallel with the line on which the first modifier is placed Observe that *very* modifies *happily* in the following sentence.

5. That young girl lives there very happily now.

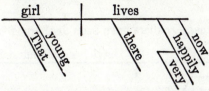

That is a definitive adjective, of the subclass demonstrative. *Young* is a descriptive adjective. Both *that* and *young* modify the noun *girl*. *There* is an adverb of place modifying the verb *lives*. *Now* is an adverb of time modifying *lives*. *Happily* is an adverb of manner modifying *lives*. *Very* is an adverb of degree modifying the adverb *happily*.

6. The old man's sight is failing.

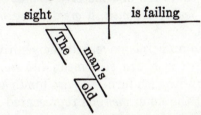

Man's is a noun in the possessive case modifying *sight*. *The* is a definite article modifying *man's*; and *old* is a descriptive adjective modifying *man's*. *Is failing* is the predicate, being the present tense, progressive form, of the verb *fail*, in the third person, singular number, indicative mode.

As a rule, one adjective cannot modify another adjective, but there are in Modern English a number of noun-words, originally followed by the genitive case, which are apparent exceptions to the general rule. Observe that the article *a* must modify *few*, not *students*, in the following sentence:

7. A few students left early.

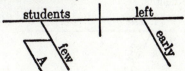

Similarly, *a* and *great* modify *many*, not *soldiers*, in the following sentence:

8. A great many soldiers have been discharged.

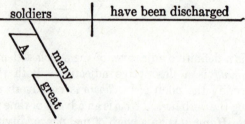

In earlier English *few* and *many* were nouns followed by the genitive case; and, in sentences such as those given in *7* and *8*, they now have the force of collective nouns. We may say *a few men* or *a few of the men*, *a great many men* or *a great many of the men*.

In Old English numerals governed the genitive plural, and hence *two hundred men* can still mean *two hundred of men*; but in its Modern English form, the *two* limits *hundred*, which limits (modifies) the noun *men*, as represented in the following diagram:

9. Two hundred persons have been invited.

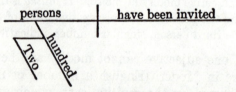

The diagram does not differentiate the transitive from the intransitive verb. Observe that one of the verbs is transitive and the other is intransitive in the two sentences which follow:

10. The horse neighs.

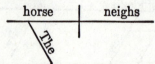

11. The horse is tied.

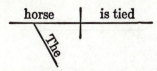

Neighs is an intransitive verb; the action does not pass over to an object. *Neighs* has no voice. *Is tied* is a transitive verb: the action passes over from a doer (some man, woman, or child) to a receiver (the horse). *Horse* is the subject of the sentence, but the object of the action. *Is tied* is in the passive voice.

When a subject or a predicate or any other sentence element is unexpressed, the implied word is represented by *x* in the diagram. Observe that the following sentence has no expressed subject:

12. Do not come in too soon.

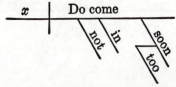

Do come is the verb, emphatic form. The subject is *you*, understood. *Not* is an adverb of negation. *In* is an adverb of direction, roughly classed as place. *Soon* is an adverb of time (more accurately of nearness to the present). *Too* is an adverb of degree modifying *soon*.

As a rule, all adverb modifiers are placed beneath the words they limit, but if the negative adverb *not* is a part of a compound verb form, as in *cannot* in the following sentence, it belongs on the base line.

13. I cannot go.

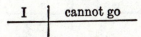

Am and *not* are always written separately, and hence should appear in the diagram as verb and adverb modifier.

14. I am not going.

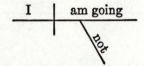

Don't, doesn't, isn't, aren't, won't, etc. should be treated as *cannot* is in the sentence given above. These contractions are used, however, only in informal emphatic or interrogative sentences:

15. I don't live here.

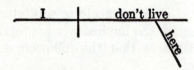

16. Doesn't he walk too fast?

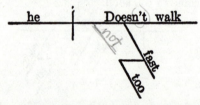

Observe that an interrogative sentence must be turned into the declarative form before it can be diagramed. The auxiliary word which begins the sentence should be capitalized in the diagram to aid in conveying the interrogative meaning.

If a contraction contains the subject and any part of the predicate verb, the line dividing the subject and predicate must separate the contraction so as to place the subject and the predicate in their proper places:

17. Here's my hand.

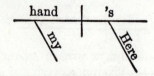

Here's (for *Here is*) is not a conventional compound word like *cannot*. In the diagram, it is correct to separate into verb ('s) and modifying adverb (*here*). A good dictionary will be found useful in answering questions in regard to the compounding of forms. *Cannot* is listed in our standard dictionaries as a compound form, but there is no single entry for *here's*.

Independent words are not attached to the subject or the predicate or to any of the modifiers of the subject or the predicate. Observe the position of *there* in the following diagram:

18. There was once a beautiful young princess.

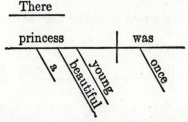

There is an expletive, grammatically unattached, the effect of which upon the sentence order is to throw the subject after the predicate.

Contrast this with *There would I live*, in which sentence *there* means *in that place*, and modifies *live*:

There I would live.

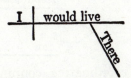

When the simple sentence contains a compound subject or a compound predicate, the base line is divided to accommodate as many parts as the compound element contains. A conjunction joining the parts of a compound subject or predicate should be placed on a dotted line extending from the line on which the first of the compound elements is placed to the line on which the last member of the group is placed. The following diagrams illustrate the more common types of the compound groups:

19. East and West shall never meet.

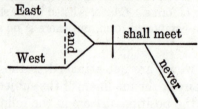

This is not a compound sentence, but a simple sentence with a compound subject.[2]

20. All the younger men and older boys have enlisted.

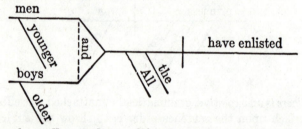

Note that *all* and *the* modify the entire compound subject, while *younger* modifies *men*, and *older* modifies *boys*.

21. She screamed and ran.

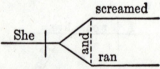

When correlative coördinating conjunctions are used to join the parts of a compound element, the correlatives are placed on separate dotted lines as *both* and *and* are in the following diagram:

---

[2] A compound sentence must contain two or more independent (principal) clauses. To diagram a compound sentence, we must draw a base line for each clause, and place the elements of each clause in their proper places. For models showing the diagram forms for compound sentences, see Compound Sentences, Lesson XV, pp. 421–432.

22. Both the ship and all its cargo have been sunk and hopelessly lost.

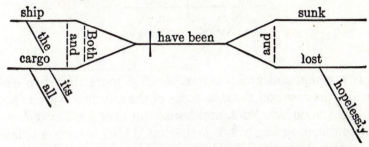

Both . . . and are correlative coördinating conjunctions. *Either . . . or* and *neither . . . nor* are similarly diagramed. *Have been sunk and lost* is an instance of two verbs in which a phrasal auxiliary, *have been,* is used with two participles, *sunk* and *lost,* in the formation of the present perfect tense.

It is important to observe here and elsewhere that *and* joins only what is coördinate; i.e., like elements, such as two nouns, two verbs, two auxiliaries, two participles, etc. It must never be made to join unlike elements.

When two or more adjectives or two or more adverbs are joined by coördinating conjunctions, the conjunctions are placed on a dotted line connecting the coördinate elements, as in the following diagram:

23. The long and dreamy night passed calmly and silently.

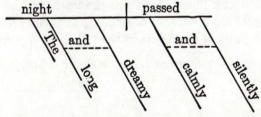

Note that *the* modifies *night.* It cannot possibly modify *long.* Articles are adjectives, and adjectives do not, as a rule, modify other adjectives. (Special exceptions to the rule are listed and analyzed on p. 208). In the following sentence *an* modifies *man,* not *old:*

24. An old man usually rises early.

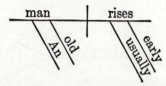

If a compound group is composed of more than two elements, the first and the last words of the coördinate group are put on the outside lines, and horizontal lines are drawn from the conjunction line (which is the dotted line) to accommodate the other elements of the compound group, as illustrated in the following diagrams:

25. The ducks, geese, and chickens were frightened.

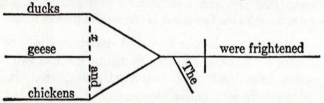

An *x* may be placed on the dotted line joining *ducks* and *geese* to indicate that the conjunction *and* is implied. The *and* which is expressed is placed between the last two elements, as in the spoken sentence.

Sometimes the parts of a compound element are arranged in pairs, and the lines which are drawn from the base line must be again divided, and horizontal lines drawn to accommodate the pairs of words, as in the following diagram:

26. I inquired and rejected, consulted and deliberated.

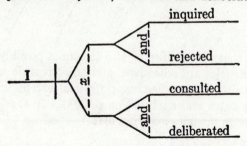

27. The poor and the rich, the weak and the strong, the young and the old must die.

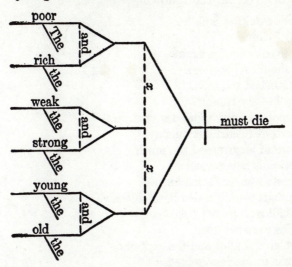

If a modifier limits all of the words of a compound adjective or adverb group, it should be placed so as to indicate that it modifies the entire unit, as *very* does in the following example:

28. The old man drives very slowly and cautiously.

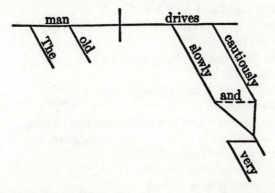

The diagram indicates here that *very* modifies both *slowly* and *cautiously*.

EXERCISE A

Analyze or diagram the following:

1. He was thinking rapidly.
2. Weep I cannot.
3. Foul deeds will rise again.
4. You should register early.
5. She returned too soon.
6. There lies my trouble.
7. The spot was now quite deserted.
8. The crowd rushed out quickly.
9. The world is governed too much.
10. Affection is never wasted.
11. Harvests were gathered in.
12. All sounds were blended harmoniously.
13. We shall restore, not destroy.
14. Politics were excluded.
15. There go the pilot and the captain.
16. Still the uneasiness existed.
17. No previous meeting had been indicated or suggested.
18. True nobility cannot long be hidden.
19. His knees shook together violently.
20. Morals are socially determined.
21. How can an art decay?
22. Michael had been hit.
23. The mob raged and roared.
24. An unusually large crop has just been harvested.
25. His works have not died.
26. Neither John nor his sister works here.
27. Thou shalt not kill.
28. The early worm is sometimes caught.
29. Where's the king?
30. A brave, prudent, and honorable man was chosen.
31. Many ill matters and projects are undertaken.
32. Children and fools cannot lie.
33. Ill weeds grow fast.
34. A short horse is soon curried.
35. Her best dress was very badly soiled.
36. Is there not another and better world?

37. A threefold cord is not quickly broken.
38. Pride, poverty, and fashion cannot live together.
39. Thrice flew thy shaft.
40. Matters are going swimmingly.
41. Justice should not be postponed.
42. The old man could not speak distinctly.
43. The candidate should dress becomingly and modestly.
44. She sang both high and loud.
45. Neither John nor his sister works hard.
46. Society advances very slowly.
47. The horses and the cows should be fed and watered regularly.
48. The elaborate luncheon was quickly served.
49. Do not smoke here.
50. Our best thoughts are seldom written down.

EXERCISE B

Correct all the violations of good usage which you find in the following sentences, and justify each correction you make:

1. Why don't he try to get another job?
2. Neither the secretary nor the treasurer were present.
3. Each of us have cast our vote against the amendment.
4. You shall, I believe, become a good teacher.
5. The captain, as well as his men, were suspected.
6. Here comes the bride and the groom.
7. I didn't like that there report we had today.
8. Have each of you decided to resign?
9. I like to have died laughing at him.
10. He attends church regular now.
11. Has the teacher rang the bell yet?
12. He bursted out laughing when he heard the news.
13. There goes the pilot and the captain.
14. She is sick physically and in her mind.
15. In applying for a job, one should be especially careful about their grammar.
16. The weather man has forecasted snow for tonight.
17. The teacher suddenly lit on me for being rude.
18. In most colleges, some form of athletics are required.
19. Every man, woman, and child like to be praised.

20. Either of these men are good painters.
21. There is no bacteria in the soil.
22. Neither Latin nor Greek are taught in our school.
23. The guest, as well as the host and the hostess, were annoyed by the child's tantrums.
24. In the refrigerator is a grapefruit and an egg which you may have for your breakfast.
25. He always has and always will be a care.

Lesson II

Prepositional Phrases

A **prepositional phrase** is composed of a preposition and a noun or a noun-equivalent, the former governing the latter; i.e., determining its case. The noun or its equivalent, which is always the principal term in the prepositional phrase, is generally referred to as the **object of the preposition.**

In the diagram, the prepositional phrase is placed on a slanting line drawn diagonally down from the word which the phrase modifies; and the object (i.e., the principal word in the phrase) is placed on a horizontal line drawn from the line on which the preposition is placed, as shown in the following model. Observe that the preposition line extends beyond the horizontal line on which the object of the preposition is placed.

1. Come to me.

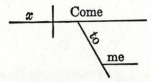

Observe that the object of *to* is the principal term in the prepositional phrase *to me*, and that it is in the objective case. In Modern English, all prepositions regularly govern the objective case.

The compounding of the object of the preposition does not affect the case of either the noun or pronoun governed. Both must be in the objective case.

219

2. He looked steadily at John and *me.*

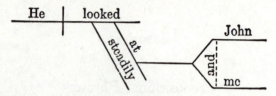

Observe that the horizontal line drawn for the object of the preposition is divided to accommodate the compound object.

By a well-established idiom, prepositions sometimes govern the possessive case (see Double Genitive, or Possessive, pp. 174–175):

3. This new friend of mine came early

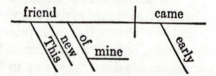

4. An important order of the Dean's has been sent out.

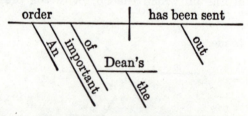

Uses of the Prepositional Phrase

Almost every preposition is capable of indicating a number of different relationships between the grammatical units which it joins. Hence prepositional phrases have a wide variety of uses as adjective and adverb modifiers. Only a representative number of these can be shown in this chapter.[1]

---

[1] For a fuller treatment of the uses and meaning of prepositions, see Part One, Chapter Seven, pp. 174–184.

ADJECTIVE USES

1. *Possession:* The purse of the unfortunate man was recovered.

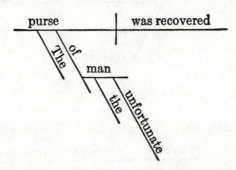

In the diagram, the modifiers of the object of the preposition are placed on diagonal lines extending from the line on which the principal term of the phrase is placed. Observe that both *the* and *unfortunate* modify *man,* and that the definite article *the* does not modify the adjective *unfortunate.*

2. *Location:* His place in the ranks has been filled.

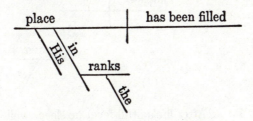

3. *Source:* The letter from home has arrived.

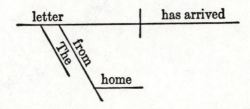

4. *Association:* His alliance with the best people had been
noted.

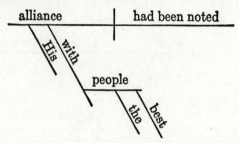

5. *Antagonism:* His fight with evil has been rewarded.

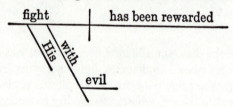

ADVERB USES

1. *Place:* Duncan is in his grave.

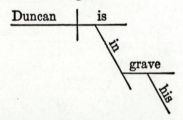

2. *Time:* After life's fitful fever he sleeps well.

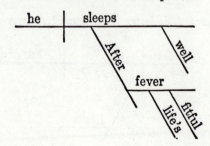

3. Manner: He dances with ease.

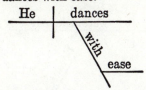

4. Degree and Source: An odor pleasant in the extreme emanated from the kitchen.

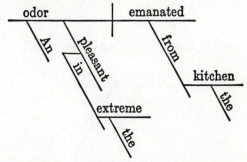

Observe that *in the extreme* is an adverbial phrase denoting degree; it modifies the adjective *pleasant.*

Prepositions may be compounded of two or more words. When the words are written separately but are used to show single relationship, they are called **phrasal (or group) prepositions.**

5. Material: The story was made out of whole cloth.

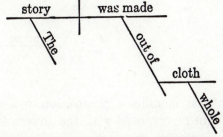

In this sentence *out of* shows relation between *was made* and *cloth,* and is almost the equivalent of *from.* Observe that neither *of* nor *out* could here be used alone.

6. Cause: Because of an accident, we were delayed.

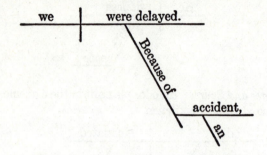

7. Purpose: The boy has gone out on an errand.

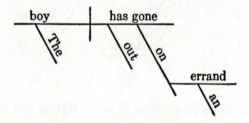

Here *out* is an adverb denoting direction; it modifies *has gone.*

8. Place: The boy came out of the house.

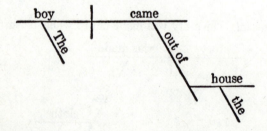

The adverb that modifies a preposition or a prepositional phrase should not be confused with the adverb that precedes the phrase but modifies the verb, as in sentence *7*, or with an adverb which is a part of a phrasal preposition, as in sentence *8*.

Most of the adverbs commonly used to modify the preposition or the prepositional phrase may be construed as modifiers of the entire phrase, though originally many of them were doubtless employed to restrict the relational meaning expressed in the preposition. In such phrases as *just before noon, clear across the stream, far behind the group, completely over the wall,* the adverbs *just, clear, far,* and *completely* seem to limit the ideas expressed in the prepositions. But in each of the following: *only for two, merely for business, even by the weakest, partly for your sake,* the adverb (*only, merely, even, partly*) modifies the entire phrase.

The following show the correct form for diagraming such adverbs:

1. They have penetrated far into the hillside.

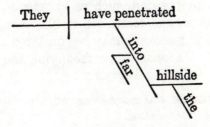

Far modifies *into.* It is an adverb of degree. One should not be surprised to discover that adverbs do modify prepositions, for most prepositions are merely old adverbs which have come to take objects, and many adverbs and prepositions are alike. Compare *He has been here before,* where *before* is an adverb, with *He came before the wedding,* where *before* is a preposition.

When the adverb modifies the entire prepositional phrase, it is placed on a diagonal line which is attached to the preposition and to the object of the preposition, as in the following diagram:

2. They march only on Saturday night.

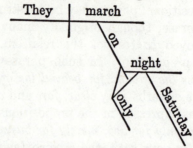

Only on Saturday night is like *only then.*   The position in the sentence of *only* is important.   Were it to precede *march,* the sentence might be interpreted as meaning that marching is the only thing they do on Saturday night (for instance, they do not play cards or attend the movies).

A phrasal preposition consisting of a prepositional phrase followed by a preposition, such as *in spite of, in accordance with, in respect to,* and many others like these, may be diagramed as one phrase; or it may be construed as two prepositional phrases, the second one modifying the object of the first, as in the following diagrams:

The appointment was made in accordance with the President's recommendation.

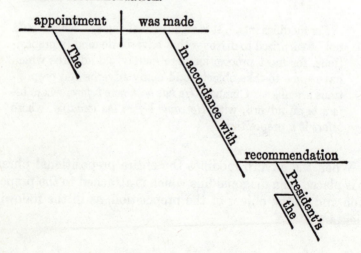

or

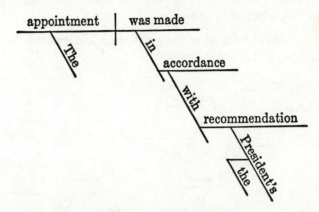

The Latin construction simply puts the noun in the ablative case without a preposition: *suis moribus* means *in accordance with their customs*.

The following diagram shows the correct form for coördinate prepositional phrases:

3. He went at great expense and without hope of financial profit.

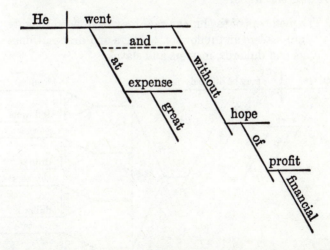

If a word or phrase modifies the objects of two different prepositions, the lines on which these are placed are brought back together, and the modifier is attached to the joined line, as in the following sentence:

4. I have lived in most of the great cities and some of the small villages of the country.

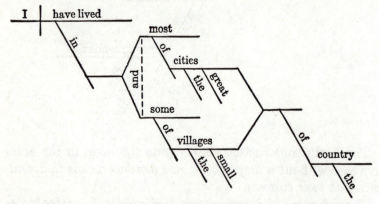

Observe that *of the country* modifies both *cities* and *villages*.

When the compound object of a preposition is grouped in pairs, the diagram indicates the grouping by dividing and subdividing the lines:

5. The members of the human race may be divided roughly into leaders and followers, workers and drones, thinkers and dullards, masters and slaves.

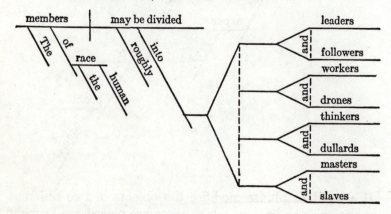

EXERCISE A

Analyze or diagram:

1. The scent of lilies was in the air.
2. The captain of the crew stepped into the light.
3. The remainder of the day passed very quickly and pleasantly.
4. A small wooden chest stood against the wall.
5. Come and sit beside me.
6. Bombs fell in our vicinity for several days.
7. The civilians on the roads and in the towns smiled and waved.
8. We were tied up along the water front of a small port near Naples.
9. In the fields were small herds of cattle, sheep, horses, and mules.
10. He came by his name in a peculiar fashion.
11. The rain was coming down in torrents.
12. With dreadful smoothness the negotiations proceeded.
13. Three of his gang were waiting for him.
14. The men of the new regiment watched and listened.
15. I went out of the laboratory and down the hill to the nearest house.
16. The result of the election may not be known until Wednesday or Thursday of next week.
17. Mother and Father came out of the front door and hurried up the street.
18. A tall man with a red face and thin gray hair was standing in front of the drawing-room fire.
19. Everything depends upon the movement of this indolent fellow in front of us.
20. What dire offence from amorous causes springs!—Pope.
21. The hours passed with unbelievable rapidity.
22. Soon with soundless steps the foot of Evangeline followed.
23. I got up and turned around in my tracks.
24. Filled was the air with dreamy and magical light.
25. The two friends were momentarily occupied with a large tin pot of tea and a kit of salt beef.
26. The earliest taboos probably centered about religious rites and duties.
27. Pride meets with provocations and disturbances upon almost every occasion.
28. In the middle of the room a round table of his own vigorous carpentry stood on a panther's skin.

29. They went in a hurry from house to house.
30. What did you decide upon?
31. The vices of the administration must be ascribed chiefly to the king.
32. In society, much depends upon the justice and fidelity, the temperance and character of the members.
33. People in affliction and distress cannot be hated by generous minds.
34. The climactic experience came shortly after the excommunication.
35. The star of love shone all about him.
36. The sun was going down far beyond the green hill.
37. There should be perfect freedom in matters of religious belief.
38. Little, frivolous minds are wholly occupied with the vulgar objects of nature.
39. The new building at the corner of Rhode Island Avenue and Fifteenth Street is nearly completed.
40. The contract was sent to you on Monday by special delivery.
41. Childe Roland to the dark tower came.
42. These costumes are worn in some rural regions and small towns on festive occasions.
43. Our civilization is being changed by democracy and by modern science.
44. They were assembling on benches, wagon seats, and boxes for the ceremony.
45. My brother stayed with us for a day, and then went on to New York.
46. A decrepit woman, old and infirm, appeared in the doorway.
47. Because of the storm, we stopped at the first house.
48. The months of July and August were named after Julius Caesar and Augustus Caesar.
49. No dew, no rain, no cloud comes to the relief of the parched earth.
50. Glass windows were introduced into England in the eighteenth century.

EXERCISE B

I. Review the sections on the Form and Derivation and the Meanings and Uses of Prepositions, Part One, Chapter Seven; and correct all violations of good usage in the following sentences.   Consult the dictionary when in doubt as to the correct form or meaning of a word.   Correct only what you consider incorrect.   Justify each change you make.

1. He jumped in the water and swam clear across the river.
2. He laughed when I asked him where the registrar's office was at.
3. I was angry at my professor when I heard him talking about his students.
4. He only smokes after meals.
5. My book is different than yours.
6. He decided to divide his income among his two oldest sons.
7. I might of gone off without you.
8. Our mailman comes at about noon.
9. I have nothing to do beside helping you.
10. He wanted to know who I was looking for.
11. I am going in town today with John and she.
12. He is ill with typhoid fever.
13. Keep off of my property.
14. I cannot remember of hearing that story.
15. The vessel was blown on the rocks.
16. The train will arrive inside of an hour.
17. There is some trouble among the teacher and his students.
18. I wonder what is the matter of him.
19. This kind of work takes longer than you think for.
20. The marriage customs of your country are very different to ours.
21. The Republicans may win out in the November election.
22. Everybody but he approved my leaving.
23. I could travel on the plane as well as the bus.
24. She sat in back of us at the concert.
25. The estate was divided between the seven sons.
26. I have great fear but no respect for men like him.
27. Due to weather conditions, the flight has been canceled.
28. The conclusion of that book was different than what I expected.
29. There was some discussion in regard to whom the property belonged.
30. I have observed in a majority of the cases that you are at fault.

Lesson III

Subjective[1] Complements

The **subjective complement** is a noun or an adjective or the equivalent of either which completes the predicate and refers to the subject. It follows either intransitive verbs or transitive verbs in the passive voice.

Those verbs which cannot predicate without the assistance of subjective complements are called **copulative** (or **linking**) verbs: they join (or link) the subject and the complement. Without its complement (completing word), a copulative verb has very little distinctive verb meaning.

When the subjective complement is a substantive, it is called a **predicate nominative.** The **predicate nominative** is a noun or pronoun in the nominative case used to complete the predicate and refer to the subject. It is always in a sense identical with the subject.

When the subjective complement is an adjective or any word or phrase used for an adjective, it is called the **attribute complement,** or when broadly classified, it may be called **predicate adjective.**[2] The **attribute complement** always de-

---

[1] The term *subjective* is here used in its strictly grammatical sense, and means *pertaining to the grammatical subject.* Similarly the word *objective* is used elsewhere in this text with the meaning *pertaining to the grammatical object.* These meanings should not be confused with those senses in which the same terms are used in the language of psychology and philosophy.

[2] Many grammarians prefer the term *attribute complement* for an adjective in this construction. The sole objection to the use of this expression would seem to be that it ignores the distinction between an attributive adjective and a predicative adjective (see pp. 81–82). The term *predicate adjective* stresses the predicating function, as distinguished from the attributive, or assumptive, one, where the adjective is a mere modifier of the noun. But not all adjectives in the predicate are subjective complements. The objective complement is often an adjective, and it is also in the predicate. See Lesson V, pp. 250–256.

fines or describes (i.e., gives some attribute of) the subject.

Predicate Nominative (a noun)

In the diagram, the subjective complement is placed on the base line immediately after the copulative verb which it assists in predicating. The verb and the complement are separated by a diagonal line pointing toward the subject to indicate the relationship.

1. I am thy father's spirit.

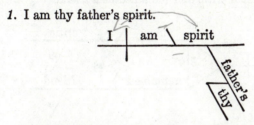

The word *spirit*, a noun in the nominative case, completes the predicate, refers to the subject, *I*, and is in a sense identical with the subject. *Spirit* is the predicate nominative. *Am* is an intransitive verb, and in this sentence means little until completed ("complemented") by *spirit*.

2. I am he.

$$I \mid am \diagdown he$$

Suppose someone has inquired, *Who is the writer of this letter?* I answer, *I am he.* I here identify myself (*I*) with the writer of the letter (*he*). *He* is a pronoun in the nominative case which completes the predicate, refers to the subject, and is in a sense identical with the subject. *He* is the predicate nominative.[3]

---

[3] The possessive case is sometimes used absolutely in the predicate as a subjective complement. It cannot properly be called a predicate nominative because it is not in the nominative case. It represents the possessor and the thing possessed.

This room is mine.

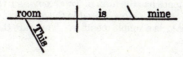

3. Washington was made Commander-in-chief.

Washington | · was made \ Commander-in-chief

Washington and *Commander-in-chief* are the same person. Both nouns are in the nominative case, the former being the subject, the latter the predicate nominative. *Was made* is a transitive verb in the passive voice.

4. Jones came as a critic and remained as a friend.

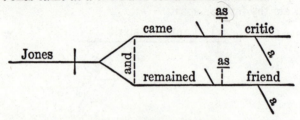

Critic and *friend* are identical with *Jones*. *As* is an expletive introducing the predicate nominative.

5. He was appointed as ambassador.

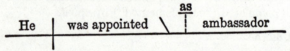

Observe that in the diagram the expletive *as* is placed on a short horizontal line, and that a dotted line attaches it to the base line between the complement and the subjective complement line.

Attribute Complement, or Predicate Adjective

1. The man became angry.

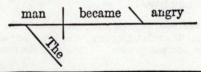

Expanded this sentence has the form of *This room is my room.* In the first sentence, the possessive pronoun *mine* is used in the predicate. In the second, or expanded form, *my* is used as a simple modifier. These are the two chief living uses of the possessive case.

Angry is an adjective which completes the predicate and modifies the subject. *Became* is an intransitive verb. *Angry* is the predicate adjective.

2. The man was made angry.

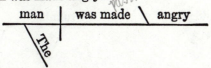

Was made is a transitive verb in the passive voice. *Angry* is the predicate adjective.

3. I feel bad.

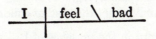

4. Rest easy and keep quiet.

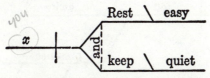

I feel bad means *I feel ill*, or *unhappy*. *Bad* is not an adverb but a predicate adjective. *I feel "badly"* would be less accurate, as it would seem to stress a manner of feeling rather than a quality of the subject. *Rest "easily"* and *keep "quietly"* would be equally absurd.

Caution: Distinguish clearly between the adverb construction and that of the predicate adjective. Do not substitute the adverb for the adjective where the sense requires the latter.

The diagram should help the student in differentiating the two parts of speech. Observe the adjective and adverb meanings in the following sentences:

1. The children are running wild.

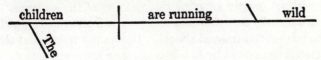

Wild is here an adjective completing the predicate. It describes the children, not their manner of running about.

2. The children are running wildly about.

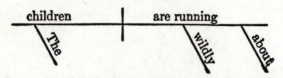

Here *are running* is a full predicating verb; it needs no completing word to convey the simple predicate meaning. *Wildly* is an adverb modifying *are running*. It tells us the manner of the running, not the kind of children spoken of.

3. He felt awkward in the presence of ladies.

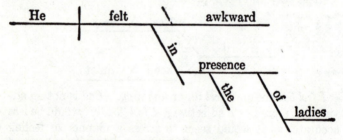

4. He felt awkwardly around for a chair.

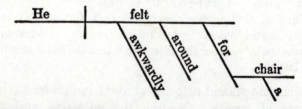

Awkward in sentence *3* is an adjective used as a subjective complement. It completes the predicate and describes the subject. *Felt* is a copulative verb, and could be replaced by *is* without greatly affecting the meaning of the sentence.

Awkwardly in sentence *4* describes the manner in which the subject felt (moved about). It does not tell us that the person represented by *he* is by nature an awkward person.

The prepositional phrase immediately following the verb and used as a subjective complement should not be confused with the adverb phrase used as a modifier of the verb. If the verb is a copulative one, the prepositional phrase will be an attribute (subjective) complement. Often the adjective phrase can be tested by substituting a pure adjective. Observe the following:

1. The ring is of gold.

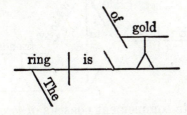

Of gold (equivalent to *golden*) is an adjective phrase used as predicate adjective. The construction resembles the Latin "genitive of material."

Observe that the prepositional phrase *of gold* is placed on a prepositional line on a standard above the base line. This form is used to show that the entire phrase is to be construed as the attribute complement.

2. The teacher is now in a very bad humor.

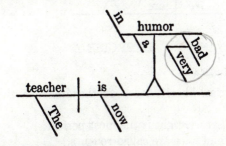

In a very bad humor describes the teacher. Compare this sentence with *The teacher is in his office*, where *is* is a full verb meaning *exists*, and *in his office* tells where the teacher is (i.e., *exists*).

The attribute complement may be a compound prepositional phrase:

3. He is out of funds and without friends.

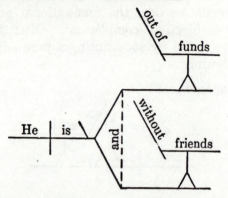

If the attribute complement consists of two or more nouns
governed by one preposition, the base line is not divided, but
the phrase is put on a standard, as in the following diagram:

4. We are out of sugar and coffee.

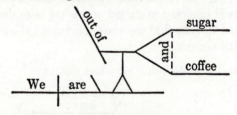

EXERCISE A

Analyze or diagram:

1. For centuries, liberty has been the dream of the brave Czech
people.

2. Of all our senses, sight is the most perfect.

3. Both rats and mice are called rodents.

4. The first and indispensable quality of a good style is clearness.

5. The rhythm of Lord Bacon's poetry is rather mechanical.

√ **6.** Anarchy and confusion, poverty and distress, desolation and
ruin are the consequences of civil war.

7. Does he come as an enemy or as a friend?

8. This is the Captain's dining room.

9. Virtuous and wise he was in all of his actions.

10. An apothecary should never be out of spirits.

11. A life of leisure and a life of laziness are two things.

12. The history of the world is the biography of great men.

13. Obscurity and affectation are the two greatest faults of style.

14. The honest fellow's eyes were full of tears.

15. A bad critic is probably the most mischievous person in the world.

16. You are desperate, full of fancies, and wilful.

17. Nathan Hale died a martyr to liberty.

18. All French nouns are either masculine or feminine.

19. The scent was of horsehair and plush and Florida water.

20. Facts were the playthings of Burke's style, and the sport of his fancy.

21. A well-bred man is quiet in dress, respectful to everybody, kind to the weak, helpful to the feeble.

22. Amusements often become the business instead of the relaxation of young persons.

23. Which one of the boys is your brother?

24. Washington was elected the first president of the United States.

25. Double-dealers are seldom in favor with honest men.

26. Andy was the eldest and the handsomest of all the boys.

27. The men in my family have always been soldiers.

28. The deep cave among the rocks on the hillside was long the secret home of a family of foxes.

29. A rainbow in the morning is the shepherd's warning.

30. Mathematical truth is not the only truth in the world.

31. Words of opposite meaning are called antonyms.

32. In rude nations, the dependence of children upon their parents is of short duration.

33. A knowledge of synonyms and of their special uses is absolutely necessary in every kind of composition.

34. The way before you is intricate, dark, and full of treacherous mazes.

35. Hurry, bustle, and agitation are the never-failing symptoms of a weak and frivolous mind.

36. Precision of speech is not altogether a matter of single words.

37. This book is presented to you as a gift from the entire family.

38. Some of our wealthiest men have lived and died bachelors.

39. Happiness is a wine of the rarest vintage, and seems insipid to the vulgar.

40. Parents are sometimes foreigners to their sons and daughters.

41. He is also called the Almighty, the Invisible, the Infinite, the Lord of lords.

42. Houses and lands, offices and honors, gold and bonds are nothing to the man at Death's door.

43. According to Mark Twain, the difference between the right word and the almost right word is the difference between lightning and the lightning bug.

44. The most important characteristic of poetical communication is rhythm.

45. A parody is a piece of imitative writing with a humorous or satiric purpose.

46. This counsellor is now most still, most secret, most grave.

47. The food looked good but was offensive to the taste.

48. Homonyms are considered among the most useful words of the language.

49. Caesar's *Commentaries on the Gallic War* is proof of his literary ability.

50. The aid of a good citizen is never without a beneficial effect.

EXERCISE B

I. In Exercise A, pick out five examples of a verb in the passive voice followed by a subjective complement, and tell whether the complement is an adjective or a noun (i.e. attribute complement or predicate nominative).

II. Pick out five examples of an intransitive verb (other than the verb *be*) followed by a subjective complement, and tell whether the complement is a predicate nominative or an attribute complement.

III. Write five original sentences containing prepositional phrases used as attribute complements.

IV. Write sentences using each of the following verbs (1) as a copulative (linking) verb and (2) as full predicating verb: *smell, taste, live, come, turn, grow, shine, run, feel, look, keep, appear, die.*

V. Write sentences containing subjective complements, using the following passive voice forms: *was called, has been made, is presented, will be named, was thought, was styled, should be considered.*

VI. Use each of the following words in the predicate as a subjective complement or as an adverbial modifier; and point out any words that can have either adjectival or adverbial use: *awkward, bad, roughly, good, homely, dead, lovely, bright, queenly, ugly, handsome, distinctly, due.*

EXERCISE C

Correct any errors which you find in the following, and give a reason for each correction you make. If the wrong form of a word is used, make a sentence to show its correct use.

1. He dresses real good.
2. She looks beautifully in her evening clothes.
3. Can you not stand more erectly?
4. I was reasonable sure about the price of the hat.
5. If I were him, I would leave at once.
6. She is a success financially and socially.
7. The ivy clings closely to the wall.
8. I feel sadly about your losing the fight.
9. The young speaker appeared very awkwardly and nervously.
10. The child speaks her speech too rapid.
11. We used to dance more modest than you do.
12. He will behave different hereafter.
13. Your walls will look well after the paint dries.
14. You must write your name legible and distinct on both copies of the contract.
15. The boy has always worked faithful.

LESSON IV

The Object Complement
(Direct Object)

The **object complement,** or **direct object,** is a noun or a noun-equivalent which completes the predicate and receives the act expressed in the verb.

It usually follows a transitive verb in the active voice; and the verb governs it; i.e., determines its case, which in English is always the objective.

In the diagram, the direct object is placed on the base line, and a short vertical line drawn to the base line separates the verb and the direct object.

1. He touched the wall.

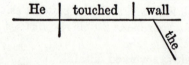

Wall is the object complement. It completes the predicate and names the object which receives the act expressed in the verb *touched.* It is commonly referred to as the **direct object:** it receives the direct action of the verb. The student would do well here to think of the object (the Latin word *objectus* means literally *thrown against*) as an obstacle, in this case actually arresting the motion of the subject expressed in the verb.

2. He saw me.

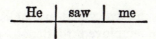

Here the object, *me*, stands in the line of vision and arrests the sight.

3. He saw the point of my remark.

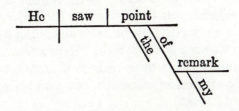

The sentence is metaphorical. *Saw* means *perceived;* and the object, *point*, stands in the line of mental vision.

It will be seen from the above illustrations that the term *object* must be interpreted broadly. The object may arrest physical action (*He caught the ball*); it may focus any sort of sense activity (*He heard me; He felt me*); it may be a mental result of figurative action (*He framed an excuse*); it may serve as the conclusion of mental aim or experience (*He attempted suicide; He tried a change of diet*).

Some verbs which are normally intransitive can be made into transitive verbs by giving them **cognate objects** (see Classification of Verbs, pp. 94–95). The **cognate object** is a noun identical in etymology (i.e., cognate) with the normally intransitive verb which governs it. Observe that the verb in *I dreamed about you* is intransitive. But note that the same verb in *I dreamed a bad dream about you* is transitive, the object *dream* being cognate in origin with the verb *dream, dreamed.* Other intransitive verbs capable of taking on transitive meaning if followed by a cognate object are *dance* (*danced the dance*), *run* (*run a race*), *play* (*played the play*), *fight* (*fought a* *good fight*), *sing* (*sing a song*), *live* (*live a good life*), and many others.[1]

A number of intransitive verbs in English become transitive when they are employed to denote causation. Such verbs are sometimes called **causative verbs.** In Germanic (e.g. Gothic) some intransitive verbs became transitive by the addition of the causative suffix (see Causative Verbs, pp. 95–96). In Modern English, the causative verb may have a suffix (e.g., *whiten; -en* is added to the adjective *white*) or a prefix (e.g., *enfeeble; -en* is prefixed to the adjective *feeble*): but many of our causative verbs have no ending whatever, as *ran* in *He ran the car into the garage.* Here a normally intransitive verb simply takes on a restricted transitive meaning. It is limited to expressing causation, *ran* here being the equivalent of *caused to run.*

Many verbs in English, such as *give, grant, allow, teach,* etc. take two objects, one the **direct object,** the other the **indirect** (see Adverbial Objectives, pp. 271–284). Either object can become the subject of the verb in the passive voice.

Sometimes the indirect object is converted into a prepositional phrase when it is placed after the direct object in the spoken sentence. See sentences *1* and *2* following:

1. I gave the money to John.

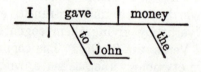

---

[1] In the diagram, the cognate object is not differentiated from other direct objects:

He dreamed a dream.

2. The money was given to John by me.

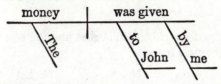

3. John was given the money by me.

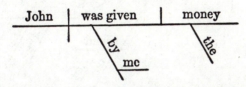

Observe that the direct object (*money*) in sentence *1* becomes the subject in sentence *2*, the verb being in the passive voice. However, in *3* the noun *John* (the object of the preposition in *1* and *2*) becomes the subject, the noun *money* being left in its original position as the direct object. Sentence *3* shows an instance of what has been called the **retained object** (or **retained object complement**: it completes the predicate and receives the direct action of the verb even though the verb is in the passive voice). This form of speech is condemned by some grammarians, but there is ample authority for its use in the practice of masters of English. Because it is sometimes awkward and heavy, it is well to guard against overworking the passive voice construction. Compare *I was taught algebra by my mother* with *My mother taught me algebra; I was allowed my expenses* with *My expenses were allowed;* and *I was given this ring* with *This ring was given to me* (or with *My roommate gave me this ring*); and *A good time was had by all at the picnic* with *Everyone had a good time at the picnic.* One should prefer the passive voice with or without the retained object only when it expresses clearly and forcefully the meaning to be conveyed. *A good time was had by all* is certainly awkward and unemphatic.

The compounding process may produce a sentence with

two or more object complements, with separate or shared modifiers:

    1. We enjoyed the old oaken bucket and the new tin dipper of our rustic friend.

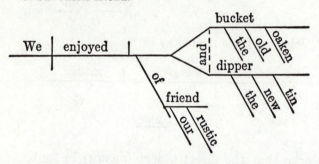

Observe that the object line is drawn vertical to the base line before it is divided to accommodate the compound object complement (*bucket* and *dipper*). Also note that the phrase *of our rustic friend* modifies both *bucket* and *dipper*, and is placed before the line is divided but at the right of the object complement line.

A verb with an object complement and one without may occur in the same predicate:

    2. He lived happily for many years, and achieved every desire of his heart.

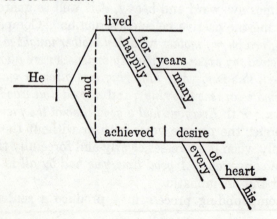

Caution: The transitive verb in the active voice governs the objective case, never the nominative.   The compounding of the object complement makes no difference in the construction of the governed substantive:

> *Incorrect:* We left Mary and she in the arbor.
> *Correct:*   We left Mary and *her* in the arbor.

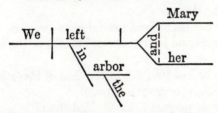

Also, in diagraming, be careful to get the modifying phrase in the right place.   *In the arbor* modifies the verb, not the object complement.

EXERCISE A

Analyze or diagram:

1. Nature hates monopolies and exceptions.
2. Plants and animals exhibit structural modifications.
3. The cat in the glove catches no mice.
4. Everything in nature contains all the powers of nature.
5. The wise man throws himself on the side of his assailants.
6. We were not allowed enough time for that examination.
7. Your bait of falsehood takes this carp of truth.
8. Few hunters or herders have developed much civilization.
9. Hope and despondency, joy and sorrow, pleasure and pain diversify life with their sudden contrasts.
10. We have been taught the basic principles.
11. Man cannot push his way through nature at will, in the absence of special knowledge.
12. Without the reindeer and the dog, the peoples of the extreme north could scarcely maintain life.
13. Tolerate no uncleanliness in body, clothes, or habitation.
14. The hand of little employment hath the daintier sense.
15. Silks and satins, scarlet and velvet put out the kitchen fire.

16. A small leak will sink a great ship.

17. Its trunk reaches up high, and spreads its boughs over the whole universe.

18. School boys can accomplish wonders in the way of deception.

19. They found the babe in a manger at Bethlehem.

20. Isolation prohibits much intermixture of different stocks.

✓ 21. With a foul traitor's name stuff I thy throat.

22. I cannot sing that song now.

23. The matter has been given careful consideration.

✓ 24. Music and measure lend grace and health to the soul and to the body.

25. At eighteen he lost his faith in the God of his fathers.

26. We blame Knox for his intolerance.

27. Like a sensible pessimist, he avoided the pitfalls of optimists.

✓ 28. He was sharply rebuked by his teacher, and took his seat in miserable silence.

29. He was granted a year's leave of absence.

✓ 30. Suddenly in the dead of the night loud noises alarmed them.

31. In the beginning God created the heavens and the earth.

32. A wise son heareth his father's instructions.

✓ 33. Cowley, with all his admirable wit and ingenuity, had little imagination.

✓ 34. Within twelve months Greece had lost her greatest ruler, her greatest orator, and her greatest philosopher.

35. Earth and sky, land and water, mountain and valley bear traces of divine workmanship.

✓ 36. Modern war destroys the healthiest and strongest men.

37. Do we want our poetry from grammarians?

✓ 38. Neither locks had they to their doors, nor bars to their windows.

✓ 39. The committee on rules has of recent years had a very singular and significant development of functions.

✓ 40. The beautiful laws and substances of the world persecute and whip the traitor.

✓ 41. The hero drew a slab of tobacco from his pocket, cut off a wedge, and pressed it into the leather pouch of his cheek.

✓ 42. He looked far up and out to the westward, and caught the glint of snow on the higher peaks.

✓ 43. Famine and sword and pestilence had devastated the fertile plains and stately cities of the Po.

44. For the sake of mere decoration, savage men and women will endure long physical agonies.

45. She never lost the child's miraculous power of wonder.

46. We resent the cold analysis and reduction of life to the commonplace.

47. We have had lessons enough of the futility of criticism.

48. For nonconformity the world whips you with its displeasure.

49. He had been forsaken by his old friends, and now could form no new companionships.

50. Suddenly one of the little Italians dropped his rod, stood up to his full height, lifted his arms very much after the manner of an orchestra leader, and joined in with me.

EXERCISE B

Correct any violations of good usage which you find in the following sentences, and give a reason for each correction you make:

1. He has lain my book on the wrong shelf.

2. He set down and talked German with us.

3. I shan't tell nobody.

4. Would you have any objections to my laying on this couch?

5. Now, that don't make no difference with me.

6. The bread will raise faster in the warm room.

7. Will every girl leave her wraps lay there?

8. The maid said she knew that the vase was broke.

9. He laid ill for more than a year.

10. Did you ask Jerry and she to go with us?

11. That puzzle is unable to be solved by me.

12. The river always raises over that bridge when the spring rains come.

13. His wife tried to cover over his faults.

14. Haven't you no friends you can ask to help you?

15. My salary has been risen twice since I came here.

16. I don't enjoy entertaining these kind of people.

17. Did you read that poem yet?

18. I have never punished the child, and never will.

19. I cannot find John and she any place.

20. I don't want to be run off from.

LESSON V

The Objective Complement

The **objective complement** is an adjective or a noun or the equivalent of either which completes the action expressed in the verb and refers to the direct object. The objective complement, if an adjective, describes or limits the object; if a noun, it is in a sense identical with the direct object.

1. The sunlight made the apple red.

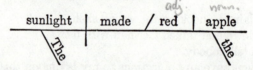

Red is an adjective used as the objective complement; it completes the meaning of the verb *made* and describes the direct object. In the diagram it is placed next to the verb which it completes (*made-red* is about the equivalent of *reddened*). It is separated from the verb by a diagonal line slanting toward the object to show that *red* belongs to the direct object, *apple.*

2. The council made Michael king.

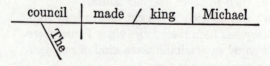

In this sentence, the objective complement is *king,* a noun. *Made-king* is the equivalent of *crowned.* It is in a sense identical with *Michael,* the direct object.

250

The action expressed in a verb may bring about a change in the nature, condition, or designation of the object. The resultant nature, condition, or designation may be represented by an adjective or a noun, which appears in the sentence as a part of the predicate.

It will be seen that in the first of these illustrations the adjective represents a new condition of the object, wrought by the action of the verb. In the second sentence, the noun represents a new status, or designation, brought about by the action of the verb: the council has made Michael a king. A verb which thus makes its object different is sometimes called a **factitive verb** (the term *factitive* is from Latin *factus*, past participle of *facere*, to make). It will be seen that the verb *make* here means *change*, not *create out of nothing*. Compare *He made the chair usable* with *He made the chair*, and note that in the first sentence only the condition of the chair was changed, and in the second the chair was made from pieces of lumber or other raw material.

In each of the following sentences the factitive idea is present in the verb, and the resulting condition or designation of the object is seen in the objective complement.

1. She dyed the wool green.

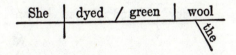

2. The news drove the man insane.

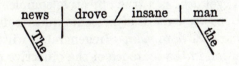

3. He appointed Harris manager.

| He | appointed / manager | Harris |

4. They named the child Martha.

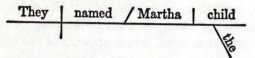

5. The frost turned the leaves yellow.

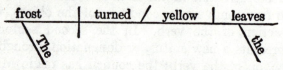

In each of these sentences, the subject as an actor causes a change in the condition of the object receiving the action of the verb, and the objective complement tells what the change was.

In *The frost turned the leaves yellow*, the subject *frost* changes what we may assume were green leaves to yellow leaves. The sentence is about the equivalent of *The frost yellowed the leaves.*

However, not all verbs which are followed by the objective complement present the factitive idea. Certain **nonfactitive verbs** also require the assistance of the objective complement for full predication.

6. They found the man dead.

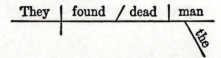

Here the action of the verb produces no change in the state of the object, yet *dead* is a true objective complement. Note that *They found the man dead* presents quite a different idea from *They found the dead man.* In general, it will be observed that the position in the sentence of the objective complement is after the object, though the former is placed at the left of the direct object in the diagram.[1] It is always true that

---

[1] Occasionally for emphasis or for variation of sentence structure, the objective complement is not placed immediately after the direct object. In an inter-

without the objective complement the verb would mean something different from what it means when the objective complement is present. *They found the dead man* conveys the idea that some persons were looking for *a dead man* and discovered the corpse; whereas *They found the man dead* indicates that those who were looking for the man had no knowledge that he was dead until they found him, and then they discovered that he was dead; i.e., they *found-dead* the man.

Other examples of the objective complement following a nonfactitive verb are the following:

1. Leave me alone.

$$x \mid \text{Leave} \,/\, \text{alone} \mid \text{me}$$

2. We thought the boat safe and sound.

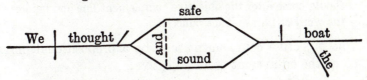

3. Do you believe him guilty?

$$\text{you} \mid \text{Do believe} \,/\, \text{guilty} \mid \text{him}$$

4. She called him a villain.

$$\text{She} \mid \text{called} \,/\, \text{villain} \mid \text{him}$$

Observe that *leave, thought, do believe,* and *called* are not true factitive ("making") verbs. The objective complements which follow them do not modify the condition of the direct

rogative sentence the direct object may be placed at or near the beginning of the sentence, as in *Whose house have I made a wilderness?* Here *house* is the direct object, and *wilderness* is the objective complement. Interrogative sentences must be thrown into the declarative form for analysis. In *Murderers they call themselves,* the noun *murderers* is the objective complement. Observe that the normal word order for this sentence would be *They call themselves murderers.*

objects.   Our thinking a person guilty does not make him guilty.   Observe that *make, made* cannot be substituted for the nonfactitive verbs.

The expletive *as* may introduce the objective complement:

5. He used his scepter as a schoolmaster's rod.

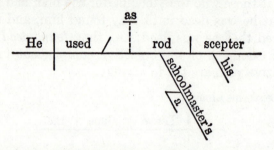

Observe that the dotted line attaching *as* to the base line should come after the objective complement line and before the word or phrase it introduces.

The objective complement may be a prepositional phrase used as the equivalent of an adjective:

1. I found my mother in good health.

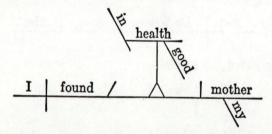

In the diagram the entire prepositional phrase is placed on a standard above the base line to indicate that the phrase is used as one grammatical unit.

Observe that *in good health* restricts the meaning of the verb and refers to and describes the object complement. The phrase is the equivalent of *well* or *healthy.*   Compare the above sentence with *I found mother in the attic,* where *in the attic* tells place and is an adverbial phrase modifying the verb *found*.

EXERCISE A

Analyze or diagram:

1. We thought your sister's remarks very unkind.
2. I find many of your answers incorrect.
3. A thief he named himself.
4. My sister has cut her hair too short.
5. Work made Mr. Blythe ill.
6. Soames thought her sweet and pure.
7. They selected St. Paul's as their church.
8. She felt herself a great liberator.
9. They have selected her as model.
10. We shall paint the walls white, and then put up our best curtains.
11. Nature keeps things in order.
12. The times made Brutus an assassin and traitor.
13. Isolation on a heath renders vulgarity well-nigh impossible.
14. I have made my heart clean.
15. Any strong wild man might have made himself poet, king, priest, or any kind of hero.
16. We will call poetry musical thought.
17. We do not now call our great men gods.
18. Kant entitled his great work *A Critique of Pure Reason*.
19. Before the war he could regard this state of affairs as normal and certain.
20. We should consider mind chiefly as conscious knowledge.
21. The doctor's medicine made both of us very sleepy.
22. I create thee here my lord and master.
23. All this makes results less certain, definite, and notable.
24. Critics will call him virile and passionate.
25. In life the true realist finds nothing insignificant.
26. Such tastes and acquirements in a man of his condition made the contrast more poignant.
27. People now call a spade an agricultural implement.
28. The great flood of the spring had swept the valley clean.
29. That author makes his paupers and porters superhuman.
30. Nature never rhymes her children, nor makes two men alike.

31. They made Carol president and director.
32. I believed him one of the best men in the world.
33. The use of new lands has made food cheap and abundant.
34. All this makes capital abundant and interest low.
35. His fatigue rendered the act an effort.
36. In some states the tramp finds himself a criminal.
37. He had always considered Lulu the most beautiful and charming girl in the universe.
38. Dost thou call me a fool?
39. I pronounce thee a gross lout and a mindless slave.
40. Grief makes one hour two.
41. My terror shall not make thee afraid.
42. We have elected as president a number of mediocre men.

EXERCISE B

Correct any violations of good usage which you find in the following sentences, and give a reason for each correction you make:

1. Are you making the edges evenly?
2. Your remark made me feel badly.
3. Of the two subjects, I find English the most interesting.
4. Rub the surface smoothly before applying the base coat of paint.
5. These students do not take these matters serious enough.
6. We thought that play the best of any play given this season.
7. She thought the two persons John and I.
8. Andrea del Sarto must of made his picture too perfectly.
9. The hot sun has made our grass terrible brown.
10. We believed him real honest.
11. She laid her plans openly before us.
12. They have done cut the grass too closely.
13. They I shall pronounce guilty.
14. Did you find your mother and she alone?
15. The maid don't wash our clothes cleanly.
16. The reference made him illy at ease.
17. You should take life more serious.
18. Who have they elected president of the club?
19. He made them soldiers stand erectly.
20. We thought she the bravest of anyone we knew.

Lesson VI

Appositives and Independent Words and Phrases

Appositives

An **appositive** (or **explanatory modifier**) is a word, phrase, or clause which is inserted in a sentence to identify or explain some other word or group of words occurring in the same sentence. The most common appositive is the noun in apposition with another noun. It is usually in the same case as the noun it explains.[1]

Appositives, or explanatory modifiers, may be **restrictive or nonrestrictive.** If they identify (i.e., restrict) what precedes them in the sentence, they are **restrictive,** and are not set off by any sort of punctuation. The **nonrestrictive appositives** give additional information, and they can be omitted from the sentences in which they occur without greatly affecting the basic meaning. These must be separated from the elements which they are in apposition with by some sort of punctuation. Observe the punctuation used to set off nonrestrictive appositives in Exercise A at the end of this Lesson.

In the diagram, the appositive is usually placed immediately after the word it identifies or explains, and it is always enclosed in parentheses. The diagram does not differentiate the restrictive from the nonrestrictive appositive when it is construed as an explanatory modifier. Sometimes the re-

---

[1] A noun having the nominative (or objective) form may be in apposition with a noun or pronoun in the possessive case, as in *I got this at Smith's, the florist; He married his brother John's sister-in-law.*

257

strictive appositive is so closely associated with the word it explains that it becomes a part of a phrasal noun; e.g., *William the Conqueror, King Alfred, President Roosevelt*, etc., and need not be enclosed in parentheses in the diagram.

1. The Manx, inhabitants of the Isle of Man, speak a Celtic tongue.

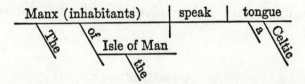

In this sentence, *inhabitants* is a nonrestrictive appositive; it explains by giving additional information about the noun *Manx*. It should be construed as being in the nominative case, since it is in apposition with the subject of the sentence. Observe that the appositive is modified by the adjective phrase *of the Isle of Man*. Note that *Isle of Man* is a phrasal noun, the object of the preposition *of*.

Many of the nonrestrictive appositives are introduced by **expletives** (fossilized conjunctions). The most common of these are *or, namely, i.e.* (*id est*, that is), *e.g.* (*exampla gratia*, for example), *as, such as, or rather, especially, for example, for instance, viz.* (*videlicit*, namely, to wit).

In the diagram, the expletive is placed just before and above the appositive it introduces:

2. Boneset, or thoroughwort, has tonic properties.

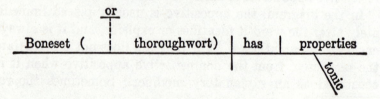

Observe that *or* here introduces a nonrestrictive appositive, which is set off by commas. Note also that the comma before *or* and the one after *thoroughwort* are important to the meaning of this sentence. If they were omitted, *or* would be a conjunction joining two nouns naming two different objects, and not an expletive introducing a different name for the same object. *Or thoroughwort* could be omitted without affecting the meaning of this sentence, but its insertion may explain *boneset* sufficiently so that a reader who knows what thoroughwort is may not need to consult a dictionary to know the meaning of the sentence. Nonrestrictive appositives often prove great time-savers for the reader.

The following sentence contains two appositives; one is restrictive, the other is not. The second, which is the nonrestrictive one, is introduced by the expletive *namely:*

3. The word *knowledge* implies three things: namely, truth, proof, and conviction.

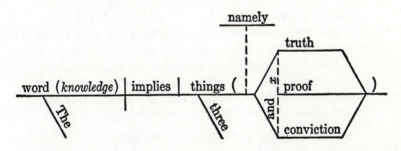

In the diagram of a compound appositive, the line is divided to accommodate the members of the compound element. Observe that *namely* is placed immediately before the words it introduces, and is attached to the line before it is divided but after the first parenthetical mark. The divided lines must be joined before the second parenthetical mark is placed to indicate that all three of the nouns are in apposition with the noun *things.*

A noun in the plural may be in apposition with two or more nouns, as in the following:

4. We should cultivate prudence, justice, temperance, and fortitude, the cardinal virtues of man.

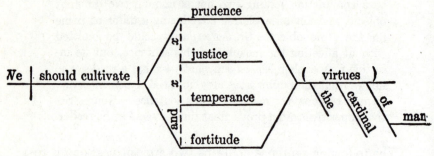

5. The word *what* has many uses.

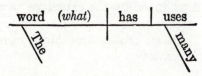

What is a restrictive appositive. Observe that it is not separated by any sort of punctuation from the word which precedes it or from the one which follows it. Also note that *what* cannot be omitted from this sentence without making the sentence obscure. In the written sentence restrictive appositives of this sort, where a word is singled out, should be underscored; in print they are italicized, not quoted.

6. My brother John is the eldest of the family.

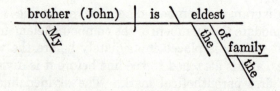

In this sentence, *John* is also a restrictive appositive. The meaning conveyed here is that the author of this sentence had other brothers and sisters, and that John is the eldest. If we set off *John* by commas, the sentence would mean that there was only one brother in the family.

If I have only one sister, I may say *My sister, Mary, lives in New York;* but if I have several sisters, and I wish to indicate that Mary is the only one of them who lives in New York, I should write *My sister Mary lives in New York.* In spoken language one makes pauses where the commas are placed in the written speech.

As we learned in our study of the compound personal (or *self-*) pronouns (Part One, pp. 52–55), the intensive use is appositional, as in the following:[2]

7. I myself did it; *or* I did it myself.

$$\text{I (myself)} \mid \text{did} \mid \text{it}$$

Observe that the position of *myself* in the written or spoken sentence does not cnange its construction. It may come immediately after the word it emphasizes (intensifies), or it may come at the end of a phrase, clause, or sentence. It frequently comes after the object complement, as in the second phrasing of sentence 7.

An adjective is sometimes used as an appositive to explain another adjective which immediately precedes it in the sentence. In the written form, an adjective appositive should be enclosed in parentheses to prevent its being construed as just another nonrestrictive adjective modifier.

---

[2] The intensive and reflexive uses of the *self*-pronouns should not be confused. Observe that *myself* in the following sentence is a reflexive pronoun:

I came here by myself.

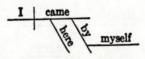

In this sentence, *myself* is in the objective case; it is the object of the preposition *by*. Observe that the personal pronoun *me* could not be used here. (For other uses of the intensive and reflexive pronouns, see Part One, Chapter Three, pp. 52–55).

8. An anaemic (bloodless) pallor was the chief fault of her complexion.

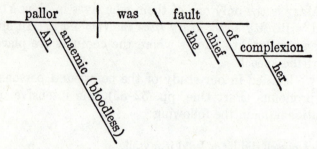

In this sentence, the adjective *bloodless* is a nonrestrictive appositive; it explains, defines, gives additional information. It could be omitted, and the sentence would convey the same meaning.

9. He is marrying my cousin John's sister-in-law

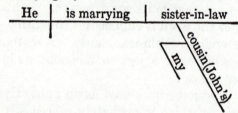

Here the possessive form *John's* is an appositive of *cousin,* which would have the possessive form if the appositive were omitted.

Occasionally a verb is an appositive (an explanatory modifier) of another verb, as in the following sentence:

10. He would syllogize (state in the terms of formal logic) the difficult matter.

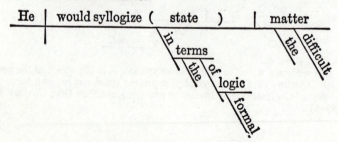

Here *state* with its complex modifying phrase *in the terms of formal logic* explains, interprets *would syllogize*. It is non-restrictive and could be omitted; but its use saves time, for one who does not know the meaning of the verb *syllogize*, by defining it.

An effective use of an appositive is to explain or summarize an entire idea:

11. She shut the door in the beggar's face—an act of unnecessary rudeness.

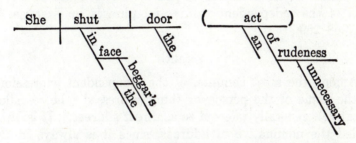

Here *an act of unnecessary rudeness* is in apposition with an entire statement, not with any single word. It is the shutting of the door in the beggar's face that is the act of rudeness.

In the diagram, the appositive of an entire idea or statement is placed after what it explains, and the chief element (the head word) in the appositive phrase is enclosed in parentheses. Observe that the line on which *act* is placed in the diagram is not in any way joined to what it explains. It is not an independent element; therefore, the parentheses in the diagram are important to differentiate it from the independent expression.

Independent Words and Phrases

Any word or phrase which does not enter into the construction of the sentence may be construed as an independent element. An independent expression may be a noun used merely to call attention to someone addressed by naming him before the sentence proper is closed. It may be an interjection used solely to convey an emotional reaction. Or it may be a worn out (fossilized) adverb or conjunction or interjection employed to introduce or to vary the word order of a sentence. It may even be a redundant, or pleonastic, expression used to secure a literary or poetic effect.

Independent expressions are usually separated from the sentence proper by some punctuation, such as the comma, the dash, or the exclamation point. Observe the punctuation of the independent words and phrases in Exercise A, pp. 268–269.

Vocative

Among the most common of the independent expressions is the name of the person or thing addressed (the so-called **vocative**), generally referred to as **direct address**. It is often called the **nominative of address,** since it is always in the nominative case in Modern English.

1. Paul, thou art beside thyself.

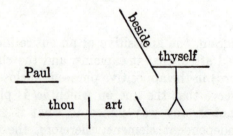

Paul is not explanatory of *thou*, but is independent. *Beside thyself* (equivalent to *mad, deranged*) is a descriptive predicate adjective, not an adverb phrase of place.

The vocative is sometimes preceded by the interjection *O,* as in the following sentence:

2. O Lord, how manifold are Thy mercies!

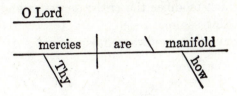

Interjections

Interjections are always independent. Sometimes they are to be interpreted as complete exclamatory sentences, as in the case of Cicero's well known exclamation, *O tempora! O mores!* (*O these times!   O these customs!*)

More often the interjection is emotionally related to what follows, though grammatically not a part of the sentence:

1. Alas, how impossible it seems!

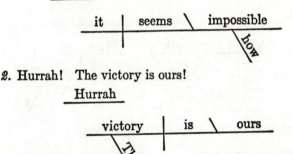

2. Hurrah!   The victory is ours!

Any isolated word or group of words uttered with much force and feeling should be treated as independent elements both in the analysis and in the diagram. *Goodness gracious! Dear me!   Behold!   Peace!   Silence!* and other expressions like these belong outside the sentence proper.

Independent Adverbs and Parenthetical Expressions

An independent adverb, like the interjection, has a rhetorical rather than a grammatical function.   It may be an expletive and merely introduce a statement, or it may be a word or phrase which modifies the entire sentence and connects it with a preceding sentence.

The expletive *there* is always independent:

There is enough for all.

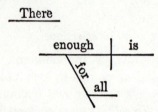

Parenthetical expressions are words or groups of words which are inserted in the sentence as asides or afterthoughts. They do not belong to either the subject or the predicate of the sentences they are in. They are always construed as independent elements.

God bless—no harm in a blessing—the Pretender.

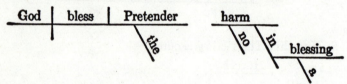

The adverbial phrase may be independent:

In short, you are wrong.

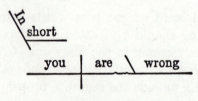

Pleonasm

The word *pleonasm* means overfullness. Rhetorically, it is a species of redundancy, the use of unnecessary words. The term *pleonasm,* however, is generally employed to describe a structure wherein for some purpose one of the main elements of the sentence is repeated. It is, therefore, not always bad, as are some other types of redundancy. An expression may be repeated for clearness or for emphasis or merely for a poetic effect. Shakespeare makes frequent and effective use of pleonastic expressions, one of the most famous of his being *To be or not to be, that is the question.* Here *that* is pleonastic, and it could be omitted, but the effectiveness of the sentence would suffer greatly by its omission.

The smith, a mighty man is he.

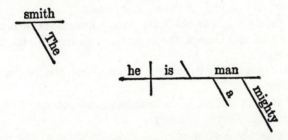

Observe that the pronoun *he* is the subject of this sentence. Its antecedent, the noun *smith,* should be construed as an independent element, not as an appositive. It is well to remember that pronouns are substitutes for nouns, and that nouns are not, as a general rule, used to explain pronouns.

EXERCISE A

Analyze or diagram:

1. Then spoke Beowulf, son of Ecgtheow.
2. The sky, or firmament, is above us.
3. Thy rod and thy staff, they comfort me.
4. The gods, sole witnesses of their battle, betted dead against him.
5. The principal characteristic of the second nephew, Adrian Harley, was his sagacity.
6. Benson, the woman-hater, was wide-awake.
7. The trader himself will take care of the supply.

8. Law and order, the basic results of government, will be somehow extended beyond national boundaries.
9. The king, our master, must be served.
10. One of the greatest forces in the world is man himself.
11. A reconstruction of life under such circumstances appears in Jack London's story *Before Adam*.
12. Allan Ramsay, the poet and wigmaker, was born in 1686 and died in 1758.
13. The book itself will not add much to the fame of Milton.
14. Unto thee, O Lord, do I lift up my soul.
15. The passover, a feast of the Jews, was nigh.
16. Woe unto you also, ye lawgivers.
17. Oh, I did not understand you.
18. The bed, or channel, of the river is wide.
19. Upon the door was an old brass plate, a useless yet precious relic.
20. I am Alpha and Omega, the beginning and the end, the first and the last.
21. She has rank, talent, wealth, beauty—all the prizes of this world.
22. The Paradiso, a kind of inarticulate music to me, is the finest part of the Divine Comedy.
23. They were the leaders of men, these great ones: the modelers, the patterns, and the creators.
24. We will look at these two, the poet Dante and the poet Shakespeare.
25. The three kingdoms, Inferno, Purgatorio, Paradiso, look out on one another like compartments of a great edifice.
26. God, the Maker of heaven and earth, is worshiped by a myriad of creatures.
27. Can a great soul be possible without a conscience in it, the essence of all real souls?
28. Hero-worship, reverence for false authorities, is itself false.
29. The verbals (participles, gerunds, and infinitives) are verb forms.
30. The destruction of Demetrius, son to Philip the Second of Macedonia, turned upon the father.
31. The topic at present was a highly popular and frequent one— the personal character of Mrs. Charmond.
32. Always use the singular demonstrative adjectives (*this* and *that*) with singular nouns.

33. Winterborne retired into the background of human life and action—a feat not particularly difficult of performance.

34. The lariat, or lasso, is not used by riders in Australia.

35. Then answered Bildad the Shuhite.

36. In short, my deary, kiss me and be quiet.

37. O mountains, rivers, rocks, and savage herds, To you I speak!

38. O shame! where is thy blush?

39. O beware, my lord, of jealousy.

40. Human nature is made up of two elements, power and form.

41. Hermione, Queen to the worthy Leontes, King of Sicilia, thou art accused of treason.

42. The letters *W. V. B.* are branded very distinctly on his forehead.

43. Hark! the shrill trumpet sounds to horse.

44. In the history of the Missouri River there were hundreds of these heroes, these builders of the epic world.

45. The world—this shadow of the soul, or other me—lies wide around.

46. Apollo and his twin sister, Artemis, were children of the goddess Leto.

47. Between you and me, his brother John stole our fruit.

48. The initials *JS* on the Roosevelt dimes stand for John Sinnock, an engraver at the Philadelphia mint.

49. Virtue, honesty, good-will, temperance—all these traits comprise manhood.

50. Behold! Behold! Ernest is himself the likeness of the Great Stone Face!

EXERCISE B

Correct all errors, including errors in punctuation, in the following, giving reasons for all corrections:

1. They did all the work theirselves.

2. We should compare the words, fatherly and paternal, with reference to origin and use.

3. Mr. Brown our gardener won't work after the sun sets.

4. I shall see you my boy before you leave for Europe.

5. John will you please help your brother.

6. Oh I cannot do that errand!

7. Let him do it hisself.

8. Milton thou shouldst be living at this hour.
9. Father, mother, brother sister all are dead.
10. The world's three greatest poems are epics *Paradise Lost*, the *Aeneid,* and the *Iliad*.
11. Greece, Rome, Carthage where are they?
12. Brabantio a rich senator of Venice had a fair daughter the gentle Desdemona.
13. I rise Mr. President to a point of order.
14. Well what shall we say in reply?
15. It is then a mark of wisdom to live virtuously.
16. In truth I have no hope of promotion.
17. The child itsself was hurt.
18. The two guests (John and me) enjoyed the surprise.
19. Between you and I the work is too hard.
20. Each of you are wrong, for it was Elizabeth and myself.

Lesson VII

Adverbial Objectives

An **adverbial objective** is a noun or pronoun or the equivalent of either used as an adverb. It is always in the objective case and modifies what adverbs modify (verbs, adverbs, adjectives, prepositions, and prepositional phrases). It requires no relational word, such as the preposition, to introduce it. A noun which is governed by a preposition is not an adverbial objective, but the principal word in a prepositional phrase, which phrase may be used as an adverb.

Indirect Object

Most prominent of the adverbial objectives is the **indirect object.** This construction occurs only with verbs meaning *give, offer,* and the like, and represents an old dative case. It is sometimes called the **dative object.** The word *dative* is derived from the perfect participle, *datus,* of the Latin verb *dare,* to give.

The **indirect object** is used with a transitive verb which has a direct object. It usually tells to whom or for whom the direct object is intended. The following sentences contain indirect objects:

1. We gave him the cup.

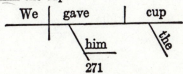

271

2. They have awarded Mary the prize.

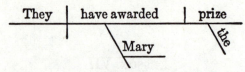

Observe that the adverbial objective is diagramed as if it were the object of a preposition. This form is suggested by the fact that most adverbial objectives can be restated as prepositional phrases. It is not true, however, that in every such instance there is "a preposition understood." In fact, the form without the preposition is older than the form with the preposition. Adverbial objectives are survivals of old case uses, and go back to a time when the use of prepositions was much more narrowly restricted than at present. Do not, therefore, in diagraming, write in an "understood" preposition where there actually should be none; nor even put in a cross, or other mark indicating a word omitted.

Some verbs which may take the indirect object are *give, grant, ask, allow, pay, loan, hand, send, allot, offer, write, tell, teach, furnish, get.* All, however, represent the giving ("dative") idea. The indirect object always represents, at least in a sense, the recipient of a gift. Such recipient may, however, be made the subject when the verb is thrown into the passive voice. When the indirect object is made the subject of a verb in the passive voice, the direct object is retained as the direct object (object complement), and is called in this construction the **retained object.** (see Object Complement, Lesson IV, pp. 244–245, for fuller treatment of the retained object.)

3. I allowed him a dollar for his work.

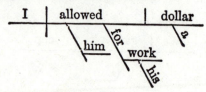

4. He was allowed a dollar for his work.

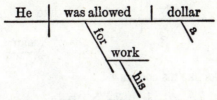

In the first of these sentences, *him* is an indirect object, and it is diagramed as a modifier of the verb *allowed*. It names the receiver of the direct object. In the second, the indirect object instead of the direct object is made the subject of the verb put in the passive voice. The direct object remains ("is retained") as a completing word for the predicate, and is still the direct receiver of the action expressed in the verb.

Other Adverbial Objectives

In Old English, adjectives and adverbs of a certain type of meaning were followed by the dative construction, and a few words of similar meaning in Modern English take the same construction.

1. Examples of such adjectives and adverbs are *like, unlike,* and *near*. In their function as adverb or as adjective, they may inflect to indicate the three degrees of comparison: *like, more like, most like; near, nearer, nearest (next)*, and words having degrees of comparison must be construed as adverbs or as adjectives. Prepositions and conjunctions have no inflection.

The following diagrams show a few of the various adjectival and adverbial uses and meanings of *like* and *near:*

a. *Like* and *Near* as Adjectives:

adj. comme

1. He is like me.

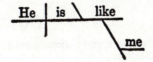

2. The candy tastes like soap.

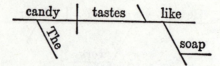

3. He looks like his cousin.

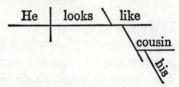

4. They are near the end.

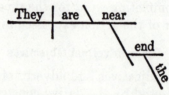

5. A fool like Jones can never be convinced.[1]

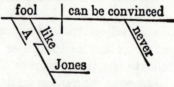

---

[1] In sentence *5, like* may be construed as a preposition:

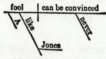

Observe that in this analysis of *like*, the sentence does not contain an adverbial objective.

But in the following sentence, *like* must be construed as an adjective:

Thou art like unto a flower.

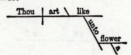

Observe that *unto a flower* is a prepositional phrase. If we omit *unto*, *flower* becomes an adverbial objective.

b. *Like* and *Near* as Adverbs:[2]

1. He runs like a deer.

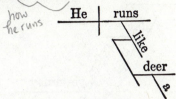

2. She is walking too near the precipice.

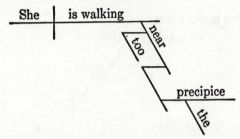

2. The adverbial objective may express *time when* or *duration* (or *extent*) *of time.* *Time when* is expressed by an adverbial objective equivalent to the Latin "ablative of time at which."

Duration of time is like the Latin accusative. Observe both types of time in the following:

a. *Time When:*

1. It happened Monday.

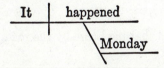

---

[2] The adverbs *like* and *near*, when not followed by prepositions, are sometimes construed as prepositions, the adverbial objectives becoming their objects; e.g., *like* in *He runs like a deer* may have the following form in the diagram when it has the force of a preposition:

2. He came the day before yesterday.

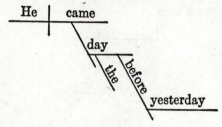

b. *Duration* (or *Extent*) *of Time:*

1. He ruled many years.

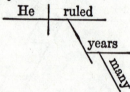

2. They worked all day.

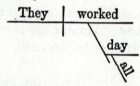

3. The adverbial objective may be employed to express *place where* (similar to the Latin ablative or locative case); *limit of motion* (similar to the Latin accusative *place to which*); and *direction,* or *way* (similar to the Latin accusative of *way*):

a. *Place Where:*

I live upstairs in that big house by the road.

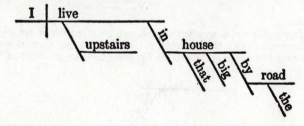

The adverbial objective is now seldom used to express *place where,* the prepositional phrase being more common and more natural.

b. *Limit of Motion:*

1. He sent her home.

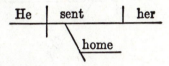

2. She has gone home.

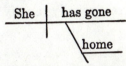

Observe that no preposition is used when the noun *home* follows a verb expressing motion. But a preposition is used when it follows verbs denoting being or a state of being. *She is home* is generally regarded as faulty English. The word *home* in the adverbial construction without the preposition can be used only after the idea of motion. *He will be home tomorrow* is acceptable English. Here *will be* has the meaning of *will come* or *will arrive.*

c. *Direction:*

I will go there the short way and return the long way.

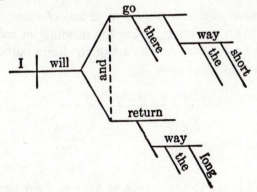

d. *Manner:* An adverbial objective expressing *manner* is the equivalent of a Latin ablative, but not derived from Latin:

Do it this way.

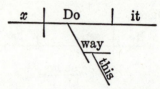

4. Adverbial objectives expressing ***degree,*** like the pure adverbs denoting degree, usually modify adjectives, adverbs, or prepositions:

a. *Modifying an Adjective:*

1. The mountain is a mile high.

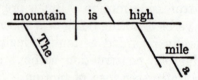

2. The saw is worth a dollar.

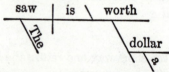

Here *dollar* expresses *degree* or *extent of value.* *Worth* is here used as an adjective having the meaning of *valuable.* It should not be construed as a part of the finite verb.

3. The child is five years old.

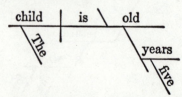

The child is *old* to the extent or degree of *five years.*

b. *Modifying an Adverb:*

They worked all day long.

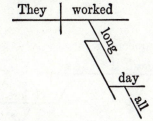

c. *Modifying a Preposition:*

He came a month before the inauguration.

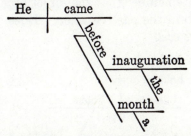

5. Adverbial objectives expressing *weight, measure, quantity,* and *value* usually modify verbs. They often convey a degree idea (as some of the following sentences will illustrate) even when modifying verbs and expressing any of the following meanings:

a. *Weight:*

The load weighs a ton.

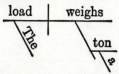

Compare this sentence with *He weighed that load of wheat,* where *weighed* is a transitive verb taking a direct object. Observe that the verb in this sentence can be put in the passive voice; as, *That load of wheat was weighed by him.* Note also that the adverbial objective in the sentence diagramed is used with an intransitive verb, which has no voice modification.

b. *Value:*

The saw cost five dollars.

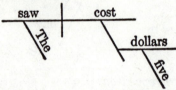

Cost is an intransitive verb.   Do not try to make it take a direct object.   Remember that the direct object becomes the subject of a verb in the passive voice.   Does one ever say or hear *Dollars were cost?*

c. *Measure:*

1. The basket holds a bushel.

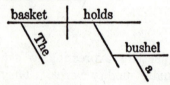

Here *hold* is an intransitive verb.   In its transitive meaning *hold* means *contain,* as in *The basket holds* (or *is holding*) *a bushel of peaches.*   We are not here told the size of the basket, as in *This basket holds* (*will hold*) *a bushel.*   One basket contains peaches; the other may be empty, but it could be used in measuring a bushel or several bushels of something.

2. The land yields fifty bushels of corn an acre.

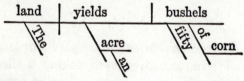

d. *Quantity.*

1. I paid a penny a stick for the candy.

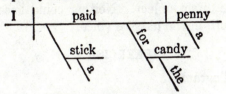

2. Butter is now selling at a dollar a pound.

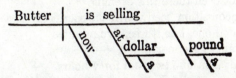

Some grammarians regard the *a* (*an*) before nouns denoting measure as in *a stick, a pound, an acre,* etc. as a preposition, a survival of the Old English preposition *an, on* meaning *at, to, on, in.* None of these prepositions seems to be a good substitute for *a* (*an*) in *That material cost a dollar a pound.* We do not now say something costs a dollar *to* (*at, in, on*) *pound.* Observe that in a different wording we say *A pound* (*one pound, two pounds, five pounds*) *will cost a dollar.* It has, therefore, seemed best to construe *a* (*an*) in sentences like these as adjectival modifiers. One should observe that if *a* (*an*) is treated as a preposition, the noun which follows it must be construed as its object, and not as an adverbial objective.

e. *Quantity and value:*

That material cost a dollar a pound.

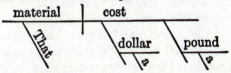

Here, as in **5, b,** *cost* is intransitive. In this sentence it is followed by two adverbial objectives: *dollar* gives us the value, and *pound* names the quantity received for one dollar.

Observe that neither of the adverbial objectives can be construed as the direct object. Neither could become the subject of the verb in the passive voice.

EXERCISE A

Analyze or diagram:

1. The Puritans gave the world not thought but action.
2. He has not been there this evening.
3. Has the acquisition been worth the sacrifice?
4. They waited one, two, three, five minutes.
5. Give me another opportunity.
6. Thou shalt continue two and forty hours.
7. Build thee more stately mansions, O my soul!
8. We have been absent twenty-three days.
9. The child is but a month old.
10. He screamed, and jumped several feet.
11. The dignity of this act was worth the audience of kings.
12. I fell into a nap about an hour ago.
13. Your predictions cannot be worth much.
14. May we all become some day perfectly useless and beautiful.
15. My poor old great-aunt died about eight months ago.
16. She arrived two months after the wedding.
17. We put the sheets on the line that night.
18. Riches make themselves wings.
19. We went two hundred yards beyond the bridge.
20. She did not appear at church the next Sunday.
21. Ten minutes after his own experience, the man made his first conversion.
22. Eddie came from a town twelve miles from Paris.
23. They drifted several miles down the river.
24. A fragrance lay like a soft mist over the park.
25. We are near the church, and but two blocks from the highway.
26. The water is ten feet deep in the shallowest place.
27. This luck continued twenty-five winter days.
28. Ice costs two cents a pound in our town.
29. Lindbergh maintained an average speed of one hundred and thirty miles an hour.
30. Strawberries cost twenty-five cents a box at the corner store.

31. During Thomas Jefferson's college term, he studied sixteen hours each day.
32. The turtle in the tub is three feet long and weighs thirty pounds.
33. All evening she sang Scotch ballads to Kennicott.
34. Kind words cost nothing, but are worth much.
35. Give every man thy ear, but few thy voice.
36. Your dress looks exactly like mine.
37. Near the "bonny Doon" stands a little clay-built cottage, the birthplace of Robert Burns.
38. I smoked a whole pack of cigarettes that morning.
39. One today is worth two tomorrows.
40. I have often walked that way on Sundays.
41. Will you wait a moment for an answer?
42. The postman comes three days a week: Monday, Wednesday, and Friday.
43. The White House has commonly cost the president all his peace of mind, and the best of his manly attributes.
44. Give him this money and these notes.
45. The board is two feet square and two inches thick.
46. Yeobright did not interrupt the preparations and went home again.
47. Rip Van Winkle assisted at the children's sports, made their playthings, and told them long stories of ghosts, witches, and Indians.
48. Five hundred miles below its source, the falls of the Missouri begin with a vertical plunge of sixty feet.
49. Nature will not spare us the smallest leaf of laurel.
50. The thread is many shades too dark for this material.

EXERCISE B

Correct any violations of good usage which you find in the following sentences, and give a reason for each change you make:

1. We are to home on Monday and Wednesday nights.
2. Will you give her and I the examination tomorrow?
3. You should take your exercise like you enjoyed it.
4. The accident cost John and she their happiness.
5. They live nowheres near our farm.

6. The instructor taught we girls to pronounce our long vowels thusly.
7. I should like to send your mother and yourself some of the refreshments.
8. The professor looks like he was angry today.
9. He gave to the youngest boy the largest share of the estate.
10. Father acted like he meant what he said.

LESSON VIII

Participles

A **participle** is a nonfinite verb (i.e., a verb not limited by person, number, or mode). The word *participle* (French *participe*, from Latin *participium*, participating, sharing) suggests the two chief functions of the participle: (1) it participates, assists in the formation of a number of the periphrastic (compound) tenses; and (2) it participates, shares its verb function with the adjective.

1. In forming the compound tenses of every full verb, the present participle is compounded with the inflectional forms of *be* in making up the progressive (or continuous) tenses; as, *He is going; He will be going; He has been helping his brother.* The past participle is employed in the formation of all the perfect tenses and of the present and past tenses, passive voice, being assisted in these formations by the finite tense forms of the verbs *be* and *have*; e.g., *I have seen, I had seen, I am seen, I was seen, I have been seen, I shall be seen, I had been seen.*[1]

When participles are combined with finite auxiliaries to make predicate verbs, they should never be separated in the diagram from the rest of the compound forms. In the following *going, gone, lifted,* and *helping* are all participles combined with finite auxiliaries to make predicate verbs:

---

[1] The student should review the forms of the participle and the inflectional forms of *be* and *have* which are combined with participles to make certain periphrastic tenses. These are listed and discussed under Tense, Part One, Chapter Five, pp. 116–118.

285

1. He is going.   *2.* He has gone.

| He | is going |

| He | has gone |

3. He is being lifted up.

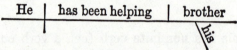

| He | is being lifted |
up

4. He has been helping his brother.

| He | has been helping | brother |
his

2. But participles have numerous constructions in which they are not parts of predicate (finite) verbs. Often they merely serve the grammatical purpose of adjectives. In this function the participle is commonly referred to as a **verbal,** or as a **verbal adjective.** Such forms as *fighting, dancing, taken, thrown, performed* are participles which may be used in the formation of compound tenses. But they may also be used as modifiers of nouns; that is, as adjectives, and, when so used, they are **verbal adjectives.** It is important to note that not every adjective which has a verbal idea as its basic meaning is to be construed as a participle. *Active, dependent, afraid* are mere adjectives. To be a true participle, a form must be a part of the actual inflection of some verb. The participle is always a verb form.

The Participle as a Verbal

The **participle as a verbal** has adjective function and adjective meaning; but it is dual in nature and retains its verbal meaning, and may therefore take any of the complements and have any of the modifiers which verbs take or have. In the sentence, the participle may be used in any of the constructions where an adjective may be used. The following sentences and their diagrams will illustrate the most common adjectival uses of the participle:

1. The Participle as Modifier of the Subject:

1. Truth kept in the dark will never save the world.

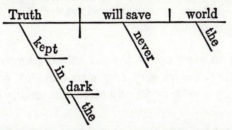

In the diagram, the participle is placed on a line much like the one used for the prepositional phrase, except that the diagonal line does not extend beyond the horizontal line. Observe the two forms in the preceding sentence. The participle is written partly on the diagonal and partly on the horizontal lines to indicate that it is something more than a mere adjective modifier. It is important to differentiate the participle and the prepositional phrase lines, because some prepositions are derived from participles, and the lines of the diagram, if correctly drawn, can distinguish the two functions.

2. Catching sight of the advancing standard, the soldiers rallied to the charge.

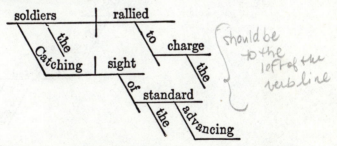

should be to the left of the verb line

The participles *kept* and *catching* in the two diagrams given above are both transitive verb forms. *Kept* is the past participle of the verb *keep*. It is a passive voice form. Its subject, the word which it modifies, receives the action expressed in *kept*. *Catching* is the present participle of the transitive verb *catch*.　It is an active voice form, and therefore must have an object complement (direct object) to complete its meaning.　Its subject is *soldiers*, the noun which it modifies.　*Advancing* is an intransitive verb, and, therefore, has no voice modification.

Note that in sentence *1* the adverbial phrase *in the dark* modifies *kept*.　Almost any sentence element which can be used to modify a verb or an adjective can modify a participle.

2. Participle as Modifier of the Object of the Preposition:

The game was played on an oblong field encased in circular concrete tiers peopled with braying lunatics incited to frenzy by howling dervishes.

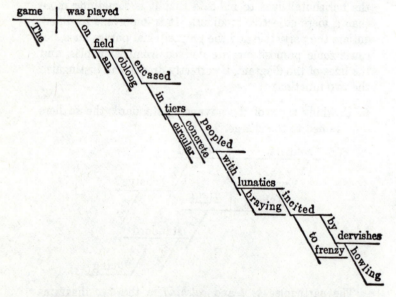

Note that *braying* and *howling* are intransitive verbs, and have no voice; no action is here transferred to a receiver. When the past participle is used as a verbal, it is, as a rule, transitive; e.g., *encased, peopled, incited.*

3. Participle as Modifier of the Predicate Nominative:

Light is the one thing wanted for the world.

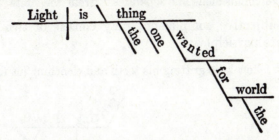

4. Participle as Modifier of the Direct Object:

I stamped and mailed the letter addressed to your friend.

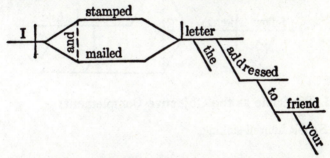

5. Participle as Attribute (Subjective) Complement:

The girl came running.

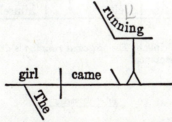

Came running, the predicate of this sentence, is derived from two verbs, *come* and *run.* *Running,* the present participle of the intransitive verb *run,* is here used as an adjective in the predicate. In the diagram, it is placed on a participle line on a standard above the base line to differentiate it from the pure adjective used as attribute complement. The subjective complement line separates it from the finite verb.[2]

The subjective complement may consist of two or more coördinate participles:

That fellow kept gritting his teeth and clenching his fists.

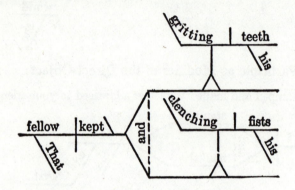

6. Participle as the Objective Complement:

He felt himself sinking.

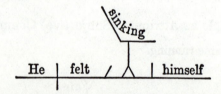

---

[2] Note that the participle in *The girl came running* is different from the participle in the following sentence:

The girl is running.

Here *is running* is a finite verb form, being present indicative, third person, singular, progressive, of the intransitive verb *run*. Observe that no line separates the auxiliary verb and the participle.

Here *sinking* is the present participle of the intransitive verb *sink*. It refers, as the objective complement line preceding it in the diagram indicates, to the direct object, which is its subject. A good rule to remember about this use of the participle is that, whenever the objective complement is a verb form, its subject is the direct object.

In this construction the object and its modifying verbal (the objective complement) have the force of a clause, though they do not constitute a true clause, for a clause should contain a finite (predicating) verb; and participles are nonfinite (nonpredicating) verb forms.

The objective complement may consist of two or more coördinate participles:

1. We saw them eating peanuts and laughing uproariously at the clown's jokes.

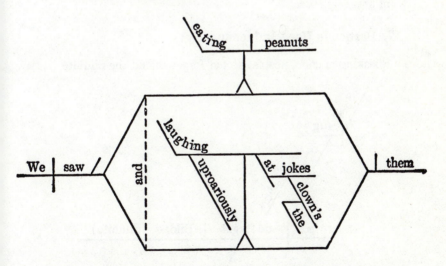

In this sentence, the participles refer to the same object; but in the one that follows they refer to different objects:

2. I felt my veins stretching and my muscles becoming tense.

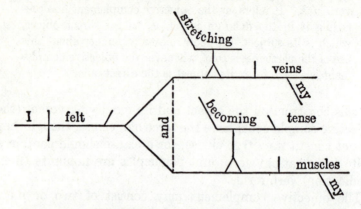

Observe that the participle *becoming* is a copulative verb. It requires a subjective complement, and therefore the line before *tense* is a subjective complement line. The objective complement line after *felt* points toward *muscles*, the subject of *becoming tense*.

7. Participle Used Independently:

Speaking of short people, do not forget Bildad the Shuhite

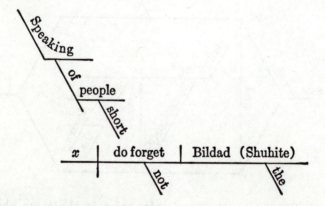

Observe that the participle in the preceding sentence is not like the one in the following sentence:

Proceeding a little farther, we came to a deep chasm.

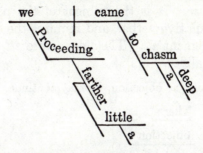

Proceeding modifies the subject, whereas *speaking* does not modify any word in the sentence. The independent participle usually comes at the beginning of the sentence, but it is well to remember that not every participle occurring at the beginning of a sentence is independent.

8. Participles in the Absolute Phrase:

An absolute phrase is an independent expression consisting of a substantive with modifying participle:

1. Hope lost, all is lost.

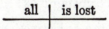

2. The teacher being ill, we had no school on Monday.

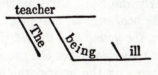

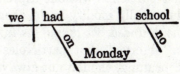

Observe that the principal word in the absolute phrase is the noun *teacher*. It is the subject of the participle *being*, which is a copulative verbal, and requires the attribute (subjective) complement *ill*. The line before *ill* points toward the word it qualifies.

3. There being no objection, we may continue.

This construction is identical with one type of the "ablative absolute" in Latin, and is called by some English grammarians the **nominative absolute**. The idea of the absolute phrase can usually be rendered as an adverb clause expressing time, cause, condition, concession, and the like:

1. When hope is lost, all is lost.
2. Because the teacher was ill, we had no school on Monday.
3. Because (*or* Since) there is no objection, we may continue.

9. Participles as Substantives:

Participles, like pure adjectives, may be used as substantives in elliptical sentences where the nouns which the participles would modify are clearly implied. Just as we may say *the poor and the rich* (for *the poor and the rich people*), *the English* (for *the English people*), *the young and the old* (for *the young and the old people*), so we may use either the present or the past participle without expressing the nouns which they would normally modify in the expanded form of the sentence; e.g., *the wounded, the dying, the injured, the suffering*, etc. It will be observed that participles so used generally convey plural meaning, though not always. Such expressions as *my betrothed, the deceased,* and the like usually convey singular meaning.

In the diagram, one may indicate the dual function of the participle by putting it on a participle line on a standard, as in the following illustrations:

1. The wounded and the dying lay helpless in the street.

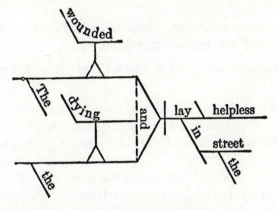

2. All the days of the afflicted are evil.[3]

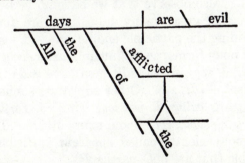

---

[3] It would be logical to construe the participle in this construction as a modifier of an understood noun, as in the following diagram:

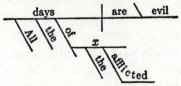

It should be noted that *wounded, dying,* and *afflicted* are verbal adjectives (participles) used as nouns. They are not verbal nouns; that is, gerunds. They do not name acts. Compare *suffering* (a participle used for a noun) and *having suffered* (a gerund, i.e., a verbal noun) in the following: *You cannot sympathize with the suffering without having suffered.* For uses of the gerund, see Lesson IX, pp. 309–321.

In the above sentences, *wounded* and *afflicted* are past participles; *dying* is a present participle.

10. Apparent Participles (Adjectives Resembling Participles):

As we have already noted in the section in this text dealing with the forms and origins of adjectives, Part One, Chapter Four, some adjectives are formed by putting prefixes or suffixes to other parts of speech. *Unshorn, unwashed, unkempt, unschooled* are all adjectives, not participles, even though they are formed by prefixing *un-* to participles. But such forms are not found in the conjugation of the verb *shear, wash, comb, school.* Also observe that we have no verb to *unshear, unwash,* etc. A great many adjectives are formed from nouns by adding the participle ending *-ing, -ed, -en, -d,* and *-t* to standard noun forms; as, *willing* in *I am willing to go* (from the noun *will* + *ing*), *silken* (*silk* + *en*), *diseased* (*disease* + *d*), *talented* (*talent* + *ed*), etc. Other adjectives similarly formed from nouns are *cultured, wooden, wretched, earthen, flaxen, wooded, woolen, golden, rotten,* and many others. These forms have been conveniently called **apparent participles** because they resemble (but are not) participles.

The apparent participle is especially common in adjectives like *bald-headed, hard-hearted, cold-blooded, far-fetched, faint-hearted, three-cornered,* where the *-ed* is added to the combination and not to the second word alone.

A number of words look like participles, but are not from verb stems nor from any nouns in the living language: *naked, sudden, wicked, dilapidated, rugged, cunning.*

Words which are of verbal derivation may have lost their active meaning and have come to represent relatively permanent characteristics. They are best regarded as adjectives. Examples are seen in such expressions as *lost articles, an interesting story, drunken men, sunken eye, cloven hoof, clean-shaven, graven image, grasping nature, captivating manner.*

A number of *-ing* words in English which are now used to modify nouns are really survivals of prepositional phrases which have lost their prepositions. They look like participles and are often treated as participles because they are from verbs and modify nouns. They can be differentiated from participles in meaning only. Such expressions as *a fishing pole, a living room, dining room, eating house, drinking fountain,* contain contracted gerund phrases. *A fishing pole* is a pole for fishing, *a drinking fountain* is a fountain for drinking, etc. These should not be called participles, nor diagramed as participles, but as mere adjectives. We should remember that a participle modifies a noun or pronoun which names the actor or agent or the receiver of the action expressed in the modifying participle. Observe that *poles do not fish; fountains do not drink; houses do not eat.* Compare these expressions with *The boy entering the house is my brother,* where the subject of the participle is the actor. Here the boy does *enter* (or *is entering*) the house.

The safest test for differentiating the pure participle from adjectives which resemble participles is meaning. Even if a word looks like a participle and may once have had the use of a participle, it should not be construed as a participle unless it has the force of a verb, and, if transitive, transfers action to a receiver. Observe that *interesting* in *The story is interesting* is an adjective, not a participle; but in the following sentence it is a participle: *He is interesting his neighbors in his new enterprise. Interesting* is here a participle, completing the progressive form of the verb *interest.* Usually, if a pure adjective can be substituted without change of meaning for the one which looks like a participle, the modifier should be analyzed as an adjective. In the first sentence, we may say *This is a good story*, and the substitution of *good* for *interesting* does not greatly change the meaning, because *interesting* conveyed no verbal action. A good dictionary should prove helpful in determining whether to call a word an adjective or a participle. Consult Webster for the meanings and uses of such words as *lasting, everlasting, shocking, living, startling, tired, wandering.*

Adjectives which look like participles, but are not, are diagramed or analyzed as simple adjectives, not as participles. The following diagrams illustrate the proper analysis of the so-called **apparent participle:**

1. The bald-headed man appeared hard-hearted.

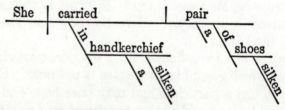

2. She carried a pair of silken shoes in a silken handkerchief.

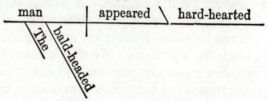

3. He was unmolested.

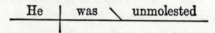

4. I never saw him unoccupied.

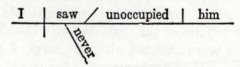

5. He came to us unshorn and unwashed.

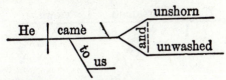

11. The Participle as a Preposition:

A number of prepositions have the form of participles, and are derived from participles. The most common of these are *excepting, respecting, concerning, regarding,* and *touching.* Some of these are still in use as verbals. In *The girl touching the wall is an artist, touching* is a participle modifying *girl,* but in the sense of *concerning* or *on,* it is a preposition, as in *The new laws touching marriage are excellent.* Note the prepositional meaning in *excepting, concerning,* and *regarding* in the following:

1. All were there excepting the leader.

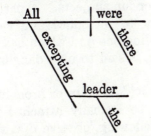

2. I shall say nothing concerning the unity of the church.

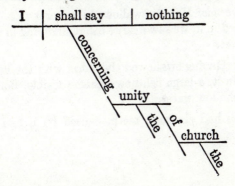

3. He entertained no false views regarding the matter.

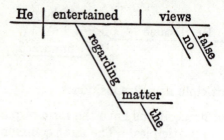

The Dangling Participle

A **dangling participle** is one which has no expressed or implied logical subject, and sometimes seems to modify what participles should not modify. Being a verbal adjective, the participle is, in the main, restricted to modifying nouns or pronouns. It should not be used as the modifier of a verb or an adjective or an adverb. As a general rule, all participles, except the independent one, should have clearly expressed noun or pronoun subjects. A participle which is not used independently to introduce and relate one sentence thought to a preceding one and which has no expressed noun or pronoun subject, is said to be a **dangling** (or **unattached**) **participle.**

The failure to provide a noun or pronoun subject to which the participle can be logically attached is often a serious blunder. In the following, observe that the dangling participles in the faulty sentences have no logical subjects:

Loose and crude: Having swallowed the worm with the hook concealed in it, we saw a large fish floundering in the shallow water.

Improved: Having swallowed the worm with the hook concealed in it, a large fish now became visible, floundering in the shallow water.

Loose: She had six good teeth, caused by a bad case of pyorrhea.

Equally bad: She had six good teeth, due to a bad case of pyorrhea. [*Due*, like *caused*, should modify a noun.]

Improved: She had only six good teeth, the loss of her other teeth being due to a bad case of pyorrhea.

Sometimes a participle is wrongly placed in the sentence, and appears to be attached to the wrong noun. In *Eating with the dog, the little girl found her pet rabbit*, the participle is misplaced. To avoid obscurity all participles should be placed as close as possible to their subjects. Put the participle *eating* immediately after *rabbit*, and this sentence is clear and grammatical.

Most dangling participles can be corrected or avoided by (1) expanding the verbal phrase into a clause, (2) placing the verbal near the word it modifies, (3) furnishing a logical subject for the verbal, or (4) changing the passive voice of the predicate verb to the active; e.g., *Going over the hill, the ocean can be seen* can be corrected by using the active voice form for *can be seen*; as, *Going over the hill, we can see the ocean.* Use the passive voice cautiously.

The Expanded Forms of the Participle

The student will discover on examining the sentences used in illustrating the various uses of the participle that the most common forms of the participle are the present and the past tense forms. But the verbal use is not restricted to these two forms. The periphrastic (expanded) tenses are more recent formations, and hence are not so well established, and therefore not so common, as the older forms in the adjective function. In the diagram, the compound forms should never be separated by any sort of line. Each of the expanded forms represents one tense, and may be used in any construction where a present or a past participle can be used.

1. The man being interviewed by the police is my brother.

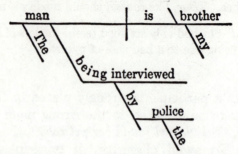

Being interviewed is a present tense, passive voice, form of the transitive verb *interview.* Its subject (*man*) receives the action expressed in the verbal.

2. Having devoured the thane, Grendel stalked away.

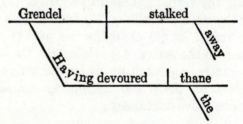

Having devoured is the present perfect tense of the transitive verb *devour.*

3. Our team having been defeated, we were depressed all evening.

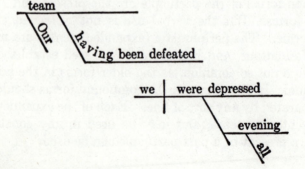

The present perfect participle is here used in the absolute phrase. *Having been defeated* is a transitive verb in the passive voice.

4. Having been singing all morning, she is very weary

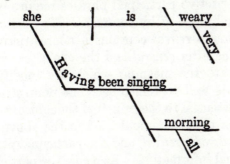

Having been singing is the present perfect progressive (continuous) form of the participle of the verb *sing*. It is here used intransitively.

Caution: Do not use unauthorized forms as participles, and never use the participle as a substitute for the finite (predicate) verb. There is no verb *enthuse*, and hence we cannot say She seemed *enthused* for *she seemed enthusiastic.* There is no verb *attackt*, and hence there can be no participle *attackted.* Consult the dictionary when in doubt as to the basic form of a verb or of any of its inflectional forms.

The past participles *taken, done, written* and *seen* are sometimes erroneously used for finite verbs. Say *I did* (not *I done) that myself; He has written* (not *He written) me; I took* (not *I taken) him for you; We saw* (not *We seen) you yesterday.*

Punctuations of Participial Modifiers

Participles, like adjectives, may be used as restrictive or as nonrestrictive modifiers. If they are restrictive (i.e., identifying), they must not be set off from the other elements of the sentence by punctuation. In *The girl wearing the red sweater is my sister*, we have a restrictive participial modifier, and hence no commas or other punctuation marks are needed. The phrase *wearing the red sweater* identifies the girl, and the sentence containing this phrase is read or spoken without any pauses.

But nonrestrictive participial phrases require punctuation. They are usually set off by commas. *The general, seeing the day lost, ordered a retreat* contains a nonrestrictive modifier, and the comma after *general* and the one after *lost* are necessary to indicate the meaning which the modifying phrase conveys. It is well to remember that nonrestrictive modifiers are not essential to the principal thought of the sentence. The chief idea to be communicated in the above sentence is *The general ordered a retreat,* and the participial phrase merely gives additional information. As a rule the participial phrase which introduces a sentence is nonrestrictive; as, *Having been offended, he refused to come.*

The independent participle and the absolute phrase are always separated from the sentence proper by punctuation (usually the comma): *Speaking of books, have you read this one? The day being dark, we ate by lamplight.* If the absolute phrase contains a nonrestrictive participle, then it will be separated from its subject (the noun it modifies) by a comma. But participles in absolute phrases are quite generally restrictive.

The subjective and objective complements are never set off by commas or any other punctuation. *He sat there staring at me* has no comma between *staring* and the verb because it is a part of the predicate. But in *Little Jack Horner sat in a corner, eating his Christmas pie,* we set the participial phrase off by inserting the comma before *eating.* This participle modifies the subject of the sentence; it is not a part of the predicate. Here the full predicate thought is conveyed in the verb *sat* and its adverbial phrase modifier, *in a corner.* Observe that in the first sentence, the verb *sat* is not a full predicating verb; it requires a completing element.

EXERCISE A

Analyze or diagram:

1. Hope deferred maketh the heart sick.
2. We sometimes find ourselves changing our minds.
3. Stolen fruits are sweet.
4. The great reality stands glaring there upon him.
5. It is a square-built gloomy palace of black ashlar marble, shrouded in awe and horror.
6. The great Heaven, rolling silent overhead, with its blue-glancing stars, answered not.
7. Thought once awakened does not slumber.
8. Books, written words, are still miraculous runes, the latest form.
9. Luther sat translating one of the Psalms.
10. Light is the one thing wanted for the world.
11. Ours is a most confused world.
12. One leaves all these nobilities standing in their niches of honor.
13. He cannot even get his music copied.
14. These people have wise and excellent laws touching marriage.
15. The day having come, he made his entry.
16. Bill and the Kid sat on a pile of rocks, looking very sullen.
17. Putting our shoulders against the powers of the screw, we pushed her out into the current.
18. Dinner being done, Tirsan retired again.
19. Then, holding the cup to his lips, quite readily and cheerfully he drank the poison.
20. Here we find conditions reeking with degradation.
21. We had found ourselves possessed of vast wealth.
22. Unguided by knowledge, the people are a multitude without order.
23. There were one or two cities stretching up the mountain.
24. The vast body of data gathered by him became the groundwork of the progress of science.
25. We find the enjoyment of values growing unassured and precarious.
26. Sparta and Athens, forgetting their jealousies and joining their forces, fought off the attack of the Persians.
27. Science and Art make life satisfying.
28. Most of his writings are notes taken by his own students.

29. The good humor of a man elated by success often displays itself towards enemies.
30. General theories are often drawn from detached facts.
31. The worth of the thing signified must vindicate our taste for the emblem.
32. Cut your coat according to your cloth.
33. I read the other day some verses written by an eminent painter.
34. An institution is the lengthened shadow of one man.
35. Spirit is matter reduced to extreme thinness.
36. He went away vexed and disappointed.
37. All men have wandering impulses, fits and starts of generosity.
38. In every work of genius we recognize our own rejected thoughts.
39. The harm of the improved machinery may counterbalance its good.
40. Character is the moral order seen through the medium of an individual nature.
41. Within the general institution of marriage developed the organization known as the family.
42. We cannot easily perceive the broad implications and abiding results of the machine age.
43. Here comes a walking fire.
44. This gentle and unforced accord sits smiling to my heart.
45. Fairest Cordelia, thou art most rich being poor.
46. He sank down in despair, thinking himself the most miserable of living creatures.
47. Shielding the house from storms, on the north, were the barns and the farmyard.
48. Faint and reeling this way and that, I got to my feet.
49. A sleeping fox catches no poultry.
50. My mind being soured with his conduct, I kept on refusing him.
51. Art is filled with creations inspired by these myths.
52. The materials used for this were ivory and gold.
53. Turning my eyes upon him, I perceived him greatly agitated.
54. Some of our people became terrified.
55. Investigation also finds the victim of society cursed with the blight of poverty.
56. I find them admirably contrived in some respects.
57. Scientific knowledge touches our lives on every hand, modifying our environment and altering our daily habits.

58. A moment later he heard the jingle of departing sleigh bells.
59. We are an honest people, keeping our contract and giving full measure.
60. She was on the couch, sobbing.
61. The unknown youth lay naked and shivering in the chilly wind.
62. Out of his mouth go burning lamps.
63. I have called Coleridge a hooded eagle among blinking owls.
64. So Job died, being old and full of days.
65. He sat beside her, smiling bravely.
66. Pleasure not known beforehand is half wasted.
67. All similes and allegories concerning her began and ended with birds.
68. Speaking of card games, what has become of *Authors?*
69. They were surrounded by dusky forms about four feet high, standing a few paces beyond the rays of the lantern.
70. Going back to an old question, was Athens really a republic?
71. Referring to your letter of the 10th, we have made the shipment.
72. Speaking of literary patrons, who "discovered" Shakespeare?
73. A hawk wheeled and swooped and floated far up in the dazzling air.
74. There is a still more fundamental cause underlying our democratic tendencies.
75. To me there is something very touching in this primeval figure of heroism.

EXERCISE B

I. Make a list of ten adjectives ending in -*t*, -*d*, or -*ed*, which are only apparent participles. b. Make a similar list of mere adjectives ending in -*ing*. c. Give the derivation of each word you list. Refer to your dictionary, if necessary.

II. In Exercise A, find ten intransitive and ten transitive participles, and name the subject of each verbal.

III. Pick out five restrictive and five nonrestrictive participial phrases in Exercise A.

IV. Give all the participles of the verb *write*, and use each in a sentence as a verbal.

EXERCISE C

Correct all errors in the following, giving reasons for all corrections:

1. While bathing at that beach, a shark frightened all of us.
2. Going over the hill, the ocean can be seen.
3. They have joined the Annanias Club, thus making them very unpopular.
4. This fur coat is for sale by a lady slightly used.
5. I have only one parent, my mother, due to the flu and a poor doctor.
6. The facts lain before us should be given due consideration.
7. A bursted balloon cannot be inflated.
8. Rowing rapidly, the river was soon crossed.
9. He reads poetry badly caused by a harelip.
10. The accused denied the charge, causing the judge to postpone his decision.
11. The children seemed enthused about moving into the city.
12. Arriving early, all the show can be seen before we leave for your train.
13. Our ice melted before we could use it, thus making us drink warm punch.
14. Standing in the mudhole, the boy left his pony.
15. He arrived late, causing the teacher to be angry.
16. Made of tapestry, she found her grandmother's bag.
17. Having studied abroad, her friends were much impressed.
18. Having made a perfect recitation, the teacher dismissed the class.
19. Huddled under the mother hen, the little girl found her lost doll and pet chicken.
20. She wrote with a pencil on scratch paper, making her papers look very untidy.
21. Many men are either very bald or prematurely gray, caused by wearing felt hats too much.
22. Thinking over all the evils of smoking, the sale of cigarettes should be prohibited.

Gerunds

A **gerund** is a word derived from a verb and performing the function of both a verb and a noun. In short, the gerund is one kind of verbal noun.[1]

Like the participle, the gerund is a nonfinite (infinite, unlimited) verb form; it is not limited by person, number, or mode; but it has tense and voice modification, which modification only verbs can have. The gerund can have a subject and take an object or be followed by any of the complements which complete finite verbs; and it can be modified by adverbs. Because it has the function of a noun, the gerund can be used in the sentence in any construction in which a noun can be used; therefore, it may be the subject of a sentence, the direct object of a verb, the object of a preposition, an adverbial objective, or a subjective or an objective complement.

The gerund cannot be distinguished from the participle except by use, for all of its forms are like corresponding forms of the participle. In fact, all of the forms of the gerund except the *-ing* form were probably participles long before they were gerunds, and may be said to be derived from the participle. The *-ing* form the participle took from the gerund (see Forms of the Gerund, Part One, pp. 134–135). The gerund must, therefore, be distinguished from the participle by use

---

[1] The gerund is not the only kind of verbal noun. Such words as *arrival*, *movement*, and *action* are also from verbs, but they have the form of nouns and the inflection of nouns. These are not found in the inflection of the verb from which they are derived. Gerunds are always verb forms used as nouns.

only.   To differentiate the two one has only to remember the function of a noun and the function of an adjective.   The gerund is a verb form used as a noun; the participle is a verb form used as an adjective.   Also in relation to their subject, the two differ; the participle modifies and qualifies its subject, and is diagramed as a modifier; the subject of the gerund is always construed as a modifier of the gerund when it is expressed as such in the gerund phrase; and is, as a rule, in the possessive case.

In the diagram, the gerund, like the participle, has a special line of its own.   It is always placed on a broken line (⌐___⌐___); and, whether the gerund is the simple -*ing* form or one of the periphrastic (expanded) forms, it is written across the step, or break, in the line.   The subject of the gerund (usually a possessive noun or pronoun) and any other of its adjectival modifiers should be placed at the left of the step; and its adverbial modifiers at the right of the step. Thus the diagram can indicate the dual nature of the gerund.

The gerund, when used as the subject or as a part of the predicate, should be put on a standard above the base line. The base line, the one on which the subject and predicate of the sentence are placed, is never broken, though it may be divided to accommodate compound elements.

1. The Gerund as Subject:

1. His running away was a mistake.

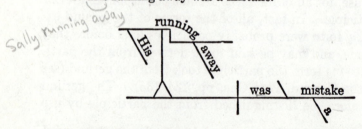

Running is a gerund, used here as the subject of the sentence.   It is present tense, intransitive.   The subject of the gerund is the possessive pronoun *his*, which is placed as an adjective modifier. *Away* is an adverb modifying the action named in *running*. In this sentence, the complete subject is *his running away;* and the complete predicate is *was a mistake.* Observe that *his*, an adjective modifier, is placed before the step; and *away*, the adverb modifier, is placed after the step.

2. His accepting too much for his services was the cause of his downfall.

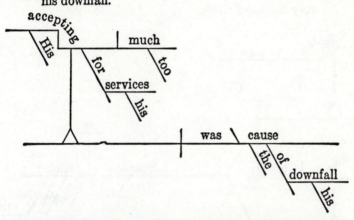

Accepting in this sentence is the gerund; it is a present tense, active voice form of the transitive verb *accept;* its object is *much*. Its subject *his*, like the subjective genitive, is analyzed as an adjective modifier; the prepositional phrase *for his service* is an adverbial modifier. Note that the complete subject of this sentence is the entire gerund phrase.

3. Your not being invited surprises me.

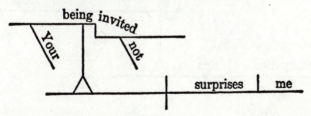

Being invited is a transitive verb form, passive voice, present tense. Its subject *your* receives the action expressed in the verbal noun. *Not* is an adverbial modifier expressing negation.

If the gerund subject is compound, the base line should be divided and each gerund put on a standard, as in the following model:

4. Eating one's cake and keeping it has been regarded as the very climax of thrift.

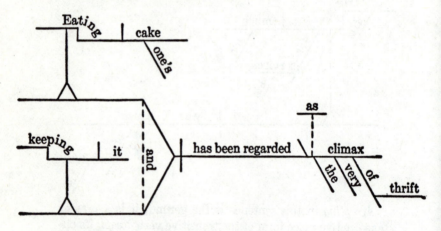

2. Gerund as Predicate Nominative:

Kingsley's favorite occupation was helping lame dogs over stiles.

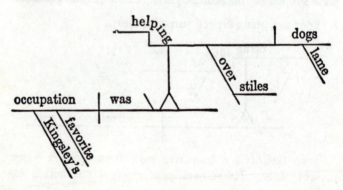

Here the subjective complement is the gerund phrase *helping lame dogs over stiles*, the chief word of which is the gerund *helping*. It is present tense, active voice. Its subject is expressed as a modifier of the subject of the sentence. Observe that we might say *Kingsley's helping lame dogs over stiles was his favorite occupation*.

In sentences of this sort, it is important to differentiate between the gerund as predicate nominative after a copulative verb (in this instance *was)* and the participle in the progressive tense form of a finite verb. In *Kingsley was helping lame dogs over stiles*, *was helping* is the finite verb; it is the past progressive tense form of the verb *help*. The predicate nominative is the same person, thing, or idea as the subject, and as such the sentence can be turned about so that the predicate nominative element becomes the subject, and the noun which was the subject becomes the predicate nominative. Observe that one would not be likely to say *Helping lame dogs was Kingsley*.

3. The Gerund as an Appositive (Explanatory Modifier):

1. Bless me! This is pleasant, riding on a rail.

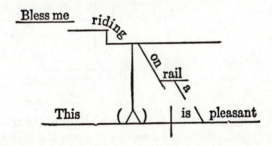

When the gerund phrase is used as an appositive, it is diagramed on a standard, and the base of the standard is enclosed in parentheses, as illustrated in model *1.* When the appositive is compound, the base line should be divided to accommodate the coördinate elements, as in the following:

2. These things are done well in haste: flying from the plague, escaping quarrels, and catching flies.

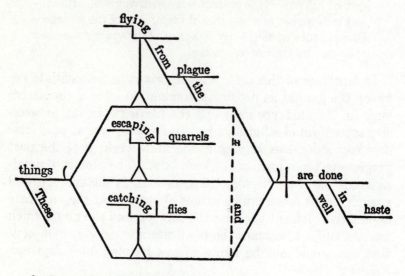

4. Gerund as Direct Object:

The children enjoyed feeding the bears.

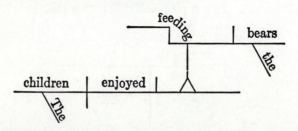

Here *feeding the bears* is the direct object of the transitive verb *enjoyed*. Sometimes we can discover the object complement by putting *what* or *whom* after the verb; as, *The children enjoyed what?* The answer should be the direct object, as it is in this sentence, *feeding the bears.* Another test of the object complement is to make it the subject of the predicate verb shifted into the passive voice as in the following: *Feeding the bears was enjoyed by the children.*

5. Gerund as Objective Complement:

1. I call that taking candy from babies.

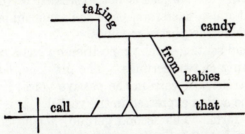

The objective complement in this sentence is the gerund phrase *taking candy from babies.* If the finite verb is put in the passive voice the objective complement becomes the predicate nominative; as, *That is called taking candy from babies.*

6. Gerund as Object of Preposition:

1. He makes his living by grinding scissors.

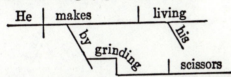

2. He was congratulated on having been honored by his neighbors and having attained his chief ambition.

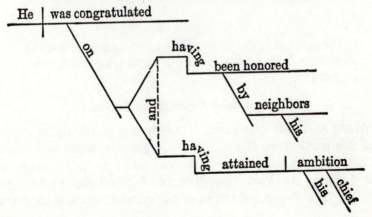

The prepositional phrases in the two preceding sentences are used adverbially. In the first sentence, *grinding* is a transitive verb. Its subject is not expressed in the gerund phrase; and it must, therefore, have the same subject as the finite verb, which the phrase modifies.

In the second sentence, the preposition *on* has a compound object consisting of two gerunds. The first one, *having been honored*, is a transitive verb in the passive voice; its subject, *he*, receives the action expressed in the verbal. It is a present perfect tense form. The second gerund, *having attained*, is also transitive; but its voice is active; its tense is present perfect. Its subject is also *he*, the subject of the sentence.

7. Gerund as Adverbial Objective:

1. The book is worth reading aloud.

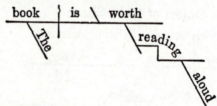

2. This water is boiling hot.

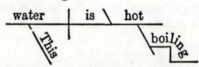

The gerunds in the two preceding sentences are adverbial objectives denoting degree. Both forms are present tense, intransitive.

The Expanded Forms of the Gerund

Along with the expansion of the tenses of the finite verbs and the participles, the gerund acquired new tense and voice forms. (For a discussion of the old and new tense forms of the gerund, see Part One, Tenses of Nonfinite Verbs, pp. 133ff.) The expanded tenses of the gerund, because they are newer, are not so common and so well established in the language as the one ending in *-ing*, which form is as old as the English language. The various forms of the gerund may be seen in the following sentences:

ACTIVE VOICE

Present Tense: Your *writing* the letter so neatly secured the position.

Present Perfect: His *having said* that is proof enough of his attitude on the matter.

Present Perfect Progressive: She questioned my *having been studying* Latin all evening.

PASSIVE VOICE

Present Tense: She enjoys *being teased.*

Present Perfect: After *having been punished* severely, he became penitent.

Intransitive verbs have the same forms as those listed for the active voice of the transitive verb.

Nouns Resembling Gerunds

To differentiate the *-ing* gerund form from a pure noun ending in *-ing*, one must rely upon the meaning of the word as it is used in a given sentence, and not upon its form. The *-ing* ending has been attached to proper nouns to suggest origin ('son of'), as in *Browning, Billings;* and to common nouns to suggest source or material; as, *clothing, tubing, roofing, bedding,* etc. Such nouns as these are not usually confused with the verbal noun, because they really convey no verbal meaning; they are the names of specific persons or objects.

There are, however, a number of nouns ending in *-ing* in the language which are derived from verbs, some of them once gerunds, which are no longer felt to be verb forms but mere abstract nouns. Many of these have forms identical with gerund forms; and only the use and meaning in a given sentence can be relied upon for the differentiation. As a rule, the noun denotes a single completed act, whereas the gerund suggests the continuation of an act.   In the following phrases, the -*ing* words are unquestionably mere nouns: *her second wedding, his earnings, a good opening, a sound understanding, in the beginning, a poor ending, good-breeding, human being.*   In the following the -*ing* words are verb forms which retain their verb meaning, and they are, therefore, gerunds: *Her **wedding** the duke was a mistake; His **earning** that prize pleased his parents; The **opening** and the **closing** of the shop is my job; My **beginning** and **ending** that project will depend upon my health.*

Frequently the pure noun has noun inflection; i.e., it can denote plural by the addition of -*s*.   The gerunds are infinite verb forms and cannot denote number or person.   Therefore, any noun-word ending in -*ing* which can indicate plural number by the addition of -*s* may be regarded as a mere noun. The following are not gerunds: *earnings, writings, spendings, feelings, human beings, warnings, shavings, savings.*

If the -*ing* form can be replaced by an abstract noun which does not end in -*ing*, one has very good proof that it is a mere noun; e.g., *living* may be the equivalent of *livelihood; building* may be used for *edifice; painting* for *picture; ending* for *end.* When an -*ing* form in a compound group is coordinated with an abstract noun, one is usually justified in assuming that it is a simple noun, as in *reading, **writing** and arithmetic; **spelling,** accountancy, and English; **typing** and shorthand;* and so forth.

When all of the suggested tests fail to aid in differentiating the gerund from the simple abstract noun, the student should consult the dictionary.   If a form is used as a pure noun, it will be listed in an unabridged dictionary as a noun, and its noun meaning will be given.

Subject of the Gerund

Much has been said and written in recent years concerning the proper case to be used as the subject of the gerund; and since usage is the law of language, we must consider as standard and correct what our best speakers and writers use. Originally the subject of the verbal idea expressed in the gerund was a noun or pronoun in the genitive case, and was called the subjective genitive (see Uses of the Possessive Case, under Nouns and Pronouns, pp. 30–31, 48–53). In Modern English, usage favors the use of the possessive case as the modifier and subject of the gerund:

1. I cannot go without my *father's* giving his consent.
2. *Your* saying that does not alter the case.
3. I object to the *children's* going there without a chaperon.
4. I do not approve that *man's* coming with Mary.

One of the chief reasons for retaining the possessive case form is that it prevents confusion with the participle. In sentence 4 above, an exchange of *man* for *man's* would change the meaning. In *I do not approve that man coming with Mary*, disapproval of the man is indicated; but if the possessive *man's* is used, it is the coming of the man with Mary which is not approved. In sentences such as this, it is important to choose the form which will convey clearly the intended meaning.

If a noun or pronoun has no possessive form, then one has no alternative, and must use the uninflected case form. The demonstratives *this* and *that* and *these* and *those* have no possessive forms, and if any one of these words is used as the modifier (i.e., the subject) of a gerund, it will not have the apostrophe followed by *s*. We must say *I object to that being changed; I am afraid of these being lost*.

When an intervening word or phrase comes between the gerund and its subject, the possessive form is not used; as, *I shall object to a son of mine being married by a justice of the peace*. Here *son* is the subject of *being married*, but the intervening phrase *of mine* makes the addition of the *'s* phonetically difficult. In such sentences as this, usage would justify the use of the noun without the possessive sign. Whether we call it a possessive form which has dropped its inflection, or regard it as an objective case form used as a modifier of the verbal noun is of little consequence.

One may find in both written and spoken English numerous examples of violations of the rule requiring the possessive case form as the subject of the gerund; but in spite of some evidence of a trend away from the possessive form, our best writers and speakers do seem to prefer and to use it consistently wherever form and sound permit its use.

When the gerund is used in sentences expressing maxims, general truths, etc., the subject is usually omitted, as in *Seeing is believing; Fretting and repining at every disappointment discovers childishness; Attempting too much and doing too little is the most common cause of failure.* In sentences of this sort, the word *one's* may be regarded as the implied subject.

Dangling Gerund Phrases

Like the participle, the gerund is a verb form which, as a rule, requires a subject expressed in the sentence or clearly implied in the context. When the subject of the gerund is the same object or person as the subject of the predicate verb in the sentence, the subject of the gerund need not be expressed in the gerund phrase. In *After playing tennis for two hours, we rested for an hour,* the gerund is the object of the preposition *after,* and the entire prepositional phrase modifies *rested.* Here the gerund has the same subject as the verb which the phrase modifies. The insertion of *our* between *after* and *playing* is unnecessary, because it does not add to the meaning or the force of the sentence. But if the subject of the gerund is not the same as the subject of the sentence or is not clearly implied, it should be expressed in the gerund phrases. In *I cannot go there without my father's giving his consent,* the subject of the gerund is not the same as the subject of the verb which the gerund phrase modifies; and hence it is expressed in the gerund phrase.

Failure to give the gerund a logical subject produces what is called the **dangling** (or **unattached**) **gerund phrase.** In a sentence such as *After catching the thief, he should be punished,* the subject of *should be punished* is not the subject of *catching,* and hence the sentence is ambiguous and faulty. If we say *After catching the thief, the police should ask the judge to sentence him,* we have a clearly expressed thought. The dangling gerund phrase occurs most frequently when a writer or speaker shifts his point of view, and has his gerund in the active voice and his principal verb in the passive. When the gerund phrase starts the sentence, one should take pains to see that his point of view does not shift from a personal to an impersonal one. Usually when the gerund phrase introduces the sentence, the subject is the agent of the action of the main verb—not the receiver of the action. Observe the following: *In baking a cake, the oven should be kept at 350 degrees.* Here *baking* requires a personal (agent) subject, not the impersonal one. If the finite verb is changed to the active voice, the sentence will have an agent (actor) subject expressed in the sentence; as, *In baking a cake, one should keep the oven at 350 degrees.*

EXERCISE A

Analyze or diagram:

1. Horse-whipping would be too good for such a scoundrel.
2. His speaking out prevented my stating the facts.
3. I was not aware of his having been dismissed.
4. She thought skiing and sliding old-fashioned.
5. I have journeyed for many months among these violent people without discovering anything but courtesy.
6. I do not doubt the teacher's being a scholar.
7. Living in a house and sleeping in a bed he now regarded as a luxury.
8. Tom continued counting the spoons and placing them in order.
9. Doubting is a very healthy sign, especially in the young.
10. He did us a good turn without knowing it.
11. Do you mind my mentioning this matter to my father?
12. My friend gives me entertainment without requiring anything on my part.

13. I was not aware of your having secured the loan for the purchase of the farm.

14. The old man had insisted upon purchasing a beautiful new rifle for Shiloh.

15. There is no use in your going any farther.

16. John's having been a student in a first-rate college should be questioned.

17. After pausing for applause and after receiving none, the speaker left the platform.

18. His having sworn by his sword is no evidence of his honesty.

19. Our being conscious of our integrity is a great solace in the time of calamity and reproach.

20. The princess avoided exposing her plans to her rival's friends.

21. John's having gone away was a signal for my return.

22. True greatness consists solely in seeing everything.

23. No alert American can visit any foreign country without noting examples of adherence to outgrown methods in industry, commerce, and transportation.

24. Socrates was executed for "corrupting" youth and for infidelity to the gods.

25. Francis Bacon impeached the medieval schoolmen for spinning out endless cobwebs of theory.

26. Being ignorant was to her the quintessence of being common.

27. The teacher called copying from another's notes cheating.

28. Mr. Springle cannot be rivaled in his shoeing of horses.

29. Her complexion was a blending of the rose and the lily.

30. William Dean Howells tried encouraging the writing of the finer kinds of romance.

31. The savage obtains food by slaying the animals.

32. There is no scientific reason for separating the man from the animal.

33. The man persisted in keeping his wife a woman.

34. He employed certain powerful restoratives suggested by no little medical learning.

35. There was no hope of rivaling them.

36. There will be sleeping enough in the grave.

37. My always keeping good hours and giving little trouble made her unhappy at parting with me.

38. To some this may sound merely like the grating of overwrought nerves.

39. Making the soul graceful is one of the powers of music.

40. The greatest living philosopher has abandoned the hope of answering that question.

41. Her mistake, whipping the child without knowing the crime, cost her her peace of mind.

42. Suffering is often caused by the thought of death.

43. The sound was like the hissing of innumerable snakes.

44. We discussed the best methods for making a beefsteak delicious.

45. Observing our faults in others is sometimes helpful for our case.

46. Planting of countries is like planting of woods.

47. Is not all the work of man in this world a making of order?

48. The answering of this question is revealing the soul of the nation.

49. We cannot look, however imperfectly, upon a great man, without gaining something from him.

50. The Lord shall preserve thy going out and thy coming in from this time forth.

EXERCISE B

I. Pick out in Exercise A, several words ending in *-ing* which seem to you to be mere abstract nouns. Explain why you do not consider them gerunds.

II. Pick out five sentences containing gerunds with no expressed subject in the gerund phrase, and tell what subject is implied or is expressed elsewhere in the sentence.

III. Write ten sentences containing the compound (expanded) tense forms of the gerund, and name the tense you use in each sentence. Use some of the gerunds as adverbial objectives, some as objects of prepositions, and some as objective complements.

EXERCISE C

Correct all errors in the following sentences, giving reasons for all corrections:

1. In reviewing the matter with him, he seemed unusually stupid.

2. After buying a car, it should be used.

3. The mother was not aware of her son stealing.

4. I object to you making light of a serious subject.

5. After eating his apple to the core, a worm was discovered.

6. I am sure of him being invited.

7. After marking the papers, the grades must be sent to the registrar.

8. I do not doubt them being interested.

9. Upon entering the parlor, the thief was seen to dash through the window.

10. Don't believe that by merely asking favors, they will be granted.

11. By waxing floors, the grain in the wood can be seen.

12. After listening carefully to his tale of woe, the subject was dropped.

13. Washington never having told a lie is sometimes questioned.

14. Pardon me asking such personal questions.

15. After baking a cake, it will be eaten.

16. While bathing baby, it fainted.

17. After cooking the frog's legs, nobody would eat them.

18. By working hard is the way to get ahead in the world.

19. In preparing and writing a formal essay, the outline should be made first and then carefully followed.

20. After having finished our dinner, the waiter brought us our change and took his tip and left.

21. In trying to do two jobs, neither is seldom done well.

22. After having escaped being drafted for three years, the Army finally called him.

23. By studying diligently and avoiding absences, the teacher may give me an A.

24. After having corrected all of these dangling modifiers, no danglers should appear in his rewritten theme.

25. Before accepting a new job, all of the advantages and disadvantages of the transfer should be carefully considered.

Lesson X

Infinitives

The **infinitive** is an infinite (Lat. *infinitus*, unlimited, boundless) verb form. Like the participle and the gerund, it has no inflection to indicate person or number. The simplest and the oldest form of the infinitive (i.e., the present indefinite tense: *go, talk, forget*, etc.) is regarded as the basic verb form, the one from which all the other verb forms, including the participle and the gerund, are derived.[1]

The **infinitive phrase** in its simplest form consists of the preposition *to* and the basic form of a principal verb: *to go, to talk, to forget*, etc. Like the gerund and the participle, the infinitive may have modifiers and complements; and, like them also, it has voice and tense modifications. The full infinitive phrase may, therefore, include many more words than the infinitive with *to*. In *To forgive is to be charitable*, the first infinitive phrase consists of *to* and the basic verb form *forgive;* but the second contains a subjective complement. One phrase is the subject of the sentence; the other is the subjective complement.

Except when the infinitive is a part of the inflectional form of a finite verb, it is always analyzed (or diagramed) as a prepositional phrase, even when the *to* is not expressed, as the following illustrations will show. In the infinitive phrase, the verb form (i.e., the infinitive without *to*) has the function of a noun and is always parsed as the object of the *to*, and in the diagram it is placed where the object of the preposition

---

[1] The student should review the forms of the infinitive and the finite verb forms which are made up by combining infinitives with auxiliaries. These are listed and discussed in Part One under Tenses of Finite and Infinite Verbs, Chapter Five, pp. 116–138.

belongs. It is proper, therefore, in analyzing the infinitive in its various verbal functions to consider the infinitive phrase as the grammatical unit performing the function of a noun, an adjective, or an adverb.

Uses of the Infinitive Phrase

1. As Subject of a Sentence:

1. To side with truth is noble.

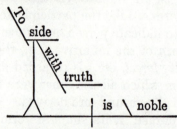

In this sentence, the infinitive phrase consists of function word *to* (diagramed as a preposition, though in this sentence it is not a true preposition; it does not show relation between grammatical units) and the infinitive *side* and its adverbial phrase modifier *with truth*. *Side* is the simplest form of the verb it represents (similar to the O.E. noun form in the nominative case). It is an intransitive verb, and is the indefinite present tense form.

The infinitive may take a direct object or be followed by a subjective or an objective complement; as:

2. To join the school orchestra was his one great ambition.

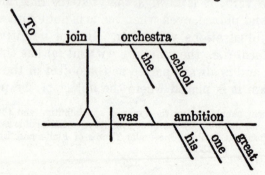

2. Infinitive Phrase as Subjective Complement:

a. *Predicate Nominative:*

His sole ambition was to succeed.

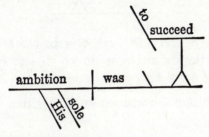

b. *Attribute Complement:*

They seemed to be drifting aimlessly about.

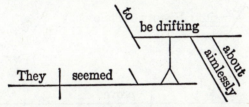

The infinitive phrase has the function of an adjective here. The predicate verb *seemed* is the past tense of *seem*, a copulative verb, which requires a subjective complement for full predication.

3. Infinitive Phrase as Direct Object (Object Complement):

1. I attempt from love's sickness to fly.

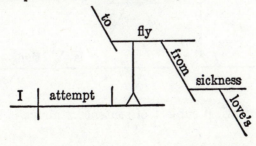

2. Dare they do it?

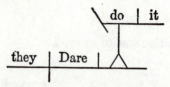

After *dare, help,* and a few other verbs the *to* is sometimes omitted before the infinitive as direct object: *He helped pay my expenses; He helps support his parents;* etc.

4. The Infinitive Phrase as an Appositive (Explanatory Modifier):

1. His grand aim, to write a History of Philosophy, proved beyond his strength.

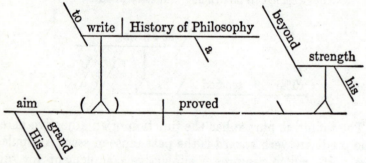

2. It is a good thing to give thanks unto the Lord.

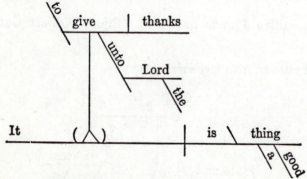

The grammatical subject of sentence *2* above is the introductory pronoun *it*, sometimes called an expletive, because its chief function is to introduce a sentence whose logical subject follows the verb. *It* has no real meaning in this idiomatic function, and could be omitted if the subject were transposed to its normal position, and made to precede the predicate verb; e.g., *To give thanks unto the Lord is a good thing.*

5. Infinitive Phrase as Objective Complement:

1. The shock caused him to lose his balance.

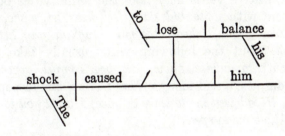

2. I believe him to be honest.

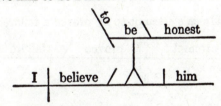

In this sentence, the infinitive *be* is a copulative verb. The adjective *honest* is a subjective complement and refers to and describes the subject of the infinitive. Observe that the objective complement line after *believe* directs the infinitive to its subject, the direct object.

This construction is sometimes called the **infinitive clause.** Observe that the infinitive and its subject can be converted into a noun clause without loss of meaning: *I believe that he is honest.* In this text, however, the term *clause* is used to identify that division of a sentence which contains a subject in the nominative case and a finite (asserting) verb.

3. Do not make me laugh.

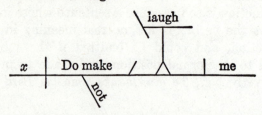

Some verbs in objective complement construction require the infinitive with *to;* others do not permit the *to.* The following transitive verbs may take the infinitive as objective complement without *to: bid, dare, feel, hear, let, make, observe, see,* and *watch;* e.g., *I heard the man laugh at you; Let me see your book.* But the following verbs usually take the infinitive with *to: advise, allow, ask, beg, compel, expect, force, forbid, want, wish,* and many others having similar copulative use; e.g., *He advised me to leave at once; I want you to come tc see me; Allow me to speak.*

6. Infinitive Phrase as a Modifier of a Noun:

1. Darius Green's attempt to fly proved a failure.

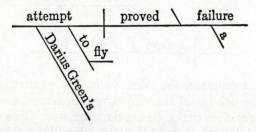

Observe that *to fly* is not an appositive. *Fly (flying)* represents the object of the verbal idea in the noun *attempt;* i.e., *he attempted flight.* Or, *to fly* may be rendered *at flying.*

2. This is a trap to catch the thief.

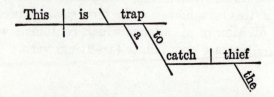

Here *to catch the thief* represents the design of the trap; i.e., *This is a trap designed for catching the thief.*

The infinitive is used with the noun *nothing* to represent a thing impossible or undesirable of accomplishment:

3. There is nothing to do.

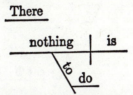

7. Infinitive Phrase Used as Modifier of a Verb

He struggled to get free.

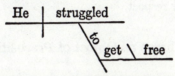

The infinitive here expresses mental direction, or purpose. When an infinitive phrase modifies a predicate verb, the subject of the finite verb is also the logical subject of the infinitive. In sentence **7**, *he* is the grammatical subject of *struggled* and the logical subject of *get*.

8. Infinitive Phrase as Modifier of an Adjective:

She is difficult to please.

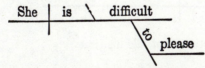

To please expresses respect, or specification; i.e., it tells in what respect she is difficult. Observe that *to eat* is also a phrase of respect, or specification, in the following sentence:

The fruit is too unripe to eat.

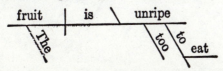

9. Infinitive Phrase as Modifier of an Adverb:

They arrived too late to catch the train.

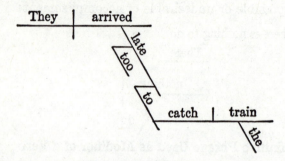

The infinitive phrase *to catch the train* also expresses specification, or respect.

10. Infinitive Phrase as Object of Preposition:

1. He was about to close his shop.

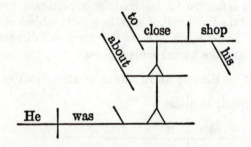

2. He did nothing but idle his time.

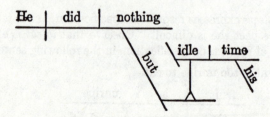

3. Nothing is left but to gather up the fragments.

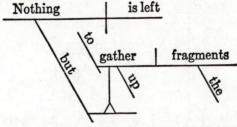

In sentence *1*, *about* has very little prepositional force, though it may be regarded as showing some relation between the subject of the sentence, to which the phrase refers, and its object, *to close his shop*. In sentences *2* and *3*, *but* is a full preposition. *Except* and *save* are often used in this construction.

Observe that in sentence *1*; the infinitive phrase is placed on a second standard to indicate that the entire phrase is the object of the preposition *about*.

The necessity of furnishing a subject for the infinitive and of throwing this subject into the objective case has resulted in the invention of an idiom wherein *for* governs an entire group, consisting of the infinitive and its subject:

1. For a man to love his neighbor is the essence of the Christian law.

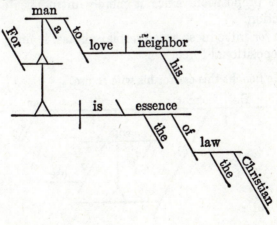

2. It now became necessary for Ruth to earn her own living.

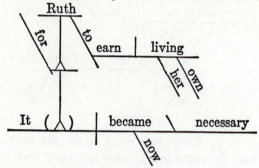

3. He said for me to come home early.

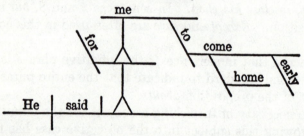

In the three preceding sentences, *for* has no prepositional (relational) meaning; but, because it is a fossilized preposition (like the *to* before the infinitive), it is always diagramed as a preposition. It may properly be called an introductory or expletive preposition, since it merely introduces a complex construction.

When *for* introduces an adverbial phrase, it may, however, have prepositional force:

4. He bought this car for his wife to use.

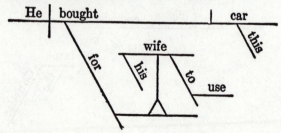

The purpose idea and the relationship expressed by *for* may be seen if we convert the infinitive phrase into a simple prepositional phrase: *For his wife to use* is about the equivalent of *for his wife's use.*

11. The Complementary Infinitive:

1. He ought to pay his debt.

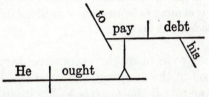

This sentence is nearly equivalent to *He must pay his debt*, where *pay* is really the complementary infinitive without *to* (though not indicated as such in the diagram because *must pay* is now regarded as an inflectional form of the verb *pay*. (See Tenses of Modal Auxiliaries, Part One, Chapter Five, pp. 128–132.)

2. The sun is going to rise.

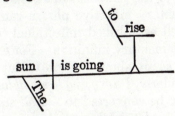

3. The group is to assemble at dawn.

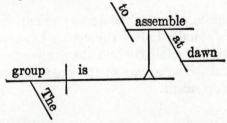

Is going to rise indicates futurity, nearly equal to *will rise.*
Is to assemble indicates futurity plus intention.

The following are further examples of the complementary infinitive:

1. I am *to do* a good turn for them.
2. Please *close* the door.
3. Need I *say* more?
4. I have *to study* on Sunday.
5. He used *to live* in this house.
6. Sunday is coming *to be* an orgy of automobile slayings.
7. I have *to leave* at once.

The infinitive with *to* in the complementary function has established itself in the language since the Old English period. The infinitive acquired the *to* after losing its distinctive suffix marking (O.E. *-an;* M.E. *-en*). The modal verbs which have been in use as auxiliaries since the Middle English period are seldom followed by the infinitive with *to* in the formation of predicate verbs. Observe that we do not say *please to study, can to study, must to study.* But our modern substitutes for the older auxiliary (or modal) verbs do have the infinitive with *to,* as many of the sentences in **11** show.

The complementary infinitive phrase can usually be converted into a well established inflectional form—this is the test of the complementary infinitive. For example, *I have to go* and *I ought to go* are about the equivalent of *I must go* and *I should go.* Similarly, *I am going to study tonight* and *I am to leave at noon* may be converted to *I shall study tonight* and *I shall leave at noon. I used to work there* means *I once worked there.*

In the diagram, the complementary infinitive phrase with *to* is put on a standard after the verb. Observe there is no line separating the auxiliary and the complementary phrase, which is construed as a part of the predicate verb, not as a subjective complement.

12. Infinitive Phrase Used Independently:

To tell the truth, I positively dislike him.

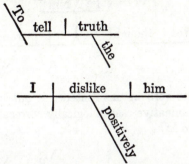

The independent infinitive phrase, like the participle phrase used independently, is not a part of the sentence proper. It has some illative (conjunctive) force in that it introduces an inference or a consequence based on what has preceded. In the diagram, the independent infinitive phrase is separated from the sentence it introduces, as in the preceding model. In the written sentence, it may be inserted within the sentence, but it is always set off from the other elements of the sentence by punctuation. Observe that in the diagram it is never enclosed in parenthetical marks; it is an independent unit, not an appositive.

The Subject of the Infinitive

The subject of the infinitive may be a noun or pronoun in the nominative or the objective case, used in any construction in the sentence where either of these cases would be proper. When the infinitive is a copulative verb requiring a subjective complement, the noun complement in this construction may be nominative or objective, the case being determined by the case of the subject of the infinitive. If we say *I thought the intruder to be he,* we fail to recognize that the subject of the infinitive (*be*) is *intruder,* the direct object, which is always in the objective case. Observe the construction in the diagram below:

We thought the intruder to be him.

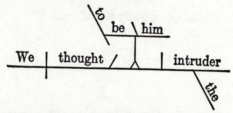

If the finite verb in this sentence is put in the passive voice, the nominative case is logically correct: *The intruder was thought to be he.*

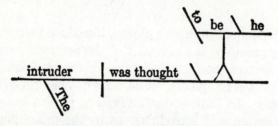

In stating general truths, the subject of the infinitive is seldom expressed: *To act openly is honest; It is wrong to laugh at another's weaknesses.* The subject *one* can be supplied in each of these sentences if we use the function word *for* to introduce it; as, *For one to act openly is honest; It is wrong for one to laugh at another's weaknesses.*

Infinitive *vs.* Gerund

In many of their uses, the gerund and the infinitive phrases are interchangeable. Since both verbals are used in the noun construction, the choice may depend on personal feeling, but in some instances idiomatic usage allows only one of these verbals. We may say *To lie is wrong,* or *Lying is wrong; He began to talk at one o'clock,* or *He began talking at one o'clock;* and convey about the same meaning with the infinitive that we convey with the gerund. But in the object position some verbs are followed by the infinitive, others by the gerund: *I like to sing hymns,* but *I enjoy singing hymns.*

Often a different meaning is conveyed when the infinitive replaces the gerund; e.g., *I hate to lie* does not quite mean *I hate lying.* The gerund is often used in making the more general statement, and the infinitive is employed in stating a personal attitude. No specific rules can be given which will aid the student in deciding when to use the gerund and when the infinitive. One must observe the speech of the best writers and speakers, and follow their usage. All such differentiations are matters of usage, not logic or formal rules.

Sometimes a prepositional phrase containing a gerund is used loosely as a substitute for the infinitive phrase as subject or as predicate nominative, as in the following:

Loose: By reading good books is the best way to improve one's mind.

Improved: To read good books is the best way to improve one's mind.

Also good: Reading good books is the best way to improve one's mind.

The preposition *by* in the "loose" sentence suggests an adverbial function. Such a phrase should modify the verb, as it does in *We improve our minds by reading good books.*

The Split Infinitive

The **split infinitive** is an expression used by some grammarians to describe the infinitive phrase when an adverb (a word or phrase) separates the infinitive and the *to.* The term *split* is really a misnomer when it is applied to this type of "splitting," because the infinitive, strictly speaking, consists only of the verb form, which is not split by putting a modifier between the function word *to* and the verb form, as in *to thoroughly enjoy, to secretly leave, to at once and for all times take,* etc.

Since the *to* is now felt to belong to the infinitive, usage on the whole favors keeping it next to the verb it introduces; but there may be times when it is better to split the phrase, especially if obscurity results from not splitting it. Many of our best writers do split their infinitives, and schooled grammarians justify the construction when it prevents awkwardness or ambiguity. *I failed to fully understand* is as graceful and clear as *I failed to understand fully.* Similarly, *I had to sit down and faithfully copy all the numbers in my notebook,* has a more natural ring than *I had to sit down and copy faithfully all the numbers in my notebook.*

Dangling Infinitives

The **dangling infinitive phrase** contains an infinitive which has no logical subject, either expressed or implied in the sentence to which it belongs. Like the dangling gerund phrase, the infinitive phrase as a modifier of the principal verb is sometimes used loosely. If we say *To repair your radio, it must be sent to the shop,* we fail to give the infinitive *repair* a logical subject; but if we say *To repair your radio, I must take it to the shop,* we supply a logical subject. The incorrect sentence is introduced by a phrase containing an infinitive in the active voice, which form suggests that an actor or agent subject is to follow; but, when the agent subject does not follow, the sentence becomes vague and confusing. As a rule, when the infinitive phrase modifies the verb, it should have for its subject the noun or pronoun which is the subject of the sentence.

EXERCISE A

Analyze or diagram:

1. We began to suspect our neighbor's children.
2. Dickens's stories made everybody laugh and cry.
3. He thinks it a virtue to be intolerant.
4. I am willing to take advice and to pay for it.
5. The teacher advised the students to study harder.
6. To help a friend is to give ourselves pleasure.
7. My sister will do anything but wash dishes.
8. A dog seems to be a nuisance in this community.

9. I am anxious for you to meet my sister.
10. These bills ought to be paid before the end of the month.
11. Is it too late for me to see your pictures?
12. The art of skating and skiing is not always easily acquired.
13. To be frank with you, I am not interested in taking out more insurance.
14. The newcomer was known to be she.
15. Women were made to be loved, not to be understood.
16. His failure is to be ascribed to his lack of tact.
17. Hitler tried to conquer the world.
18. We were sufficiently calm to survey the whole case.
19. Harriet had known women to turn cold at the sight of a new gown.
20. The writer must make his heroes die triumphantly.
21. The error of the romantic school was to idealize the victims of society.
22. I ought to tell you about my trip to Europe.
23. The prisoner is about to receive his death sentence.
24. Is it possible for a person to overcome the fear of thought?
25. His wife always seemed to be half asleep.
26. I am going to like him.
27. I am making you talk more logically.
28. The master wanted his servant to lie for him.
29. The maid dared to do the unkind act.
30. What is there to confess?
31. The poorest students often want to be excused from the final examination.
32. Let the old man rave all day.
33. She helped them make picnic suppers for the men.
34. It has always been a disastrous policy to rob some for the support of others.
35. To admire the book is to admire the author.
36. He gave them bread from heaven to eat.
37. It is an honor for a man to cease from strife.
38. Labor not to be rich.
39. To light a fire is an instinctive and resistant act of man.
40. Knox strove to make the government of Scotland a theocracy.
41. I have come to clear away the cobwebs.
42. There had come, at last, to be a kind of madness in him.
43. To choose time is to save time.

44. Ordinary expense ought to be limited by a man's estate.
45. The chief business of mankind is to discover the truth.
46. To be masters of the sea is an ambition of Englishmen.
47. To die is not sport for a man.
48. It is a most exciting thing to be alive in this world.
49. To attempt theorizing on such matters would profit little.
50. His wife had volunteered to go with him and to die with him.
51. The greatest of faults is to be conscious of none.
52. Religion teaches us to be resigned to circumstances.
53. In all ways we are to become perfect through suffering.
54. It is a subtle compliment to have book agents and tramps frequently at one's door.
55. He made the world seem almost empty and very lonesome.
56. It took very little imagination for me to feel the whirlwind of battles.
57. This process of fitting things properly into one's cosmos seems to be one of the chief aims of conscious life.
58. For a long time no technical words were invented to give aloofness and seeming precision to philosophic and scientific discussion.
59. It is foolish to lay out money in the purchase of indulgence.
60. All children should be taught to swim.
61. Let honesty and industry be thy constant companions.
62. Only one Quaker, Mr. James Morris, appeared to oppose the measure.
63. I went to see him at his printing house.
64. He wished to please everybody.
65. To mix comedy with tragedy is like mixing water with wine.
66. It is possible to be poetic in dealing with poems.
67. The election plea at its worst is to let well enough alone.
68. He watched his fair rose wither.
69. The Devil hath power to assume a pleasing shape.
70. He himself was powerless to change his fate.
71. Even his enemies did not wish to have him fail.
72. I shall try to furnish you with the necessary information.
73. It was customary to explain the object of a building by a short motto placed over the door.
74. To get any complete idea of exchange, we must view, in some of its main aspects, the development of transportation.

75. God will not have his work made manifest by cowards.
76. Experience causes each man's individuality to develop.
77. I happen to be a Baptist preacher.
78. He defended his right to speak the dark truth.
79. To be good does not mean to be obedient and harmless.
80. I said nine *Ave Marias* to obtain his cure.
81. Do not fail to make a pilgrimage to Mecca.
82. The heavens always find means to break your heart.
83. So these men ceased to answer Job.
84. Thou shalt not stir one foot to seek a foe.
85. The writers of the best literature have used and are still using these myths to illustrate and to illuminate their thought.
86. There is little evidence to support the doctrine of the transmission of acquired characteristics.
87. There is no reason to doubt the continuity of animal society.
88. To be frank with you, I once objected to cards and dancing.
89. She does nothing but complain of her husband's shortcomings.
90. Her request, to go home a month before Christmas, was not granted.
91. To tell the truth, I did not invite him to bring his dog.
92. The dogs did nothing but bark at us.
93. To sum up, the total loss was almost a thousand dollars.
94. He will do little in the way of charity except to feed tramps.
95. I come to bury Caesar, not to praise him.
96. To live in the hearts of those left behind is not to die.
97. Her avocation—namely, to tat and embroider—netted her enough cash to buy her jewelry.
98. To be sure, I was somewhat embarrassed by his frank questioning about such personal matters.
99. History is coming to be a race between education and catastrophe.
100. Teach me, my God and King,
     In all things Thee to see.

EXERCISE B

I. Change ten of the infinitive constructions in Exercise A to gerund constructions. Comment on any changes in meaning which the shift produces.

II. You will find a treatment of the split infinitive in the following texts: Curme's *A Grammar of the English Language*, Vol. I and II; Jespersen's *Essentials of English Grammar;* Fowler's *A Dictionary of Modern English Usage;* and the *Oxford Dictionary*. Consult two of these texts, and report your findings.

III. Give the subject of each infinitive in the following sentences in Exercise A: 1, 2, 5, 8, 16, 25, 33, 39, 53, 65, 98, 100. Find five infinitives which have no expressed subjects, and tell how they are used.

IV. Give the tense and voice (if the verb has voice) of the infinitives in the following sentences in Exercise A: 6, 10, 15, 17, 32, 33, 45, 49, 61. In which of these sentences do the names of the tenses fail to name the time expressed by the infinitives?

EXERCISE C

Correct any violations of standard usage which you find in the following sentences. If you find no violations in a sentence, do not make any changes. Comment on any constructions or forms about which grammarians may differ.

1. To securely fasten the door, you should use the night lock.
2. She read her lesson over several times to thoroughly master the facts.
3. In order to successfully teach English grammar, the student should know Latin and Greek.
4. The boy was too young to properly make use of his time.
5. Through economizing is his rule for success.
6. The way to keep the flies out of the house is by screening it.
7. To never realize one's ambition is discouraging.
8. He promised to not only quit smoking himself, but to also see that the other boys stopped.
9. My uncle intends to again run for governor.
10. To keep the butter cold, it is usually kept in the ice box.
11. In order to plainly talk, the parrot's tongue should be split.
12. By working is the best way to keep out of mischief.
13. The best method to teach syntax is by diagraming.
14. She offered the services of her child to partly pay for the back rent.

15. This medicine seems to really help the patient.
16. To learn to swim, the water should be quite deep.
17. She seemed to fairly float through the air.
18. Some children seem to really appreciate their parents.
19. To keep that hen from flying over the fence, her wings should be clipped.
20. To thoroughly understand poetry and appreciate poetry, it should be studied while young.
21. To be fully informed on current topics, the newspapers must be read.
22. I wanted to at least have your opinion on this matter.
23. My mother intends to have in the fall completed her art course.
24. His formula for reducing was through exercise.
25. To successfully make cake of this sort, the eggs should be beaten separately.
26. To find the etymology of these words, a dictionary should be consulted.
27. To make sure this letter is delivered immediately, a special delivery stamp should be used.
28. The committee ought to more closely examine the credentials of every applicant.

COMPLEX SENTENCES

LESSON XI

Adjective Clauses

The sentences presented for study and analysis in the ten preceding assignments were all simple sentences. Some of them may have seemed long and involved, but none contained more than one complete subject and one complete predicate. Some were composed of compound elements, such as compound subject, compound predicate, and compound modifiers; but no sentence presented for analysis in the A Exercises in Lessons I–X inclusive contained more than one clause; that is, no two grammatical elements serving as the subject of any sentence had separate predicates. The assignments which follow will introduce and present for analysis sentences made up of two or more clauses. The next four lessons will treat of the various forms of the **complex sentence.** Each sentence in these assignments will contain one principal clause and one or more adjective, noun, or adverb clauses.

Any clause which performs the function of an adjective may be called an **adjective clause;** and any sentence which contains one principal (independent) clause and one or more adjective clauses will be called a **complex sentence.** This is, however, only one type of complex sentence (see Noun and Adverb Clauses, pp. 370–420).

Adjective clauses may be introduced by a **relative pronoun or a relative adverb,** either of which may be expressed or implied. The **relative pronoun** and the **relative adverb** perform dual functions in any sentence in which either occurs. The **relative pronoun** stands for a noun expressed or clearly implied in a preceding clause, which clause is principal to the

349

one introduced by the relative pronoun. The **relative adverb** has a still more complex nature: it stands for a prepositional phrase containing a relative pronoun as its principal word. In addition to their functions as pronoun and adverb, the relative pronoun and the relative adverb have the force of conjunctions in that they also join clauses.

Both the relative pronoun and the relative adverb belong to and are a part of the adjective clauses which they introduce. In picking out and identifying the adjective clauses in complex sentences, one must always include the relative pronouns and the relative adverbs which introduce them. The student will observe that in the diagram the relative pronoun is placed where the noun for which it stands would be placed if the adjective clause were converted into a principal clause or into a simple sentence. The relative adverb is placed as an adverb modifier of the verb or some word which adverbs modify. It always modifies what the prepositional phrase would modify if the relative adverb were converted into a phrase containing a relative pronoun; and in the converted sentence it is joined to what would be the antecedent of the relative pronoun.

In the diagram, the relative pronoun and the relative adverb are joined to their antecedent by dotted lines drawn diagonally to denote the modifying nature of the clauses. The dotted line also indicates the conjunctive function of the relative word. It is important to note that the principal clause is diagramed first, and that the adjective clause is placed below it, never above it.

Adjective Clauses Introduced by Relative Pronouns

A **relative pronoun** agrees with its antecedent in person, number, and gender, but not in case. Its case will be determined by its use in the adjective clause to which it belongs. Observe the agreement of the relative pronoun with its antecedent in the adjective clauses analyzed and diagramed and in those presented for analysis in Exercise A.

1. I met the girl who is substituting for your brother.

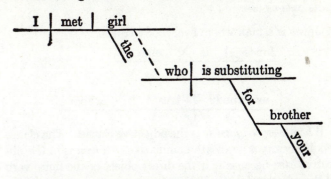

Who is substituting for your brother is the adjective clause; it describes and identifies *girl,* the object complement of the principal clause. *Who* is the relative pronoun which connects (relates) the two clauses. It is nominative case because it is the subject of the adjective clause. It is third person and singular number, because its antecedent is third person singular. The gender of *who* is important in this sentence because the reference pronoun *her* agrees with it and its antecedent in gender, both therefore being feminine. Observe that the case of *who* is nominative, but that its antecedent is objective, the case of each of these words being determined by its use in its own clause.

2. Any man who would steal would lie.

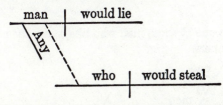

Who would steal is the adjective clause. The clause is introduced by the relative pronoun *who,* which agrees with its antecedent in person, number, and gender, though none of these modifications can be determined by the inflectional form of any word in the adjective clause. The case of *who* is nominative, but it does not have this case because of any sort of agreement with its antecedent, but because of its use in its own clause.

3. Jones is a man whom everybody trusts.

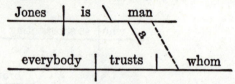

Whom everybody trusts is the adjective clause.   The clause modifies *man,* a predicate nominative.   *Whom* is in the objective case because it is the direct object of the finite verb in the adjective clause it introduces.

4. He dances well to whom fortune pipes.

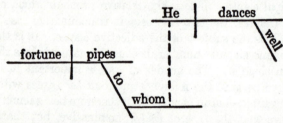

Whom is the correct case form in this sentence because it is used as the object of a preposition.   Its person, number, and gender are not denoted by its form, but the antecedent tells us that it is third person, singular number, masculine gender.

5. Smith is one of those men who like to see their names in the papers.

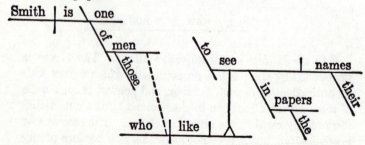

In this sentence, it is important that we recognize the antecedent of the relative pronoun *who*, because its person and number govern the person and number of the personal pronoun *their*, which modifies *names*. Also the verb in the adjective clause must agree with its subject in person and number. We, therefore, have the plural verb *like*, not *likes*.

6. I am the only one of the men who enjoys baseball.

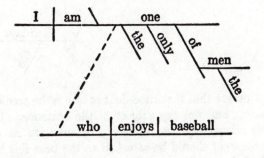

Here the antecedent of *who* is *one*, not *men;* therefore, the verb in the adjective clause is third person singular to agree with *who*, whose person and number are determined by its antecedent *one*.

7. It is I who am at fault.

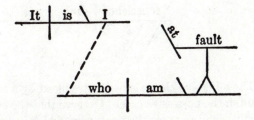

Here the verb *am* shows us that the relative pronoun agrees with its antecedent in person and number.

8. It is my brother and sister who are coming for the holidays.

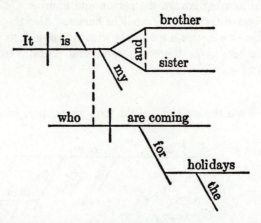

Observe that the antecedent of *who* is the predicate nominative, and not the subject of the sentence. The dotted line connecting the relative pronoun with its compound antecedent should be attached to the base line before it is divided.

9. Jones is one man whose conscience does not permit him to lie.

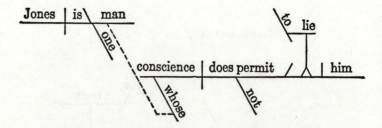

The adjective clause is here introduced by a relative pronoun in the possessive case. Observe that the entire clause modifies and restricts the noun *man*, which in turn refers to and is identical with *Jones*. In the diagram, the dotted line is drawn from *man* to *whose*, as shown in the illustration.

10. Uneasy lies the head that wears a crown.

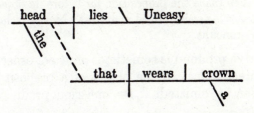

Observe that this sentence has inverted word order, and that the subject of the principal clause comes after its predicate. The relative pronoun *that* does not inflect to indicate person, number, or gender; but its use in its clause tells us that it is nominative case; and its antecedent, *head*, tells us that it is neuter gender, singular number, third person.

11. This is the man that I voted for.

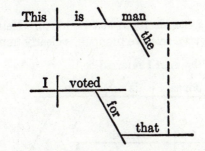

Though *that* in this sentence has the same form as it had in sentence *10*, its meaning and use are different, because its antecedent and its construction in the sentence are different. Here *that* is objective case, because it is the object of the preposition *for*. It is masculine gender, singular number, third person. Its antecedent denotes these meanings for us.

Observe that this sentence ends in a preposition and that it is a well-phrased grammatical sentence. The preposition has a function in the sentence, and could not for euphonic reasons be placed before *that* in the spoken sentence. All prepositions must be put in post-position when they govern the relative pronoun *that*.   If we substitute *whom* for *that*, we can then place the preposition *for* before its object; but the sentence is not improved in any way by the exchange of relative pronouns.

The relative pronoun is sometimes omitted, especially when it is the direct object or the object of a preposition; but it should never be omitted, if its omission produces any obscurity.

12. Have you read the book I gave you?

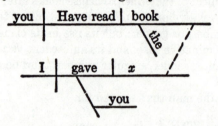

Here the x stands for a *that* or *which*.   Neither is expressed because a relative pronoun is clearly implied.

13. Jones is the man I referred to.

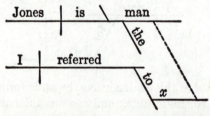

Here again, the relative pronoun is understood.   This type of omission is limited to restrictive clauses (see discussion of restrictive and nonrestrictive adjective clauses, pp. 363–365).

The conjunctions *as* and *but* sometimes serve as relative pronouns.   *As* has the function of a relative after the adjectives *such* and *same*, and is used to refer to persons, animals, or things.   *But* is sometimes employed as a negative relative, the equivalent of *that not*.

14. I have the same place as my father held.

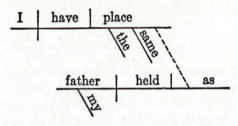

15. He has no neighbor but will recommend him.

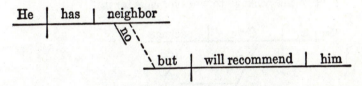

(For other sentences containing *but* and *as* used as relative pronouns, see Uses of the Relative Pronouns, Part One, Chapter Three, pp. 61–64.)

The Indefinite Relative Pronouns

The antecedents of the indefinite relative pronouns are often implied, seldom expressed. All of the compound indefinites (*whoever, whichever, whatever, whosoever, whatsoever, whichsoever*) and the indefinite relative *what* regularly refer to unexpressed antecedents, which, if expressed, would be indefinite pronouns, such as *anyone, anything, that, it*. Sometimes *who* and *which* are also used indefinitely, and refer to implied antecedents having very indefinite meaning.

In the analysis of the sentence, the antecedents of the indefinite relatives should be supplied in order to give full meaning to the principal clause. In the diagram, an *x* represents the understood antecedent. Observe that each of the relative pronouns with unexpressed antecedents in the following sentences belongs in the adjective clause, and the clause modifies the word which the *x* represents.

1. I shall send whoever will go.

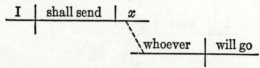

In this sentence *whoever* is equivalent to *anyone who*, and if we supply the antecedent, the *whoever* becomes *who*, and in the converted sentence the meaning becomes more definite. *Whoever* is nominative, because it is the subject of the adjective clause.

2. Give the package to whoever calls for it.

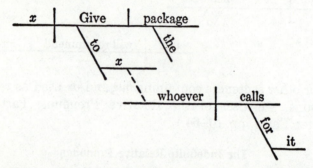

Observe that the preposition *to* here governs the unexpressed antecedent of *whoever;* it does not govern *whoever*, which must be in the nominative case because it is the subject of the adjective clause.

In the following sentence *whomever* is the proper form, because the relative pronoun is the object of the verb *see.* Its antecedent is the implied object of the preposition *to.*

3. Give the package to whomever you see.

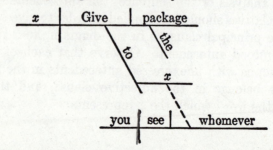

4. Take whichever you choose.

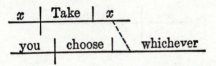

Unlike *whoever*, *whichever* does not have different forms for the nominative and the objective. Its antecedent, if supplied, would be *that, anything*, or some other equally indefinite pronoun.

5. That is what I said before.

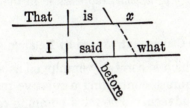

6. Do what is right.

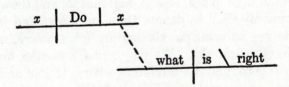

What is here the equivalent of *that which*. *Whatever* could be used here instead of *what*. Both are indefinite relatives.

7. Who steals my purse steals trash.

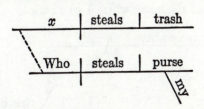

When *who* is used as an indefinite relative pronoun, it has the meaning of *whoever*, which could replace *who* in this sentence without loss of meaning.

8. Whom the court favors is safe.

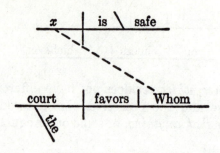

Whom is the equivalent of *whomever* here. Its antecedent may be *anybody* or *anyone*, represented in the diagram by the *x*.

Adjective Clauses Introduced by Relative Adverbs

Any adverb which is correctly employed as a substitute for a prepositional phrase containing a relative pronoun may be called a **relative adverb.** The most common relative adverbs which can be used to introduce adjective clauses are those which denote time, place, reason, and means; and the adverbs most commonly used to denote these meanings and join adjective clauses to principal clauses are *when, where, whereof, wherewith, why, whereby.* We may say *I remember the house where I was born,* and use a relative adverb to join and relate the clauses; or we may say *I remember the house in which I was born,* and use a relative pronoun to introduce our adjective clause. The two sentences have identical meaning.

1. I remember the house where I was born.

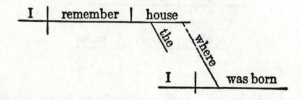

Observe that the relative adverb *where* is placed on a line made up of two parts to indicate its dual nature. The upper part is dotted to represent *where* as a conjunction connecting the adjective clause to *house;* and the lower part is made solid to represent it as an adverb modifying *was born.* If we convert *where* into a prepositional phrase containing a relative pronoun, the phrase would modify the same grammatical element as the relative adverb, and the clause would modify the same noun.

2. Spring is the season when all nature seems glad.

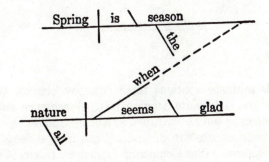

3. This is the reason why you failed.

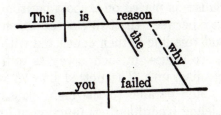

Why is sometimes implied in sentences of this type.

Coördinate Adjective Clauses

The things which we ourselves most admire and which we
speak of with the deepest emotion may be the very things
which leave our neighbors absolutely cold.

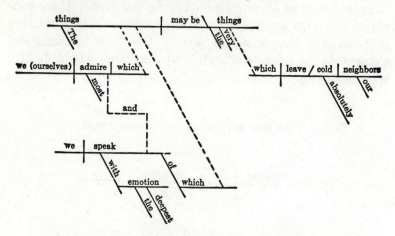

This sentence contains three adjective clauses, two of
which are coördinate (compound). A sentence such as
this one must not be construed as a compound sentence: the
coördinate clauses are dependent, not independent (principal) clauses. (See Compound Sentences, Lesson XV, pp.
420–426).

In the diagram, the conjunction *and* which joins the two
coördinate clauses is placed on a short horizontal dotted line
drawn halfway between the two clauses which the conjunction joins; and this line is then connected with the principal
verbs in the two clauses in such a way as to form a step, as
shown in the diagram. The dotted line on which the *and*
is placed is made parallel to the main clause lines to suggest its paralleling (coördinating) function in joining two like
elements. The dotted line is attached to the verbs chiefly
for convenience, but partly because the predicate verbs in
clauses are very important grammatical elements.

Restrictive and Nonrestrictive Clauses

Adjective clauses, when analyzed as to the particular way in which they modify nouns and pronouns, may be classed as restrictive and nonrestrictive.[1]

Restrictive clauses limit or identify: *These are the boys who (or that) deserve promotion.* Out of a group of boys certain ones are selected, distinguished. The extension of meaning or application in the word *boys* is here lessened, restricted. The restrictive clause is essential to the meaning of the sentence. If we say *Mother found the book which you lost,* we refer to a particular book, which is identified by the adjective clause *which you lost.* If we toss out a statement containing only the principal clause *Mother found the book,* someone is certain to ask *which book,* and the identifying element must then be added. Observe the restrictive meaning in the following sentences:

1. This is the house *that was sold* (one house is singled out in a row or group of houses).
2. These are the citizens *who deserve well of their neighbors* (certain persons are chosen out of all citizens, good and bad).
3. This is the room *where the tragedy occurred* (one room is distinguished among all the rooms of the house).

Observe that the restrictive clause is not set off by any punctuation.

Nonrestrictive clauses do not limit or identify. They do not affect the intention, nor restrict the number of the nouns or pronouns they modify: *Sunlight, which is necessary to plant growth, was plentiful that season.* The clause applies to all sunlight; it merely gives a bit of information concerning sunlight as an agency in life stimulation. *The eldest son, who had been abroad for some time, was hastily called home* contains a clearly marked nonrestrictive clause. *Son* is not restricted

---

[1] For a discussion of restrictive and nonrestrictive appositives, see Lesson VI, pp. 257–259; and for discussion of restrictive and nonrestrictive participial phrases, see Lesson VIII, pp. 303–304.

by the clause, having been already restricted, even identified, by the adjective preceding and modifying it. Observe that the principal clause does not depend upon the subordinate clause to convey the principal idea. We may even say *The eldest son was called home.* But if we say *The son who was in Europe was called home,* we refer to one son of perhaps several as the one who was called home. Observe that the adjective clauses in the following sentences are nonrestrictive; they do not identify or restrict the persons or objects named in the antecedents of the relative words, and these antecedents are the nouns which the clauses modify:

1. The sophomores, *who had no intimation of the trick,* walked right into the trap (Here all sophomores are included; all of them walked right into the trap).
2. The lower animals, *which have no complete and formal language,* must converse by rude signs and noises.
3. Moscow, *where Napoleon's campaign ended,* is the ancient capital of Russia.

Observe that the nonrestrictive clauses are always set off by commas.

A few words should be said here about the pronouns which may introduce the restrictive and the nonrestrictive clauses. Almost any relative pronoun or any of the relative adverbs may be employed in introducing the restrictive clauses; but some of the relatives are not generally used to introduce non-restrictive clauses.

The relative pronoun *that* and the indefinites (*whoever, whichever, whatever, what,* etc.) are used chiefly in restrictive clauses. *But* and *as,* when used as relative pronouns, introduce only restrictive clauses. *Who* and *which,* when used for one of the indefinite pronouns (i.e., with antecedents understood), belong in restrictive clauses. Any pronoun which has an implied antecedent has restrictive force, and the clause it introduces will be restrictive: *Who steals my purse steals trash.*

If the relative pronoun is not expressed (a *that* being implied), the relative clause will be restrictive, and hence will not be set off by commas: *I met the man you hired; I bought the house you wanted.*

Who and *which* as relative pronouns may introduce either restrictive or nonrestrictive clauses; and punctuating clauses containing these pronouns sometimes requires special attention. Usually, if one of these is used to introduce a restrictive clause, a *that* can be substituted for either *who* or *which.* We may say *The book which* (or *that*) *I bought is lost,* and know that the clause is restrictive because the *that* can be used for the *which.* Similarly, *I saw the man who* (or *that*) *bought your house.* Another test is to see if the pronoun can be omitted; and if it can, the clause will be a restrictive one: *I found the book which you bought* (or *the book you bought*).

The relative adverbs *where, when, why,* and *whereby* may introduce either restrictive or nonrestrictive clauses, the meaning which is to be conveyed being the test. Often if the definite article or some other similar modifier precedes the noun-antecedent, the clause which follows will be restrictive; e.g., *the place where I lived, the time when, the means whereby, the reason why.* If the antecedent is a proper noun, the clause which follows is likely to be nonrestrictive; as, *Washington, where the Capitol is, is a beautiful city; Berlin, where we once lived, was almost destroyed.*

In the diagram, there is no difference between the two types of clauses. As we learned in Lesson I, the diagram has no way of showing the proper punctuation of the sentence. It shows only the structure and relation of the grammatical units of the sentence.

Dangling Adjective Clauses

A **dangling adjective clause** is one which is unattached or is attached to the wrong grammatical unit. As we have already noted, adjective clauses should modify nouns or pronouns, and these should be expressed or clearly implied in the principal clause. If we say *I arrived late, which made everyone angry,* the relative pronoun *which* has no noun antecedent.

Such a sentence can be improved by converting it into a simple sentence containing a gerund subject; as, *My arriving late made everyone angry.* If we say *He failed three subjects, which caused his father to take him out of school,* we attempt to make the verb *failed* the antecedent. Here again the sentence would be improved if we turn the adjective clause into a gerund phrase; as, *His failing three subjects caused his father to take him out of school.*

Sometimes a clause is misplaced, and the meaning of the sentence is obscure or illogical. If we say *There was a poem in the book which I read and liked,* someone may want to know whether it was the poem or the book which was read and enjoyed. Similarly, in *I delayed writing the letter which made him angry,* the *which* may refer to the delay or to the letter, for, as this sentence is phrased, either meaning could be inferred. In *Father told me to put my money in the bank, which I didn't like,* the *which* may refer to bank or to the idea of putting money in a bank. We may say *I do not like the bank which my father recommends,* or *I do not like Father's telling me to put my money in the bank.* The rule should be: Avoid ambiguity.

EXERCISE A

Analyze or diagram:

1. Scorn the proud man that is afraid to weep.
2. Silence is a friend that will never betray.
3. There was a man in the land of Uz, whose name was Job.
4. The sex which reads the more novels reads the fewer newspapers.
5. The God who gave us life gave us liberty at the same time.
6. The number of those who undergo the fatigue of judging for themselves is very small.
7. This novel, which is called *Don Quixote,* is perhaps the greatest work of human wit.
8. His students were school teachers who wanted to own tea rooms, clerks who wanted to be sales managers, clergymen who wanted to be newspaper men.
9. The room was filled with a multitude of both sexes, who talked in low tones.

10. All who study will improve.
11. These friends of yours have displayed a senseless enmity toward me for which I am at a loss to account.
12. I gave her such clothes as I could spare.
13. There are three things I have always loved, and never understood—painting, music, and women.
14. Labor shuts the door and closes all the avenues whereby a temptation may enter.
15. She always succeeds in getting whatever she wants.
16. These students receive the same salary as the master.
17. There is not a book in his library but has some value.
18. The young hydra, which grows like a bud, fights for prey.
19. Let us go to the house where Chaucer was born.
20. There are times when the brain is tired with study and thinking.
21. Lay up for yourselves treasures in heaven, where neither moth nor rust doth corrupt, and where thieves do not break through and steal.
22. Bad and good are the prejudices which the eternal reality cannot recognize.
23. Who is that young man who talks so loud?
24. Those who could not come to him wrote to him.
25. We have here the unusual occurrence of a philosophy that is at once naturalized and spiritual.
26. He that increaseth knowledge increaseth sorrow.
27. The heart has reasons of its own, which the head can never understand.
28. He does me double wrong that wounds me with the flatteries of his tongue.
29. He jests at scars that never felt a wound.
30. They stumble that run fast.
31. Tristram, whose look became every moment more threatening, turned to the recluse.
32. Music and poetry—all the deepest and purest sentiments of the heart—are fed greatly upon the memory of things that were but can never be again.
33. What is there about the tang of wood smoke in a lonesome place that fills one with glories that seem half memory and half dream?
34. Oh, blessed is he who is negatively rich!

35. A great many will be found that can fiddle very cunningly.

36. Occasionally we find a man that has stirred up some vast commotion but does not himself persist.

37. The world has to obey him who thinks and sees in the world.

38. The poet who could merely sit in a chair and compose stanzas would never make a stanza worth much.

39. What is this unfathomable thing I live in, which men name Universe?

40. The images which Dante employs speak for themselves.

41. Romance, which relates to the beings of another world, ought to be at once mysterious and picturesque.

42. Every girl who has read Mrs. Marcet's little *Dialogues on Political Economy* could teach Montaigne or Walpole many lessons in finance.

43. We could accept whichever we chose without leaving our direct path of research.

44. There is not a boy in town but knows that tale.

45. Whoso belongs only to his own age, and reverences only its gilt Popinjays or soot-smeared Mumbojumbos, must needs die with it.—Carlyle.

46. The play's the thing wherein I'll catch the conscience of the king.

47. Whatever is worth doing at all is worth doing well.

48. The young men among us always talk of a time when they will be rich.

49. The reason why I am making this confession ought not to be generally known.

50. Unto whomsoever much is given, of him shall much be required.

51. The day is always his who works in it with serenity and great aim.

52. Speech is genuine which is without silliness, affectation, or pretense.

EXERCISE B

I. Classify as restrictive or nonrestrictive the adjective clauses in the following sentences in Exercise A: 3, 4, 7, 12, 18, 19, 20, 23, 27, 31, 40, 41, 50, 51, and 52.

II. Substitute participles for the adjective clauses in the following sentences: 6, 7, 9, 14, 23, 30, 39, 40, and 41.

III. Pick out ten sentences in Exercise A containing relative adverbs, and convert each relative adverb into a prepositional phrase containing a relative pronoun as the object of a preposition. Note whether the change modifies the meaning of the original sentence.

IV. Write out ten original sentences containing restrictive clauses and ten containing nonrestrictive clauses. Be sure that each sentence is correctly punctuated. Let some of your sentences contain relative adverbs and some relative pronouns.

EXERCISE C

Correct any errors you find in grammar and punctuation in the following sentences, giving reasons for all changes:

1. He failed in four of his subjects which caused his parents to take him out of school.
2. She wears short skirts which no other woman does now.
3. Whoever he saw he criticized.
4. My mother works which helps with the general expenses.
5. This is the house, that Jack built.
6. Denver where my uncle lives is at the foot of the Rockies.
7. Al Smith who was once governor of New York never became president.
8. The house, where I was born, lies in ruin.
9. Professor Brown is one of the teachers who doesn't believe in examinations.
10. You may refer the matter to whoever you choose.
11. He is the only one of the students who do not cheat.
12. This is the instructor which refused to help me.
13. Give the prize to whomever deserves it.
14. The man, who has done most for his age, is Chaucer.
15. He told me to give the money to whoever he sent.
16. Father suggested that I keep my money in a bank, which I have been doing.
17. It is I who is making the complaint.
18. He was born and reared on a farm, which explains his attitude.
19. She put the new rug on my floor which I did not like.
20. He wishes to buy an estate with tenants on it that will be in good condition.

Noun Clauses

Any clause which performs the function of a noun is called a **noun** (or **substantive**) **clause**. It may substitute for a mere abstract noun or for a noun-equivalent (e.g. a gerund or an infinitive phrase). We may say *His honesty has never been questioned*, and have the abstract noun *honesty* for the subject of our sentence; or we may say *That he is honest has never been questioned*, and have a noun clause for the subject of the sentence. Similarly, we may say *I know that he is honest*, and have a noun clause as the object of our principal verb; or we may convert the clause into a noun object followed by an infinitive; as, *I know him to be honest*. In the converted sentence, the infinitive phrase, *to be honest*, is the objective complement, and the direct object, *him*, is the subject of the infinitive. The noun clause may replace a gerund phrase; e.g., *His being honest has never been questioned* is almost identical in meaning with *That he is honest has never been questioned*.

Noun clauses may be introduced by any of the following:

1. Expletives: *that, but that, whether, if.*[1]

2. Interrogative pronouns: *who, which, what.*

3. Interrogative adjectives: *which, what.*

4. Interrogative adverbs: *why, when, where, how.*

Sometimes the expletive *that* is omitted when the sense of the sentence is clear without it, but *whether*, *but that*, and *if* should, as a rule, be expressed with any type of clause they

---

[1] For a discussion of the origin and the uses of these expletives and others like them, see Subordinating Conjunction in Part One, pp. 193–195.

introduce. The interrogative words which introduce noun clauses should not be omitted; they always have important functions in the clauses they introduce.

Uses of the Noun Clause

Noun clauses may be used in any of the more important constructions of nouns, such as subject, direct object, predicate nominative, object of preposition, appositive, or adverbial objective.

1. Subject of the Sentence:

1. That he was no friend became painfully apparent.

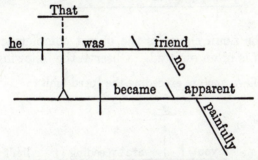

Here the noun clause is introduced by the expletive *that*. In the diagram, the noun clause is placed on a standard above the line on which a simple noun subject would be placed. The expletive *that* is put on a short horizontal line above the noun clause line, and is attached by a dotted line to the clause line as shown in the illustration.

2. Who is to go first has not been determined.

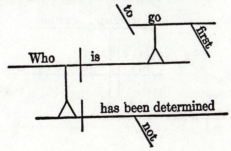

In this sentence the interrogative pronoun *who* introduces the noun clause. *Who* is the subject of the clause it introduces, and is therefore nominative.

2. Object Complement:

1. I know that my Redeemer liveth.

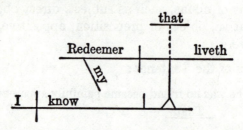

When the noun clause is the object complement, the expletive *that* is often omitted. Observe the following:

2. I believe you are exceeding the speed limit.

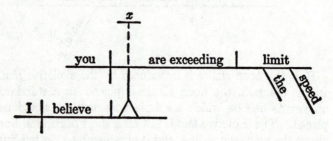

Here the *x* represents the implied expletive *that*.

3. We wondered whether you had left the city or not.

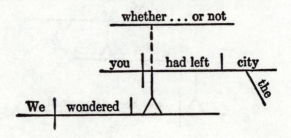

The expletive *if* could here replace *whether or not.* The noun clause may be expanded to read *whether you had or had not left the city;* and, when so expanded, the *or* would be analyzed as a coördinating conjunction joining the two verbs. But since the expression *whether or not* is idiomatic, it simplifies the analysis to treat the entire phrase as a fossilized phrasal conjunction, and call it an expletive. The *or not* is frequently not expressed, and could be omitted in the sentence given here.

4. He would not tell me who he was.

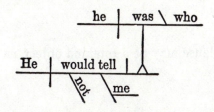

Who he was is an indirect question used as the object complement. *Who* is an interrogative pronoun. Note that *he* and *who,* the subject and predicate nominative respectively of the noun clause, appear in different order in the sentence and in the diagram. Before analyzing the indirect question, one should convert it to the statement form (*he was who,* or *he was John Smith*).

5. I wonder what he will say.

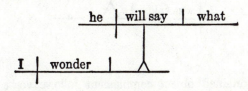

What he will say is also an indirect question used as the object complement. *What* is an interrogative pronoun.

The same construction appears in the following:

1. I asked him *which* (interrogative adjective) piece of property he would have.

2. I cannot learn *why* (interrogative adverb) he failed to appear.
3. He has never told me *how* (interrogative adverb) he made the ascent.
4. She desires to know *whether* (expletive) we are coming.
5. He ought to say *if* (expletive) he intends to buy the land.
6. I shall try to find out *when* (interrogative adverb) they are leaving, *where* (interrogative adverb) they are going, and *how* (interrogative adverb) long they intend to stay.
7. He has not yet said *whom* (interrogative pronoun) he will appoint.

The noun clause may be a **retained object,** as in the following:

6. I was told that my answer was wrong.

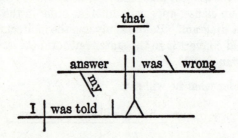

The **retained object** complement follows verbs in the passive voice. This construction results when the active voice is converted to passive, and the indirect object is made the subject of the verb in the passive voice. (For a discussion of the retained object, see Object Complement, Lesson IV, p. 245.)

3. Predicate Nominative:

1. The belief of the Sadducees was that there is no resurrection of the dead.

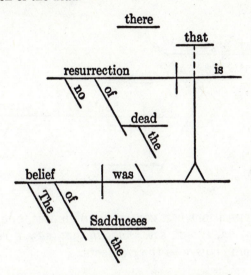

2. The question is whether he can be nominated.

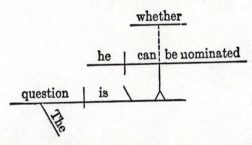

The indirect question in this sentence is introduced by the expletive *whether*. If the clause is converted into a direct question, the *whether* will be omitted, and the sentence will read *The question is, Can he be nominated?* The direct question needs no introductory word. The interrogation is indicated by placing the auxiliary *can* before the subject of the clause.

4. Object of Preposition:

1. They argued about whether they should make the attempt.

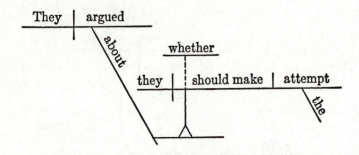

Not all prepositions can govern noun clauses, but *about, as to, over, upon, on, except, save, notwithstanding* are commonly used with noun clauses as their objects.

2. Your promotion will depend upon how well you do your assignment.

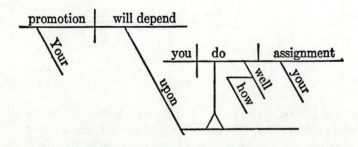

Here the noun clause is introduced by the interrogative adverb *how.* Observe that interrogative words (pronouns, adjectives, adverbs) in indirect questions have important functions in the clauses they introduce.

3. I am in doubt as to which book I should keep.

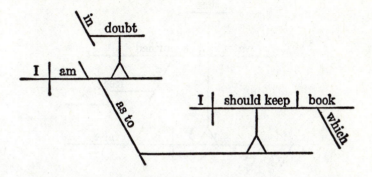

Here the prepositional phrase, the principal term of which is the noun clause, *which book I should keep,* modifies the subjective complement, which is the prepositional phrase *in doubt.* The noun clause is introduced by the interrogative adjective *which.*

5. Appositive (Explanatory Modifier):

1. There is much meaning in the following quotation: "Books are embalmed minds."

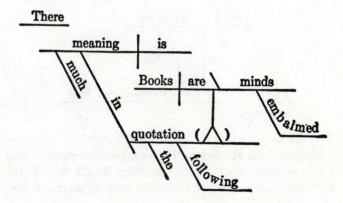

2. The popular idea that water is purified by freezing is false.

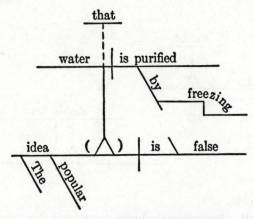

Observe that the noun clause *that water is purified by freezing* is a restrictive appositive, and should not be set off by commas. If we convert the sentence into a different sentence pattern, we may see more clearly the appositive meaning; e.g., *That water is purified by freezing is a false idea;* or, *It is a false idea that water is purified by freezing.* See the analysis of the idiomatic subject *it* in illustration *4* below.

3. His fear that he might never win overcame him.

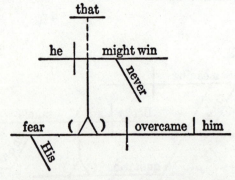

Here we have another restrictive appositive clause. It is a true restrictive explanatory modifier; it tells us what the fear was that overcame him. We may convert the sentence into a different pattern, and note the substantive meaning of the clause; as, *The fear which overcame him was that he might never win.*

4. It became painfully apparent that he was no friend.

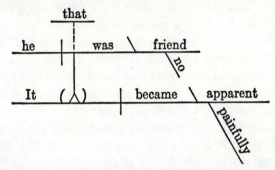

The explanatory modifier of the pronoun *it* used with impersonal verbs is one of the most common appositive uses of the noun clause. Such expressions as *it is true, it is important, it is right, it is possible,* and *it is wrong* are commonly followed either by infinitives or by substantive clauses explaining the idiomatic subject *it.* Observe that in the diagram the clause must be placed after *it* in parentheses to indicate its appositive function.

6. Adverbial Objective:

1. I am afraid that he will refuse this offer.

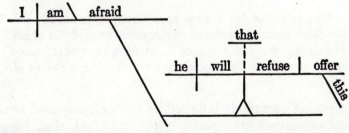

The substantive clause used as an adverbial objective after an adjective expressing mental attitude is very common in all levels of English. Many of the adverbial objective clauses can be converted into gerund phrases used as the objects of prepositions. For example, we may say *I am afraid of his refusing this offer*, and convey the meaning of the noun clause. Observe that the gerund phrase is governed by the preposition *of*, and that the noun clause used as an adverbial objective is not governed by a preposition.

Some of the noun clauses now used as adverbial objectives doubtless originated by analogy with clauses used as direct objects of verbs. *I am afraid that he will refuse this offer* means *I fear that he will refuse the offer*, the clause in the second sentence being the object of the verb *fear*.

Other adverbial objective clauses probably originated as objects of prepositions, or as appositives of the objects of prepositions; e.g., *I am afraid of **this*** (*that he will refuse the offer*); and *Is he aware of this **fact*** (*that I am his guardian*)? If we omit *of this* in the first sentence and *of this fact* in the second, we have noun clauses used as adverbial objectives.

   2. He is certain that he cannot fail.

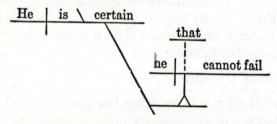

   That he cannot fail is what he is certain *of* or *about*. On the other hand, the noun clause represents the object of his certainty. Were it a simple substantive, it would correspond to a Latin "objective genitive"; i.e., he is *certain of success*.

Adjectives commonly followed by noun clauses used as adverbial objectives are *certain, afraid, confident, glad, happy, sure, positive, aware, doubtful, sorry*, and other adjectives having meanings similar to these.

It is important to observe that the adverbial objective clause modifies what adverbs modify. It will not modify nouns. In *I have no idea that the story is true*, the noun clause *that the story is true* is a restrictive appositive clause. It explains and identifies the meaning of the noun *idea*. Similarly, in *This event afforded proof that Fortune assists the brave*, the noun clause is an appositive. Here the clause explains and restricts the noun *proof*. For other illustrations of the noun clause as a restrictive appositive, see **5** p. 377.

7. Coördinate Noun Clauses:

I must learn when they are leaving, where they are going, and how long they will be away.

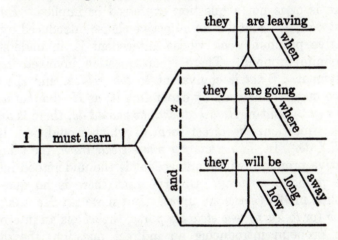

It should be noted that the noun clause is always a part of some other clause, and that the principal clauses containing noun clauses cannot logically be separated from them, because such principal clauses must include the noun clauses. In the above sentence, the entire statement must be given as the principal (or main) clause; and the noun clauses here constitute the subordinate (or dependent) element, and make the sentence complex.

Differentiating Noun and Adjective Clauses

Because the same words sometimes introduce adjective clauses and sometimes noun clauses, one should pay especial attention to the use and meaning of these words. When *who, which,* and *what* are relative pronouns, they introduce adjective clauses and have antecedents in clauses which precede them. But these words are also interrogative pronouns, and they may be employed in introducing indirect and direct questions used as noun clauses. The direct question seldom confuses the student; but indirect questions and adjective clauses introduced by these words are sometimes confused, especially if the relative pronouns have indefinite understood antecedents. The differentiation must depend upon whether there is or is not a question expressed or implied. *He did what was right* contains an adjective clause introduced by the relative pronoun *what,* whose antecedent is an understood indefinite pronoun. There is no question involved in the statement. *What* is equivalent to *that which,* and the sentence may be analyzed by expanding it; as *He did that which was right.* But in *He asked what he should do,* there is an indirect question, the direct form of which would be, *"What shall I do?"* In *Who steals my purse steals trash,* the *who* is a relative pronoun, whose antecedent is the understood indefinite pronoun *anybody.* Observe that there is no question implied in *Who steals my purse.* But if we say *He wanted to know* (or *to learn*) *who stole his purse,* the *who* is an interrogative pronoun introducing an indirect question, the direct form of which would be *"Who stole my purse?"*

The compound relative pronouns *whoever, whichever, whatever,* etc. are never employed in standard English as interrogative pronouns; and hence they are not used to introduce noun clauses. Because their antecedents are not, as a rule, expressed, clauses introduced by these indefinite relatives are sometimes construed as noun clauses. We say *John asked me who went for the mail,* but not *John asked me whoever went for the mail,* because the clause is an indirect question, and should be introduced by an interrogative word. If the simple relative pronouns *who, which,* and *what* are substituted for the indefinite compound relatives, their antecedent will be implied, not expressed. Observe that we may substitute *whoever* for *who* in *Who steals my purse steals trash* without modifying the meaning of the original sentence.

As a general rule, interrogative pronouns, interrogative adjectives, and interrogative adverbs introduce direct questions or indirect questions depending upon expressions of *asking, considering, telling, believing, doubting, knowing, perceiving, thinking, wondering,* and the like. The following sentences contain indirect questions, and therefore noun clauses:

1. I want to know *what you are saying.*
2. *Who is to be the next president* will be decided in November.
3. I am wondering *what he will do.*
4. I do not know *whose house she is buying.*
5. Can you tell me *what he said to offend you?*
6. I wish I knew *which of these books I should order.*
7. He wants me to find out *who is invited.*
8. The old man could not tell us *who he was* or *where he was going.*

The following sentences contain adjective clauses introduced by compound indefinite relatives or by simple relatives having the force of indefinite compound relatives.

1. *Whoever would find pearls* must dive deep.
2. *Whatever is,* is right.
3. Give the money to *whoever calls for it.*
4. *Who desires to be safe* should be careful to do *what is* right.
5. *Whom the court favors* is safe.
6. *What we acquire with greatest difficulty,* we retain the longest.
7. We should store in youth *what is to be used in old age.*
8. Take *whichever is the lightest.*

Some Substandard Uses of Noun Clauses

Every noun clause should perform a proper and idiomatic grammatical function:

1. A noun clause should not be made the object of an intransitive verb.

> *Loose:* Look out what you do there.
>
> *Improved:* Be careful what you do there.

2. One should not use a noun clause where the sense and the construction require an adverb clause:

> *Substandard:* She failed in the examination on account (*or* due to) she had a headache.
>
> *Improved:* She failed in the examination because she had a headache.

3. The relative adverbs *when, where, how,* and *why* should not be used after the verb *be* to introduce definitions or any clause or phrase in the predicate nominative construction; nor should they be substituted for the expletive *that* to introduce noun clauses in any other construction. They should not, therefore, be confused with interrogative adverbs, which may introduce noun clauses.

> *Loose:* An indictment is where the grand jury formally charges somebody with an offense.
>
> *Improved:* An indictment is a formal charge of offense brought on by the grand jury.
>
> *Loose:* I read in the paper where you had had an accident.
>
> *Improved:* I read in the paper that you had had an accident.
>
> *Loose:* His being there is why I am leaving.
>
> *Improved:* His being there is the reason why I am leaving.

4. The subordinating conjunction *because* is not used by our best writers and speakers for *that* in introducing noun clauses. *Because* is properly employed to introduce adverbial clauses expressing cause or reason.

> *Substandard:* Because you are the oldest is why you should go first.
>
> *Standard:* Because you are the oldest, you should go first.
>
> *Substandard:* The reason he failed was because he lost his courage.
>
> *Standard and formal:* The reason he failed was that he lost his courage.
>
> *Also correct:* He failed because he lost his courage.

5. *But what* as a substitute for *but that* is not sanctioned by good usage. The expression *but what* consists of the preposition *but* and the indefinite relative pronoun *what*. In *I did nothing but what I was told to do, but what* is correctly used. Here *what* introduces an adjective clause; it is used as the object of the infinitive *do;* its antecedent is the understood object of the preposition of *but*. (For the diagram of the adjective clause containing the relative, see Adjective Clauses, p. 359.)

> *Substandard:* I don't know but what you are right.
>
> *Standard:* I don't know but that you are right.
>
> *Substandard:* I could hardly believe but what he would return.
>
> *Standard:* I could hardly believe but that he would return.

6. *As* is not used in standard speech as a substitute for *that* to introduce noun clauses:

> *Substandard:* I don't know as I'll go to your party.
>
> *Standard:* I don't know that (or *whether*) I shall go to your party.

EXERCISE A

Analyze or diagram:

1. I say great men are still admirable.

2. That foot soldiers could withstand the charge of heavy cavalry was thought utterly impossible.

3. The men and women who do the hard work of the world have learned from Ruskin that they have a right to pleasure in their toil.

4. Tell us what we shall do.

5. Whether we are busy or idle will not be discussed.

6. Anaxagoras said that he was in the world to admire the sun.

7. Perchance you know who it was.

8. He was confident that recognition would come.

9. She had no idea but that he would succeed.

10. We have agreed that you should pay half of the expense of the trip.

11. I am very sorry, good Horatio,
    That to Laertes I forgot myself.

12. He had a vague impression that he would cut a ridiculous figure in that garb.

13. I wondered what those men would say to me.

14. I do not doubt but that he put the money in a good place.

15. Let us know among ourselves what is good.

16. I am sorry that my speech offends you.

17. Myths reveal motives and ideals, and permit us to see what comes from the latter.

18. I have said, thou art my father.

19. They who have seen him shall say, "Where is he?"

20. I was not conscious of what you were saying.

21. It was strange that the girl did not seem aware that her guests were leaving.

22. Dull people are not sure that the story of our own life is good literature.

23. I hoped that the Almighty would answer me.

24. Do tell me that this beverage owes its superior flavor to the introduction of molasses.

25. I am not informed about how the matter will be settled.

26. He wrote that he would come to lunch the following day.

27. Michael said suddenly, "Where were you born?"

28. She reflected that Mrs. Vopni, whose husband had been killed by a train, had ten children.

29. I am afraid this would put an end to all criticism.

30. I am sure that his curiosity was based on genuine interest in the subject.
31. She noted that he did not apologize for his rudeness.
32. I understood that he was offering me a night's shelter at the farm.
33. The moralists have never been satisfied with the old adage that knowledge is power.
34. We could not be sure whether it was a comfort.
35. The critic is often offensive without knowing that he is so.
36. Descartes was very careful to say that philosophic doubt is not to be carried over to daily conduct.
37. The church always argued that there were no new heresies.
38. This notion, that knowledge makes men good, is one of the superstitions of the nineteenth century.
39. The ancient Greeks believed that the chariot of the sun was driven daily across the sky by Apollo.
40. I am sorry that he must be severely punished.
41. The employer should realize that at last he has succeeded in teaching his employees to be strictly businesslike.
42. He was glad to know that you were afraid to come home alone.
43. We must remember that knowledge has widened and deepened.
44. My own opinion is that she actually did go by our gate.
45. I believe this must be true of everyone.
46. This does not mean that thinking is a disease.
47. Glad am I Your Highness can hear tidings.
48. Right glad I am he was not at this fray.
49. I am sure there is no force in eyes.
50. Our ancestors thought they knew their way from birth through eternity.
51. One can test any book and see whether the author puts one off with abstractions.
52. I am sorry I offend you by speaking so frankly.
53. That somebody had just left the room he was certain.
54. She had learned that a great deal went on under the bonnet.
55. We merely ask that the characters portrayed in fiction be human.

EXERCISE B

I. Pick out all the direct and all the indirect questions in Exercise A.
II. Write five sentences containing noun clauses introduced by interrogative adjectives, five by interrogative adverbs, and five by

interrogative pronouns. Let some of your sentences contain direct and some indirect questions.

III. Pick out from Exercise A ten instances in which the tense of a verb in the noun clause is made past by "attraction" to the tense of the principal verb. (Review Sequence of Tenses, Part One, pp. 138–141.)

IV. Write sentences containing noun clauses after the following expressions: *We fear . . . ; He said . . . ; I asked . . . ; Have you heard . . . ? My hope is . . . ; The question is . . . ; His cry was . . . ; Let us ask . . . ; Do you believe . . . ? Can you discover . . . ?* Account for any punctuation you use before or after your noun clauses.

V. Construct sentences containing noun clauses in apposition with the nouns or pronouns in the following: *The report . . . is true; The news . . . has not been published; The fact . . . proves nothing; He made the assertion . . . ; I must quote the saying . . . ; The suggestion . . . was not kindly received; It is clear . . . ; It is not right . . . ; Have you heard the proverb . . . ?* Tell which of your noun clauses are restrictive, and which, if any, are nonrestrictive.

EXERCISE C

Improve any substandard expressions you find in the following, and give reasons for any changes you make:

1. Who know but what this is the true story?
2. I don't know as I have any objection to your leaving.
3. Because he was at fault is no reason for punishing his family.
4. The reason he couldn't learn grammar was because he had never studied Latin or Greek.
5. I see in the *Evening News* where the people are blaming the president for the depression.
6. The only excuse I can now offer is because she didn't have the means.
7. Income tax is where you pay a tax on the excess over a certain amount.
8. I don't know but what I should go back home.
9. Laziness is when you are able to work and don't want to.

10. Irony is where you imply a meaning contrary to the literal sense of the words you use.
11. I cannot believe but what he intended to offend us.
12. The reason I failed was because the teacher disliked me.
13. Astigmatism is when you have a defect in your eye.
14. In the church and school is where we find some honest people.
15. A metaphor is where one object is called by the name of another.
16. Because Ann's house is small is why we are having the party at your place.
17. Because he is a preacher does not excuse his immoral conduct.
18. I don't know as you have any right to object to what I do.
19. He asked had I been working for you.
20. The teacher told me how he thought I was wrong about this.

Lesson XIII

Adverb Clauses

Any clause which performs the function of an adverb is called an **adverb clause.** Like simple adverbs, adverb clauses may be classified according to the meanings they convey, these meanings being indicated chiefly by the connectives (expressed or implied) that introduce them and join them to principal clauses.

Adverb clauses expressing **time, place, manner,** and **degree** are usually introduced by relative adverbs (sometimes called half-conjunctions because they both join and modify).

1. Adverb Clauses of Time:

a. Adverb clauses expressing time are most frequently introduced by one of the following relative adverbs: *after, as, before, ere, till, until, when, whenever,* and *while:*

When I became a man, I put away childish things.

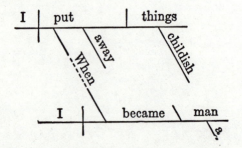

When I became a man is an adverb clause denoting time. The relative adverb *when* performs the function of an adverb and a conjunction: it modifies and joins. It has the force of two prepositional phrases into which it can be expanded without modification of meaning; as, *I put away childish things* **at that time at which** *I became a man.*

In the diagram, *when* is put on a diagonal line connecting the two clauses. The line is made solid where it joins the two verbs to indicate that it stands for two phrases which, if expressed, would modify these verbs. The dotted line connecting the two solid lines denotes the conjunctive function of *when*. It is important to observe that in the diagram the adverb clause is always placed below the clause it modifies, though it may come first in the spoken or written sentence.

b. Often the thought of a sentence containing an adverb clause of time may be expressed with added emphasis on the temporal idea by the inclusion of a simple adverb (see Correlative Adverbs, pp. 167–168):

When I became a man, then I put away childish things.

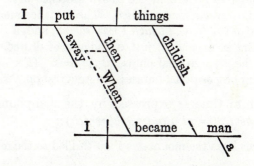

When the correlative adverbs in sentences like this one are expanded, the *then* represents the phrase *at the time*, and *when* the phrase that contains the relative adverb. Since *then* . . . *when* is the equivalent of *at the time at which*, the subordinate clause is attached to *then*. If we expand the adverb clause into an adjective clause, the *then* in the principal clause must be converted into the prepositional phrase *at the time*. Observe that in the diagram, *then* modifies *put,*

and *when* modifies *became*. One is a simple adverb; the other, a relative adverb. The dotted line used to denote the conjunctive nature of the relative adverb is attached to the line on which the simple adverb is placed, and thus suggests the correlative force of the two adverbs.

c. Sometimes an adverb denoting degree modifies a relative adverb. Observe the meaning and the construction of *just* in the following sentence:

He came just as I was leaving.

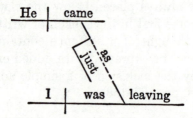

The relative adverb in the above sentence may be expanded into *at the time at which*. The sentence means *He came just at the time at which I was leaving;* and, if the sentence were so expanded, *just*, an adverb of degree, would modify the prepositional phrase *at the time*. (For adverbs modifying prepositional phrases, see Adverbs, pp. 225–226.)

d. Indefinite time is expressed by the compound relative adverb *whenever* (= *at any time at which*):

Whenever I see the mountains I am thrilled to the marrow.

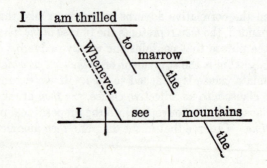

e. A number of words now used as relative adverbs are derived from prepositions, the most common of these being *after, before, since, till, until.* *He came before the sun had set* means *He came **before the time at which** the sun had set.* In earlier English, the connective in this construction was clearly a preposition governing a noun or pronoun followed by a restrictive adjective or an appositive noun clause; as, *He came before the time that* (or *when*) *the sun had set.* Some grammarians prefer to treat the *before, after, since, till,* and *until* as prepositions governing noun clauses. But since they can perform the function of joining, relating, and modifying, it seems logical to analyze them as relative adverbs. Our dictionaries and most of our school grammars list these words as prepositions when they govern simple nouns and as conjunctions (or conjunctive adverbs) when they introduce and relate clauses.

She remained after he had left.

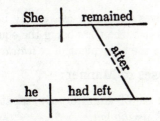

Here *after* has the meaning of *beyond the time at which.*

2. Adverb Clauses of Place:

a. Adverb clauses expressing place are introduced by the relative adverb *where* or other adverbs having the meaning of *where,* such as *wherever, whither,* etc.:

Where thou lodgest, I will lodge.

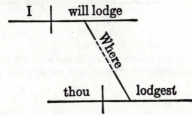

Where, like *when* in a under Clauses of Time, is a relative adverb and performs a dual function in the sentence. *I will lodge where thou lodgest* may be expanded into *I will lodge in the place in which thou lodgest,* the relative adverb *where* being the equivalent of *in the place in which.*

b. When the place idea expressed in the adverb clause is to be stressed or made more definite, *where* may correlate with *there.*

Where MacGregor sits, there is the head of the table.

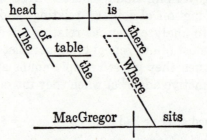

The correlatives *there . . . where* may be expanded into *at the place at which,* the *there* being the equivalent of *at the place,* and *where* the equivalent of *at which.*

3. Adverb Clauses of Manner:

a. Adverb clauses of manner are most commonly introduced by *as, as if, as though:*[1]

Speak the speech as I pronounced it to you.

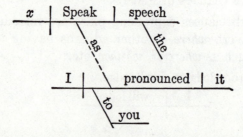

---

[1] In colloquial speech, *like* is sometimes used as a conjunction (relative adverb) to introduce an adverb clause of manner, but cultured speakers prefer *as, as if,* or *as though.*

The manner meaning may be seen when the relative adverb *as* is expanded into *in the manner in which*.

b. The conjunctive adverb *as* sometimes correlates with *so* in denoting manner, as in the following:

As goes the leader, so goes the pack.

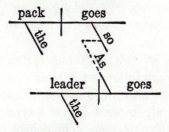

If the *so . . . as* in this sentence is converted into two prepositional phrases, the *so* will have the meaning of *in the manner*, and the *as* the meaning of *in which*.

c. The phrasal conjunctions *as if* and *as though* are frequently used to introduce clauses expressing manner:

He acts as if he were the leader.

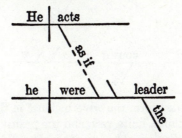

This sentence is elliptical, the older and fuller form being *He acts as he would act if he were the leader.* Observe that in the expanded and older form the verb in the condition clause was in the subjunctive mode, and that this mode is preserved in the contracted sentence. Note that as a result of the ellipsis two conjunctions (*as* and *if*) are brought together. (For Uses of the Subjunctive Mode, see Part One, pp. 112–116.)

In the older sentence the *as* conveyed the manner meaning, which is the meaning now expressed by *as if*.

4. Adverb Clauses of Degree:

Adverb clauses of degree may be introduced by the relative adverbs *than, as, that,* and *the.* All of these except *than* correlate with simple adverbs belonging in principal clauses. The chief correlatives are *as . . . as, so . . . as, so . . . that,* and *the . . . the.*

a. The relative adverb *than* has restricted meaning and use. It must always follow an adjective or an adverb in the comparative degree and must introduce an elliptical adverb clause containing an implied (never expressed) adjective or adverb in the positive degree. The degree clause will modify the adjective or adverb in the comparative degree, always expressed in the principal clause. In analyzing sentences containing *than*-clauses, one must supply the omissions.

1. He is older than his cousin.

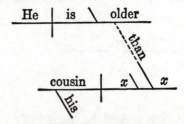

In its expanded form the adverb clause in the above sentence will contain a finite verb and the positive form of the comparative adjective *older;* as, *He is older than his cousin is old;* and to indicate the degree meaning of the clause, the expanded sentence may now be converted into a sentence containing phrases expressing degree; as, *He is old beyond the degree in which his cousin is old.* Since the relative pronoun phrase would here modify the adjective in the subordinate clause, the relative adverb *than* in the analysis of the sentence is made to modify the unexpressed positive form; and in the diagram the line joining the clauses is made solid where it is attached to the adverb clause to show that *than* modifies the understood positive *old*. It is important to note that the subordinate clause modifies the adjective *older*.

2. He will arrive earlier than I.

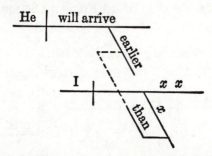

Here the subordinate clause may be expanded into *than I will arrive early*, *early* being the positive form of the adverb *earlier*.

3. I had rather go than stay.

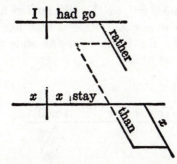

The old positive form of *rather* is *rathe* (now obsolete), but for analysis the sentence may be expanded to read *I had rather (= had better) go than I had (or would) rathe stay*, which is about the equivalent of *I would go more gladly than I would stay gladly*. The elliptical subordinate clause modifies the adverb *rather*.

b. *So . . . as* and *as . . . as* introduce clauses of degree of comparison. In general, it may be said that *as . . . as* is used in comparing similar objects, conditions, qualities, etc.; and *so* . . . *as* is used in comparing unlike objects, conditions, qualities, etc.; or, if stated differently, *so* . . . *as* generally follows negative expressions, and *as* . . . *as* follows positive ones. (For special affirmative and negative uses of these two correlatives, see the Oxford English Dictionary, at *as* and *so*.)

1. She is as wise and good as she is fair.

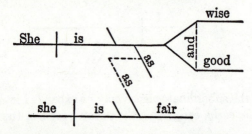

Here the first *as*, the one which modifies the adjectives *wise* and *good* can be expanded into *in the degree*, and the one which modifies *fair*, which is the relative adverb, can be expanded into *in which*. Observe that like qualities are here compared. But in the following sentences the qualities compared are unlike:

2. You are not so small as I.

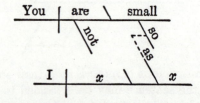

Here the subordinate clause is a contraction of *as I am small.* The first correlative, *so* (= *in the degree*), modifies *small;* and the second correlative, *as* (= *in which*), modifies the unexpressed adjective *small*, which, if expressed, would be the attribute complement in the subordinate clause. The above sentence conveys the following meaning: *You*

are not small in (or *to*) *the degree in* (or *at*) *which I am small.*

3. The engine was so hot that the car would not run.

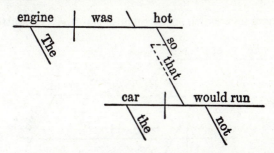

So . . . that is here the equivalent of *to the degree at which.*

c. The correlatives *the . . . the* always introduce clauses indicating comparison. One *the* is a simple adverb modifying the comparative form of an adjective or an adverb in the principal clause; the other *the* is the relative adverb, which also modifies an adjective or an adverb in the comparative degree. The student should observe that in the *the . . . the* comparisons, the subordinate clause is always written or spoken first; and therefore, in the spoken sentence, the first *the* is always the relative adverb; it can be expanded into the prepositional phrase containing the relative pronoun. In the diagram, the second clause, which is the principal clause, is always placed above the subordinate, or modifying, clause. Observe the position of the clauses when the sentence is diagramed:

The wealthier he grew, the stingier he seemed.

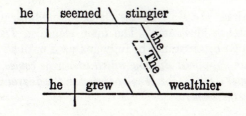

Rephrased, this sentence may have the following pattern: *He seemed stingier* **in the degree in which** *he grew wealthier.* (For a good discussion of the origin and meaning of the adverb *the*, see the Oxford English Dictionary, at *the*.)

The more he tried to speak plainly, the worse he stuttered.

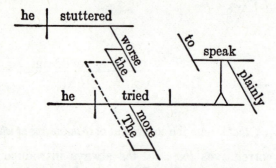

Here both the simple adverb *the* and the relative adverb *the* modify comparative forms of the adverbs *badly* and *much*. The degree meaning may become more apparent when the sentence is expanded: *By how much more he tried to speak plainly,* **by that much** *worse he stuttered.*

The sooner he comes the better.

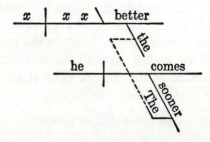

Sometimes the *the . . . the* clauses are elliptical, as the this sentence illustrates. The main clause in *The sooner he comes the better* cannot be fully analyzed until all omitted words are supplied: *By how much sooner he comes,* **by that** *much better it will be;* or *It will be better* **in the degree in which** *he comes the sooner.*

Complex Adverb Clauses

The relative adverb may introduce clauses containing subordinate clauses.   Observe the complex clauses in the following sentence:

When I said that I would die a bachelor, I did not think I should live till I were married.—Shakespeare.

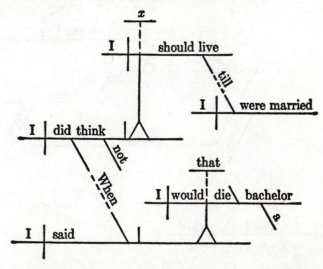

Here the subordinate clause *when I said that I would die a bachelor* is a complex clause because it contains a noun clause as the object of *said*.   Observe also that the principal clause contains a noun clause and an adverb clause subordinate to the noun clause.   The entire principal clause is *I did not think I should live till I were married.*

Coördinate Adverb Clauses

Relative adverbs may be employed to introduce two or more coördinate (compound) adverb clauses.   Observe that the following sentence contains two adverb clauses of time, which are introduced by the relative adverb *when.*   These adverb clauses are joined by the coördinating conjunction *and:*

When darkness gathers over all,
And the last tottering pillars fall,
Take the poor dust thy mercy warms,
And mould it into heavenly forms!—Oliver Wendell Holmes.

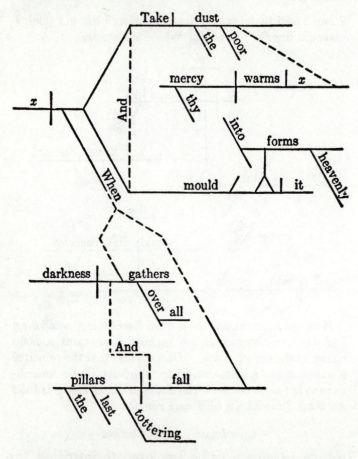

In this sentence, *when* subordinates the two coördinate adverb clauses, and in the diagram it is placed on the relative adverb line before it is divided.

In the following sentence, each subordinate clause is introduced and subordinated by a *when*. The coördinating conjunction *and* is, however, not expressed here, but it is clearly implied:

> When faith is lost, when honor dies,
> The man is dead!—Whittier.

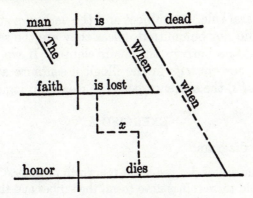

Elliptical Clauses

An **elliptical clause** is one which has a part or parts of its construction understood. Good usage does not demand that we express all of the words and phrases which are necessary for the full grammatical analysis of our sentences; but it does demand that all important omissions be clearly implied. The inflectional forms and the constructions of all words omitted should be indicated in the context; otherwise, the grammar will be faulty, and the proper meanings will not be conveyed. Note the ellipses in the following sentences:

1. When in college (= When I was in college), I lived very economically.
2. While fighting in Germany (= While he was fighting in Germany), John was seriously injured.
3. The more the merrier (= The more there are, the merrier it will be).

An elliptical adverbial clause which cannot logically be expanded to its full form and be attached to the main clause may be called a **dangling clause**:

Illogical and vague: While working on the railroad, my wife
divorced me.

Logical and clear: While I was working on the railroad, my
wife divorced me.

As a general rule, the subject and the verb of a subordinate
clause should not be omitted unless they are the same as the
subject and the verb in the main clause. If we substitute
the word *I* for *my wife* in the illogical sentence and change
me to *my wife*, the sentence becomes clear and logical.

EXERCISE A

Analyze or diagram:

1. When the well is dry, we know the worth of water.
2. As he said these things unto them, the scribes and the Pharisees
began to urge him vehemently.
3. My sighing cometh before I eat.
4. When thou liest down, thou shalt not be afraid.
5. When pride cometh, then cometh shame.
6. Whither thou goest, I will go.
7. It is more blessed to give than to receive.
8. Walk while ye have the light.
9. Love thy neighbor as thyself.
10. These notes were found in his pockets when they undressed him.
11. When a woman once dislikes another, she is merciless.
12. She believed in me when no one else would.
13. Hero-worship endures forever, while man endures.
14. While life lasts, hope lasts for everyone.
15. Universities arose while yet no books were procurable.
16. When we call a thing human, we have a spiritual idea in mind.
17. Let shame come when it will.
18. Bring me where they are.
19. I knew you would be edified by the volume ere you had finished
reading it.
20. I cannot be silent when I think Your Highness wronged.
21. After the student has found a subject, he must determine how
long his composition is to be.

22. As he drew near it now, his thoughts made a pathway for his feet.
23. When we fall asleep, we do not lay aside the thoughts of the day.
24. When he took his seat in the schoolroom and looked out upon the children, they had never seemed so small, so pitiful.
25. Talk and writing are disagreeable when they depart from the current standards of respectable behavior.
26. When one begins to fear, he has already lost the battle.
27. A third kind of thinking is stimulated when anyone questions our beliefs or opinions.
28. When you are nothing but pretty, you can get into nothing but trouble.
29. Fleur said we would kill the fatted calf when I had got my speech off.
30. When you have had your breakfast, you will be more forgiving.
31. So man lieth down, and riseth not till the heavens be no more.
32. Where words are scarce, they are seldom spent in vain.
33. The doctor says they were quite gone before they were out of the water.
34. Then, as he opened the door, he beheld the form of a maiden.
35. Laziness travels so slowly that poverty soon overtakes it.
36. Yet this evil is not so great as it may appear at first sight.
37. He knew that as they had worshiped some gods from love, so they worshiped others from fear.
38. Before the battle was over and while the result was still in doubt, the general ordered a retreat.
39. Her dress seemed made of materials as delicate and fleecy as the fringe of a sunset cloud.
40. As the Father hath loved me, so have I loved you.
41. There is nobody so poor as these professional fellows who have failed.
42. They say he can speak French as fast as a maid can eat blackberries.
43. She was as unconcerned at that contingency as a goddess at a lack of linen.
44. Napoleon does by no means seem to me so great a man as Cromwell.
45. As the boat drew nearer the city, the coast which the traveler had just left sank behind into one long, low, straw-colored line.—Ruskin.

46. Long and curious speeches are as fit for dispatch as a robe or a
mantle with a long train is for a race.

47. So still were the clear waters that we seemed midway between
two skies.

48. Simple and brief was the wedding, as that of Ruth and Boaz.

49. The fewer words he spoke the more pungent his expression became.

50. The further I advance in age, the more I find work necessary.

51. The paper is so nearly perfect that it must have the maximum
mark.

52. The author who speaks about his own books is almost as bad as
the mother who talks about her own children.

53. I will be as harsh as truth and as uncompromising as justice.

54. The more money he loaned her, the more she seemed to need.

55. It is much easier to be critical than correct.

56. Life may not be so simple as it used to be.

57. When Freedom from her mountain height
Unfurled her standard to the air,
She tore the azure robe of night,
And set the stars of glory there.—Joseph Drake.

58. In the beginning of the thirteenth century, when the clouds and
storms had come, when the gay sensuous pagan life was gone,
when men were not living by the senses and understanding,
when they were looking for the speedy coming of Antichrist,
there appeared in Italy, to the north of Rome, in the beautiful
Umbrian country at the foot of the Apennines, a figure of the
most magical power and charm, St. Francis.—Ruskin.

EXERCISE B

I. In Exercise A pick out six sentences containing correlative adverbs, and name the simple adverb and the relative adverb in
each sentence.

II. Classify the adverb clauses in the following sentences in Exercise A as to meaning: 2, 6, 10, 40, 52, 55, 56, 57, 58.

III. Pick out ten elliptical clauses in Exercise A, and complete the
omissions.

IV. Write ten original sentences, five of which will contain elliptical
clauses introduced by *when* or *while*, and five of which will show

ellipses in clauses of place, degree, or manner. Be sure that no clause you write is a dangling one.

V. Write five sentences containing complex adverb clauses, and five containing coördinate adverb clauses.

EXERCISE C

Correct all errors in grammar and punctuation in the following, giving reasons for all corrections:

1. When in Europe, my health was very poor.
2. My brother is brighter than him.
3. She and myself have different ideas on religion than them.
4. This is all the farther I got in this story when you came in.
5. She acts like she enjoyed playing cards.
6. He gives more money to beggars than his family.
7. This man is so old to plan to go abroad.
8. No sooner had I said what I thought, when I realized that I should have kept quiet.
9. I believe this material is different than what I bought last week.
10. Small oranges make better, or as good marmalade, as the large ones.
11. While painting a car, the garage should be free of dust.
12. The second edition of the book is superior than the first one.
13. We like the circus as much, if not more than, the concert.
14. I prefer being fat than dieting.
15. Even on the dirt roads I felt like I was driving on a paved street.
16. Scarcely had I finished dinner than company came.
17. You should lock your door before you retire like Father told you to.
18. While attending church last Sunday, our home was robbed.

Adverb Clauses (continued)

Adverb clauses of **condition, cause, purpose, concession, and result** or **effect** are introduced by full (or pure) subordinating conjunctions, which may be expressed or implied.

1. Adverb Clause of Condition:

Adverb clauses of condition are introduced by *if, unless,* or some word or phrase having the meaning of *if.* The most common substitutes for *if* are *provided* (or *provided that*), *in case* (or *in case that*), *supposing* (or *supposing that*), and *once. Unless* is the equivalent of *if not,* and is employed only in clauses denoting negation.

Condition clauses may have verbs in the indicative or in the subjunctive. The mode of the finite verb in the condition clause will be indicative if the clause merely indicates that the idea which it expresses may or may not be true. The subjunctive mode is employed when the clause states a condition that is contrary to fact.

1. If this prisoner is guilty, he will receive a severe sentence.

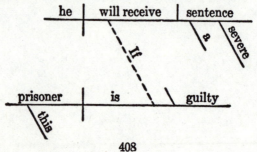

The verb in the condition clause in this sentence is in the indicative mode. Observe that there is some question in the mind of the author of this sentence as to whether or not the prisoner is guilty.

In the diagram, the conjunction *if* is placed on a diagonal dotted line attached to the lines on which the verbs of the two clauses are placed. All pure (or full) subordinating conjunctions should be placed on dotted lines like the one on which *if* is placed. Pure conjunctions are not modifiers. They cannot be expanded into modifying phrases. Their function is restricted to joining and subordinating clauses.

2. If I were you, I would not go.

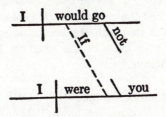

If I were you states a condition contrary to fact—one person cannot possibly be another person—and hence the subjunctive *were* is used instead of the indicative *was*. Observe differences in the grammatical tense and the time meaning of the subjunctive and the indicative. Compare *If he were here, I could leave now* with *If he was there, I did not see him.*

3. Unless you want to be burned, do not put your hand into the fire.

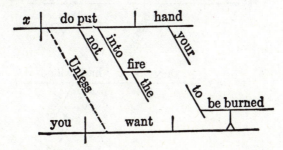

Unless you want to be burned is the equivalent of *If you do not want to be burned.*

4. "Should you care to dance, I can pipe," said he.

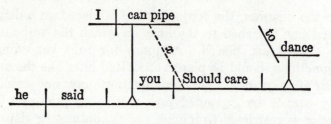

If is omitted when the auxiliary verb is placed first in the sentence. *Should you care to dance* becomes *If you should care to dance* when the conjunction *if* is inserted. *Care* is a transitive verb in this sentence, being the equivalent of *like* or *want.* An *x* is used in the diagram to indicate the omitted conjunction.

2. Adverb Clauses of Cause:

The conjunctions used in introducing clauses of cause are *because* and other words or phrases having the meaning of *because,* the chief substitutes being *since, as, for, inasmuch as,* and *forasmuch as:*

They missed the engagement because they had dallied too long.

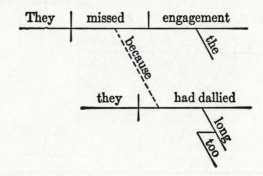

3. Adverb Clause of Purpose:

The conjunctions *that, lest, so that,* and *in order that* are used to introduce clauses expressing purpose:

1. I go that I may prepare a place for you.

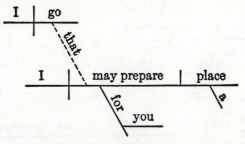

Lest is the equivalent of *that not* and is employed only when the purpose idea is expressed negatively.

2. Walk softly, lest he awaken.

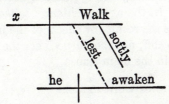

The clause *lest he awaken* has the meaning of *that he may not awaken.*

3. I have warned you so that you may be on your guard.

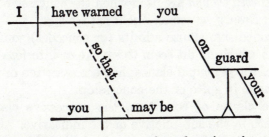

So that and *in order that* are phrasal conjunctions equivalent to *that.*

4. Adverb Clauses of Result or Effect:

Adverb clauses expressing result or effect are usually introduced by *so that:*

> A portion of the cliff had fallen down, so that the road was impassable.

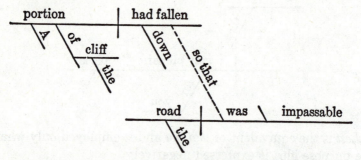

Adverb clauses of result and purpose must be differentiated by the meaning, not by the conjunctions which introduce them. In the above sentence, *so that the road was impassable* gives the result (or effect) of the falling down of a portion of the cliff, not the purpose nor the reason for the assertion made in the main clause.

5. Adverb Clause of Concession:

Concessive clauses are generally introduced by *though* or *although* or by words or phrases having the meaning of *though. If* and *while* are sometimes employed as substitutes for *though. Even if* and *even though* are used when the concessive meaning is stressed: *Even if he comes, I will not see him.*

Every concessive clause admits (or concedes) some fact or supposition which might seem to revoke or interfere with the assertion of the principal clause; but the assertion of the main clause is made in spite of the concession.

Like the clause of condition, the concessive clause may have its verb in the subjunctive or the indicative. If the dependent clause states a pure supposition, the subjunctive mode should be used; but if it admits a fact, then the indica-

tive should be used. In *Though he slay me, yet will I trust in
him, slay* is present subjunctive; the present indicative form
would be *slays.* Compare the concessive clause in this sentence with the following: *Though he is my brother, I shall not
vote for him.* The author of the first concedes a supposition
which might take place; the author of the second sentence
admits a fact before making his main assertion.

1. Though her features are regular, her face is not beautiful.

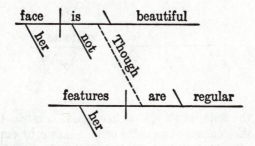

The author of this sentence admits that the girl's features
are regular, and yet he concludes *her face is not beautiful.*
The mode in this concessive clause is, therefore, indicative.
Although could be used here in place of *though.* For emphasis, *even* could be used with *though,* but not with *although.* *Yet* may also be used for emphasis with either
though or *although* in concessive clauses of this type.

2. While he is most terrible in appearance, I do not fear him.

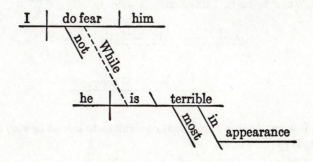

While in the sense of *though, although*, introduces a clause of concession; otherwise, a clause of time.

3. If he is not a college graduate, he is a highly educated man.

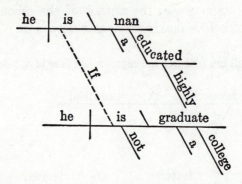

If in the sense of *though*, as here used, is rare. In oral speech, the concessive meaning of *if* is shown by emphasis on the verb: *If he isn't a college graduate*. For emphasis in the written sentence *even* may be inserted before *if*.

Various indefinite pronouns and adjectives ending in *-ever* or *-soever* (*whoever, whichever, whatever, whosoever, whichsoever, whatsoever*, etc.) are sometimes employed in introducing concessive clauses. The conjunction *though* may be regarded as meant but not expressed.

4. Whoever he is, I like him.

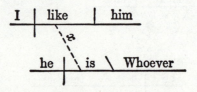

Whoever he is is here about equivalent to *though he may be anybody you please*.

5. Whichever he chooses, he will wish he had taken the other.

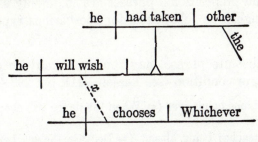

Here *whichever* is a compound indefinite pronoun, but it may also be used as an adjective in introducing a concessive clause; as, *Whichever book he takes, he will wish he had taken the other.*

Ellipses in Clauses Introduced by Pure Subordinating Conjunctions

Clauses introduced by pure subordinating conjunctions, like those introduced by relative adverbs, are frequently elliptical. All the elliptical words must, however, be supplied before the clauses can be fully analyzed. In the diagram an *x* is used to indicate the omission of a word or phrases necessary to the analysis of the sentence. Note the ellipses in the following:

1. If (it is) necessary, I could go with you.
2. Though (he is) a thief, he is generous.
3. See (If you see) a pin and let it lie,
   You'll want a pin ere you die.
4. You may stay if you want to (stay).
5. His speech was good, though rather brief (= though it was rather brief).
6. Sick as he is (= Though he be as sick as he is), he will want to go with you.
7. His critics, though outvoted (= though they have been outvoted), have not been silenced.
8. However busy (= However busy he may be), my doctor never seems to be in a hurry.

Clause Substitutes

Verbal and prepositional phrases are commonly used in all levels of English as substitutes for the various types of adverb clauses:

1. The absolute phrase may replace an adverb clause of time, cause, or condition (see Lesson VIII, pp. 293–294):

1. The dance being over (= When the dance was over), we left.
2. The teacher being absent (= Because the teacher was absent), we had no school yesterday.
3. Weather permitting (= If the weather permits), we shall go tomorrow.

2. The independent participial phrase frequently replaces a clause:

1. Confidentially speaking (= If I may speak confidentially), he is not the type of man I should employ.
2. Counting the maid (= If one counts the maid), there will be twenty to provide for.

3. The infinitive phrase may be an abridged clause:

1. I shall go early so as to get a good seat (= I shall go early in order that I may get a good seat).
2. To tell the truth (= If I tell you the truth), I must admit I do not like him.

4. The prepositional phrase may convey the meaning of a full clause. The preposition in the phrase may govern a pure noun or any of the noun-equivalents:

1. Because of these absences (= Because you have these absences), you must repeat the course.
2. Even with his brother's help (= Even if his brother helps him), he will not finish this job today.
3. I cannot go without my father's giving his consent (= I cannot go unless my father gives his consent).
4. By being late (= Because I was late), I missed the plane.

Caution: It is the habit of certain uncultured writers and speakers—particularly the latter—to begin what should be a sentence with a subordinate clause; and then fail to provide a principal statement to which the subordinate one may be attached. The following is an example of the incomplete sentence, there being no principal clause:

> Although by the practice of extemporaneous speaking one is relieved, in a great measure, of his self-consciousness before an audience, and is able to think on his feet.

The sentence completed might read as follows:

> Although by the practice of extemporaneous speaking one is relieved, in a great measure, of his self-consciousness before an audience, and is able to think on his feet, no amount of self-confidence can take the place of ample preparation.

EXERCISE A

Analyze or diagram:

1. If you tax too high, the revenue will yield nothing.
2. He is obeyed because the majority choose to be governed thus.
3. If you put a chain around the neck of a slave, the other end fastens itself around your own.
4. Though he was rough, he was kindly.
5. The truth is, that colonies are burdens unless they are plundered.
6. Since I am a dog, beware my fangs.
7. I'll cross it, though it blast me.
8. I liked the old man well enough, though he was as rough as a hedge.
9. Providence is nothing if not coquettish.
10. My son, if sinners entice thee, consent thou not.
11. Had ye believed Moses, ye would have believed me.
12. If you wish a thing to be well done, you must do it yourself.
13. If ye believe not his writings, how shall ye believe my word?
14. If I am not worth the wooing, I surely am not worth the winning.
15. Discussion is forbidden in certain clubs, because it results in a clash of feelings.
16. They pardoned though they could not approve.

17. Be he a prince or be he a pauper, every guest is welcome here.

18. As his life is not complicated, his mental processes do not have to be so.

19. Once you are accustomed to the place, it no longer seems charming.

20. Love not sleep, lest thou come to poverty.

21. You will pardon, I am sure, because I am commanded away in haste.

22. Were it not for leaving thee, my child, I could die happy.

23. We could not remember anything unless we forgot almost everything.

24. Since moments are precious, let us husband them.

25. We cannot forgive the poet if he spins his thread too fine.

26. If you maintain a dead church, you contribute to a dead Bible society.

27. He might have been happier had he stayed there.

28. In case I am not invited, how will you get to this reception?

29. During this period the buffalo increased rapidly, because the hunters were so few.

30. Do not suppose that your education is over because you have received your diploma from the Naval Academy.

31. If time be of all things the most precious, wasting time must be the greatest prodigality.

32. The works of Milton cannot be comprehended or enjoyed unless the mind of the reader coöperates with that of the writer.

33. Provided a man look sharply and attentively, he shall see fortune.

34. It is an abomination to kings to commit wickedness: for the throne is established by righteousness.

35. Human mother love is also instinctive, though among some of the lowest peoples it does not last long.

36. There is a remedy for everything, could men find it.

37. Though the speaker be a fool, let the hearer be wise.

38. Every rich man has usually some sly way of jesting which would make no great figure were he not a rich man.—Sir Richard Steele.

39. Our schooling was erratic, partly because both my father and my mother belonged to the generation that was overschooled. —Kathleen Norris.

40. Though we must sigh and acquiesce in the building of Babel, we have some right to examine the bricks.—Quiller-Couch.

41. Since you accept my hospitality, you cannot have so bad an opinion of it.—Bernard Shaw.

42. Though I have, like the rest of mankind, many failings and weaknesses, I have not yet, by either friends or enemies, been charged with superstition.—Samuel Johnson.

43. If we encounter a man of rare intellect, we should ask him what books he reads.—Emerson.

44. If men could only know each other, they would never idolize or hate.—Elbert Hubbard.

EXERCISE B

I. Classify the adverb clauses in Exercise A as clauses of condition, concession, cause, purpose, etc.

II. Write original sentences containing adverb clauses of concession introduced by the following words: *however, whoever, whichever, whatever, if,* and *while.*

III. Give the mode (subjunctive or indicative), and explain why it is used in each of the subordinate clauses in sentences in Exercise A numbered as follows: 4, 6, 7, 19, 22, 25, 28, 33, 37, 40, 42, 43, and 44.

IV. Write five sentences containing dependent coördinate (compound) clauses introduced by pure subordinating conjunctions.

EXERCISE C

Correct all errors in the following, giving reasons for all corrections:

1. If the chairman of the social committee be present, will he give us his report?

2. She is an actress, while her brother is a musician.

3. Our car is not newer, but just as good as yours.

4. While turning the corner, the accident occurred.

5. I don't know as I will have time to read your book.

6. The reason I am not calling the doctor is because he is out of town.

7. Although generally considered successful, his character shows him to be a failure morally.

8. If I was young like you are, I would join the Navy.
9. The accident would not have happened if he had have taken my advice.
10. Although, while he was a student in my class, there was no evidence that he was a Communist.
11. I would sure punish you, if I was your father.
12. If he know grammar, why is he taking this course?

Compound Sentences and Parenthetical Clauses

A **compound sentence** is one which is composed of two or more coördinate principal (independent) clauses. The principal clauses in a compound sentence may contain any number of subordinate (dependent) clauses.

A compound sentence which contains no dependent clauses is sometimes called a **simple compound sentence;** and one which contains one or more dependent clauses is sometimes called a **complex-compound** (or **compound-complex) sentence.**

The coördinate clauses are usually connected by coördinating conjunctions, of which *and, or,* and *but* are most frequently used.

The analysis of compound sentences snould not prove difficult. If the coördinate clauses are simple clauses (i.e., clauses which contain no dependent clauses), each will be of the nature of a simple sentence. In the diagram the coördinate independent clauses follow the same pattern as coördinate dependent clauses.

The coördinating conjunction, whether it is expressed or merely implied, suggests the relation in thought between the two coördinate clauses.

1. Additive (or **cumulative**) ideas are joined by *and, both . . . and,* or other words having the meaning of *and* (e.g., *also, too, now, well,* etc. See **5**, p. 425).

God spake, and it was done.

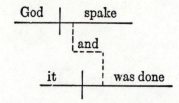

The student will observe that this compound sentence contains two simple clauses, each of which is diagramed as if it were a simple sentence. *And* joins the two clauses and indicates additive (or cumulative) meaning.

In the diagram, *and* is placed on a short dotted horizontal line drawn midway between the two clauses. A dotted line from base line of each clause connects the line on which *and* is placed in such a way as to form a step, as shown in the diagram. For convenience, the coördinating conjunction line is attached to the verbs in the clauses it joins. It is important to note that the second clause does not modify any element in the first clause. It merely adds to what has been mentioned in the preceding clause.

2. Clauses expressing **alternative** or **disjunctive** thoughts are usually joined by the coördinating conjunctions *or, nor, either . . . or,* and *neither . . . nor;* or by other words having the meaning of *or* or *nor* (e.g., *else, otherwise.* See **5,** p. 425).

 1. You must get another watch, or I must get another secretary.

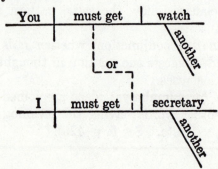

2. Either he will hate the one, and love the other; or he will hold to the one, and despise the other.

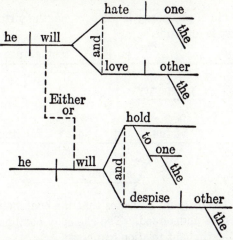

Either could be omitted in this sentence without greatly modifying the thought. The chief function of the first of the coördinating correlatives is to introduce and suggest the alternation before the choice of action is fully presented.

3. Clauses presenting **adversative** (**contrasting**) ideas are usually joined by *but,* which may be expressed or implied; or by other words having the meaning of *but,* such as *however, nevertheless, whereas, still, yet,* etc.

Prosperity asks for fidelity, but adversity imperatively demands it.

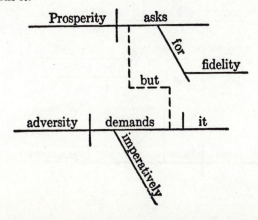

4. Any coördinating conjunction may be omitted if the relation between the clauses is clearly implied in the context.

1. The virtue of prosperity is temperance; the virtue of adversity is fortitude.

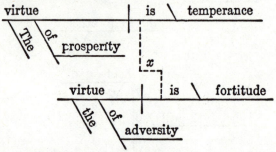

An *x* in the diagram indicates that the conjunction (*and* or *but*, here) is understood.   The choice of conjunction depends on the thought relation expressed.

When the compound sentence consists of more than two coördinate clauses, the conjunction is usually omitted between the first two, as in the following:

2. Some are born great, some achieve greatness, and some have greatness thrust upon them.—Shakespeare.

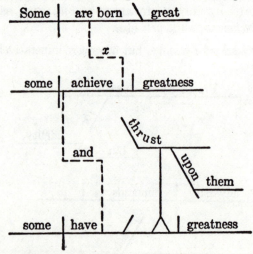

The conjunction may be omitted between the last two clauses also, as in the following:

3. I came, I saw, I conquered.

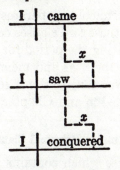

In sentences containing short simple clauses, the omission of the conjunction gives special emphasis to the last clause.

5. The idea of relationship between coördinate clauses may be suggested by a **transitional adverb** (*moreover, therefore, consequently, nevertheless, hence, otherwise, conversely, still then, yet,* etc.). Such an adverb may be interpreted as serving a rhetorical rather than a strictly grammatical purpose. Its connective function need not, therefore, be indicated in the diagram. In sentences of this type a coördinating conjunction may be supplied without change of meaning.

He must rally his forces at once; otherwise he will suffer defeat.

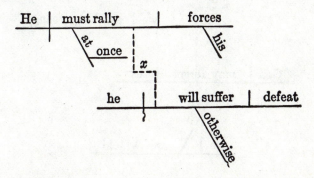

In this sentence no conjunction is needed because *otherwise* suggests the alternative meaning. The *x* in the diagram stands for the obviously understood conjunction *or*.

Observe that the semicolon separates the two clauses. In connected discourse, these two clauses could be treated as two sentences by substituting the period for the semicolon. (For a fuller discussion of the uses and meanings of adverbs used as transitional, illative, conjunctions, see Part One, Chapter Six, Adverbs, pp. 164–165 and Chapter Eight, Conjunctions, p. 191.)

Complex Principal Clauses

Any principal clause which contains an adjective, a noun, or an adverb clause will be a **complex clause**; and a principal clause may contain all three types of dependent clauses, some of which may or may not be coördinate. (For the analysis of coördinate subordinate clauses, see Adjective Clauses, pp. 349–369; Noun Clauses, pp. 370–389; and Adverb Clauses, pp. 390–420.)

We must remember God when we are young, or God may forget us when we are old.

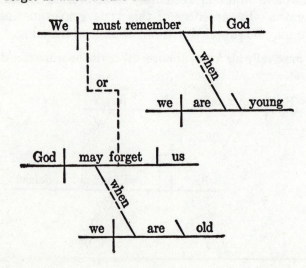

In this sentence, each principal clause may be classified as a **complex clause,** because it contains a modifying adverbial clause; and the sentence, therefore, may be called a **complex-compound** (or **compound-complex**) sentence.

There is no limit to the number of complex clauses which a sentence may have. The chief requirement of a good sentence is clearness; and clearness cannot be secured unless the coördinate and subordinate relations are clearly indicated.

Independent Parenthetical Clauses

A**n** **independent parenthetical clause** is an interpolated statement forced into the sentence as an aside to explain some idea mentioned or suggested by some word or phrase in the main statement. In the written sentence, such a clause is usually enclosed in parentheses or dashes. In the analysis or diagram, it should be construed as an independent element.

Act well thy part—there all the honor lies.

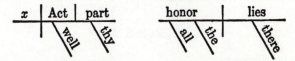

Observe that the following sentences also contain independent parenthetical clauses:

1. Forth he went—no longer would he tarry—to the town.
2. Prosperous people (there are none that are happy) are often thoughtless of the mutability of fortune.
3. He leaped (as it were) from billow to billow.
4. We know the uses—and sweet they are—of adversity.

Ellipses in Compound Sentences

A compound sentence may contain one or more elliptical clauses. Words and phrases necessary for the full analysis of the sentence may be omitted if they are clearly implied in the context. When two coördinate clauses have the same subject and the same verb, one or both of these may be omitted in the second clause, and by the omission monotonous repetition may be avoided. Observe the ellipses in the following:

1. A man of real information becomes a center of opinion, *and therefore of action* (= and therefore a man of real information becomes a center of action).
2. Individuals sometimes forgive; *but society never does* (= but society never does forgive).

If the second clause demands a different inflectional verb form from the first, no part of the predicate verb should be suppressed. In sentence 2, the omission of *forgive* shortens and strengthens the sentence; but if we say *Individuals have forgiven; but society never does*, we fail to suggest the proper inflectional form of *forgive*. Therefore, if we wish to put these two clauses in the same sentence, we should complete the predicate of the second; as, *Individuals have forgiven; but society never does forgive*.

EXERCISE A

Analyze or diagram:

1. Our life looks trivial, and we shun to record it.
2. We talk of choosing friends, but friends are self-elected.
3. Stolen fruits are sweet: undeserved rewards are exquisite.
4. He tells a fine story finely, but he cannot tell a plain story plainly.
5. Something is lost in accuracy; but much is gained in effect.
6. A soft answer turneth away wrath, but grievous words stir up anger.
7. Do not say all that you know, but always know what you say.
8. I admit that you have done me many favors; nevertheless, I must now do what I think is right.
9. No one else will go to law with authority; therefore he will.
10. Prosperity doth best discover vice, but adversity doth best discover virtue.
11. "Live and learn" may be a good motto, but many people find it necessary to live and unlearn.

12. He would like to believe in immortality, but he finds it difficult.
13. Seek ye first the kingdom of heaven, and all these things shall be added unto you.
14. This valuation was brought to a peak by Jesus, and with him every man had equal rights.
15. In sleep the brain feeds; but the will requires no work.
16. Our democracy is right at heart, and you cannot fool all the people all the time.
17. We might think in terms of molecules and atoms, but we rarely do.
18. Pleasure must succeed to pleasure; else past pleasure turns to pain.—Browning.
19. The English have mind enough, but they have not taste enough.
20. The foolish man wonders at the unusual, but the wise man at the usual.
21. Great men undertake great things because they are great; fools, because they think them easy.
22. We ought not to destroy critics, we ought to reform them.
23. We are not accustomed to eat dogs, but among some primitive peoples dogs are regarded as great delicacies.
24. Make yourself an honest man, and then you may be sure that there is one rascal less in the world.—Carlyle.
25. Without self-denial there is not merit, and the greater the self-denial the greater the merit.
26. Waste neither time nor money, but make the best use of both.
27. Know how to listen, and you will profit even from those who talk badly.—Plutarch.
28. Everything in nature is bipolar; it has a positive and a negative pole.
29. We have seen many counterfeits, but we are firm believers in great men.
30. A gentleman never dodges; his eyes look straight forward.
31. There the richest was poor, and the poorest lived in abundance.
32. A gem cannot be polished without friction, nor a man perfected without trials.
33. Our energies do not clash or compete; each is free to take his own path to knowledge.
34. I will lift up my eyes to the hills; but I will not lift up my body to the hills, unless it is absolutely necessary.

35. Plain glass doesn't harm the sight; and it really has a focusing value.

36. Give me insight into today, and you may have the antique and future worlds.

37. Beware of expenses; a small leak will sink a great ship.—Franklin.

38. Absolve yourself, and you will have the suffrage of the world.

39. Discontent is want of self-reliance: it is infirmity of will.

40. Revolutions are not made; they come.

41. The heavens declare the glory of God; and the firmament showeth his handiwork.

42. Lot's wife looked back from behind him, and she became a pillar of salt.

43. I have lost everything, and I am so poor now that I cannot afford to let anything worry me.

44. Man is stark mad; he cannot make a worm, and yet he will be making gods by the dozens.

45. Aspiration sees only one side of every question; possession, many.

46. A prating barber asked Archelaus how he would be trimmed; and he answered, "In silence."

47. Were I a nightingale, I would act the part of a nightingale; were I a swan, the part of a swan.

48. We may give advice, but we cannot inspire conduct.

49. You ask but small favors of your great friends; yet your great friends refuse you even small favors.

50. Let us have faith that right makes might; and in that faith let us dare to do our duty as we understand it.

51. Youth is a blunder; manhood a struggle; old age a regret.

52. If I am Sophocles, I am not mad; and if I am mad, I am not Sophocles.

53. Cowards do not count in battle; they are there, but not in it.

54. Talent is that which is in a man's power; genius is that in whose power man is.

55. The harder you throw down a football and a good character, the higher they rebound; but a thrown reputation is like an egg.

56. I do not love thee Sabidius, nor can I say why; this only I say, I do not love thee.

57. Avoid extremes; forbear resenting injuries as much as you think they deserve.

58. The people may be made to follow a path of action, but they may not be made to understand it.

59. We sometimes fancy that we hate flattery, but in reality we hate only the manner of flattering.

60. Time present and time past
Are both perhaps present in time future,
And time future contained in time past.—T. S. Eliot.

61. Speak well of your friends; of your enemies say nothing.

62. A man who leaves home to mend himself and others is a philosopher; but he who goes from country to country, guided by the blind impulse of curiosity is a vagabond.—Goldsmith.

EXERCISE B

Correct any errors you find in grammar and punctuation in the following, and justify each correction you make:

1. Egdon Heath was wild in character, brownish in cast, and most people hated it.

2. If I get a good place to park, I must wade through mud which ought not to be necessary in this age.

3. She was the type of person easily provoked to wrath, and who held a grudge for a long time.

4. She is not only deaf, but her sight is poor.

5. His purpose being to improve the morals of the community, and he had the support of his neighbors.

6. He weighs three hundred pounds, but which does not prevent his romping with the children.

7. I have already bought three pairs of shoes, but neither fits me very well.

8. He was late to dinner, but the family did not object but was rather glad.

9. The furniture was put in my mother's room, whom we not only expect tomorrow, but who will bring my little nephew with her.

10. We chose John because he was a veteran and on account of his loyalty also.

11. Our companion at first was not interested in taking a trip but after coaxing he decided to go.

12. I did not find the lecture too helpful, therefore I don't think you missed too much.

13. The story deals with knights, lords, and ladies and etc.

14. We played indoor tennis, went to parties, dances, went skiing, sledding, ice-skating, and had a wonderful time.

15. My friend not only gave me advice but also help.

16. A story should have a good plot, good characters, and work up to a definite climax.

17. A nicer person than she I have never met and probably never will.

18. His father had money, so he went to Europe.

19. When making fudge, it should not be stirred while boiling, or it will be grainy.

20. Having made good marks in his hardest subject, the father gave his son an automobile.

21. These novels should be read through once very carefully, then reviewing afterwards important details.

22. While bathing the baby, it went to sleep, and while sleeping, the mother baked a cake.

23. We came not only too early, but stayed too late.

24. He was determined his son should become an architect, which he did to please his father, but writing verse, dancing and playing the fiddle to please himself.

25. I am a Methodist, while my father and mother are Baptists.

26. Nature tells me, I am the image of God, as well as the Scripture.

General Review Exercise

The following sentences, excerpted chiefly from the writings of men and women whose usage may be regarded as standard, are presented for further practice in the analysis of the various types of sentences examined in Part One and Part Two of this text. The student who has completed Lessons I–XV in Part Two should be able to diagram or analyze and parse any of the following:

1. The only man who never makes a mistake is the man who never does anything.—Theodore Roosevelt.

2. It is not the man who has too little, but the man who craves more that is poor.—Seneca.

3. All things are admired either because they are new or because they are great.—Bacon.

4. "The present interests me more than the past," said the lady, "and the future more than the present."

5. Was it not Admiral Nelson who said, "No captain can do very wrong if he places his ship alongside that of an enemy"?

6. Greater love hath no man than this, that a man lay down his life for his friend.—New Testament.

7. To the primeval men, all things and everything they saw exist beside them were emblems of the Godlike.—Carlyle.

8. Unto everyone that hath shall be given, and he shall have abundance; but from him that hath not shall be taken away even that which he hath.—New Testament.

9. Resolve to perform what you ought; perform without fail what you resolve.

10. Next to seeing you is the pleasure of seeing your handwriting; next to hearing you, is the pleasure of hearing from you.

11. An object in possession seldom retains the same charm that it had in pursuit.

12. Since it is reason which shapes and regulates all other things, it ought not itself to be left in disorder.

13. Words, phrases, and clauses should be placed as near as possible to the words with which they are grammatically connected.

14. Whatsoever is counted a pleasure answers all the capacities of pleasure.

15. If we had no faults ourselves, we should not take so much pleasure in remarking them in others.

16. Cato wondered how that city is preserved wherein a fish is sold for more than an ox.

17. When our passions have forsaken us, we flatter ourselves with the belief that we have forsaken them.

18. Truly there is a tide in the affairs of men; but there is no gulf stream setting forever in one direction.

19. Perseverance is more prevailing than violence; and many things that cannot be overcome when they are together yield themselves up when taken little by little.

20. Minds of moderate caliber ordinarily condemn everything that is beyond their range.

21. Whatever fault your friend has, he cannot be accused of neglecting his family.
22. Our ideas, like orange plants, spread out in proportion to the size of the box which imprisons the roots.—Bulwer-Lytton.
23. It is as easy to deceive oneself without perceiving it as it is difficult to deceive others without their perceiving it.
24. Quarrels would not last long if the fault were always on only one side.
25. Having been asked whether it is better to marry or not, Socrates replied, "Whichever you do, you will repent it."
26. The question was put to a great philosopher, what hope is; and his answer was, "The dream of a waking man."
27. I speak the truth, not so much as I would, but as much as I dare; and I dare a little the more as I grow older.
28. Socrates thought that if all our misfortunes were laid in one common heap, whence everyone must take an equal portion, most persons would be contented to take their own and depart.
29. Never esteem anything of advantage to thee that shall make thee break thy word or lose thy self-respect.
30. Nothing is more characteristic of a man than the manner in which he behaves toward a fool.
31. Whatever punishment does to a nation, it does not induce a sense of guilt.
32. The greatest mistake you can make in life is to be continually fearing you will make one.
33. Whoever wishes to attain an English style, familiar but not coarse, and elegant but not ostentatious, must give his days and nights to the volumes of Addison.—Johnson.
34. An old Chinese proverb says, "You cannot prevent the birds of sorrow from flying over your head, but you can prevent them from building nests in your hair."
35. There is no more miserable human being than one in whom nothing is habitual but indecision.—William James.
36. In a certain sense Whitman interpreted America to Europe; and to America he tried to interpret the Universe.—William L. Phelps.
37. The hell to be endured hereafter, of which theology tells, is no worse than the hell we make for ourselves in this world by

habitually fashioning our character in the wrong way.—William James.

38. It is a custom of pedagogues to be eternally thundering in their pupils' ears.—Montaigne.

39. A sharp temper never mellows with age, and a sharp tongue is the only edged tool that grows keener with constant use.—Washington Irving.

40. We ought to see far enough into a hypocrite to see even his sincerity.—C. K. Chesterton.

41. Resolve to be thyself, and know that he who finds himself loses his misery.—Matthew Arnold.

42. I am a man; nothing that concerns mankind is alien to me.—Terence.

43. I am as bad as the worst, but thank God I am not so good as the best.—Walt Whitman.

44. Players are the only honest hypocrites.—William Hazlitt.

45. Though I speak with the tongues of men and of angels, and have not charity, I am become as sounding brass and a tinkling cymbal.—Saint Paul.

46. In the noon and afternoon of life we still throb at the recollection of days when happiness was not happy enough, but must be drugged with the relish of pain and fear.—Emerson.

47. Strait is the gate, and narrow is the way that leadeth unto life, and few there be that find it.—New Testament.

48. Whenever God erects a house of prayer,
The Devil always builds a chapel there;
And 'twill be found upon examination,
The latter has the larger congregation.—Bunyan.

Miscellaneous Errors in Grammar

Correct all violations of good usage in the following sentences, and justify each correction you make:

1. That was sure good food we had.
2. He will likely accept your offer, if he is badly in need of money.
3. Even if he was a Democrat, he wouldn't vote for me.
4. He always has and always will be a care.
5. The boy is attending class regular now.

6. All humans are liable to make errors.
7. Our sheeps' wool is carded and spun in this town.
8. He seems more contenteder than formerly.
9. Our anglo-saxon ancestors came from Germany.
10. Give this umbrella to whomever needs it.
11. My teacher told me that the reason I was poor in Spanish was because I had had no Latin.
12. It certainly looks like it is going to snow.
13. I saw Louis's the Sixteenth's statue in the Louvre.
14. John acts as if he was running our show.
15. How is your brother and wife making out now?
16. I saw John and she at the circus.
17. She must go with John and I.
18. I am sure pleased with my purchases.
19. I was kind of disappointed in the report you gave.
20. Who are you referring to?
21. She dresses neat for a working woman, but she speaks awfully bad English.
22. Her daughter was drownded in that pond.
23. The power behind the throne, my brother says, is her.
24. John is learning to aviate.
25. He was hung for killing his daughter.
26. I am going to emphasize this point stronger than before.
27. Stand still and speak distinct when you are addressing the class.
28. His *is* and *ns* look exactly alike.
29. I have some literature on the making of hooked rugs.
30. I might go home with you if I have enough money for my ticket.
31. This is not the man who you spoke to yesterday.
32. I have got two brothers and one sister.
33. He looked sourly at us when we approached the group, and seemed pretty much out of patience with all of us.
34. Our president came from somewheres in the South.
35. I don't know but what that was the wrong thing to do.
36. If I was in your place, I would quit complaining.
37. Kentucky and the South is vividly portrayed in this story.
38. I object to him coming and taking things that belong to me.
39. We lost our baggage and we were in a terrible fix.
40. That fellow that acted as the leader was from Georgia.
41. I do not like that sort of a person.

42. The Rockies are more higher than our mountains in the East.
43. I had ought to have taken the prize when it was offered to me.
44. He is one of the teachers who was dismissed last week.
45. I wish I could of been there when he was giving that report.
46. I only paid half of your traveling expenses.
47. Our preacher is nowhere near so good as the one we had last year.
48. I did not suppose that tall person to be she.
49. She is plenty old enough to speak for herself, but she is so shy.
50. This was boughten before the end of the war.
51. Was it Edward and the Duchess who is being entertained at the White House?
52. I would have gone to the wedding if I had have been invited.
53. I do not know if he will come.
54. John and yourself should get another car.
55. That was the finest of any speech I have heard this year.
56. Mother gave me a pair of beads for Christmas.
57. If you have only one memoranda, you need not report it.
58. Our mountains are not as tall as the Rockies, but they look like they were taller.
59. Being as you are not busy, why don't you read to me?
60. You will not leave this room until you have finished your home work.
61. This summer I either want to teach or get a job as a hostess at some resort.
62. Her friend is very good looking; he is tall and dark complected.
63. You should measure the cloth lengthways.
64. I didn't see none of your friends at the circus last night.
65. By constructing a park, the appearance of the town might be improved.
66. I have as many books in my library, if not more than, you.
67. This here map is too old to be of much value.
68. Your friend is so pretty and so refined.
69. I haven't gotten what I came for, and I had ought to give up.
70. Please leave me do the dishes while you visit with your guests.
71. The teacher was unwilling to so much as repeat the question.
72. I was all ready in New York when the message came.
73. Most everything that we shipped was lost.
74. Many will seek admittance, and only a few will be admitted.

75. Our arguments are likely to end up in a fight.
76. Every instructor must be in their office before the last bell rings.
77. If you have a pencil or pen, bring them.
78. The class was in their room before the teacher arrived.
79. I met a man in Japan knows you and she.
80. The party who was with us had nothing to say in our defense.
81. We had a heap of fun at the circus, but everybody spent too much dough.
82. The work was different than what we had anticipated.
83. The child was so miserable that the parents had no alternatives than to move away.
84. Will Roger's stature is in the Hall of Fame in the United States Capital.
85. We could not have our party at the church because the Reverend would not approve it.
86. Who did you see in town today?
87. I do not know whom you are.
88. One should be especially careful about their grammar.
89. When you are complimented, you act like you had been insulted.
90. I do not doubt but what he has plenty of money.
91. We decided to go to the dance, as we knew you would want us to go.
92. Erase that out and put this here problem on the board.
93. I seldom ever see any of my college friends.
94. Father thinks I had ought to go and register for this course.
95. His grandmother sets there all day long watching the crowds go and come.
96. The examination was mighty hard, and I don't think I did real well.
97. He said you are a capable person and that you were in need of work.
98. I do not know but what it would be better for me to go there unaccompanied.
99. That was a funny kind of a talk for a preacher to make.
100. Your cakes are always mighty good.

Bibliography

Baugh, Albert C., *A History of the English Language.* New York: D. Appleton-Century Company, 1935.

Bloomfield, Leonard, *Language.* New York: Henry Holt and Co., 1933.

Bright, James W., *An Anglo-Saxon Reader*, Revised Edition. New York: Henry Holt and Co., 1917.

Curme, George O., Kurath, Hans, *A Grammar of the English Language*, 3 vols. Vol. II, *Parts of Speech and Accidence;* Vol. III, *Syntax.* Boston: D. C. Heath and Co., 1931, 1933. (Vol. I, *History of the Language*, has not yet appeared.)

Emerson, Oliver Farrar, *The History of the English Language.* New York: Macmillan and Co., 1895.

Emerson, Oliver Farrar, *A Middle English Reader.* New and Revised Edition. London: Macmillan and Co., 1938.

Encyclopaedia Britannica, Fourteenth Edition. Chicago: Encyclopaedia Britannica, Inc., 1929.

Fowler, H. W., *A Dictionary of Modern English Usage.* Oxford: Clarendon Press, 1926.

Fries, Charles Carpenter, *American English Grammar.* New York: D. Appleton-Century Co., 1940.

Grattan, J. H. G., and Gurrey, P., *Our Living Language.* New York: Thomas Nelson and Sons, 1935.

Greenough, James Bradstreet, and Kittredge, George Lyman, *Words and Their Ways in English Speech.* New York: Macmillan Co., 1920.

Hall, J. Leslie, *English Usage.* Chicago: Scott, Foresman and Co., 1917.

Horwill, H. W., *A Dictionary of Modern English Usage.* Oxford: Clarendon Press, 1935.

Jespersen, Otto, *Essentials of English Grammar*. New York: Henry Holt and Co., 1933.

Jespersen, Otto, *Growth and Structure of the English Language*, 4th ed. New York: D. Appleton and Co., 1929.

Jespersen, Otto, *Modern English Grammar*. Heidelberg: Carl Winter, 1928–31. 4 vols.

Jespersen, Otto, *Philosophy of Grammar*. New York: Henry Holt and Co., 1924.

Kennedy, Arthur G., *Current English*. New York: Ginn and Co., 1935.

Kennedy, Arthur G., *English Usage*. New York: D. Appleton-Century Co., 1942.

Kenyon, John S., *American Pronunciation*, 6th ed. revised. Ann Arbor: George Wahr, 1935.

Kenyon, J. S., and Knott, Thomas A., *A Pronouncing Dictionary of American English*. Springfield, Mass.: G. and C. Merriam Co., 1944.

Kittredge, George Lyman, and Farley, Frank Edgar, *An Advanced English Grammar*. New York: Ginn and Co., 1913.

Krapp, George Philip, *Modern English: Its Growth and Structure*. New York: Charles Scribner's Sons, 1909.

Krapp, George Philip, *The Knowledge of English*. New York: Henry Holt and Co., 1927.

Kruisinga, E., *A Handbook of Present-Day English*. Pt. I, 1 vol., 4th ed. Utrecht: Kemink, 1925. Pt. II, 3 vols., 5th ed. Groningen: Noordhoff, 1931–1932.

Leonard, Sterling Andrus, *Current English Usage*. English Monograph No. 1, National Council of Teachers of English. Chicago: Inland Press, 1932.

Leonard, Sterling Andrus, *The Doctrine of Correctness in English Usage*, 1700–1800. Madison, Wisconsin: *University of Wisconsin Studies in Language and Literature, No. 25*, 1929.

Mallery, Richard D., *Our American Language*. Garden City, New York: Halcyon House, 1947.

Mencken, H. L., *The American Language*, Fourth Edition. New York: Alfred A. Knopf, 1936. Supplement I and Supplement II, 1945, 1948.

Morris, Rev. Richard, *Elementary Lessons in Historical Grammar*, Revised by Henry Bradley. New York: Macmillan Co., 1898.

Murray, James A. H., *et al.*, *New English Dictionary on Historical Principles*. Oxford: Clarendon Press, 1884–1928. 10 vols. Later corrected and re-issued as *The Oxford English Dictionary*, 1933. 12 vols. and supplement.

Nesfield, J. C., *English Grammar, Past and Present*, Revised Edition. London: Macmillan and Co., 1931.

Onions, C. T., *An Advanced English Syntax*, Fifth Edition. New York: Macmillan Co., 1929.

Perrin, Porter G., *Writer's Guide and Index to English*. New York: Scott, Foresman and Co., 1942.

Poutsma, H., *The Character of the English Verb*. Groningen: P. Noordhoff, 1921.

Poutsma, H., *A Grammar of Late Modern English*. Groningen: P. Noordhoff, 1904–1926.

Reed, Alonzo, and Kellogg, Brainerd, *Higher Lessons in English*, New Edition. New York: Charles E. Merrill Co., 1909.

Robertson, Stuart, *The Development of Modern English*. New York: Prentice-Hall, Inc., 1938.

Sapir, Edward, *Language*. New York: Harcourt, Brace and Co., 1921.

Skeat, Walter W., *Etymological Dictionary of the English Language*. Fourth Edition. Oxford: Clarendon Press, 1910.

Sweet, Henry, *A New English Grammar*. Oxford: Clarendon Press, 1924.

Vizetelly, Frank, *How to Use English, A Guide to Correct Speech and Writing*. New York: Funk and Wagnalls Co., 1932.

Webster's New International Dictionary, Revised Edition. Springfield, Mass.: G. and C. Merriam Co., 1934.

Weekley, Ernest, *English Dialect Dictionary of Modern English*. New York: Dutton and Co., 1921.

Weekley, Ernest, *Etymological Dictionary of Modern English*. New York: Dutton and Co., 1921.

Wright, Joseph, *English Dialect Dictionary*. London: Frowde, 1898–1905.

Wright, Joseph, and Wright, Elizabeth Mary, *An Elementary New English Grammar*. New York and London: Clarendon Press, 1928.

Wright, Joseph, and Wright, Elizabeth Mary, *An Elementary Middle English Grammar*. New York and London: Oxford University Press, 1924.

Wright, Joseph, and Wright, Elizabeth Mary, *Old English Grammar*, Third Edition. New York and London: Clarendon Press, 1925.

Index

Italic and **boldface** references are to paragraphs.

P